MUSIC PUBLISHING

MW00561734

THE COMPLETE GUIDE

STEVE WINOGRADSKY

Alfred

Alfred Music
P.O. Box 10003
Van Nuys, CA 91410-0003
alfred.com

ISBN-10: 0-7390-9687-7
ISBN-13: 978-0-7390-9687-1

13 14 15 16 17 9 8 7 6 5 4 3 2 1

*This book is dedicated to
my lovely wife, Rosemary,
who knew this book
existed long before I did.*

v

ACKNOWLEDGMENTS

There are many people I wish to acknowledge for their friendship, wisdom, guidance, and contributions to this book.

There were many people from whom I learned about music publishing, but there were two people who taught me not only about publishing but even more about the subject of life. Martin "Mutt" Cohen was an attorney in Los Angeles who first invited me to co-teach a music publishing class at UCLA. Andreas "Andy" Budde was my first major publishing client. Both passed away far too early but they were kind enough to share some of their wisdom and knowledge with me before doing so.

Several people graciously contributed to sections of the book, as follows: Michael Perlstein and Amy Mitchell Pooley on copyright; Jeffrey Brabec on songwriter agreements; Teri Nelson Carpenter on foreign sub-publishing; my law partner Ron Sobel on digital media; Michael Simon of The Harry Fox Agency, Inc. for the summary of the 2008 Section 115 settlement analysis; Bobby Rosenbloum and Charmaine Smith of Greenberg, Traurig, LLC in Atlanta for the summary of the 2012 Section 115 settlement; and Professor Carey Christensen of California State University, Northridge for his review and suggestions for the book. I appreciate their generosity with their time and information.

Special thanks to Mike Tolleson and the Texas State Bar Entertainment and Sports Law Section (TESLAW). I have been fortunate enough to have been invited to speak at their annual Entertainment Law Institute for 20 years, honing both my writing and lecturing skills. In 2012, I was honored to receive the Texas Star Award for contributions to legal education in Texas and was also named an Honorary Texan by Governor Rick Perry. Yee-haw, y'all!

Thanks also to Pascale Cohen-Olivar and the staff at UCLA Extension for allowing me to teach for 17 years (and counting) and for the academic freedom to conduct the classes as I deemed appropriate. With over 600 students passing through my classrooms, I am proud to see so many of them actively working in the music industry.

And a big thank you to my 2012 summer legal intern (and future attorney), Kari Wilberg, who assisted with research, formatting, and editing of the final version of the manuscript.

TABLE OF CONTENTS

INTRODUCTION

The entire music business starts with a musical composition or song. Without those elements, there are no songwriters, composers, recording artists, music publishers, record companies, and no music on the radio, Internet, television, or in motion pictures. Try to imagine watching a program without any music in it. It's not easy to imagine, which is why even silent films were accompanied by music when they played in theaters.

Music adds so much to our daily lives without us even realizing it sometimes. Music is all around us, not only in the mass media described above but also in shopping malls, restaurants, schools, and churches. Walk down almost any street, or travel on buses, trains, and airplanes anywhere and you will see people with headphones on, listening to music in their own little world. Music is said to be the universal language and understanding how the music business works is crucial for its survival. If songwriters couldn't get paid for their efforts, songwriting would turn out to be nothing but a hobby, not a profession, and far fewer people would be able to have the time or inclination to do it.

That's where music publishers come in. In speaking with a publishing colleague from Italy several years ago, I mentioned that I taught classes in music publishing. He asked how someone could be taught to be a music publisher. I responded that what I taught was not how to be a music publisher but what the functions of a music publisher are. Whether the publishers are large multi-national companies or individual songwriters who own their own creations, music publishers manage the business and legal aspects of songs for the benefit of the authors as well as for the publishing companies.

Music publishing has both creative and business aspects to it. Finding a talented songwriter and getting their songs recorded, on the radio, or placed in television and film productions are the more creative functions of our industry and very subjective. I've been in the music business for a while and, although I know what I personally like, I would be hard-pressed to pick a hit record out of the songs that pass my desk.

What I can do, and what this book hopes to teach the reader to do, is show how to conduct the business aspects of the music publishing industry and how to maximize the opportunities presented, not only from a financial standpoint but in terms of the benefits that exposure of a song can bring as well. The book begins with a discussion on copyright—the protection granted to creators under federal law—without which creators of any kind of intellectual property would be unable to make any money from their art.

Speaking of money, we will then discuss the various sources of licensing and revenue for music publishers and songwriters, including **mechanical** royalties from the sale of audio-only product; **synchronization** license income from the use of music in audio-visual productions, such as television and motion pictures; **public performance** royalties from music on television and radio, live performances, and music played in public places such as shopping malls, nightclubs, and banquet halls; and **print** royalties for sheet music, music for choirs, or band and orchestra arrangements.

The business agreements between the songwriters, publishers, co-publishers, and foreign sub-publishers will all be discussed in great detail, with explanations about the terms of these deals and why some are better than others. Other areas, such as production music libraries and companies that pitch and place a writer's music, will also be included. Lastly, a discussion on digital distribution, either by downloading or streaming, and "new media" (however that is defined on what seems to be a minute-by-minute basis) will be included, fully realizing that, because of the rapidly changing landscape we now face, whatever is written today may soon be out of date.

One of the things I've done is to explain these major areas that a music publisher must be concerned with and offer a number of sample agreements, not only for review of the contractual language but also with a detailed description of what the major clauses mean in context of the overall agreement. Having access to form agreements is always helpful, but without any explanation, they are of little value. This is a very specialized industry and there are terms of art as well as customs and practices that a publisher must understand to make the most of the opportunities to exploit their music. A failure to understand these principles could result in granting rights beyond what the publisher believes they are granting, or charging fees that are too low (or too high) for the rights being granted, all of which are detrimental to the publisher and their writer clients.

I've also added some real world examples from my own experience to illustrate how these principles come into play on a daily basis and the ramifications of certain types of negotiations and contract terms. And in some instances, I've included a "bad" agreement (and indicated as such) to show the contrast between the way business is sometimes done and the way it should be done.

To be a successful music publisher, it is important to understand not only the publishing business, but also all the ancillary businesses that utilize music. Without the knowledge of how record companies work and structure artist agreements, how television programs and motion pictures are created and distributed, and how changes in "new media" affect the songs that a publisher might control, a publisher would be working in a vacuum and unable to understand and structure deals that would benefit themselves and their writers. So although this is a book focusing on music publishing, there will also be discussions about these ancillary industries for a more well-rounded analysis of the issues facing this portion of the music industry.

This book is intended as a textbook for students in college music business programs, law students interested in the music business, and a reference book for music industry professionals and attorneys who are looking for detailed information on a very complicated subject. Some of the other books currently available are aimed at artists and songwriters, therefore covering the material only in its most basic form, or focus only on particular aspects of the industry, such as income or song plugging. The information and contract analysis contained herein, with the positions of both sides of the negotiation being presented and discussed, make this book a bit unique from the others. Upon reading it, I hope you feel the same.

CHAPTER 1

COPYRIGHT BASICS

Introduction

The Copyright Act (Title 17, United States Code) protects works of authorship in any tangible medium of expression. It is important to note that *ideas* are not protectable, only the *expression* of those ideas. Under this law, creators of (among other things) books, theatrical works, computer programs, motion pictures, music, lyrics, choreography, works of art, and recordings are granted certain exclusive rights to these works.

Copyrights, along with patents and trademarks, are sometimes also called "intellectual property." While some may debate the "intellectual" qualities of some forms of expression, such as recordings by the Spice Girls or the motion picture *Beavis and Butt-head Do America*, the key concept is one of a property right. Like other kinds of property, such as real property and personal property, the owner has certain rights in how the work is utilized. It may also be sold or licensed to third parties.

The History of Copyright

In medieval times through the Renaissance, creative persons such as composers, playwrights, authors, and artists were supported by the state, the church, or privately by wealthy patrons. As such, their works were made available to the public without cost since the needs of the artists were taken care of. With the demise of the ruling and the wealthy classes, certain limited rights were granted to these creators so as to encourage and reward them to continue their artistic endeavors. These rights gave the creators a proprietary interest in their work so that they could sell or license it for reproduction.

In 1710, the British Parliament passed the Statute of Anne, which provided the right to prevent the copying of "writings" for 14 years (renewable for another 14 years), vested in authors and their assigns. French laws of 1791 and 1793 encompassed other works of "fine art," granting authors rights to control the copying, distribution, and sale of their works plus a fixed term of rights after each author's death.

Copyright in the United States

The concept of protection for creative works in the United States has been a part of our law since our country was born. Article I, Section 8 of the United States Constitution states,

"The Congress shall have the power . . . to promote the progress of science and useful arts, by securing for limited times to authors and inventors the exclusive right to their respective writings and discoveries."

It is these rights that are contained in the current Copyright Act. Let's break down this clause phrase by phrase:

The Congress shall have the power — the Copyright Act is a federal law and only Congress has the right to amend it (and the Supreme Court the ultimate right to interpret it);

to promote the progress of science and useful arts, — it is in the best interests of the public at large to encourage the development of scientific discoveries as well as encourage artists to create;

by securing for limited times to authors and inventors — as will be discussed below, "creators" are given a limited and defined period of time to exploit their creations for monetary purposes. There are those who believe that the time period is too long and that the public should be given free access to these creations, but Congress has stated otherwise;

the exclusive right to their respective writings and discoveries — as discussed immediately below, there are exclusive rights granted to creators, and they have the sole right to control the use of their creations.

The Copyright Act

Section 106 of the Copyright Act of 1976, which took effect January 1, 1978, grants to copyright owners the exclusive rights to do and to authorize any of the following:

1. To reproduce the copyrighted work in copies or phonorecords (audio-only devices, such as records, compact discs, or audio cassettes);

2. To prepare derivative works based upon the copyrighted work, such as converting a book into a movie;

3. To distribute copies or phonorecords of the copyrighted work to the public by sale or other transfer of ownership, or by rental, lease, or lending;

4. In the case of literary, musical, dramatic, and choreographed works, pantomimes, motion pictures, and other audiovisual works, to perform the copyrighted work publicly. The performance may be live, by broadcast, or over loudspeaker in a public place (store, museum, etc.). "Public" is defined as persons outside of your family or immediate circle of acquaintances;

5. In the case of literary, musical, dramatic, and choreographed works, pantomimes, and pictorial, graphic, or sculptural works, including the individual images of a motion picture and other audiovisual works, to exhibit the copyrighted work publicly; and

6.   In the case of sound recordings, to perform the work publicly by means of a digital audio transmission. (The sixth exclusive right flows from the Digital Performance Right in Sound Recordings Act ["DPRA"], which was adopted by Congress in 1995.)

It should be noted that, even though this book focuses on music publishing and musical composition, there is often a second copyright in the master recording that must also be considered when licensing the musical composition. While a song has only one set of writers and publisher, the same song may be recorded by multiple artists. The copyrights to the master recordings by those artists are generally controlled by the record company to whom the artist is signed.

There are some exceptions to these exclusive rights, such as reproduction by libraries and archives, educational and religious uses, Fair Use, and the right of first sale. Each of these is defined (more or less precisely) by the Act and by the cases brought involving each exception.

But what do these rights really mean? It means that any person wishing to use a copyrighted work must secure the permission of the copyright owner and negotiate a fee for the use intended. Determining who owns the copyright is not always that easy. As a property right, copyrights can be bought and sold, therefore the ownership may change hands many times over the years. There may be multiple owners, each of whom may need to be contacted. Some agreements between co-owners allow for one controlling party to administer the entire copyright. Others require separate administration by each party for their respective shares.

With rare exceptions, permission and fees for the use of a copyright are totally negotiable. Those exceptions are the statutory mechanical rate for phonorecords and ringtones, and rates for certain types of uses on the Internet, such as tethered downloads and interactive streaming, which are based upon a compulsory license. Use without permission and negotiation with all relevant parties is infringement and can subject the offender to both monetary damages and an injunction against further distribution, to be discussed in more detail below.

Term of Copyright

How long does copyright protection last? The rights discussed above are granted to the copyright owner for a limited time. After the expiration of that time, the work falls into the "public domain," which means that anyone can use or copy the work without permission or payment.

Under the 1976 Copyright Act, which became effective January 1, 1978, works created after 1978 were protected for the life of the author plus 50 years. If there is more than one author, the term was 50 years after the death of the last surviving author. In 1998, Congress passed legislation (the so-called "Sonny Bono Extension Act") to extend protection to life of the (last surviving) author plus 70 years.

Post-1978 Works

Life of Author	Plus 70 Years

Under the previous Copyright Act of 1909, works created had an original term of 28 years plus a renewal term of an additional 28 years. Prior to 1992, a failure to properly renew a copyright in the 28th year threw the work into the public domain. In 1992, however, a bill was passed that automatically renewed a work copyrighted between January 1, 1964, and December 31, 1977, which served to benefit the widows and children of creators who may not have been familiar with the laws about copyright and music publishing.

The 1976 Act added 19 years to this term, which may be claimed in the United States by the author or their heirs, and another 20 years was added in 1998, for a total of 95 years. These additional 19- and 20-year terms only apply, however, to works created after 1923. Anything created prior to that was already in the public domain when the extensions provided for in the 1976 Act were passed.

Copyright Term for 1923–1977 Works

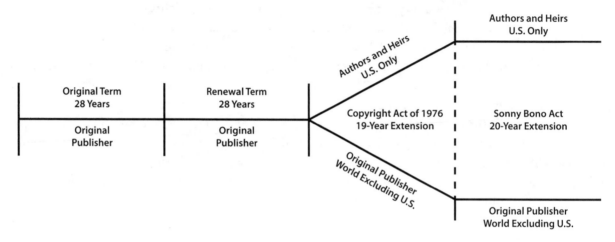

The term for a "work made for hire" is 95 years from date of publication or 120 years from creation, whichever comes first. A "work made for hire" is (1) a work prepared by an employee within the scope of his employment or (2) a work specially ordered or commissioned for use as contribution to a collective work, such as a motion picture. For copyright purposes, the employer is considered the "author" of work and at no time does the creator have an ownership interest in the work.

The terms of copyright in foreign territories vary, although they are based upon the "life plus X years" concept. In the European community, the term is generally life of the author plus 70 years. In other territories, it may extend to life plus 99 years. Because of these different terms, a work could go into the public domain in the United States and still be protected in foreign territories, or *vice versa*.

Under the current Act, copyright protection exists in original works of authorship "fixed" (see definition in §101 of the Act) in any tangible medium of expression from which they can be perceived, reproduced, or otherwise communicated for a period of more than transitory duration. This means that a song that is sung, but not recorded or written down, is not protected.

The so-called "poor man's copyright," in which you mail a sealed copy to yourself and never open it, is of limited value. While it allegedly establishes the date of the postmark as proof of the date of creation, it is not a substitute for proper registration.

Termination and Recapturing of Copyright

Under the 1976 Act, the grant to publishers of the copyrights for works created both under the 1909 Act and the 1976 Act (see §203 and §304) may be terminated in the United States at certain points in time, with the remaining copyright term in the United States being recaptured and controlled by the writer or their heirs.

For works created after 1978, a window exists whereby the authors (or their heirs) may terminate a transfer of rights (such as from a songwriter to a publisher) commencing 35 years after the date of the transfer and ending 40 years after the date of the transfer. These transfers must be made by the original author, not the author's successors. Notice must be given to the copyright proprietor no less than 10 years, nor more than 2 years prior to the effective date of the termination. In other words, notice may be given as early as year 25 after the transfer, but no later than year 38 after the transfer. Once a transfer is completed, the new rights holder has control over the copyright for the remainder of the term. In the event that the author has a surviving spouse but no surviving children or grandchildren, then the termination right is owned entirely by the author's spouse. If the author dies leaving a spouse and children, then the termination interest is owned 50% by the author's spouse and 50% by the author's children on a *per stirpes* basis. In the event of multiple authors as part of the same grant, a majority of them must file for termination in order for the rights to revert to ANY of them. If a majority of the parties cannot agree on the termination, it is possible for the original publisher to retain all rights, as the heirs are unwilling to cooperate in a joint effort to recapture the rights.

Termination of Post-1978 Works

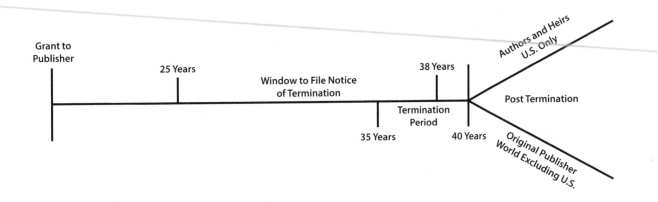

In one of the first lawsuits based on this right of termination, *Scorpio Music S.A., et. al. v Victor Willis*, first decided in 2012, Victor Willis, lead singer for The Village People, filed notice of termination for songs co-written by him post 1977, including "YMCA" and "In the Navy," and assigned his copyright interests to Can't Stop Music, sub-publisher for Scorpio Music, the original French publisher. Willis translated lyrics from the original French language songs, so his grant to Scorpio was independent of the grant by the original writers. Scorpio argued that Willis was the only author to file notice of termination and that, under §203(a)(1), a majority of all authors who transferred rights must join in the termination. The U.S. District Court for the Southern District of California held that, since the grants were separately made, Willis' individual grant made him eligible to terminate his share of the rights granted in the songs.

2013 is the first date that these terminations can take effect, as 2013 is 35 years after the commencement of the current Act in 1978.

For works created before 1977, the rules for termination are a little more complicated. Remember that for these works, the term was 28 years plus a 28-year renewal, with an additional 39 years added under the 1976 Act and Sonny Bono extension.

In most older songwriter/publisher agreements, the writer granted the publisher rights for the initial term and all renewals or extensions to which the writer became entitled. If the writer was still alive at the end of the first 28-year term, the original agreement granted the renewal term to the publisher. The termination "window" under this section is a 5-year period beginning at the end of the 56th year from the date that copyright is secured and continuing through the last day of the 61st year from the date copyright is secured.

If, however, the writer was deceased prior to the expiration of the initial term, the renewal right had not yet vested in year 29, so the renewal grant in the original term did not vest in the writer, the renewal grant by the writer was invalid and the heirs (which could be the writer's spouse and both legitimate and illegitimate children) could file notice of termination and regain the copyright for the second 28 years as well as the remaining 39-year extension. If there is more than one author of the work, and only one author is deceased, that author's heirs can regain his share of the work, with the remaining share kept by the copyright holder.

Termination of 1923–1977 Works

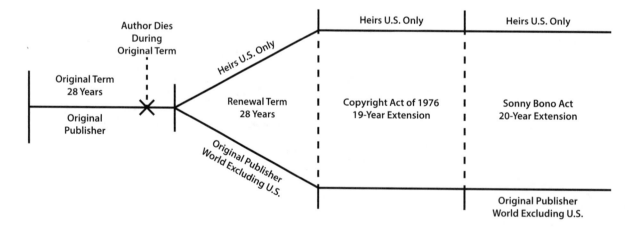

§304(a)(1)(C) of the Act designates the persons entitled to renew a copyright registration in the event that the author has died prior to the commencement of the renewal term: "(ii) the widow, widower, or children of the author, if the author is not living, (iii) the author's executors, if such author, widow, widower, or children are not living, or (iv) the author's next of kin, in the absence of a will of the author." Children of the author could be either legitimate or illegitimate children. In the event that the author has a surviving spouse but no surviving children or grandchildren, then the termination right is owned entirely by the author's spouse. If the author dies leaving a spouse and children, then the termination interest is owned 50% by the author's spouse and 50% by the author's children on a per stirpes basis.

If the author survives in the renewal period, the copyright owner retains ownership through the second 28 years. Upon expiration of the 56-year period, however, the author or their heirs again has the right to terminate the grant to the publisher and regain the balance of the copyright term by filing notice with the copyright owner within five years of the end of the 56-year term.

While there is no specific form that must be used for termination either for §304 or §203, there are certain elements that must be contained in the notice. The party terminating must specify under which provision they are terminating to allow the current copyright owner to evaluate the validity of the intended termination. The notice must contain the name of the grantee (or their successor in interest) whose rights are being terminated. Notice must also contain the specific titles to be terminated, the name of at least one of the authors, the date the copyright was originally secured and, if available, the original copyright registration number. All of this information verifies that there is no confusion about which song's copyright is being terminated. Notice should also set out the effective date of the termination, which is set by the terminating party so long as it falls within the termination window. Notice should also list the party filing for termination and, if not the author, the relationship of the party seeking termination, such as a widow or surviving child. Lastly, the notice of termination should be filed with the Copyright Office for proper registration.

Under either scenario, once the copyright grants have terminated, the author or their heirs have the full rights accorded to copyright owners in the United States. They can administer the copyrights themselves, engage an administration company, assign the copyrights to a new publisher, or enter into a new agreement with the previous publisher on more favorable terms.

It should be noted that these terminations only apply to the rights to the copyright in the United States. Although the statute does not limit this termination to the United States, only the United States has these rights of renewal and termination, so industry custom is to limit the rights of the heirs to U.S. rights. The grantee of the original rights remains as the copyright owner in all territories outside the United States, leading to multiple copyright owners of the same work. As will be demonstrated in subsequent chapters, this can have an effect on potential licensing deals for the work.

Copyright Infringement

The improper use of a copyrighted work, either without the permission of the owner or in violation of the terms of a compulsory license, is an infringement of that copyright. Infringement takes two basic forms: (1) the use of a copyrighted work without the necessary license, and (2) plagiarism.

For use without the necessary license, it is a relatively easy matter for the owner to prove the use and the lack of a license. It is in these situations where the defenses of Fair Use and parody usually come into play to alleviate the need for a license.

For plagiarism, proving the illegal copying is more complex. There are three key elements to proving a claim of plagiarism: (1) proof of ownership of the work allegedly being infringed; (2) that the allegedly infringing work is "substantially similar" to the original work; and (3) the defendant had "access" to the original work in order to have copied it. These are issues for the trier of fact to determine and must be proved by the plaintiff in that sequence, i.e., if there is no substantial similarity, access doesn't matter.

The classic case regarding plagiarism involves former Beatle George Harrison, *Bright Tunes Music v. Harrisongs Music*, 420 F. Supp. 177 (S.D.N.Y. 1976). One of Harrison's first solo works after the breakup of The Beatles was a song called "My Sweet Lord," recorded in 1970. Shortly after the release of the song, Harrison was sued by the publishers of a song titled "He's So Fine," which was written by Ronnie Mack and recorded by The Chiffons in 1962. Following the release of Harrison's version of "My Sweet Lord," musical similarities between it and "He's So Fine" were remarked on almost immediately—*Rolling Stone*'s album review of January 1971 even referred to "My Sweet Lord" as an "obvious re-write of the Chiffons' 'He's So Fine.' " By March, proceedings were under way for what became a prolonged copyright infringement suit, lasting over 10 years.

In September 1976, a U.S. district court decision found that Harrison had "subconsciously" copied the earlier tune. One of the theories was that, since the members of The Beatles were known to be fans of American music, Harrison probably heard "He's So Fine" when it was popular in the early 1960s, thereby inferring access and satisfying the two-part test.

In 1978, before the court decided on damages in the case, Harrison's former manager Allen Klein, who had represented him earlier in the proceedings, purchased the copyright to "He's So Fine" from Bright Tunes. In 1981, the court decided the damages amounted to $1,599,987, but that due to Klein's duplicity in the case, Harrison would only have to pay Klein $587,000 for the rights to "He's So Fine"— the amount Klein had paid Bright Tunes for the song. At some point later, Harrison purchased the copyright to "He's So Fine," which his company still owns today.

Damages for Infringement

Under §500, et seq. of the Act, the remedies for infringement are described. One remedy described in §502 is for a court to "grant temporary and final injunctions on such terms as it may deem reasonable to prevent or restrain infringement of a copyright," which would include preventing any further distribution or sale of the infringing product.

Another remedy, as described in §503, is for the infringing articles to be impounded and destroyed. This would include all copies of phonorecords, films, DVDs, or other products that contained the infringing work.

Still another remedy is actual damages to the copyright owner or profits made by the infringer. For example, if an infringer sells 10 copies of a CD, and the mechanical rate for the publisher would be $0.091 for that copy, the actual damages would be $0.91. If for those same 10 CDs, the infringer made a profit of $5.00 per CD, the profits would be $50.00. Neither of these amounts would warrant bringing a lawsuit for copyright infringement. In either case, the court could decide to impose statutory damages that would exceed those amounts, as described below.

If the court finds, however that the infringement was committed willfully, the amount of statutory damages can increase dramatically.

Statutory damages are provided in §504 (c) of the Act. Basic damages for copyright infringement are currently between $750 and $30,000 per work, at the discretion of the court; however, plaintiffs who can show willful infringement may be entitled to damages up to $150,000 per work. Defendants who can show that they were "not aware and had no reason to believe" they were infringing copyright may have the damages reduced to $200 per work.

Lastly, per §505, the court in its discretion may allow the recovery of full costs by or against any party other than the United States or an officer thereof. The court may also award a reasonable attorney's fee to the prevailing party as part of the costs.

In the real world, however, many claims of copyright infringement are settled between the parties before litigation commences or before a verdict is reached at trial. The parties can mutually agree on a remedy that compensates the owner of the infringed work for something less than what the statutes might require but also alleviates both parties of the time and expense that would be devoted to a trial as well as the risk of success and failure. A noted judge once told me, "The best compromise is one that leaves both parties slightly unhappy." A settlement is just that: a compromise that resolves the issues between the parties while compensating the infringed party in a manner that they deem acceptable under the circumstances.

Exceptions to the Exclusive Rights of Copyright Owners

There are certain uses of copyrighted material that do not require permission or licensing from the copyright owner, as set out by various sections of the Act limiting the exclusive rights granted to the copyright owner.

A. The right of first sale: Once a copy of a copyrighted work is obtained legally, either through purchase or license, that copy may be resold by the purchaser to a third party without the permission of or compensation to the original copyright owner. See §109. Effect of transfer of particular copy or phonorecord.

   If a party buys a CD containing musical compositions as well as performance by an artist, that party has the right to sell or transfer that particular copy of the CD, but does not have the right to reproduce copies of any of the copyrighted material on the CD. See §109(a).

   The same concept would apply to a piece of art. The purchaser of a painting has the right to sell that painting but not the right to make posters or other reproductions of the painting. That said, there is a little-known California law called the "Resale Royalty Act" (_California Civil Code §986_). What this law essentially states is that when a person purchases fine artwork and then resells it for more than $1,000, such seller must pay five percent (5%) of the "gross sales price" to the artist who created the artwork. See the code section for more details.

   In late 2011, a bill was introduced in Congress that would amend §106 of the Act and provide similar compensation to living artists throughout the country for artwork sold by auction houses for more than $10,000. See H.R.3688—the proposed Equity for Visual Artists Act of 2011. As of the date of this writing, this bill has not passed.

   However, in the spring of 2013, the Supreme Court held that the first-sale doctrine applies to copies of copyrighted work lawfully made and purchased abroad. In _Kirtsaeng v. John Wiley & Sons, Inc._, No. 11-697 (U.S. Mar. 19, 2013), the court held that textbooks originally purchased in Thailand could be resold in the United States, as the purchase of the books was made legally.

B. Reproduction by libraries and archives: it has been determined that libraries and other repositories of copyrighted works shall have the right to make copies for archival purposes but not for distribution. For example, UCLA has a large library of old films and television programs that are currently on film or videotape that is deteriorating. Under this principle, UCLA is allowed to make digital copies of these films so that they may be viewed by researchers or members of the general public at the UCLA facilities. UCLA may not, however, make copies of these productions for distribution or sale to the public. See §108.

C. Certain uses by educational and religious organizations are also protected under these exceptions to further their goals. §110 (1) of the Act allows for the "performance or display of a work by instructors or pupils in the course of face-to-face teaching activities of a nonprofit educational institution, in a classroom or similar place devoted to instruction." For example, a teacher in a literature class may make copies of a verse from a poem as an instructional aide for her lessons. This would be permissible, while copying an entire book by the poet in question would not be.

§110 (3) of the Act allows for "performance of a nondramatic literary or musical work or of a dramatico-musical work of a religious nature, or display of a work, in the course of services at a place of worship or other religious assembly" if the performance is free or the proceeds are used for religious purposes.

✱ D. Fair Use: This is one of the most difficult and misunderstood sections of the Act. §107 explains that the use of copyrighted material for purposes such as criticism, comment, news reporting, teaching (including multiple copies for classroom use), scholarship, or research, is not an infringement of copyright. In determining whether the use made of a work in any particular case falls under this doctrine, the factors to be considered shall include (quoting §107):

(1) *the purpose and character of the use, including whether such use is of a commercial nature or is for nonprofit educational purposes;*

(2) *the nature of the copyrighted work;*

(3) *the amount and substantiality of the portion used in relation to the copyrighted work as a whole; and*

(4) *the effect of the use upon the potential market for or value of the copyrighted work.*

These are *very* subjective tests that are the basis for many court decisions. But the Fair Use doctrine is often misquoted as an excuse to infringe copyrights by parties that know the term "fair use" but not its meaning under the law. In some cases, the party making the claim feels that it isn't "fair" that they can't use the copyrights of very successful musical artists who have a lot of money, while the user has very little. In the TV and film world, often the producers use the doctrine as an excuse to use a copyright for which they cannot get permission to use for a reasonable fee or permission is denied altogether.

Benefits of Registration

While copyright registration is not a condition of copyright protection, there are certain advantages to registering your copyrights with the Copyright Office.

1. Registration is a prerequisite to filing an infringement suit in court for works of U.S. origin.

2. If registration is made within three months after publication of the work or prior to an infringement of the work, statutory damages and attorneys' fees will be available to the copyright owner. Otherwise, the copyright owner may only obtain an award of actual damages and/or profits of the infringing party.

3. Registration establishes a public record of the copyright claim, and, if made before or within five years of publication, registration will establish *prima facie* evidence of the validity of the copyright.

4. Registrations may be recorded with the U.S. Customs Service for protection against the importation of infringing copies. For more information, go to the U.S. Customs and Border

Protection website at www.cbp.gov/xp/cgov/trade/priority_trade/ and click on "Intellectual Property Rights."

Basic Registration Process

1. *Select Method of Registration:* Paper, Form CO, or Electronic. Form CO is a new fill-in form for basic registrations, which replaces Forms TX, VA, PA, SE, and SR. It is basically a hybrid of the electronic filing and paper filing system because you fill in the form on your personal computer, but then you print and mail the form to the Copyright Office for processing.

   If filing with Form CO, go to the Copyright Office website at www.copyright.gov and click on "Forms." If filing electronically, access eCO by going to the Copyright Office website and clicking on "Electronic Copyright Office."

2. *Select Proper Form:* If filing by paper, you must call the Copyright Office at (202) 707-3000 and request that they mail you the proper form—Form TX (literary works); Form VA (visual arts works); Form PA (performing arts works, including motion pictures); Form SR (sound recordings); and Form SE (single serials). Certain applications must be completed on paper, such as Form RE renewals of copyright claims and forms for group submissions. These forms are still available on the Copyright Office website at www.copyright.gov/forms/.

3. *Complete Application:* The application may be completed by the (1) author, (2) the copyright claimant, (3) the owner of exclusive right(s) or the authorized agent of such author, (4) other copyright claimant, or (5) owner of exclusive right(s). Under certain circumstances, multiple works can be registered with one application and one fee.

   In what is referred to as a "compilation copyright registration," multiple works can be registered using the same form and paying the same single fee if all the works have the same copyright claimants. If there are different claimants, those works must be registered separately although, if there are multiple works with these same "different" claimants, they can all be registered together as well.

   This usually works best for works that have not yet been released to the public. Once released, for maximum protection the works should then be registered individually.

4. *Pay Fees:* Effective August 1, 2009, registration fees for basic claims are $65 for paper filings, $50 for Form CO filings and $35 for eCO filings. The method of accepted payment varies based on the type of filing. Basic claims include (1) a single work; (2) multiple unpublished works if they are all by the same author(s) and owned by the same claimant; and (3) multiple published works if they are all first published together in the same publication on the same date and owned by the same claimant.

5. *Submit Deposit:* Pay special attention to the deposit requirements as they vary based on the type of work being registered. Generally, unpublished works and works first published outside of the U.S. require a deposit of one complete copy or phonorecord. Works first published in the U.S. on or after January 1, 1978, require two complete copies or phonorecords of the "best edition." The Copyright Office has interpreted this to mean that eCO filers may still need to mail in a hard copy or copies to comply with the "best edition" language of the Copyright Act. For example, if you are applying for registration of a published CD on eCO, you must currently mail in hard

copies of the CD as the actual CD is considered the "best edition" of the published work (not the electronically uploaded files). You must print out a shipping slip from the eCO website to accompany such deposit.

6. *Receipt of Registration Certificate:* The Copyright Office website states that 90% of electronic (eCO) filers should receive a certificate within 6 months of completing their application; Form CO-filers within 8 months; and paper filers within 18 months. Regardless of the time needed to process the application, the effective date of registration is the date that the Copyright Office receives *all required elements in acceptable form.* Therefore, it is very important to read all instructions on the application to make sure you are submitting the application, fees, and deposit in the manner indicated, which is always subject to change. This is especially true now that there are three distinct methods of applying for registration.

For the latest information on the registration process for copyright, see **www.copyright.gov/eco/faq.html.**

CHAPTER 2

PUBLIC PERFORMING RIGHTS ORGANIZATIONS:
Inside the PROs—What They Do and How They Do It

Performing rights organizations (PROs) are a major source of income for creators and copyright owners of musical compositions, whether for music created for television and motion pictures or popular songs performed in a variety of ways. The United States has three PROs serving writers and publishers, unlike most other countries in the world that only have one PRO. The function of the PROs is to collect royalties for the public performance of music and distribute these royalties to the creators and owners. Unofficial estimates are that the PROs collect about $2 billion, most of which is paid to their members.

Copyright Law Basics for Public Performance

The right of public performance is one of the exclusive rights of copyright owners granted pursuant to Copyright Act of 1976 (USC 1700):

§ 106. Exclusive rights in copyrighted works

Subject to sections 107 through 120, the owner of copyright under this title has the exclusive rights to do and to authorize any of the following:

(4) in the case of literary, musical, dramatic, and choreographic works, pantomimes, and motion pictures and other audiovisual works, to perform the copyrighted work publicly;

Per § 101. Definitions:

To perform or display a work "publicly" means—

(1) to perform or display it at a place open to the public or at any place where a substantial number of persons outside of a normal circle of a family and its social acquaintances is gathered;

The key here is the definition of "public." The number of parties who are capable of hearing the music is not the key. If 500 invited guests gather for a wedding at the groom's family home, that is not public. If a single person sits in a nightclub open to anyone and music is played, this is a public performance. This also includes other public venues, such as music services played in shopping malls, grocery stores, restaurants over a certain size (see more below), concert halls, etc. One exception, unique to the United States, is that motion picture theaters do not require a performing rights license due to a 1948 case, *Alden-Rochelle v. ASCAP*, 80 F. Supp, 888.

> *(2) to transmit or otherwise communicate a performance or display of the work to a place specified by clause (1) or to the public, by means of any device or process, whether the members of the public capable of receiving the performance or display receive it in the same place or in separate places and at the same time or at different times.*

This clause addresses public performances via various media, such as television, radio, and the Internet, where members of the "public" can receive a transmitted performance simultaneously with other parties.

These are also sometimes referred to as "small performing rights," which are different from the "grand rights" that are granted for the use of music in stage plays or musicals and are licensed directly from the publisher, not through the PROs.

Also, per § 101:

> *A "performing rights society" is an association, corporation, or other entity that licenses the public performance of nondramatic musical works on behalf of copyright owners of such works, such as the American Society of Composers, Authors and Publishers (ASCAP), Broadcast Music, Inc. (BMI), and SESAC, Inc.*

Historical Perspective

The first PRO was founded in France. A composer, Ernest Bourget, was dining in the most fashionable café-concert at the time, *Les Ambassadeurs*. His music was being played in the café and he realized that he was not receiving any compensation for it. According to the story, he ate dinner and then walked out of the restaurant without paying his bill. When asked by the owners why he refused to pay, he was said to reply that since they were not paying for his music, he was not paying for their food. He had the courts recognize these legitimate rights founded in revolutionary laws. The provisional union of authors, composers, and publishers of music was thus established in 1850, and one year later, the professional union became a society [*société civile*] comprised of members—authors, composers, and publishers who divided the author's rights collected amongst the members in an equitable way, and this rule has been maintained to the present day. And so the *Société des Auteurs, Compositeurs et Editeurs de Musique* ("SACEM") was founded.

Performing rights organizations in the United States came into being in 1914, when a group of composers, including Victor Herbert, Jerome Kern, Irving Berlin, and John Philip Sousa, founded the **American Society of Composers, Authors and Publishers**, (otherwise known as **ASCAP**). It was formed in response to a 1909 amendment to United States copyright law that explicitly provided for performance rights as opposed to mechanical rights (royalties paid to publishers for *phonorecords*, i.e., CDs, digital downloads, etc.) or synchronization rights (music synchronized to pictures). The law—and ASCAP—were given new force when Herbert, then a celebrity composer for Broadway, sued a New York restaurant called Shanley's after hearing one of his compositions performed there. The case took a couple of years to wind through the courts, but in the end, Supreme Court Justice Oliver Wendell Holmes decided for Herbert. "If music did not pay, it would be given up," Holmes wrote. "Whether it pays or not, the purpose of employing it is profit and that is enough."

The **Society of European Stage Authors and Composers** (now known just as **SESAC**) was founded in New York in 1930 by German immigrant Paul Heinecke in an effort to help European publishers with their American performance royalties. SESAC helped broadcasters satisfy FCC requirements, supplying them with quality recordings of SESAC's substantial gospel catalog. SESAC later began signing country writers, and then songwriters from all genres.

In 1939, radio broadcasters, irked at paying royalties set by ASCAP, which was then pretty much a monopoly due to the small amount of music controlled by SESAC, founded their own PRO, **Broadcast Music Inc. (BMI)**. This they did by rounding up the many songwriters excluded from ASCAP's umbrella: what at the time were called "race musicians," toiling away in the genres of jazz, country, blues, and later, rock 'n' roll. Today, BMI represents some 400,000 songwriters from all genres as well.

ASCAP and BMI, the two largest PROs, are non-profit organizations, while SESAC (by far the smallest of the three) is a privately owned, for-profit company. Despite that difference, their goals are the same: to license the public performance rights of their respective repertoires on behalf of their writer and publisher affiliates and members to venues and broadcasters using their music, collect royalties from their licensees, and to distribute the royalties based upon their individually unique methodologies and business models.

The PROs make separate, but equal, distributions to the writers and publishers. These are the so-called "writer shares" and "publisher shares" and are the only source of music publishing income paid separately to writers, as all other income is collected by the publisher, who then divides it with the writer pursuant to their agreement.

It is important to note that the writer's ability to collect these royalties is not mandated by the Act, but by contract as well as custom and practice. <u>Writer agreements with publishing companies or production companies should clearly state that the writer has the ability to collect these royalties directly.</u>

All three PROs have offices in the major music centers of the United States and a robust Internet presence (www.ascap.com, www.bmi.com, and www.sesac.com) in order to service their members, educate potential licensees, and provide information for those seeking to use their catalogs, such as audiovisual producers for television, film, and other media.

How to Join a PRO

In order for their music to be represented by a PRO, writers and publishers must become members of the organizations. A writer may only belong to one PRO (although they may switch at some point in time to a different PRO) and their music must be published through a publisher affiliated with the same PRO. In other words, an ASCAP writer's music must be published by an ASCAP publisher, etc. As publishing companies may have writers that belong to all three PROs, they may form three separate companies, each affiliated with a different PRO, in order to follow this protocol.

All of the PROs have writer and publisher applications available on their websites and require similar information about the applicant. In the case of the publisher application, a potential member will be asked to provide four to five possible names for their publishing company, as the names must be cross-checked against the name of that PRO as well as the others. This is to make sure that there is little chance of it being too similar to another existing company and minimize errors in which royalties are paid to the incorrect party (ex.: Steve's Music and Steves Music would be too similar and the second name filed would probably be denied). If filing with all three PROs, multiple names must be devised, as the same name cannot be with the different societies.

If a writer owns their own copyrights, it is not enough to just join as a writer. It is in the best interest of the writer to join a PRO as both a writer and publisher member to ensure that both income streams get paid to them properly.

In many jurisdictions, in order to comply with local laws and, on a practical level, to open a bank account in

---

Case Study #1

Once, when trying to locate the publisher for a new female artist in order to clear a song for a TV show, I called the number listed in the ASCAP database. A woman answered and I asked if this was the number of the publisher for the artist. "Who the hell is this?" was the response. I identified myself and asked who I was speaking to. "This is (the artist)—how did you get my cell phone number?" I explained that she had listed it in the ASCAP database for the world to see and politely suggested she change it. It was changed a few days later.

Moral of the story: when registering with a PRO, do not use your personal address or phone number. Use a P.O. Box and an answering service or number of your business representative.

---

the company name, a party must file a Fictitious Name Statement (also sometimes commonly known as a "DBA" or "Assumed Name" statement). This allows the publisher to deposit checks made payable to the publishing company. This should be filed only *after* the PRO gives you the clearance to use one of the names submitted.

Once a membership is established, the member can set up online access to their account, which will allow them to register their songs, check their catalog, view their statements online, and take advantage of the other services that their PRO makes available to members.

Registering Songs

Once the writer and publisher become members of their chosen PRO, it is necessary to advise the PRO of the songs written by the writer and controlled by the publisher, and their respective shares, in order for the PRO to be able to monitor the uses of those songs, verify the writer and publisher information, and pay out accordingly. There have been many occasions in which parties have complained that they haven't received any royalties despite becoming members, but when asked if they have registered their songs, they have no idea what is being talked about. The parties have to populate the databases of the PROs in order for the songs to be tracked and for them to be paid properly.

Registering the songs can also be done online. The registering party will be asked to supply the title of the song, the writers, their shares, and their PRO affiliations, as well as the publisher names, shares, and PRO affiliations. Historically, the writer and publisher are, in most cases, each entitled to equal shares of music publishing income, or a 50/50 split. In the cases of ASCAP and SESAC, the combined shares of the writers and publishers must equal 100% (50% for the writers and 50% for the publishers), while BMI works on a 200% system (100% for writers and 100% for publishers). If the combined shares for writers and publishers do not equal the total percentage necessary for each system, the song will not be accepted.

Maintaining this information and keeping it current is crucial for the members, as outdated information can result in improper credit and/or non-payment of royalties. For example, if a member moves and the PRO is not notified, any payments will be sent to the member's old address and returned as undeliverable, costing the member all royalties until the information is current. As the PROs will only retain the unclaimed income for a limited period of time (12–18 months), delays in updating the current information may result in loss of the income for the unclaimed periods.

Once the songs are registered, if they show up in the monitoring methods of the PRO (see below for more details), the PROs will issue payments to the writers and publishers, no matter when the songs were created, recorded, or first broadcast on radio or television. Any music that is broadcast, no matter when created, can continue to earn these royalties. This is why these types of royalties are sometimes called "mailbox money," because every quarter, a check can show up for a song recorded or licensed years ago to a television program or film. This is also known as "back end" income, as it comes after the initial sales or license fees are paid for the use of the music, and it can go on for the entire term of copyright of the music.

Monitoring the Uses of Music

Each PRO uses a variety of methodologies to gather data on the use of music in order to determine the value of each song and to pay the writers and publishers their respective share. While the specific methods of each PRO are too complicated to list here, below are some examples of how they collect data from television and radio.

CENSUS: In the case of most of the major free (i.e., broadcast), pay, and basic cable television networks and the larger local television stations, the PROs conduct a census to track the shows being broadcast 24 hours a day, 365 days a year. By using this broadcast data and matching it with the music cue sheets supplied by the production companies (music cue sheets list the title, composer, and publisher of each piece of music in the program—see Chapter 4: Synchronization for Audio-Visual Productions for an example of a music cue sheet), they can determine what music was performed in these programs. By factoring in the number of times the music was performed, the circumstances under which it was performed (i.e., was it a feature or background use, was it in a program or in a commercial or promo), the timing of each use, the time of day it was broadcast (prime time is weighted higher than daytime) and the number of stations on which it was performed, the PROs use sophisticated metrics to assign a value to each "unit" of measurement, then multiply those units by a financial factor based upon how much money the PRO earned during that accounting period (usually quarterly).

SURVEY (or SAMPLE): In this situation, used for some local television stations and virtually all radio stations, the stations report to the PROs their programming and music played for a specific "sampled" period of time. By using that data, the PROs extrapolate the actual uses to estimate the potential uses. By way of hypothetical example, if you assume that Top 40 stations in New York and Los Angeles would probably be playing the same music, if a song shows up in a sample of an L.A. radio station in January, it will be assumed

---

Case Study #2

In 1951, a television program about a Cuban bandleader and his wacky redheaded wife debuted. *I Love Lucy* was an instant hit, as was the theme song composed by Eliot Daniel. Several years later, lyrics were written by Harold Adamson and, from that day forward, the writer's share of royalties for both the instrumental and vocal versions was divided between Daniel and Adamson.

In the U.S., there was a time when *I Love Lucy* was broadcast at least once a day in every city in the country that had a television station. Over 60 years later, as the program is still airing in some markets, the writers' shares of income just from performing rights is about $200,000 per year.

Case Study #3

Many years ago, the company I worked for was doing music clearance for a TV movie. The producers wanted to use pop songs but didn't have the budget to license them. The owner of the company and I were both musicians and songwriters and offered to write original songs for the film, licensing them for free to the producer on the condition that we kept ownership of the publishing. The song I wrote took me an hour. The next week, we went into the studio with some musician friends and a singer and cut two tracks in four hours. The song I wrote was included in this TV movie as well as a second TV movie. My first checks from ASCAP for the initial network broadcast were about $3,500 combined for writer and publisher shares. Over the course of 25 years, I have earned approximately $100,000 in performance royalties and still get statements to this day for small amounts of money. This for a song that has not sold a single record, never been played on the radio and, to be honest, I might not recognize if I heard it today.

that it is also on the N.Y. station during the same period. Similarly (and hypothetically), if music is performed in 50 of the top 100 television markets, it will be assumed that it is also in 50 of the second 100 stations.

These hypothetical examples are, of course, over-simplified examples of how the systems actually work, but representative of the research and statistical analysis used by the PROs to gauge the music on over 1,700 local television stations and over 14,000 radio stations. If all of these stations were monitored on a census basis, the amount of employee hours needed to process all of the data would consume most, if not all, of the revenue collected by the PROs. So, while not a perfectly accurate system, it allows for a representative allocation of income balanced with reasonable costs and labor.

As a result of these methods, whenever a song is played on radio or television and is picked up by the PROs, the writers and publishers receive a royalty, no matter how old the song or television program is. As mentioned before, this mailbox money means checks could appear years after the songs were written or the television programs first aired. Consider the money that might be earned from a song that gets a lot of radio airplay and is licensed into television programs and motion pictures multiple times.

Blanket vs. Per Program Licenses

The rates the PROs charge television and radio broadcasters are set by negotiations between the parties. When they are unable to agree, however, ASCAP and BMI are subject to proceedings before the Justice Department to set the rates. SESAC, as a much smaller player in this area, is not yet subject to rate courts but, as of this writing, there is litigation pending to have them included under a consent decree, as ASCAP, BMI, and the broadcasters feel that not being included in the same process gives SESAC a competitive advantage in negotiating fees.

For the national networks, the PROs issue blanket licenses that, for an annual fee, cover their entire repertoire publicly performed on that network. On the local television level, the stations have the choice of a blanket license, as above, or "per program" licenses.

The per program license allows a station that believes that it does not use enough music to warrant the cost of a blanket license to pay only for those programs that actually use music from a particular PRO. For example, if a station only has four hours of programming with music from ASCAP, paying for a blanket license for 24-hour coverage is probably more that it would cost if the programs were paid individually.

The local stations can decide on an annual basis as to which license they wish to use. If they choose the per program basis, they must report each program that utilizes music from that PRO and pay the mandated fee. The fee is calculated at the blanket rate broken down on a daily basis, divided by 24 hours and multiplied by 140%. At some point, depending on how many hours of programming utilize that PRO's music, the 140% fees are either higher or lower than the "daily rate."

Hypothetically (and to make the math easier), if the blanket daily rate was $2,400/day, the hourly rate would be $100/hour. Multiplied by 140%, the per program rate is $140/hour. If the station in fact has only four hours of programming using that PRO's music, the savings can be considerable, as the new per program license fees would equal $640/day instead of $2,400/day. The "break-even" point, therefore, is at about 17 hours a day of programming with music from that particular PRO. Stations with less than 17 hours of either ASCAP, BMI, or SESAC music would be better off with the per program rate from the PROs.

In a situation like this, the money paid for each program goes to the PROs but is then paid to the writers and publishers of the music in those programs, outside the "normal" distribution analysis mentioned above. As each broadcast of show is individually monitored, the amount of performance income can be substantially higher than if the station used the blanket method and was monitored on a survey basis.

Source Licensing or Direct Licensing

For some stations, and for some types of programs, a policy has been instituted by the broadcaster that they wish to bypass entirely the PRO licenses and obtain performing rights licenses directly from the owner of the music. The owner could be the production company that supplies the program or a publisher who controls a catalog being used by the producer, such as the creators of packages of music typically used in local news broadcasts. The agreements of both writers and publishers with the PROs are non-exclusive, which means that the writers and publisher have the right to negotiate and grant these rights directly if they so choose.

In this model, the station negotiates with the owner of the music (either the program producer or a publisher of the music) for a performing rights license and fee. The fee is paid directly to the publisher instead of the PROs, and can be based upon whatever criteria are agreed upon by the parties. Under this scenario, because they are getting paid directly by the broadcaster, it is possible for a publisher and writer to make more money than if the music was licensed through the PRO. However, it also possible for a broadcaster to pay substantially less than what a PRO would pay.

Composers of music for television are in an unusually precarious position when it comes to direct licensing unless they own their own publishing. For many television programs, the producer owns the music, not the writer, and the producer has the most to gain from a direct license, even if they are supposed to split the license fees with the writers. Let's look at some possible scenarios using similar fact patterns:

1. A broadcaster wishes to purchase the rights to broadcast a particular program, for which a license fee will be paid to the producer. For purposes of discussion only, assume that a one-hour program would cost the broadcaster $100,000 per episode. The broadcaster tells the producer that he will pay the $100,000 per episode, but it must include the public performance rights in the music. If the producer agrees to those terms, none of that fee is allocated towards the cost of performing rights and the composer would earn nothing from those broadcasts.

2.   Same program, same broadcaster. In this case, the broadcaster also insists on getting all performing rights in the music for the program but is willing to pay $100,200 per episode as the license fee for the program. Even though there is additional money being paid, it is not designated as "music income," so the composer may not receive any share of the increased fee, again earning nothing.

3.   Same program, same broadcaster, same license fee. In this case, however, the extra money is paid separately to the music publishing company of the producer, who splits the $200 with the writer, as is custom and practice.

4.   Same program, same broadcaster, same license fee, same split with the composer. The question must be asked, however, if the $200 allocated to the license fee for the music is fair market value for the music, based upon industry custom and practice. If the fee is equal to or higher than what the PROs would have collected and paid out, then the composer is in good shape. But if the fee is lower, the composer will earn less than they would have if the money went through the PROs. In addition, this extra fee is paid only once for each episode, not for every broadcast, so multiple broadcasts of the program diminish the composer's position even further.

Imagine what would have happened if Eliot Daniel had been asked to directly license the music from *I Love Lucy*, especially if the producers had asked for a one-time buyout of his writer's share.

In the event that a writer or publisher enters into a direct license, they must advise their PRO of the license so that the PRO does not include this program in their accountings and pay the writer and composer for these broadcasts. There have been instances where the writer or publisher failed to report the direct license, collected from both sources, and then got notice from their PRO of the double payment. The PRO then had to be reimbursed for royalties that they should not have paid out.

Non-Broadcast Uses

While the PROs license non-broadcast venues—such as concert halls, nightclubs, coffee shops, restaurants over a certain size, sports arenas, shopping malls, etc.—all over the country, these other uses of music, except for the top-grossing concerts each year, have not been reported in either a census or survey due to the overwhelming number of venues and the amount of tracking necessary. The money collected from these licensees goes into a general fund and is distributed based mostly on the same basis as money from radio and television. As such, singers who perform their own songs in clubs 300 days a year but have no television or radio exposure could end up not earning anything from their PRO. Again, the amount of manpower needed to process all of the data would consume much, if not most, of the revenue collected by the PROs.

With regard to restaurants, only those that are larger than 3,750 square feet are required to obtain performing rights licenses. This is a result of a compromise that was caused by the National Restaurant Association (or as we in the music industry like to call it, the "other NRA") objecting to having any licenses at all, claiming that music was so ancillary to the dining experience that it should not have to be paid for. The counterargument made by the music industry was that colored napkins and parsley on a plate also did nothing to enhance the diner's experiences but was a cost item to the restaurants anyway. When the Sonny Bono Copyright Term Extension Act was being debated in Congress, this exception to smaller restaurants was added as an amendment to the extension bill and, rather than lose the fight for 20 years of additional copyright protection, the music industry allowed the amendment to stand.

In 2011, however, BMI instituted BMI Live, a program designed to allow songwriters performing in live music venues to receive royalties at every stage of their careers. Songwriter/performers (not their publishers) must register their concerts and set lists online to be considered for payment. BMI will pay royalties to both writers and publishers via direct deposit. The distribution from BMI Live will be made quarterly.

SESAC pays its writer and publisher affiliates for live performances at venues of all sizes across America through its Live Performance Notification System. There, writers and publishers can list the venue name, address, size of venue, date of performance, and registered SESAC songs performed.

In October 2012, ASCAP launched ASCAP OnStage, similar in nature to the programs above. This program will allow members to submit claims for live performances to ASCAP via Member Access and receive quarterly distributions for these royalties. Each submission requires a set list so that payments can be attributed to performed works. According to ASCAP, it will have a much simpler submission process and allow for a much greater distribution in its first year.

Electronic Detection Methods

In recent years, there have been developments in electronic detection methods that, in the long run, will allow for a substantial increase in accuracy in monitoring the uses of music on television and radio. Two different methods have been developed: watermarking and fingerprinting.

Watermarking is the embedding of a digital identifier into the recording of a composition. It is the recording that is marked, not the composition itself, as there may be different recordings of the same composition, all of which would have a different watermark.

Fingerprinting is the analysis of the wave forms of the recording to uniquely identify that recording and the underlying composition. In effect, it is taking the unique "fingerprint" of that recording and giving it a tag by which it can be identified in the future. The recordings must be submitted to the fingerprint company for analysis and then the data is used to recognize the song. The smartphone application Shazam is a form of fingerprint recognition technology.

All three PROs use a form of fingerprint technology as part of their song identification and tracking techniques, but it has its limitations in the real world, such as:

(a) Not every recording has been analyzed, so not every recording can be identified. This is especially the case in music in television programs or motion pictures, in which there are 80 years of films and 60 years of television programs, many that have not, and probably will not, be submitted for analysis due to cost;

(b) If there are several recordings used, as in a sampling situation, the software may not be able to identify each unique element;

(c) Similarly, where there is dialog or sound effects over the music, the software may not be able to identify the music in this "dirty" audio;

(d) If the music on television or in the film is performed by a live act or by an actor, there is no reference recording to be analyzed unless the program submits this recording to the fingerprinting companies for review;

(e) The technologies need to be able to sample the song for a certain amount of time in order to identify it. While this time period has shrunk considerably in the past few years, it still has not been perfected;

(f) Many composers and artists use sample libraries of beats or other musical elements. If there are multiple songs that use the same underlying recording of a beat, false results might be triggered, as the technology will not necessarily be able to distinguish the different uses of the same track.

In addition to the issues listed above, in the production music library world as well as in pitching and placement agreements, it is not uncommon for a work to be given a new second title to distinguish it from the original for royalty purposes. When this happens, the recognition technologies cannot differentiate between the original title and the newly titled work, so there is a good possibility that the incorrect party may be credited and paid the performing rights income. See Chapter 10: Production Music Libraries.

Performing Rights and the Internet

The PROs are committed to licensing to websites that feature music in order to collect and distribute as much money as possible to their members.

Historically, the PROs required license fees from sites that both streamed and downloaded music. Streaming audio or audio-visual content is, indeed, a public performance of the music, similar to radio. The PROs also insisted that a download was a performance, as the music was "transmitted" to the user's computer. The courts have held, however, that downloads are considered a reproduction, not a public performance and therefore do not require licensing from the PROs. *U.S. v. ASCAP*, 485 F. Supp. 2d 438 (S.D.N.Y. 2007)

In addition, there is an exception to the need for a streaming license from sites that offer a 0:30 sample of the music for review prior to a possible purchase. This covers, for example, the iTunes-style function of being able to hear a portion of a track prior to deciding whether to purchase. A recent policy change has iTunes now offering a sample of 1:30 instead of 0:30.

There are two different types of streaming audio from the Internet: interactive and non-interactive. Non-interactive is akin to radio where, once a "station" or type of music is selected, the user has no control over what music is played. Even if the user can reject the song played, as with Pandora, this is still considered non-interactive. There are, however, limits to the input the user has to remain non-interactive. Using Pandora as the model, the user selects a "station" based upon the music of a particular artist. The program will play a limited amount of music by that artist but also music the program determines the user might like that is similar in some way. As such, it is not only that artist's music that is played, but other artists that the user has no control over. In addition, the user can only reject a certain number of songs within a specific time period in order for Pandora's non-interactive status to be maintained.

Interactive streaming gives the user control over what they hear. Spotify is a good example, as the user can select exactly which songs they wish to hear if they so choose.

These two streaming models are treated differently in terms of how license fees are calculated, as well as how the earnings to the writers and publishers are paid, with interactive fees being higher.

With listeners getting more and more music from the Internet, while it is still a small part of the PRO income, this is becoming a very important area of growth for writers and publishers and is being monitored very closely by the PROs for licensing opportunities. As with live venues, however, finding all the websites and getting license fees is a challenge.

Once streaming became more practical because of increased bandwidth and processing speed, many terrestrial radio stations began to simulcast their signals both over the air and on the station website. As the PRO licenses only covered the stations' broadcasts in their local areas, this new transmission could go worldwide (remember what the "www" stands for in website URLs). As such, until new license fees could be negotiated, many radio stations had to eliminate music from their websites or face penalties for infringement.

An additional issue is the streaming of audio-visual content online. Many television broadcasters, either free television networks or cable companies, offer their program on demand for streaming online. There are independent online services like Hulu that license programming for streaming as well. The issue facing the PROs is how to license those performances in addition to the traditional broadcasts and what those performances are worth. While initially the broadcasters' licenses included their online streams, the PROs are negotiating for additional fees for these streamed exhibitions, as they are often advertiser-supported and earn money for the broadcasters. As with almost everything on the Internet, these are rapidly changing developments. For more information on how the PROs determine Internet rates, see Chapter 13: Digital Media—Part 2.

Foreign Performance Royalties

Public performance royalties are collected through performance rights societies in each territory. Much as ASCAP, BMI, and SESAC collect these royalties in the United States, most major territories have their own PROs. These PROs are almost like quasi-governmental bodies and license performing rights to the radio stations, television stations, and (unlike the United States) motion picture theaters in their territory.

These foreign PROs monitor the broadcasts in their territories and calculate the value of the performances, much like the U.S. PROs. They conduct surveys (i.e., a statistical sampling instead of a census) of local television and some cable stations, but many foreign PROs are able to provide a virtual census for the main terrestrial stations, which is certainly preferable to a sample survey. In addition, in most foreign countries, there is monitoring of live music in concert halls, clubs, and sports stadiums, providing more detailed and accurate accountings of music performed in the territories.

Unlike the 50/50 division between writers and publishers in the U.S., the foreign royalties are divided into $^{12}/_{12}$ outside the United States. $^{6}/_{12}$ (or, in some territories, $^{8}/_{12}$) are paid by the local performing rights society directly to the U.S. performance rights societies (ASCAP, BMI, and SESAC) as the writer's share of these royalties, and the U.S. societies pay the writers directly as they do for domestic income. The remaining $^{6}/_{12}$ (or $^{4}/_{12}$) represent the owner's and sub-publisher's share of the performance income which is paid 100% to the sub-publisher. In the event that there is no sub-publisher representing the original publisher, the foreign PRO will send the publisher's share of royalties back to the domestic PRO, who will then distribute to the publisher.

Other than in mechanicals, the local adapter's (local lyric writer, arranger, and others) share of performance royalties is automatically deducted by the local societies out of the U.S. writer's share of performance royalties before payment is made to the U.S. performance rights societies (ASCAP, BMI, and SESAC). This is usually equal to $^{2}/_{12}$ of the writer's $^{6}/_{12}$ share.

CHAPTER 3

MECHANICAL LICENSING FOR AUDIO-ONLY PRODUCT

The sale of "records" has, and continues to be, the most profitable revenue source for music publishers and writers. Pursuant to Section 106 of the Copyright Act of 1976:

Subject to sections 107 through 122, the **owner of copyright** *under this title has the* **exclusive rights to do and to authorize** *any of the following:*

> *(1) to reproduce the copyrighted work in copies or phonorecords;*

> *(and)*

> *(3) to distribute copies or phonorecords of the copyrighted work to the public by sale or other transfer of ownership, or by rental, lease, or lending;* [bold added]

A mechanical license is necessary in order to manufacture and distribute sound recordings, or **phonorecords**. Phonorecords are defined in Section 101 of the Copyright Act as *"material objects in which sounds, other than those accompanying a motion picture or other audiovisual work, are fixed by any method now known or later developed, and from which the sounds can be perceived, reproduced, or otherwise communicated, either directly or with the aid of a machine or device."* The term "phonorecords" includes the material object in which the sounds are first fixed. In simpler terms, phonorecords are audio-only devices, such as vinyl records, audio cassettes, and compact discs. More recently, this definition has been expanded to include **digital phonorecord delivery (DPD)**, a music file delivered via digital download.

Of the types of licenses discussed in this book, the mechanical license is the only one where the Copyright Act specifically sets out a method whereby a party may obtain a valid license without the consent of the copyright owner, subject to certain procedures being followed, and a statutory rate of payment. As with all other types of licensing, however, the possibility exists to negotiate the terms of a mechanical license on a basis more favorable to the publisher or the record company.

Any mechanical license should apply to a particular recording of the copyright by the named artist and only on the record described in the agreement. This will prevent the record company from including this song on any other record, either by this artist or on a compilation album, without securing another license. It should also be noted that a publisher in the United States can only grant a mechanical license for U.S. rights. In other countries, the mechanical rate is set by statute (usually a percentage of something similar to the wholesale sales price, divided among the copyright owners on the recording) and collected by a local mechanical rights organization similar to a performing rights society. These organizations are quasi-governmental and control all royalties for sales of records manufactured within their territory.

A Brief History of Phonorecords

The term "mechanical" comes from the earliest days of the ability to reproduce music in a form other than by printed music. Perforated paper was used to create piano rolls that were used by player pianos to recreate the music as performed by a pianist. These piano rolls were created by machines, i.e. by a mechanical process. Later, as perfected by Thomas Edison in 1878, the *phonograph* was a device with a cylinder covered with material such as tin foil, lead, or wax on which a stylus etched grooves.

The stylus created grooves of varying depths corresponding to changes in the sound waves created by the original sound. The recording could be played back by tracing a needle through the grooves and amplifying, through mechanical means, the resulting vibrations. A disadvantage of the early phonographs was the difficulty of reproducing the phonograph cylinders in mass production.

This changed with the advent of the gramophone, which was patented by Emile Berliner in 1887. The gramophone imprinted grooves on the flat side of a metal disc rather than the outside of a cylinder. Instead of recording by varying the depth of the groove, as with the phonograph, the vibration of the recording stylus was across the width of the track. The depth of the groove remained constant. Berliner called this audio disc a "gramophone record," although it was often called a "phonograph record" in the United States.

These flat discs were created and mass produced using stampers that took the grooves from the metal discs and embedded the wax discs with grooves that were able to transmit the sound by using a needle and speaker. Wax eventually was replaced by vinyl to create phonograph records as we know them today and that are still manufactured using stampers. After vinyl records came magnetic audiotape in cassette form, then compact discs where the music was embedded digitally on the discs. But all of these media required some kind of machine to create multiple copies of the original recording.

The Compulsory License

A compulsory license for phonorecords was first codified in the Copyright Act of 1909, which allowed anyone to make a mechanical reproduction (i.e., phonorecord) of a non-dramatic musical composition without the consent of the copyright owner provided that the person adhered to the provisions of the license. The rationale behind this was the growing popularity of the player piano, uncertainty about a copyright owner's right to control the licensing of the composition, and the fear that one company could have a monopoly on the licensing process. Congress was concerned enough about this that they decided that, rather than the right be exclusive to the copyright owner, they would create a compulsory license which would allow any person to make "similar use" of the musical work upon payment of a royalty of two cents for "each such part manufactured." 1909 Act, Section 1 (e)

There were, however, certain conditions under which parties could avail themselves of the compulsory license. No one could obtain a compulsory license unless the copyright owner had authorized the first reproduction of the work. Notices also had to be filed with the Copyright Office by both the copyright owner once the copyrighted work had been reproduced and by the potential licensee in order to signify their intention to use the license. The license had a provision that the royalty to be paid was two cents per copy, a royalty that remained in effect until the Copyright Act of 1976 and acted as a ceiling for licenses that were negotiated as well as those under the compulsory license provision.

§ 115. Scope of exclusive rights in nondramatic musical works: Compulsory license for making and distributing phonorecords

Section 115 of the Copyright Act of 1976 provides for a compulsory license to make and distribute phonorecords (audio-only devices, such as vinyl records, audio tapes, compact discs, and digital phonorecord deliveries [DPDs]), subject to the following:

1. **When phonorecords of a nondramatic musical work have been distributed to the public in the United States under the authority of the copyright owner;**

   Like the 1909 Act, it should be noted that a compulsory license is only available *after* a work has previously been distributed to the public under a valid license. This allows the music publisher to determine and control the terms by which the first recording of a composition may be released. For example, the publisher of a new song may shop the song to several artists in the hope of obtaining a recording. If a major artist expresses an interest in recording the song, the publisher has the right not to allow anyone else to record the song prior to the release by the major artist. (This is known as "putting a song on hold.") Once a song has been released, however, any other artist may record the song without the consent of the publisher, subject to the terms of the compulsory license.

2. **Any person wishing to obtain a compulsory license must serve notice of intention to do so on the copyright owner before or within 30 days after making and before distributing any phonorecords of the work;**

   The notice provision now only applies to the party wishing to obtain the compulsory license. If the registration or other public records of the Copyright Office do not identify the copyright owner and include an address where notice can be served, it shall be sufficient to file the notice of intention to the Copyright Office. A failure to provide such notice makes the distribution of the recording an act of infringement under Copyright Act section 501 and fully subject to the remedies provided by sections 502 through 506 and 509.

3. **The statutory rate must be paid for each phonorecord made and distributed, with accountings on a monthly basis.**

   The statutory rates (see chart below) were set by the Copyright Royalty Tribunal or, more recently, the Copyright Royalty Judges, and are adjusted periodically. As of this writing in 2012, the statutory rate for mechanical royalties is 9.10 cents per copy for a recording up to 5 minutes. For recordings over 5 minutes in length, the current statutory rate is 1.75 cents per minute, or portion thereof. For example, if a recording is 5:05 in length, the royalty is 1.75 cents X 6 minutes = 10.50 cents per copy. Royalties are due and payable on a monthly basis. These royalty rates have recently been extended until December 31, 2017.

   The language "made and distributed" is also worth noting. A phonorecord is considered "distributed" if the person exercising the compulsory license has voluntarily and permanently parted with its possession. In laymen's terms, once a manufacturer has shipped a copy of the recording, the copy is considered "distributed" and a royalty is owed to the copyright owner beginning with the first unit distributed. This differs significantly from a negotiated mechanical license, the terms of which are discussed below.

4. **A compulsory license includes the privilege of making a musical arrangement of the work to the extent necessary to conform it to the style or manner of interpretation of the performance involved, but the arrangement shall not change the basic melody or fundamental character of the work, and shall not be subject to protection as a derivative work under this title, except with the express consent of the copyright owner.**

    Under this condition, an artist may change the composition to fit their unique style: it can be played faster or slower; it can be performed in a different key signature; it can be played in a different musical style, such as hard rock or a ballad; it can be sung by a man or a woman. The main point is that the underlying composition must remain the same. No material changes in melody, harmony, or lyrics are permitted under a compulsory license. By custom and practice, there are allowances made for minor changes in pronouns, such as changing "he loves you" to "she loves you," but not much more is allowed. Any material change in the composition requires the consent of the copyright owner to create a derivative work.

Negotiated Licenses

Despite the availability of a compulsory license, many times a potential licensee will negotiate a license with the copyright owner on different terms than those mandated in the compulsory license. This allows the parties to modify the terms of the compulsory license to fit a particular circumstance or the business practices of the parties. Some of the most commonly negotiated terms are:

1. Royalty rate: With consent of the publisher, a royalty can be set to be less than the statutory rate. There are several instances where, despite the rate being set by statute, a publisher will agree to a reduced rate. This reduction is often 75% of the statutory rate, sometimes known as a "¾ rate," but it can be any percentage of the full rate, or even a waiver of any royalties whatsoever.

    One example of where a reduced rate would be negotiated is where an older song is being included on a low-budget compilation album with more than the usual amount of songs. In this case, unless the rates were reduced, the "record company" could not afford to distribute the album with that many songs or at the lowered retail sales price. It might be to the publisher's advantage to have their song in this compilation, even with the reduced rate, especially if the record company will pay an advance on a certain number of units. Getting paid money up front, even at a reduced rate, is sometimes better than having to wait for quarterly or semi-annual royalty payments.

    Another example of a publisher granting a reduced rate is for a charity project of some kind, where the proceeds from the recordings are being donated to a worthy cause. In both of the situations above, the publishers will usually request (and be granted) a Most Favored Nations clause, guaranteeing that all parties have agreed to the reduction (or, in some cases, a complete waiver of any royalties) and no one publisher or song is getting paid more than another. A failure to grant a reduction in these cases usually means that the song in question will not be used due to the ramifications of the Most Favored Nations clause by having the rates for all other songs in the project raised to meet the highest rate.

2. Date the royalty rate is set: Under variations of the mechanical license agreement, the date that the royalty rate is set is spelled out by contract, either at a fixed rate or as the rate is adjusted pursuant to the rate proceedings. For example, some agreements state that the rate is set at the time recording of the composition is commenced, with no adjustments. Other agreements set the rate at the time of the first release of the recording, again with no adjustments. Lastly, some agreements set the rate at the time of distribution of the recordings, with periodic adjustments to match the subsequent dates of distribution.

Given that mechanical rates have, to this date, always been adjusted higher, setting the date of the royalty as early as possible and fixing it permanently is in the record company's best interest, in case the rate goes up at a later date. This was one of the problems with pre-1978 recordings where the rate was set at two cents per copy and not adjusted after the rates began to escalate in 1978.

Case Study #1

Several years ago, I was working on a project that was raising money to combat breast cancer. A television network produced a program called *Women Who Rock* featuring a number of prominent female artists. The charity behind the project was producing a compilation CD that would be available for sale at a major retailer for $5.00, with all proceeds benefiting the charity. My job was to negotiate mechanical licenses for 50% of the statutory rate. For 9 out of the 10 songs, this was easy. The 10th song was controlled by an "old school" publisher in Nashville, and the party who worked in their licensing department claimed that they never granted reduced rates. I explained again that the proceeds were to help the fight against breast cancer and again the publisher told me that they didn't reduce their rates.

As a last resort, in an attempt to shame them into reconsidering, I stated that, since they were unwilling to fight breast cancer, they must be **in favor** of breast cancer. Needless to say, that didn't work. However, a call to the head of the company resulted in a phone call to me in which the licensing person said, "Oh, I'm sorry, did you say breast cancer?" and granted the reduced rate.

Moral of the story: almost everything is negotiable if the argument is valid.

---

3. In most negotiated licenses, royalties are paid on units "sold and not returned," instead of "manufactured and distributed" as in the compulsory license. By custom and practice, most record retailers of physical goods (as they still exist) have provisions in their agreement with distributors and record companies that they are able to return for full credit any and all units that have not sold. Under this construct, the record company only owes royalties on units that have permanently left their possession and will not be returned for credit. Obviously, there is a huge difference between these two models, but it's acknowledged that making payment of royalties to the

publisher on returned units is an unfair burden on the record company, since they did not collect any fees for these returned units.

4. Because of the return policy above, the record company will want to keep a portion of the royalties earned in a reserve account in the event that the returns in a particular accounting period are larger than the royalties earned. Reserves should be limited to a maximum of 25% in any accounting period, with the reserves to be disbursed within one year from the date of withholding. In the case of digital distribution (to be discussed in more detail below), no reserves should be allowed, as there are no returns.

   Something that publishers must beware of, however, is to check the royalty statements received from the record companies to see if the royalty rate for returns is the same as for prior sales, especially in periods where the royalty rates have changed. For example, from January 1, 2004, until December 31, 2005, the royalty rate was 8.5 cents per copy. After January 1, 2006, the rate increased to 9.1 cents per copy. Records distributed prior to January 1, 2006, would have earned 8.5 cents per unit, but if returned after that date, the royalty rate had increased and, with it, the calculations or royalties made by the computers for the record companies would have also increased. Potentially, a unit returned in 2006 (but distributed in 2005) would have been credited at the higher rate, even though the publisher was paid at the lower rate, resulting in a net loss of 0.6 cents per unit to the publisher for each unit sold and returned under this scenario. This is a prime example of where a "desk audit" by the publisher could reveal discrepancies in the reporting practices of the record companies.

5. "Free goods": Copies of the records can also be given away as part of retail sales incentives. For example, if a retailer buys 10 copies, the record company then ships 12 copies. The additional two copies may be sold by the retailer without payment to the distributor. Where this gets tricky for the publisher auditing the record company is that not all units sent by the distributor to the retailer will be accounted for due to these special free goods. For example, if the retailer buys 10 copies and is shipped 12 copies, when the retailer returns six of these copies, they are only charged with four copies sold, not six. The six copies not returned (because they are in the hands of customers who have paid for them) include the two "free" copies for which the retailer is not charged and the record company pays no royalties.

6. "Special free goods": Record companies often distribute copies of recordings to radio stations, TV and film producers, nightclubs, and disc jockeys for promotional purposes. The record company will want a waiver of royalties on these so-called "free goods," but a limit on the number of units distributed without paying royalties can be negotiated.

7. Lyric reprint rights: Often, the lyrics of the song will be printed on a CD sleeve or offered electronically with DPDs. This is a right not covered under the mechanical license, so it must be requested by the record company and granted by the publisher. As the publisher and writer often want the lyrics printed, there is usually no additional fee for this right.

8. Audit rights: The publisher should have the right to audit the books and records of the record company to verify that the royalty payments are accurate and up to date. Typical language requires the publisher to give reasonable notice of their intent to audit and usually limits audits to once per calendar year. The audit clause allows the publisher a certain period of time after the statement has been issued to audit that statement, with a failure to audit within that time period

being deemed an acceptance of the statement. In addition, any statement may only be audited once. The penalty for under-reporting of royalties could be termination of the agreement, but is usually just a payment of the royalties. Sometimes, a publisher will be able to negotiate language that says that, if the underpaid royalties exceed a certain percentage of the royalties paid, the record company will pay for the costs of the audit.

Digital Phonorecord Delivery (DPDs)

The compulsory license provision also allows for the right to distribute or authorize the distribution of a sound recording by means of a digital transmission, which constitutes a digital phonorecord delivery under Section 115(C)(3)(a). There had been some debate as to whether a DPD, in addition to being a reproduction and subject to a mechanical license, was also a public performance requiring licenses from the performing rights organizations. The argument made by the PROs was that the transmission of the audio file from a server to the consumer constituted a public performance similar to the transmission of a television program or radio.

This has been determined by the courts not to be the case (*U.S. v. ASCAP*, 485 F. Supp. 2d 438 [S.D.N.Y. 2007]). A download is not contemporaneously perceived because it is simply a transfer of electronic file(s) containing copies from an online service to a local drive. The downloaded songs are not performed in any perceptible manner during the transfer; the user must take some further action to play the songs after they are downloaded. Since the electronic download itself did not involve a dance, an act, or recitation, rendering, or playing of the musical work encoded in the digital transmission, the download was not a performance of that work. As such, no public performance licenses are necessary for DPDs that are permanently stored on a user's device.

The Controlled Composition Clause

A controlled composition clause ("CCC") is a provision, usually two to three pages in length, contained in most artist agreements with a record company. The CCC applies to any composition written, published, or owned (i.e., "controlled") by the artist. In the case of an artist/songwriter, this could include songs written by the artist, the record producer, a spouse, or a long-standing songwriting partner. If a writer is also a recording artist, an essential piece of information that the music publisher must also have is knowledge of the artist's agreement with the record company, as it will severely impact the amount of mechanical royalties paid by the record company to the publisher for the writer's compositions.

Attached to this chapter is a sample of a CCC, annotated to show the details of the clause and the potential ramifications to the artist/writer and publisher. Beginning in the late 1960s and early 1970s, the record companies, in an attempt to reduce the amount of royalties paid out to artists, arbitrarily decided that an artist who writes his own material should allow the record company to pay his publisher a reduced rate for mechanical royalties and has made this a standard clause in recording contracts. The record companies have taken this a step further by sometimes placing a ceiling on the amount of the mechanical royalties they will pay on an album to 10 times 75% of the statutory rate. If an artist does not control all the compositions on his album, the difference between this rate and the actual royalties payable is deducted from the compositions he does control.

For example, if an artist wrote six of the songs on his album and used six songs written by other outside or non-controlled writers, the six songs written by others would receive the full statutory rate of

9.1 cents per copy sold, for a total of 54.6 cents. But because the record company has instituted a ceiling of 68.25 cents (75% of 9.1 cents = 6.825 cents X 10 songs), the six songs controlled by the artist would be paid only a total of 13.65 cents, or 2.275 cents per song—only 25.28% of the statutory rate! This fee would be reduced even further if the artist co-wrote his material with another writer who would receive full rate for his share of the composition. This example already takes into account the fact that, as is often the case since the advent of the compact disc, more than 10 songs are included on an album, yet the album ceiling is still based on a vinyl phonograph maximum.

MECHANICAL ROYALTIES AND THE CONTROLLED COMPOSITION CLAUSE HYPOTHETICAL ILLUSTRATION #1		
Current Statutory Rate (in cents)		9.1000
75% of the Statutory Rate		6.8250
Album Ceiling = 10 × 75% of Statutory Rate	10 × 6.825 cents	68.2500
Album = 12 Songs		
6 Non-controlled Songs	6 × 9.1 cents	(54.6000)
Available Royalties Remaining		13.6500
6 Controlled Songs	13.65 cents ÷ 6 Songs	2.2750 per song
Percentage of Statutory Rate per Controlled Song		25.28%

In the event that the artist uses more non-controlled songs than the example above, the situation for artist and publisher royalties can become even worse. For the next example, the artist records nine non-controlled songs and three controlled songs.

MECHANICAL ROYALTIES AND THE CONTROLLED COMPOSITION CLAUSE
HYPOTHETICAL ILLUSTRATION #2

Current Statutory Rate (in cents)		9.1000
75% of the Statutory Rate		6.8250
Album Ceiling = 10 × 75% of Statutory Rate	10 × 6.825 cents	68.2500
Album = 12 Songs		
9 Non-controlled Songs	9 × 9.1 cents	(81.9000)
Available Royalties Remaining		**(13.6500)**
3 Controlled Songs		**0.0000**
Percentage of Statutory Rate per Controlled Song		**0.00%**

In this case, the non-controlled songs not only take up the entire mechanical royalty allotment, the songs exceed the allotment by 13.65 cents per album. This overage will be taken from the artist royalties (or deemed an additional advance by the record company against the artist's account), making it even harder than usual for an artist to recoup their advance from the record company and earn any additional artist royalties. More to the point for the publisher is that the three controlled songs will earn **no mechanical royalties** whatsoever, due to the cap on royalties already having been exceeded.

It should be noted that some record company agreements try to use mechanical royalties earned by the controlled compositions to recoup advances the artist received under the recording agreement. This "**cross collateralization**" should not be allowed by the artist, their representatives, or the artist's publisher, as mechanical royalties should be treated as a separate income stream to the publisher and paid from the first units sold, without recoupment by the record company. And with the increasing use of "360 deals," in which where the artist signs with the same company for their record deal, music publishing, touring, and merchandising, cross collateralization is even more complicated, as the companies may try to use income from **all** of these sources to recoup any and all advances that may be paid.

Sometimes a record company will agree to pay a full statutory rate on the artist's song on the condition that the artist enters into a co-publisher agreement with the label's publisher. In such a scenario, the label's co-publisher would receive ½ of the publisher's share of income, or 25% of the license fee, with the artist's publisher and writer shares combining for 75% of the royalty. While this seems to be no different that the artist receiving 75% of the statutory rate, this model gives the label's publisher 25% of

ALL sources of publishing income, not just mechanical royalties. As such, this is a significantly worse deal for the artist.

Needless to say, the music publishing community has long fought against the concept of the CCC. But artists are sometimes so desperate to sign a recording agreement, they will agree to almost anything, such as this clause.

The United States is the only country in the world that allows a reduction in the mechanical rate by virtue of this type of contract language. This has caused some friction between the United States and foreign countries as to how mechanical royalties and publishers are treated here and abroad.

In addition, there are provisions in the Copyright Act that provide that the full statutory rate shall be paid for DPDs. Sections 115(c)(3)(E)(i) and (ii) jointly provide that no reduction from the full statutory rate may be taken for digital copies. The language is VERY confusing and not many record companies are familiar with it (or admit to it), but this mandates the full statutory rate be paid on DPDs.

The Harry Fox Agency

The Harry Fox Agency (HFA) (www.harryfox.com) is an organization that administers the issuance of mechanical licenses and collection of royalties for a large number of U.S. publishers. Based in New York City, it is an arm of the National Music Publishers' Association, a non-profit group and the largest U.S. music publishing trade organization. In 1927, the National Music Publishers' Association established HFA to act as an information source, clearinghouse, and monitoring service for licensing musical copyrights.

HFA represents its publisher clients/licensors for the licensing, collection, and distribution of these mechanical licenses and royalties to the record company/licensees wishing to distribute recordings featuring songs owned and controlled by HFA-affiliated publishers. By affiliating with HFA, publishers have access to services to assist them in administering their catalogs. HFA is not a publisher, nor does it own copyrights. It merely administrates mechanical rights on behalf of its publisher clients. As a large number of publishers are affiliated with HFA, record company licensees are often able to license a majority of their recordings through HFA.

As noted above, publishers in the U.S. can only issue licenses for products manufactured and distributed in the U.S. (including territories and possessions). HFA issues licenses for these rights, but only to U.S. manufacturers or importers with a U.S. address. A foreign entity must obtain licenses in their home territory. HFA does, however, provide collection and monitoring services for its publisher clients for music distributed and sold in over 90 territories around the world through reciprocal agreements with mechanical societies in those territories.

How HFA Works

A publisher must join HFA as a publisher affiliate, which can be done for no fee. This allows the publisher to register their songs with HFA (much as a publisher does with one of the PROs) so that a potential licensee can find them on the HFA website and obtain a license electronically. A record company or distributor may also join as a licensee in order to access HFA and the licensing tools it has.

Once the licensee has established an account, it can research the HFA database to locate the correct songs, titles, writers, and publishers, and request that a license be issued for a particular project. At this point in time, separate licenses must be requested for physical and digital product, although that may streamline in the future. Licenses will be issued listing the song being licensed, the project to which it is being licensed, the parties on both sides, and all other licensing terms and restrictions.

Due to the large number of independent labels and artists that might sell very few copies, HFA also has a process for licensing for a small number of copies by paying for these copies in advance with a credit card. "Songfile" (www.harryfox.com/public/songfile.jsp) is the HFA tool for this type of licensing, which allows for licensing of 25–2,500 copies of a song at the full statutory rate plus a small handling fee.

It should be noted that HFA is merely a licensing agent and does not have the full powers of an administrator. It is unable to negotiate for a reduction in the mechanical rate. This must be done directly with the publisher by the licensee. HFA will honor any reduction granted by the publisher but will require permission from the publisher in writing.

For the services provided, HFA charges a commission based on the royalties earned. This royalty fluctuates, depending on expenses and any lobbying efforts being undertaken by the NMPA. As of this writing, the current rate is 6.75% of all royalties (except for those services which are on a commission-free basis). There is also currently a supplementary commission of 1% to fund the work of the NMPA in lobbying efforts regarding royalty issues before Congress or in the courts.

Other Services and Licenses

HFA also represents publishers for the licensing of ringtones, ringbacks, and mastertones as well as limited downloads and interactive streaming. These areas will be discussed in more detail in Chapter 12: Digital Media—Part 1.

One of the most important services provided by HFA is the regular auditing of record companies. HFA conducts royalty compliance examinations of record company licensees utilizing HFA staff as well as outside accountants to verify the accuracy of royalty statements reported and payments remitted by licensees. These audits, if conducted by an individual publisher, would be prohibitively expensive and time consuming. HFA conducts these audits on behalf of all of their publisher members, which greatly reduces the costs.

MECHANICAL RATES		
Effective Date	**Flat Rate** (up to 5:00 in length)	**Per-Minute Rate** (over 5:00 in length)
March 23, 1905	2.000¢	N/A
January 1, 1978 (per Copyright Act of 1976, effective January 1, 1978)	2.725¢	0.500¢
January 1, 1981	4.000¢	0.750¢
January 1, 1983	4.250¢	0.800¢
July 1, 1984	4.500¢	0.850¢
January 1, 1986	5.000¢	0.950¢
January 1, 1988	5.250¢	1.000¢
January 1, 1990	5.700¢	1.100¢
January 1, 1992	6.250¢	1.200¢
January 1, 1994	6.600¢	1.250¢
January 1, 1996	6.950¢	1.300¢
January 1, 1998	7.100¢	1.350¢
January 1, 2000	7.550¢	1.450¢
January 1, 2002	8.000¢	1.550¢
January 1, 2004	8.500¢	1.650¢
January 1, 2006	9.100¢	1.750¢
January 1, 2008 – December 31, 2012	9.100¢	1.750¢
January 1, 2013 – December 31, 2017	9.100¢	1.750¢

CONTROLLED COMPOSITION CLAUSE

This clause would be found in an artist agreement with a record company, but would be binding on the music publisher for the artist/writer. Some of the capitalized terms in this clause are found elsewhere in the artist agreement but will be described in the comments below as well.

11.   LICENSES FOR MUSICAL COMPOSITIONS

(a)(1)   You (Artist) hereby grant to Record Company an irrevocable license under copyright to reproduce each Controlled Composition on Records and distribute them in the United States.

> Although a mechanical license is usually issued by the music publisher, in this case the agreement requires the artist to issue the license. While the license may not actually be issued by the artist, the net effect is that the artist must instruct their music publisher, who controls the music, to issue the license on these terms.

(a)(2)   For that license, Record Company will pay Mechanical Royalties, on the basis of Net Sales, at the following rates:

> "Net Sales" is usually defined as "units sold and not returned" and also excludes free goods and other non-royalty bearing units.

(A)   On audio Records manufactured for distribution in the United States:

> U.S. publishers can only grant rights for records sold in the U.S.

The rate equal to seventy five percent (75%) of the minimum compulsory license rate

> Also known as a "¾ rate."

(regardless of playing time) applicable to the use of musical compositions on audio Records under the United States Copyright Law at the

> The long song formula for songs over 5:00 will not be used.

(b)   The total Mechanical Royalty for all Compositions (including Controlled Compositions) shall be (1) with respect to each single disc LP (or the equivalent thereof), not more than ten (10) times the amount which would be payable on it under clause (a)(2) if it contained only one Controlled Composition;

> The album rate is set at 10 x 75% of statutory, regardless of how many tracks are on the album.

(2)   with respect to each single Record released hereunder, not more than twice that amount;

> 2 x 75% for singles.

(3)   with respect to any EP released hereunder, not more than five (5) times that amount; and

> 5 x 75% for an EP.

(4)   with respect to Multiple Record LPs (if any), the maximum aggregate Mechanical Royalty shall not be more than the maximum Mechanical Royalty applicable to a single disc LP or the equivalent Record (as set forth above) multiplied by a fraction, the numerator of which is the Suggested Retail List Price of such Multiple Record LP at the commencement of the accounting period when such LP is initially released, and the denominator of which is the Suggested Retail List Price of "top-line" singles disc LPs at the time of initial release of such Multiple Record LP.

> For multiple CDs, the ceiling will be based on a formula comparing the price of the multiple CD to a single CD. For example, if a multiple CD sells for $27 and a single CD sells for $18, the ceiling for the multiple CD will be 1.5 times the ceiling for the singles CD = 15 x the 75% rate, again without regard to the actual number of tracks on the multiple CD.

With respect to the exploitation or sale of Records as described in paragraphs 7.02 other than with respect to EPs, Singles and Multiple Record LPs, 7.03 (other than with respect to club sales through third parties such as the RCA Record Club where a separate license is negotiated between such club and the copyright proprietor and paid by such club) and 7.96,

This applies to mid-priced or budget CDs or sales to military bases.

the Mechanical Royalty maximum shall be three-fourths (¾) of the amounts prescribed in this subparagraph. Any amounts in excess of the applicable maximums pursuant to this sub-paragraph (b) shall be treated as described in subparagraph (f) below.

¾ of 75% for these units.

(c)   Mechanical Royalties shall not be payable with respect to Records otherwise not royalty bearing hereunder,

Excludes royalties on free goods.

with respect to non-musical material or with respect to Composition of one minute or less in duration.

Excludes royalties on extremely short songs.

No Mechanical Royalties shall be payable in respect of Controlled Compositions which are in the public domain or are arrangements of Compositions in the public domain

Excludes royalties for songs in the public domain.

except if such arrangement is credited by ASCAP or BMI, then the Mechanical Royalty otherwise payable hereunder will be apportioned in the same ration as used by ASCAP or BMI in determining the credits for public performance of the work, provided you furnish the record company with satisfactory evidence of that ratio.

For copyrighted arrangements of public domain songs, the record company will pay royalties on the same basis as ASCAP or BMI credit works of this type, i.e., usually as a small percentage of an original composition.

(d)   Record Company will compute Mechanical Royalties on Controlled Compositions as of the end of each calendar quarter period in which there are sales or returns of Records on which Mechanical Royalties are payable to you on or before the next May 15, August 15, November 15, or February 15, Record Company will send a statement covering those royalties and will pay any net royalties which are due.

Quarterly accountings. Some record companies account semi-annually instead.

THE HARRY FOX AGENCY LICENSE

The Harry Fox Agency license, although widely used, has certain flaws in the language of the agreement. That said, the language is generally non-negotiable due to the immense volume of licenses HFA generates.

The Harry Fox Agency Inc.   601 West 26th Street, 5th Floor, New York, NY

This sets out to whom the license is being issued and identifies the specific license for future reference.

To: _____   License No. _____

_____   Date: _____

_____   TRX. NO. _____

Refer to provisions hereof reproduced in (E) varying terms of compulsory license provision of Copyright Act. The following is supplementary thereto:

Sections A and B identify the particular song being recorded, the writers and publishers of the song.

A.   SONG CODE: XXXXXX

  TITLE: _____   WRITERS: _____

B.   INCOME PARTICIPANT (S):
  PUBLISHER NAME _____
  ADMINISTRATIVE SHARE: _____

C.   RECORD NO.: _____

  ARTIST: _____

  ROYALTY RATE: STATUTORY
      PLAYING TIME: _____ MINUTES _____ SECONDS

  ALBUM: _____

  DATE OF RELEASE: _____
  RECORD LABEL: _____

  CONFIGURATION CODE: CD – COMPACT DISC (ALBUM)

Section C provides information about the specific recording of the song listed above. Keep in mind that a mechanical license is only valid for the recording and release for which it is issued. If this same record is re-released on a soundtrack album or greatest hits record by the same artist, a new license would be necessary.

D.   ADDITIONAL PROVISIONS:

  THE AUTHORITY HEREUNDER IS LIMITED TO THE MANUFACTURE AND DISTRIBUTION OF PHONORECORDS SOLELY IN THE UNITED STATES, ITS TERRITORIES AND POSSESSIONS AND NOT ELSEWHERE.

Mechanical licenses issued in the United States can only grant rights for records manufactured and distributed in the United States. Other territories have their own licensing bodies and royalty rates.

CREDIT: IN REGARD TO ALL PHONORECORDS MANUFACTURED, DISTRIBUTED AND/OR SOLD HEREUNDER, YOU SHALL USE YOUR BEST EFFORTS TO INCLUDE IN THE LABEL COPY OF ALL SUCH PHONORECORDS, OR ON THE PERMANENT CONTAINERS OF ALL SUCH PHONORECORDS, PRINTED WRITER / PUBLISHER CREDIT IN THE FORM OF THE NAME OF THE WRITER(S) AND THE PUBLISHER(S) OF THE COPYRIGHTED WORK.

Credit to the songwriter and publisher is usually required as part of a mechanical license.

E.   GENERAL VARIATIONS OF COMPULSORY LICENSE PROVISION:

You have advised us, in our capacity as Agent for the Publisher(s) referred to in (B) supra, that you wish to obtain a compulsory license to make and to distribute phonorecords of the copyrighted work referred to in (A) supra, under the compulsory license provision of Section 115 of the Copyright Act.

Recognition of the notice requirement for compulsory licenses, even though this is actually a negotiated license, due to the modifications below.

Upon your doing so, you shall have all the rights which are granted to, and all the obligations which are imposed upon, users of said copyrighted work under the compulsory license provision of the Copyright Act, after phonorecords of the copyrighted work have been distributed to the public in the United States under the authority of the copyright owner by another person, except that with respect to phonorecords thereof made and distributed hereunder:

This grants the licensee all the rights under a compulsory license with the following modifications.

1.   You shall pay royalties and account to us as Agent for and on behalf of said Publisher(s) quarterly, within forty-five days after the end of each calendar quarter, on the basis of phonorecords made and distributed;

Quarterly accountings instead of monthly accountings under the compulsory license. Note, however, the language for payments for phonorecords "made and distributed" (the language in a compulsory license), rather than "sold and not returned" that would usually be found in a negotiated license.

2.   For such phonorecords made and distributed, the royalty shall be the statutory rate in effect at the time the phonorecord is made, except as otherwise stated in (C) supra;

The rate is set as of the date the recording is made, with no adjustments in the event the statutory rate changes in the future.

3.   This compulsory license covers and is limited to one particular recording of said copyrighted work as performed by the artist and on the phonorecord number identified in (C) supra; and this compulsory license does not supersede nor in any way affect any prior agreements now in effect respecting phonorecords of said copyrighted work.

License applies to this recording only.

4.   In the event that you fail to account to HFA and pay royalties as herein provided for, said Publisher(s) or his Agent may give written notice to you that, unless the default is remedied within 30 days from the date of the notice, this compulsory license will be automatically terminated. Such termination shall render either the making or the distribution, or both, of all phonorecords for which royalties have not been paid, actionable as acts of infringement under and fully subject to the remedies provided by, the Copyright Act.

In the event that the licensee fails to make payments, they are given cure period of 30 days from the date of written notice. If they continue to fail to pay, the license is terminated and the licensee is subject to a claim of copyright infringement.

5.   You need not serve or file the notice of intention to obtain a compulsory license required by the Copyright Act.

6.   Additional provisions are reproduced under (D) supra.

As HFA has been notified of the intent to obtain a license, no notice needs be filed with the Copyright Office or publisher, as required by the Act.

MECHANICAL LICENSE (I)

This is a negotiated license drafted from the perspective of the publisher.

PUBLISHER NAME
STREET
CITY, STATE, ZIP

[Date]

RECORD COMPANY (OR "LICENSEE") NAME
STREET
CITY, STATE, ZIP

Title: _____
Composer(s): _____
Publisher and Copyright Date: _____
Performance Rights Affiliation: _____
 Artist: _____
Record Title & Catalog No.: "__" - _____
ISRC # _____

Song Timing: _____
Date of Release: _____

Gentlemen:

You have advised us that you wish to use the above captioned copyrighted musical composition (hereinafter referred to as the "copyrighted work"), under the compulsory license provision of the United States Copyright Act (hereinafter referred to as the "Copyright Act"), to wit: Title 17, U.S.C. Section 115, upon the parts of instruments serving to reproduce mechanically the copyrighted work.

We hereby grant to you

a non-exclusive license pursuant to the compulsory license provision of the Copyright Act to use the copyrighted work or any portion thereof, whether words and/or music, including the title thereof, in the manufacture, production, recording, distribution and sale of records upon the terms and conditions hereinafter set forth.

Mechanical licenses are granted for one composition, performed by one artist, on one recording, so these details are filled in here. Note the fields for catalog numbers and ISRC numbers, to verify the single use. Any other uses of this recording (such a compilation or soundtrack album) require a new, unique license.

Song timing and date of release identify the basis for the amount of the statutory royalty.

Per Section 115, the record company sent a Notice of Intention to obtain a compulsory license.

Rather than strictly rely on the compulsory license provision, the publisher is granting a negotiated license to the record company, which will modify some of the terms of the compulsory license while retaining others.

All mechanical licenses are non-exclusive.

You shall have all rights which are granted to, and all the obligations which are imposed upon, users of the copyrighted work under the compulsory license provision of the Copyright Act after use or permission or knowing acquiescence by us in the use of the copyrighted work upon the parts of instruments serving to reproduce mechanically the work (viz: phonograph records) by another person, except that with respect to recordings manufactured by you:

1.   The territory of this license is limited to the United States of America, its territories and possessions.

> Publishers in the U.S. can only grant rights for the U.S., as other countries have mechanical rights societies that collect royalties directly from the record companies or distributors.

A.   You agree, for all rights and privileges granted to you hereunder, to pay us for each record **manufactured and actually sold or otherwise distributed.**

> The language here is unclear as to whether the quantity of records paid is on "manufactured and distributed" or "sold and not returned," as the term "actually sold" would indicate the ability to credit returns.

by you or your licensee, serving to reproduce mechanically any portion of the copyrighted work, subject to the provisions set forth in Paragraph 11 hereof, at the full statutory rate (based upon timing) provided for in the Copyright Act in effect at the time of such sale or other distribution.

> Royalty rate set at the full statutory rate (based upon timing) in effect at the time of sale or distribution.

B.   With regard to records manufactured and sold or distributed as "free" and "bonus" record through any mail order and/or club operation carried on by you or your subsidiaries, affiliates or licenses, no reductions in the rate specified in Paragraph 1.A will be allowed.

> No reduction in royalties for free goods, which must be paid at the full rate.

2.   You shall render to us within sixty days, after June 30 and December 31 of each year hereafter, a written statement setting forth the amount of accrued royalties earned in the preceding three month period. You shall concurrently therewith remit and pay to us the amount of money to which we have become entitled during said period.

> Semi-annual accountings. Some agreements call for quarterly accountings.

3.   We, or our designated agents or representatives, shall have the right to examine your books and records, and those of your licensees and distributors, at reasonable times and upon reasonable notice in order to verify the accuracy thereof, and the statements based thereon.

> Publisher shall have the right to audit the books of the record company for accuracy.

4.   In the event you fail to fully and accurately account to us and pay royalties to us based thereon, we shall have the right to repudiate and revoke this agreement by giving you written notice to such effect. The effect of any such repudiation and revocation shall not relieve you of your obligation to account and pay royalties to us hereunder which have been earned through and including the date of such repudiation and revocation or which may be earned by reason of your exercise of any of the rights granted hereunder through and including the date of such repudiation and revocation.

> A failure to account, or a discrepancy in accounting, gives the publisher the right to terminate this license, subject to the record company still having the obligation to pay for any royalties earned as of the date of termination. Any distribution of records after the date of termination could be deemed an infringement of publisher's copyright, which typically has stronger penalties than just a breach of contract action.

5.   This agreement covers and is limited to one particular recording of the copyrighted work as performed by the artist(s) and on the record described hereinabove. This agreement does not supersede nor in anyway affect any prior agreements now in effect respecting recordings of the copyrighted work.

> See note above regarding one recording/one artist.

6.   This agreement shall not be assignable by you and any attempted or purported assignment by you shall be void and of no force or effect.

> This agreement is with this particular record company and may not be assigned to another party.

7.   You need not serve or file the notices required by the Copyright Act.

> As this is a negotiated license, notice to the Copyright Office is not needed.

8.   You shall imprint the correct title, name(s) of writer(s), on the label of each and every single record, or in the case of LP-records, on the label or the back liner of the album cover, manufactured by you hereunder; in the event any of the foregoing is omitted or appears incorrectly on the records, you shall immediately correct any such errors and/or omissions upon notice of same.

> Credit information for CDs. Usually for DPDs, this information is embedded in the digital file as "metadata" and viewable by various means.

9.   Notwithstanding anything to the contrary contained in this agreement, no other licensor of musical compositions shall be accorded appropriate credit on any LP-record manufactured by you hereunder in any manner whatsoever which is more favorable than the manner in which appropriate credit is accorded to us. Moreover, no other licensor of musical compositions shall be dealt with by you in any respect whatsoever in a manner more favorable than the manner in which we are dealt with herein, including without limitation, the amount, manner of payment, and manner of accounting for payment, of royalties hereunder.

> A Most Favored Nations clause regarding credits.

10.   In the event more favorable terms are granted to any third party than are contained herein, this agreement shall be deemed amended to incorporate same as of the date when such higher rate is paid or such more favorable terms are granted to such third party and continuing for the duration of the period during which such higher rate is so paid or such more favorable terms are granted.

> A broader MFN clause regarding other elements, including royalty rates. This is often used when a reduced royalty is granted for compilations, charity CDs, and other reductions not required by a controlled compositions clause.

11.   In connection with the manufacture, sale or other distribution by you of your licensees of records hereunder, you shall take all steps necessary to prevent any copyright held by us in and to the copyrighted work from being dedicated to the public domain. Notwithstanding the generality of the foregoing, if all or any part of the work, or any elements thereof, is reproduced in any written form, in connection with such manufacture, sale or other distribution, you shall place or require to be placed adjacent thereto the appropriate copyright notice in our name. You shall indemnify and hold us harmless of and from any and all loss, damage and expense, including attorney's fees and costs, arising from or in connection with your failure to comply with this provision.

12.   The term "record" as used in this agreement shall be deemed to include all conventional type of phonograph records now in use, as well as compact discs, reel-to-reel tapes, audio-only cassettes, digital audio tape (DAT), eight-track recordings and digital phonorecord delivery (DPD). Said term does not, however, include sound motion pictures, audio-visual (video) cassettes, CD-ROM, CD-I or any other devices by which both picture and sound may be transmitted to the audience simultaneously.

> The definition of record, which includes all forms of audio "now in use" but specifically excludes all forms of audio-visual devices.

13.   You shall forward to us, free of charge, upon the first sale or other distribution of the work, five (5) copies of each record in each configuration manufactured by you hereunder. In addition, we may purchase promotional copies of records from you at the lowest promotional price charged by you to music publishers for promotional copies.

> Often, publishers request copies of the recordings for their files and also to be able to pitch the songs for other uses.

14.   We may assign this agreement, any part thereof and any rights hereunder. You agree that you shall not pledge, hypothecate, mortgage or in any way encumber the license hereby granted. No modifications or extensions of this agreement shall be binding unless in writing and signed by the party sought to be bound.

15.   This license is binding upon the successors, assigns, heirs and representatives of the parties hereto. This licensing agreement is made in the State of California, United States and its validity, construction and effect shall be governed by the laws thereof.

> Sets the jurisdiction for any court proceedings.

16.   In the event that either party hereto files a suit in any way connected with this agreement, the unsuccessful party shall pay to the prevailing party attorney's fees and any and all costs incurred.

> The possibility of having to pay the other party's attorneys fees can act as a deterrent to the filing of a lawsuit and encourage settlement of any claims.

17.   It is understood by the parties that all the remedies provided for in the Copyright Act and otherwise provided by law shall be applicable to this agreement. Any such remedies set forth herein shall be in addition to such statutory or other remedies.

18.   In the event that you manufacture a record hereunder, containing a new arrangement of the work, all right, title and interest therein, including such material and universal copyright therein, and extensions and renewal thereof, shall remain vested in and be deemed to be our sole and exclusive property.

Nothing contained in this agreement shall be construed to permit you to add lyrics to the work without prior written permission from us.

19.   This license is effective upon the date specified hereinabove.

Very truly yours,

_____

By: _____

APPROVED AND ACCEPTED:

_____

By: _____

Title: _____

See section in this book on copyright infringement and the possible remedies and penalties. It can be found in Chapter 1: Copyright Basics.

A new arrangement could be considered a derivative work, which requires the consent of the copyright holder. This language ensures that any new version is owned by the publisher and that the arranger cannot claim either partial ownership or a share of the royalties.

No new lyrics may be added to the song without the consent of the publisher.

MECHANICAL LICENSE (II)
ROYALTIES REDUCED DUE TO CONTROLLED COMPOSITIONS CLAUSE

This is a negotiated license drafted by a record company and is weighted in their favor.

PUBLISHER NAME
STREET
CITY, STATE, ZIP

[Date]

RECORD COMPANY (OR "LICENSEE") NAME
STREET
CITY, STATE, ZIP

Artist: _____
Record Title & Catalog No.: "_____" - _____
ISRC # _____
Date of Release: _____

See comments to previous license for comments on this section and other sections below that are not annotated.

Gentlemen:

You have advised us that you wish to use the copyrighted musical compositions listed on Schedule "A", attached (hereinafter referred to as the "copyrighted works"), under the compulsory license provision of the United States Copyright Act (hereinafter referred to as the "Copyright Act"), to wit: Title 17, U.S.C. Section 115, upon the parts of instruments serving to reproduce mechanically the copyrighted work.

We hereby grant to you a nonexclusive license pursuant to the compulsory license provision of the Copyright Act to use the copyrighted work or any portion thereof, whether words and/or music, including the title thereof, in the manufacture, production, recording, distribution and sale of records upon the terms and conditions hereinafter set forth.

You shall have all rights which are granted to, and all the obligations which are imposed upon, users of the copyrighted work under the compulsory license provision of the Copyright Act after use or permission or knowing acquiescence by us in the use of the copyrighted work upon the parts of instruments serving to reproduce mechanically the work (viz: phonograph records) by another person, except that with respect to recordings manufactured by you:

1)   The territory of this license is limited to the United States of America, its territories and possessions.

2)   a)   You agree, for all rights and privileges granted to you hereunder, to pay us for each record manufactured and actually sold and not returned by you or your licensee, serving to reproduce mechanically any portion of the copyrighted work, subject to the provisions set forth in Paragraph 11 hereof, at eleven (11) times seventy-five (75%) percent of the minimum statutory rate (with no regard to timing) provided for in the Copyright Act in effect at the time of such sale or other distribution.

> Due to a controlled compositions clause in the artist's agreement with the record company, the royalties are reduced to 75% of the statutory rate, **irrespective of timing**, with a ceiling of 11 times 75% for the entire album.

(i)   On commercial videos sold, seventy-five (75%) percent of the above rates as applicable in the territory of sale.

> Although not a synchronization license *per se*, this agreement has language addressing royalties for the sale of music videos at 75% of the rate listed above.

(ii)   On records sold through a direct mail or mail order distribution method or through any combination of the foregoing, the royalty rate will be the lesser of (A) the otherwise applicable royalty rate, or (B) fifty (50%) percent of the net receipts from the sale of those records.

> For direct sales via mail order, the royalty rate is 75% of statutory or 50% of the net receipts from the sale of the record, whichever is less.

(iii)   On mid-price records the royalty rate will be eighty (80%) percent of the otherwise applicable royalty rate.

> A reduction for mid-priced sales to 80% of the 75% rate.

(iv)   On budget records the royalty rate will be fifty (50%) percent of the otherwise applicable royalty rate.

> A further reduction for budget sales to 50% of the 75% rate.

On multiple albums, the royalty rate will be the lesser of: (A) the otherwise applicable royalty rate and (B) the otherwise applicable royalty rate multiplied by a fraction, the numerator of which is the PPD of the multiple album and the denominator of which is the product of the PPD of a top-line single-disc record and the number of discs contained in the multiple album.

> "PPD" is published price to dealers, or what we call wholesale (as opposed to retail), which is the price paid by the distributor or record store to the record company. This clause is similar to the clause in the controlled compositions clause above, but uses PPD as the measure of pricing instead of the suggested retail list price.

(vi)   On records sold in the form of electronic transmissions, downloads or any other so-called new configurations the royalty rate will be seventy-five (75%) percent of the otherwise applicable royalty rate, provided however that the royalty rate payable to you under this subparagraph shall increase to one hundred (100%) percent of the applicable royalty rate if the percentage of electronic transmission of the overall turnover of your recordings sold hereunder shall exceed twenty-five (25%) percent, commencing in the immediate following accounting period such turnover was reached.

> Despite the language of section 115 (c)(3)(E)(ii)(I) providing for full statutory rates for DPDs, this clause allows for a further reduction from the reduced rate above to 75% of 75%, as it was part of the artist's controlled composition clause with the label. Note, however, the increase in the rate back to the original 75% of statutory if digital sales meet a certain percentage of overall sales. For a publisher, this is a horrible clause to have to accept but was mandated by the artist agreement.

(vii)   Notwithstanding the foregoing: (1) No royalties or mechanical royalties will be payable on records furnished as free or bonus records or on records distributed for promotional purposes to radio stations, television stations or networks, record reviewers, or other customary recipients of promotional records;

on so-called "promotional compilations" records; on records sold as scrap or as cut-outs,

or on records sold at less than fifty (50%) percent of their regular wholesale price to distributors, subdistributors, dealers, or others, whether or not the recipients thereof are affiliated with you, or for records for which you are not paid, provided however that you shall always adhere to the mechanical rights regulations of the respective collecting societies.

b)   You will have the right to maintain reasonable reserves of a maximum of twenty (20%) percent of the sales in each accounting period against returns and other adjustments, and will liquidate each reserve in equal parts within four (4) accounting periods after it is initially retained.

3)   You shall render to us within ninety days after June 30 and December 31 of each year hereafter, a written statement setting forth the amount of accrued royalties earned in the preceding six month period. You shall concurrently therewith remit and pay to us the amount of money to which we have become entitled during said period.

4)   We, or our designated agents or representatives, shall have the right to examine your books and records, and those of your licensees and distributors, once during the four (4) year period after the rendering of that statement; at the end of such four (4) year period (whether or not we have performed an audit), each statement will become binding and not subject to objection for any reason, unless, prior to such time, we provide you with a specific objection, in writing, setting forth in reasonable detail the basis for such objection.

We agree that any claim we make against you will be limited to a claim for amounts payable to us hereunder, and we will not seek equitable relief.

No mechanical royalties on free goods.

"Promotional compilations" are CDs created by the labels featuring a number of their artists to promote the label's catalog as a whole, not a particular artist.

No royalties paid on records sold for less than 50% of the wholesale sales price (or less than so-called "budget" CDs).

The record company is able to keep 20% of the royalties earned in any period as "reserves" against future returns. Reserves will be disbursed over a period of four accounting periods.

Accountings are semi-annual, with payments due 90 days after the end of the period.

The publisher has the right to audit the record company for up to four years after the issuance of the statement.

An underpayment of royalties will not entitle the publisher to terminate the agreement.

In the event any such audit shall reveal an underpayment by you of five (5%) percent or more, you shall make good such underpayment and reimburse us for the reasonable costs of such audit.

If the discrepancy is over 5%, the label will be responsible for paying the costs of the audit.

5)   In the event you fail to fully and accurately account to us and pay royalties to us based thereon, we shall have the right to repudiate and revoke this agreement by giving you written notice to such effect. The effect of any such repudiation and revocation shall not relieve you of your obligation to account and pay royalties to us hereunder which have been earned through and including the date of such repudiation and revocation or which may be earned by reason of your exercise of any of the rights granted hereunder through and including the date of such repudiation and revocation.

A failure to account, or a discrepancy in accounting, gives the publisher the right to terminate this license, subject to the record company still having the obligation to pay for any royalties earned as of the date of termination. Any distribution of records after the date of termination could be deemed an infringement of publisher's copyright, which typically has stronger penalties than just a breach of contract action.

6)   This agreement covers and is limited to one particular recording of the copyrighted work as performed by the artist(s) and on the record described hereinabove. This agreement does not supersede nor in anyway affect any prior agreements now in effect respecting recordings of the copyrighted work.

7)   This agreement shall not be assignable by you and any attempted or purported assignment by you shall be void and of no force or effect.

The license may not be assigned to any third party.

8)   You need not serve or file the notices required by the Copyright Act.

9)   You shall imprint the correct title, name(s) of writer(s), on the label of each and every single record, or in the case of LPrecords, on the label or the back liner of the album cover, manufactured by you hereunder; in the event any of the foregoing is omitted or appears incorrectly on the records, you shall immediately correct any such errors and/or omissions upon notice of same.

10)   Notwithstanding anything to the contrary contained in this agreement, no other licensor of musical compositions shall be accorded appropriate credit on any LPrecord manufactured by you hereunder in any manner whatsoever which is more favorable than the manner in which appropriate credit is accorded to us. Moreover, no other licensor of musical compositions shall be dealt with by you in any respect whatsoever in a manner more favorable than the manner in which we are dealt with herein, including without limitation, the amount, manner of payment, and manner of accounting for payment, of royalties hereunder. In the event more favorable terms are granted to any third party than are contained herein, this agreement shall be deemed amended to incorporate same as of the date when such higher rate is paid or such more favorable terms are granted to such third party and continuing for the duration of the period during which such higher rate is so paid or such more favorable terms are granted.

11) In connection with the manufacture, sale or other distribution by you of your licensees of records hereunder, you shall take all steps necessary to prevent any copyright held by us in and to the copyrighted work from being dedicated to the public domain. Notwithstanding the generality of the foregoing, if all or any part of the work, or any elements thereof, is reproduced in any written form, in connection with such manufacture, sale or other distribution, you shall place or require to be placed adjacent thereto the appropriate copyright notice in our name. You shall indemnify and hold us harmless of and from any and all loss, damage and expense, including attorney's fees and costs, arising from or in connection with your failure to comply with this provision.

12) The term "record" as used in this agreement shall be deemed to include all conventional type of phonograph records now in use, as well as compact discs, reeltoreel tapes, audioonly cassettes, digital audio tape (DAT), and eighttrack recordings. Said term does not, however, include sound motion pictures, audiovisual (video) cassettes, DVD, CD-ROM, CD-I or any other devices by which both picture and sound may be transmitted to the audience simultaneously.

13) We may purchase promotional copies of records from you at the lowest promotional price charged by you to music publishers for promotional copies.

No free copies to publisher.

14) We may assign this agreement, any part thereof and any rights hereunder. You agree that you shall not pledge, hypothecate, mortgage or in any way encumber the license hereby granted. No modifications or extensions of this agreement shall be binding unless in writing and signed by the party sought to be bound.

15) This license is binding upon the successors, assigns, heirs and representatives of the parties hereto. This licensing agreement is made in the State of California, United States and its validity, construction and effect shall be governed by the laws thereof.

16) In the event that either party hereto files a suit in any way connected with this agreement, the unsuccessful party shall pay to the prevailing party attorney's fees and any and all costs incurred.

17) It is understood by the parties that all the remedies provided for in the Copyright Act and otherwise provided by law shall be applicable to this agreement. Any such remedies set forth herein shall be in addition to such statutory or other remedies.

18)   In the event that you manufacture a record hereunder, containing a new arrangement of the work, all right, title and interest therein, including such material and universal copyright therein, and extensions and renewal thereof, shall remain vested in and be deemed to be our sole and exclusive property. Nothing contained in this agreement shall be construed to permit you to add lyrics to the work without prior written permission from us.

19)   This license is effective upon the date specified hereinabove. Very truly yours,

PUBLISHER
    Federal ID Number: _____

By   _____

APPROVED AND ACCEPTED:

RECORD COMPANY

By   _____

Title   _____

SCHEDULE "A"

Selection Number   CD   123456   "ALBUM TITLE"

Artist: ARTIST

Publisher: PUBLISHER

Song Title *Writer(s)*	Timing	Share	Penny Rate
"Title 1" *(Writers)*	5:01	100%	$0.06825
"Title 2" *(Writers)*	3:55	100%	$0.06825
"Title 3" *(Writers)*	5:39	100%	$0.06825
"Title 4" *(Writers)*	4:23	100%	$0.06825
"Title 5" *(Writers)*	6:41	100%	$0.06825
"Title 6" *(Writers)*	7:04	100%	$0.06825
"Title 7" *(Writers)*	4:38	100%	$0.06825
"Title 8" *(Writers)*	7:33	100%	$0.06825
"Title 9" *(Writers)*	4:27	100%	$0.06825
"Title 10" *(Writers)*	14:24	100%	$0.06825
"Title 11" *(Writers)*	4:32	100%	$0.06825
		Total	**$0.75075**

75% of the statutory rate of $0.091 in effect at the time of release.

Despite a timing of over 5:00, the "long song" rate of $0.0175 per minute is not in effect, due to the language of the controlled composition clause.

If the statutory "long song" rate was in effect, this song alone would earn $0.2625 per sale.

CHAPTER 4

SYNCHRONIZATION LICENSING FOR AUDIO-VISUAL PRODUCTIONS

Sometimes a television or film producer will want to use a popular or recognizable (or even unknown) song in a production to add a specific flavor to the scene or because of the secondary meaning attached to it. Movies that take place in a certain time period may wish to use music from that era (i.e., *Forrest Gump*). Certain song lyrics can be used as a substitute for dialogue to convey a message left unspoken by the characters (*One Tree Hill*). A nightclub scene may have a band or recording playing in the background with the actors dancing (*Pulp Fiction*).

When copyrighted music is included in an audio-visual production, be it a television program, motion picture, home video, video game, or interactive media, there are potentially two separate copyrights involved that need to be licensed: (1) the musical composition, typically owned by the music publisher; and (2) the specific recording of that composition, typically owned by the artist's record company. Licensing of these two copyrights is generally called synchronization (sync) rights and master recording rights, respectively.

Licensing sync rights from the music publisher might be possible without needing master rights from the record company if the music is recorded specifically for the production, such as being sung on camera or recorded by the underscore composer. However, any time a master recording is used, a sync license must also be obtained for the song, unless the composition is in the public domain. Because any one song may have several different recorded versions, the owner of the sync rights will remain constant while the owner of the master may vary, depending on which recorded version used. For example, the song "Yesterday," by John Lennon and Paul McCartney, has been recorded by approximately 6,000 different artists. Each artist's record company controls

Case Study #1

Reality competition programs, such as *American Idol* or *The Voice*, license synchronization rights from the publishers of the songs performed. Since the songs are being sung by the contestants, there are no separate master recording licenses necessary, as no master recordings are being used.

In a similar fashion, in a television program like *Glee*, the cast members sing popular songs as part of the script and, because the actors are singing, again there are no master recordings being used.

the rights to that artist's master recording, but the publisher of the song remains the same, no matter which version is used.

For both music publishers and producers of audio-visual productions, clearing and licensing music is an area that requires a certain amount of knowledge regarding copyright, the policies and practices of the potentially numerous parties involved, and the parameters of the terms necessary to structure the deal correctly. There are companies who specialize in this area, can offer expert opinions and guidance, and actually perform the function of clearing the music on behalf of production companies.

Copyright Law Basics for Sync Licensing

Licensing the use of a copyright in copies of audio-visual works is part of the right of reproduction granted exclusively to copyright owners in Section 106 of the Copyright Act (Title 17 U.S.C.). Although the word "synchronization" is not mentioned specifically, Section 106 gives the copyright owner the exclusive right to reproduce and authorize others to reproduce the copyrighted work in copies, such as television programs, motion pictures, and home videos. "Synchronization" is the right to reproduce an audio representation of a copyrighted work with a visual image on film, tape, or other visual media. The visual image is "married" or "synchronized" to the music, so that every time the same scene is shown the same music is heard. (With the exception of video games, most licenses do not allow for the manipulation of the audio track to be shown with a different scene than the one being licensed.)

Many producers are under the mistaken impression that a small portion of a song may be used without obtaining a license. One often hears, "You can use (a) up to X number of measures of music (b) up to X seconds of music or (c) up to X notes for free." **This is totally false.** Any part of copyrighted music reproduced in a production must be licensed. This includes lyrics that are spoken instead of sung, since the lyrics are copyrighted as part of the song and cannot be used without clearance even though there is no music accompanying them.

That said, you often hear lines from songs spoken in these productions. While no exact rules exist, as a rule of thumb, if the dialog is such that normal people would speak the same words in the course of conversation, this may not require clearance. But if the use of the lyric is unusual for conversation, the song must be cleared. As an example, if one character says to another, "She loves you," that is normal. But if one character says, "She loves you" and the second character says, "Yeah, yeah, yeah," that may require clearance of The Beatles' song.

In this context, the "Fair Use" doctrine (17 U.S.C. ' 107), as discussed in Chapter 1: Copyright Basics, does not apply except in rare instances. Also, distinguish between a comedic use and a true parody, which must make fun of the work that is the subject of parody. Keep in mind also that the Fair Use and parody exceptions are defenses to claims of copyright infringement for an unauthorized use and are part of United States law only. Other countries, which have adopted the concept of "*droit moral*," or moral rights, will not recognize the defense to an unauthorized use on these grounds. This could have a significant impact on a producer's ability to distribute the production throughout the world.

Identifying the Owners

The first step in licensing music for a production is identifying the copyright owners of the material. Titles of songs are not protectable, so there can be many different songs with the same title, or many different recordings of the same song. Since copyrights may be split, with ownership by several parties, making sure that the production company is able to locate all parties that have an interest in any particular song is essential to the licensing process. On a practical level, publishers should know who their co-publishers are and how to reach them. As discussed in the first chapter, songs may be divided both by ownership percentage or territory, or both, resulting in multiple owners. With the increased awareness of the value of music publishing, it is not uncommon for the interests of each writer of more recently created compositions to be controlled by separate publishers.

ASCAP, SESAC, and BMI have websites that allow the user to access some of their contact and ownership information for research. This can usually provide the composer and publisher names and many of the addresses and telephone numbers. The publishers' duty is to provide accurate information to the PROs to allow users to contact them. That includes supplying and maintaining current address, phone, and email information. Many publishing companies have information on their websites as well. Caution should be exercised, however, as the information in the performing rights societies' databases only applies to the copyright owners of the United States rights and is not always accurate. If there are owners of rights outside the United States, a producer searching these databases would be unaware of the additional parties and might think they are obtaining all the rights they need from only the U.S. publishers.

In cases where there are multiple owners of a song, a good practice for publishers to follow is to advise the production company representative of that fact and supply as much contact information as is available. If a production company cannot locate all co-publishers of a song, the more likely it is that the song cannot be cleared and will not be used in the production.

Issues with Multiple Publishers

If there are multiple publishers, in most cases the producer will need to obtain permission and negotiate a fee with each party separately. Each of the multiple parties has the right to grant or deny permission, which means if one publisher grants approval and one publisher denies approval, the producer cannot use the song, as he will be unable to obtain rights to 100% of the composition.

Under common law principles, if there is no agreement between the parties otherwise, any co-owner can grant rights on behalf of the entire copyright without consulting his co-publishers, subject to a duty to account to the other parties. In the real world, however, most publishers are reluctant to grant rights for another party because (1) the other party may be more likely to grant rights without them next time, and (2) there is a duty to account to the other party. A producer will not know if an agreement between the parties for separate licensing and administration exists, so the prudent thing to do is to negotiate with each party separately.

There was a recent example of multiple parties owning a song where a major music publisher owned and controlled 0.5% of a song by a major artist. **0.5%?** One has to ask what the contribution to that song was that entitled the writer and his publisher to earn 0.5% of the song. Did the writer add a word to the lyrics? Did he bring the donuts to the recording session? Was this a tip to the pizza delivery guy? In this instance, with the total license fee being $750.00, a check was written to the major publisher for $3.75, which they then had to split with the writer.

For older songs, copyright terminations and reversions under both domestic and foreign copyright laws may cause a split in the ownership of the copyright. For example, one company may have rights for the United States while another may have rights for the balance of the world. With the relatively recent practice of sampling, there can be 10–15 publishers of a single song, all of which administer their own shares and need to be contacted.

Using Most Favored Nations Clauses

In the same fashion that each party can grant or withhold approval, once approved, each party can set the fees for its share. A common practice, however, is for co-publishers to set fees on a Most Favored Nations ("MFN") basis, so that each party receives an equal fee, pro rata to their share of the song. Sample MFN language is as follows:

> *In the event that Producer grants more favorable terms including, without limitation, additional consideration in any form, to the co-publisher(s) of the Composition(s) (where applicable) licensed hereunder or any third party granting rights with respect to use of musical compositions in the Program, Producer shall notify Publisher thereof, and this Agreement shall be deemed amended to incorporate same as of the date when such higher rate is paid or such more favorable terms are granted to such third party, and to continue for the duration of the period which such more favorable terms are granted.*

It would not be uncommon for the MFN clause to also include the owner of the master recording, so that the record company and publisher(s) receive equal treatment. In rare cases, the MFN will be for all music in the production, not just with co-owners, as the producer may suggest fees based upon certain budgetary criteria, or the nature of the program is such that having all parties treated equally benefits both publishers and producers. For example, for a concert show where an artist is performing all of his No. 1 records, it makes sense to have all songs treated the same. On shows like this, it is always amazing when a publisher will say, "My song was No. 1 for six weeks while some other songs were only No. 1 for two weeks, so I should get more money." At this point, the producer has the option of dropping this song, because increasing the price of this one song increases the price of all the others in the program.

There are also times where an MFN clause can be used to reduce fees instead of increasing them. For example, for a particular song, there are two publishers, each with a 50% interest in the song. One quotes $1,000 and the other quotes $1,500, both quotes based on 100% of the composition, with each publisher taking their *pro rata* share of the fee. The first publisher's share would be $500, while the second publisher's share would be $750. If the first publisher had an MFN clause, however, that share would be increased to $750 to match their co-publisher. However, in an attempt to reduce the fees, a producer might go to the second publisher and ask that the quote be lowered from $750 to match the $500 quote of the first publisher, and offer an MFN clause to ensure that both parties are being treated equally.

Key License Terms

Other than the specific contract language, to be discussed later in this chapter, negotiating for a sync license involves two main elements: permission and a determination of the license fee. As an exclusive right of the copyright owner, **permission** *must* be secured for the reproduction of the work in the program. There is no such thing as a compulsory license in sync licensing as there is in mechanical licensing. A publisher has absolute discretion to grant (or deny) permission, for any reason whatsoever, or for no reason at all.

Setting a **license fee** is also within the discretion of the publisher, as there is also no statutory rate as in mechanical licensing. Each production has its own licensing needs and each song has its own unique value to the publisher, so these negotiations are a one-to-one process between the publisher and the production company.

For the use of a composition in a single production, the primary components of the license terms consist of (1) media, (2) territory, and (3) length of the term of the license.

Media describes the method by which the production will be made available to the public. For example, there are various forms of television:

Free or broadcast television, such as CBS, NBC, ABC, and local stations that are available over-the-air without charge to the viewer;

Basic cable television, such as CNN and MTV, which is available to cable customers as part of the basic package they receive upon signing up with the cable service;

Pay or subscription television, such as HBO or Showtime, for which an additional fee is paid by the viewer for access to the pay networks' programming on an all-you-can-eat basis;

Satellite television, which incorporates many of the features of basic cable and pay TV but is delivered via satellite rather than by cable;

Pay-per-view events ("PPV"), such as one-time major sporting events or concerts, for which the viewer pays a fee for that individual program;

Video-on-demand ("VOD"), in which the viewer is able to watch a program at their convenience instead of waiting for the program to be run according to the networks' schedules; and

Pay video-on-demand ("PVOD"), for which the viewer pays a fee for the right to view at their convenience.

There are also theatrical exhibition (publicly performing for profit or not-for-profit in motion picture theaters, film festivals, and other places of public entertainment where motion pictures are customarily exhibited), non-theatrical exhibition (on common carriers such as commercial airlines, trains, ships, and buses, as well as in educational, religious and penal institutions, health care facilities, libraries, museums, hospitals, military bases, oil rigs, marine and industrial installations, clubs, bars, restaurants, and similar non-theatrical venues where there is typically no direct charge imposed for viewing), home video (audio-visual products for personal use), Internet streaming and downloading (electronically delivered copies regardless of the means of data retention), as well as receiving programming via wireless mobile devices.

Territory is the geographic area where the production will be distributed. It could be as small as a local television market or as broad as throughout the universe. Common intervals between those extremes would be for the United States, U.S., and Canada; world excluding U.S. and Canada; or specifically named territories.

Term would be the length of time the producers want to exploit the production. It could be as short as a few weeks or in perpetuity, depending in the distribution of the production. Again, common intervals could be one year, five years, 10 years, or any other time period requested by the producers.

Below is a grid showing how the items listed above can be mixed and matched, by selecting the media, territory, and term from each column to match what the producer needs and is requesting:

MEDIA	TERRITORY	TERM
Free Television	United States	1 year
Free and Basic Cable Television	United States & Canada	5 years
Pay & Subscription Television	World excluding United States & Canada	10 years
All Television Media	Worldwide	Duration of copyright term owned and controlled by publisher
All rights in all media	Universe	Perpetuity

Everything else being equal, the more media, territory, or term requested by the producers, the higher the fee will be. One important point to remember as a publisher is that producers have distribution requirements that they must meet, which involve all of the elements discussed above. While the publisher has the right to deny the use of the music on the license terms requested by the producers, rarely can the publisher modify the license terms without the producer deciding *not* to include the song in the production, as to do so on terms that do not meet the needs of the production will require re-editing of the program, taking it out of distribution or breaching the distribution agreement. A publisher who thinks that a 10-year term is too long can either refuse to license or add to the fee to compensate for the additional time period. The same concept applies to the other terms.

This is the function of the marketplace, where buyers determine what they want and sellers determine what terms they will accept. To use a non-music example, a customer wants to buy five steaks at the grocery store. If the grocer doesn't want to sell five steaks, he might try to persuade the customer to buy only three. But if the customer needs five steaks, they will go to a different store that will sell them five steaks instead of trying to modify their purchase. The same principle applies to music licensing, in that the producer has certain needs and will find a publisher of a different song to agree to his terms.

Additional Information for a Publisher to Consider

In determining whether permission will be granted and what license fee will be requested, a publisher will want to know, and the producer should expect to supply, the following information regarding the project into which the music will be licensed:

> Name of the production
> Name of the production company
> Actors starring in the production

Director and writer
Film budget/music budget
Synopsis of the film
Specific scene description where music will be used (script pages may be requested)
Usage (visual or background, vocal or instrumental) and approximate timing

All of these factors are important to the publisher, with the last three items of most importance in determining permission and fees. For example, when asked how the song is being used, a producer may say that the scene is a young man and woman, sitting in a car, listening to the radio when the song is played. This sounds innocent enough, so the publisher grants the approval. The writer calls all his family and friends to tell them about the use of the song and everyone tunes in to watch. What transpires is the following: a young man and woman are sitting in a car, listening to the radio when the song is played. The woman says, "I hate that song!" This is not the result that the writer or the publisher had hoped for. By not asking for more detailed information, such as seeing script pages, the publisher has embarrassed the writer and injured not only the value of the copyright but the relationship with a creative partner.

As for usage and timing, all things being equal, the longer the use, the higher the fee. If the song is sung on camera, as opposed to being used in the background, this will raise the fee as well.

Each publisher can value their own songs on whatever criteria they choose. More popular songs, or songs by more popular artists, will tend to earn higher fees than less popular songs. For new artists, there are times when there will be opportunities to license songs to a television program, but the producer will insist that they do so only for no fee to the publisher or artist.

Despite my natural objection to licensing music for free, there are valid reasons to do so, especially if there is value in other ways that the artist might receive. If the artist feels that the exposure on the program is important, or that the exposure might drive sales of the song, this is worth something to the artist and publisher. If the program lists the song in the credits, or features the song and artist on an "art card" (a card at the end of the program that says "This episode of the program featured music by [*band name*]"). Perhaps the program website will list the songs with a link to the artist's iTunes page. These all have value to the artist that don't require the production to pay a fee.

Case Study #2

One of our artists was approached about having their song in a very popular television program. The producers offered a fee of $6,000, which was a reasonable fee for this type of use. We counter-offered with a fee of $12,000 because we knew that the program really wanted the song. The producers then countered with a fee of $0, but an art card at the end of the program. Half of the band members wanted the art card, half of them needed the money and wanted the fee. A fistfight broke out in our offices between the band members. By time the issue was resolved, another artist accepted the art card and our artists missed a great opportunity.

The Quotation Process

Generally, the production company (or its representative) will want to contact the publisher as soon as the music is being considered for use. Most companies will require a request in writing, with email being the preference these days. As there are sometimes several approvals necessary, the more lead time available, and the more information supplied, the higher the chance of negotiating a reasonable fee in a timely manner. The publishers will quote a fee that is contingent on the music actually being used in the production. There is generally no obligation to pay a publisher for music not used. Obtaining these quotes is free, i.e., there is no "option" fee for setting the price, only the requirement of payment if used. Quotes are generally valid for a reasonable period of time (60–90 days) but may be extended, especially if the producer knows that his post-production schedule will require a longer period. This can be part of the negotiation.

After receiving a fee quotation, the producer should issue a letter of confirmation, setting out the key deal terms as he understands them, to ensure that there is no miscommunication between the parties. This also offers the publisher the opportunity to dispute any of the deal points in the confirmation letter prior to the song being used in the production.

Sync licenses are typically non-exclusive, meaning that the same song can be licensed to multiple productions at the same time. Licensing of the copyright does not generally include the right to utilize the title of the song as the title of the production or to incorporate the story of the song into the production. These rights must also be specifically negotiated with the copyright owner. An example of this is the film *Ode to Billie Jo*, from the Bobbie Gentry song of the same name, which used the story of the song as the underlying plot of the film.

As indicated in the titles of each of the sample agreements at the end of this chapter, these different agreements are drafted both from the perspective of the publisher and the producer. While there are differences in substantive licensing terms for television and motion pictures, these agreements, taken together, give a representative idea of the positions taken by both parties in this type of negotiation. Keep in mind, everything is negotiable.

Motion Picture Licensing

In licensing for motion pictures, producers generally will want to acquire rights for "any and all media, now known or hereafter devised, throughout the universe, in perpetuity" for a one-time flat fee price (" buyout"). In simpler terms, everything, everywhere, forever. This includes media not currently known or developed. This is a major negotiating point.

In the days before home video, licenses either had language allowing the studios to distribute the films "in any and all media" or the license was silent on this point. When these films began to be released on video, the music publishers and record companies were unable to combat the studios with regard to additional payment for video.

Now, with the advent of all types of new media platforms, such as video on demand, iTunes video, mobile devices, and the Internet, movies can be shown on a personal computer, smartphone, or television screen and be manipulated in ways never dreamed of even five years ago. Most of the studios are requesting rights "in any and all media, *whether now known or hereafter developed*," without wishing to pay any additional fees to music publishers and suggesting that any copyright proprietor who does not grant these rights will not have their music used in these films.

Despite a philosophical objection to this, virtually all publishing and record companies have had to agree with this grant, not only for films but also for television programs. In some cases, the license will allow for future technologies but only where the film can only be shown in a linear manner, as opposed to media in which the film's images can be manipulated and rearranged.

One other difference in motion picture sync licenses is a grant of public performance rights for theatrical exhibition in the United States (currently, there is no right of public performance in master recordings except for digital transmissions). By court consent decrees entered into between the Justice Department and the performing rights societies, music copyright owners are required to issue domestic public performance licenses to movie producers on a per-film basis. This goes back to a case from 1948 (*Alden-Rochelle, Inc., et al. v. American Society of Composers, Authors and Publishers et al.*, 80 F. Supp. 888) when the owners of movie theaters brought suit against ASCAP for anti-trust violations, claiming that ASCAP, in representing the publishing interests of the motion picture studios that produced the films, paid a large portion of the monies collected from the theater operators back to the same studios. As a result, performing rights societies in the U.S. do not license movie theaters as the foreign societies do in their respective territories. Sync licenses should include a provision granting public performance rights directly to producers for U.S. theatrical exhibition but should also state that television broadcasts in the U.S. should be subject to the stations having performing rights licenses as well as.

With low-budget independent films, the amount of the license fee is always an issue. Sometimes, a small film will have to be shown at festivals in order to acquire distribution. While the exposure of the film is minimal, it still requires a valid license. The producers will want to exhibit the film in what they feel is the final version, with all the desired music included in the film. To achieve that, sometimes music publishers will grant limited rights for festivals for a nominal fee with an additional pre-negotiated fee as an option if the film gets distribution. Also, sometimes the license fees will be determined on the basis of a "step deal." In this scenario, a small fee is paid upon distribution of the film, with additional payments paid in "steps" based upon the earning of revenue by the film. For example, the initial fee could be $5,000.00, with an additional $2,000.00 payment when the film reaches $5,000,000.00 in box office, another payment at $7,500,000.00, etc., until the license fee equals (or exceeds) what would normally have been charged. The theory here is that small films (with small budgets) also need music but when the film starts earning money, the music publishers will receive additional compensation.

If there is a soundtrack album for the film, this can also have an impact on licensing fees. Many publishers will reduce their fees if they are included on the soundtrack album. The reasons should be obvious: the soundtrack album is another source of potential revenue.

Licensing for Television

As a right of reproduction, a publisher needs to understand what type of television program requires (or does not require) a license. All programs shot on film, a reproductive medium by definition, require a license. However, because there is no reproduction, live programs, such as news programs, sports, and specials such as the Academy Awards do not require a license.

In addition, certain programs recorded on videotape do not require a license. An "ephemeral recording" is a reproduction of a work, in the form of a copy or phonorecord, produced by an entity legally entitled to publicly perform the work, made solely for the purpose of later transmission by a broadcasting organization legally entitled to transmit the work. Section 112 of the Copyright Act allows a transmitting organization (such as a television network) to make an ephemeral recording of no more than one copy of a particular transmission program if (1) the copy is retained by the transmitting organization and no further copies are made; (2) the copy is used solely for the transmitting organization's own transmissions; and (3) unless preserved exclusively for archival purposes, the copy is destroyed within six months from the date of transmission. The ephemeral recording privilege would extend to copies or phonorecords made in advance for later broadcast, as well as recordings of a program that are made while being transmitted and are intended for deferred transmission or preservation. Thus, the exemption applies whether the images and sounds to be broadcast are first recorded (on a videotape, film, etc.) and then transmitted, or the program content is transmitted live to the public while being recorded at the same time.

In this case, programs like *The Tonight Show*, which are recorded on videotape earlier in the day for broadcast at a later time, do not require a license. Extending this provision by custom and practice, neither do the first-run episodes of other network programs on videotape, such as some of the situation comedies currently running. Reruns of videotaped programs, however, do require a license, since the very fact that they are broadcast again means that they were reproduced outside the scope of Section 112. As a practical matter, since almost all prime time programs are repeated, many television producers of videotaped programs negotiate for sync and master licenses prior to taping their programs in order to have some negotiating leverage and to prevent the use of a song that may not be licensable, either because the use may be denied after the program is already completed, or the fee may be higher than the producer wants to pay. Once the program is completed, the producer's ability to remove the song or negotiate a reasonable fee diminishes greatly, making clearance in advance a practical necessity.

An interesting point here is that, while a program may fall under the exception for the first broadcast, a re-broadcast will violate the exception, as the program (in order to be re-run) had to be recorded for purposes of further broadcasts. In cases like this, many publishers will insist that any license include not only the rebroadcasts, but the first broadcast as well. As such, the license term and media might need to be adjusted to take the first broadcast into account.

Licensing Terms for Television Programs

Because of the changing patterns and uncertainty of television distribution, producers commonly negotiate for a number of different licensed rights, both for immediate broadcast needs and no-cost options for future exploitation, in order to fix their costs as the outset of production. As stated previously, for the use of a composition in a single episode of a television program, the license terms consist of (1) media (e.g., free television, basic cable television, pay television, home video); (2) territory (e.g.,: world, United States, world excluding United States); and (3) length of license term (e.g., one year, five years, perpetuity vs. life of copyright vs. duration of copyright owned and controlled by publisher). All of these, including the use and duration of use of the copyright, go into determining whether permission will be granted and what fee will be charged.

Because of the some of the recent changes caused by additional methods of exploitation, such as video on demand, iTunes video, transmissions to mobile devices, and Internet exhibition, both with streaming and downloading, many of the major production companies are now acquiring all rights in all media (excluding theatrical exhibition), now known or hereafter devised in order to avoid having to make additional payments or secure additional rights each time a new distribution method is developed. This is potentially beneficial to publishers and songwriters as the fees are paid up front instead of having to wait for a variety of options to be exercised. The detriment, of course, is that no new revenue streams will develop if additional forms of distribution are devised.

Licensing for Home Video

For projects being distributed in the home video market, either by physical goods or digital downloads, the process of clearing music is the same as above. One potential difference, however, is the method of payment. For home video licenses, there are three main ways of paying license fees:

1. A per unit royalty: Similar to the process for mechanical royalties, the publisher will set a per unit price for the use of their song in the project. Often, this price is coupled with an advance payment based on a certain number of units, with accountings to the publisher on a quarterly or semi-annual basis for all units sold once the advance is recouped;

2. A buyout: This is a one-time flat fee payment for as many units of the video as the producer can sell. In some ways, this is a gamble by both sides: the producer hopes he sells millions of units for this one-time fee, making the per unit cost go way down. The publisher, on the other hand, hopes that the project sells very few units, making the per unit cost go up; and

3. A rollover, or rolling advance: This technique combines the two scenarios above, where the producer pays an advance for a certain number of units and, once that threshold has been met, pays another advance, and so on. This allows the producer to somewhat avoid the costs of regular accountings and allows the publisher to get larger payments instead of incremental royalties on a lesser number of units.

Video games follow the same model as above, but are one of the rare instances in which the publisher will allow the manipulation of the visual images with the music, as video games are more "interactive" than traditional programming.

As home video productions are for private, not public viewing, there are no public performance royalties generated from the distribution and sale of these programs. Streaming over the Internet, however, could generate some performance income.

Licensing for Commercials

Licensing music for commercials has become one of the most lucrative areas for music publishers and writers, as the use of popular music has grown in recent years. Sponsors realize that having a popular song attached to a product has a benefit and actively seek the right music to provide that benefit.

In the world of commercials, the term can be as short as a few weeks in a local market for a test period to see if an audience responds favorably to the commercial and the music. In many cases, the initial term is for 13 weeks, but sometimes up to a full year. With viral marketing now a reality, rights are obtained not just for television and radio but also for online and mobile uses. In addition, in many situations, the sponsor will obtain options for additional terms for an additional fee. Usually, this fee for the additional term is more than the original fee and is determined by an increase based on a percentage of the original fee, i.e. year two is 15% higher than year one, year three is 15% higher than year two.

This is one of the few areas where exclusivity is requested by the parties licensing the music, as they don't want the same song used to promote another product during their campaign. In most cases, however, the exclusivity is limited to products in the same type of product, sometimes called "category exclusivity." In this instance, if the publisher is licensing music for a soft drink, they may not license it to another soft drink company but are free to license it to a car company.

Writer Approvals for Commercials

This area of licensing is the most sensitive for writers. As noted in Chapter 6: Songwriter Agreements, the right of approval for uses in commercials is one that is almost automatically granted to the writer upon request. By allowing the music to be used in a commercial, the writer is almost endorsing the product. If the product is one that the writer might object to, the publisher should avoid granting permission for the use. For example, a vegetarian would not want to license music to a burger chain, and a writer with a family history of alcoholism would not want to license to a beer company. For many years, Carole King, who wrote "(You Make Me Feel Like) A Natural Woman," has not allowed her song to be licensed for feminine hygiene products.

Case Study #3

One of the most interesting denials in recent years involves the group The Doors. In the late 1960s, when Jim Morrison was still alive, he refused to allow one of their songs to be used for a car commercial. Many years later, long after Morrison's death, The Doors were approached again about licensing for a car commercial for Cadillac, which would feature the song "Break on Through (To the Other Side)" and use the song as the tag line for the commercial. As approval required unanimous consent by all the members of The Doors (or their estates), one of the members denied the use on the basis that, since Jim had denied a similar use more than 30 years prior, he would have denied the use today as well. This member exercised his right not to approve based upon the "wishes" of his deceased bandmate. The members of Led Zeppelin had no such qualms, however, and Cadillac went on to use their song "Rock and Roll" instead, paying several million dollars for the privilege.

Collecting Public Performance Royalties

In order to collect the public performance royalties generated by distribution of the motion picture, television program, or commercial to which you have licensed music, a **music cue sheet** needs to be filed with the performing rights organizations (PROs). This is a document created by the production company which lists every piece of music in the program, in show order, with the title, composer, publisher, performing rights affiliations, usage, and timing of each piece of music. (A sample cue sheet follows this chapter.) The description of the usage (i.e., VV = visual vocal, IB = instrumental background, etc.) is a factor in what the PROs use in determining the value of the use according to their weighting formulas. The PROs use this document to track the broadcasts or foreign theatrical exhibitions of the production and match it with the music in the productions to determine how much in royalties each composition earns. This music cue sheet is part of the delivery requirement for the production and travels around the world with it to provide the same information to the foreign PROs. The PROs around the world use broadcast data from a variety of sources to determine when, where, and how often a program is broadcast. While the producer's responsibility is to file these documents, a synchronization license should have a provision requiring the publisher to receive a copy as well. This allows the publishers to file with the PROs on their own to ensure that the PROs get this information and allows the publishers to provide copies to their foreign sub-publishers so that foreign performances can be tracked as well.

For commercials, the process is a little more complex. Because broadcast data is not readily available from the same sources that track television programs, a publisher must obtain a copy of the commercial and media buy information from the sponsor. The media buy information contains the stations, dates, and times that the commercials were run, thereby allowing the PROs to do the same type of analysis as they do with regular programming and allocate credits to the music in the commercials. Some sponsors are hesitant to provide this information, as their belief is that their marketing plans are proprietary. Nevertheless, most will provide the information, even if it takes a little while after the campaign finishes to receive it.

Common Music Licensing Problems

There are a number of reasons why producers may have trouble when trying to license music for their productions. Knowing how this area of the business works can be crucial to the process. Music clearance may not be brain surgery, but it does require knowledge and experience to do it right. Often clients question the cost of doing music clearance. After all, isn't it something they could do themselves? Of course, they probably could do it, if they had enough time to learn how to contact all the parties and what each party's policies are. What music clearance companies sell is their expertise. While a producer might need to make 10 phone calls to find out who owns a song, a clearance specialist might need only three (or fewer). This might not seem important until the producer suddenly needs a song for the next day's shooting, when the right knowledge and contacts might be able to make the deal in time.

The most easily controllable problem is the time factor. As is becoming increasingly more common, record companies and music publishers are required to get approval from their artists/songwriters in order to license their music. This, of course, takes time, especially if the artist is on the road and not easily available. With multiple songwriters, this only adds to the time required. In television especially, due to short production schedules, time is a crucial factor. A publisher should try to have their writers pre-approve certain types of programs so that the turnaround time can be kept to a minimum. It's at this stage that a good working relationship and a level of trust between writers and publishers come in handy.

Multiple copyright owners also add to the problems. Simply stated, the more parties that have to be contacted, the longer the approval process. One co-owner can grant rights on behalf of all the owners *only* if there is no co-administration agreement between them. Most agreements of this kind call for each party to administer its own share directly. In addition, there may be disputes as to the respective shares of each owner. Until these are resolved, a producer may face the possibility of licensing (and paying for) more than 100% of the copyright, if the parties are willing to enter into negotiations at all prior to resolution of the ownership splits. In this scenario, as long as all parties are paid for whatever share they think they are entitled to, no one has a right to complain about the fees being paid to their co-owners. Sometimes, if all the ownership parties will agree, a deal can be made for a certain fee, subject to each party receiving its respective share once the ownership splits are finalized.

Along the same line, one co-owner may require a fee disproportionate to its ownership interest. This is especially troublesome if the other co-owners have granted fees on a Most Favored Nations basis, where, despite their willingness to accept a lower and more reasonable fee, they will receive their pro rata share of the higher fee quoted by one owner.

Because licensing terms are totally negotiable, the producer may be at the mercy of a copyright owner who demands unreasonable terms. For example, there is one publisher who, as part of its motion picture license, has a clause making the failure to provide two tickets to the premiere of the movie a material breach, subject to an injunction against distribution and release. While complying with this requirement may not seem like a big deal, the parties responsible for licensing the music for the production company generally have no control over who is invited to the premiere, leaving open the possibility of a breach.

Often, the specific approval of the writer or artist may be necessary. As all approvals are discretionary, the writer or artist may deny the usage of a song for any reason. Sometimes the reasons have to do with the context in which the song is used or the terms of the deal. Occasionally, however, it has to do with the financial status of the writer/publisher company relationship. For example, if a writer's royalty account is unrecouped, the license fee will be credited to the account, but the writer may not see any of the income. Therefore, there is no incentive to agree to the use. Sometimes the writer and publisher will reach some accommodation regarding a division of the income from the license fee so that the writer will receive a portion of the fee directly and an approval will be given. The producer is at the whim of the other parties regarding that determination.

Producers must also be aware that not all music is available for licensing. Just because it can be heard on the radio or in the context of a live broadcast does not mean that a song can be licensed for your production. As mentioned above, live broadcasts do not require permission and radio is covered under blanket licenses from ASCAP, BMI, and SESAC. In addition, the copyright owner may not approve of the context in which the music is being used. Nudity, profanity and the politics of the artist/songwriter all contribute to the use of a song being denied.

A common practice today is for the music editor, when a rough cut of the film is available, to prepare a temporary soundtrack to the film so that the director can see it with some music behind it and get a better sense of the rhythm and feel of the film. These "temp tracks" can cause some problems, however. Often, the director gets so used to seeing his film with a particular piece of music that he feels that only

Case Study #4

On a low-to-medium budget ($15 million) film from several years ago, the director felt he "had to, had to, had to" have a piece by noted composer Nino Rota. The publishing was owned by an Italian publisher, but was administered in the United States by one of the major publishing companies. Upon contacting them, the clearance company was advised that the Italian publisher never responded to licensing requests and that the producer client should choose something else.

After several months and several requests, the clearance company attempted to directly contact the Italian publisher. Again, after several faxes and phone calls over a period of time, there was either no response, or they were told that the owner of the company was frequently out of town on business.

Still, the creative parties did not want to give up. The music supervisor also made contact with the publisher and faxes were sent directly to the owner of the company. Finally, the day before the final dub of the film for release, the head of the distribution company (a major independent film company) called the Italian publisher directly, who advised his good friend that, of course the song was available and could be licensed for $100,000. All of a sudden, nine months after production began, this piece of music was no longer that important to the film.

On this same film, there was a decided difference of opinion about the direction the music should take. One side wanted a jazz feel and the producers cleared a lot of music by Chet Baker. The other side wanted a more contemporary, R&B, and pop feel. As previews were held and different versions of the film screened, no clear choices emerged. Two nights before the premiere, two different versions were previewed. In the three weeks preceding the final dub, 28 additional songs were cleared for the film.

Moral of the story: the easiest way to get a director to fixate on a song is to tell him he can't have it.

that music will be acceptable for the film. This is sometimes referred to as "temp love." At that point, the music needs to be cleared and licensed. Unfortunately, because of the director's emotional investment in the music, a deal may have to be struck with publishers on terms that are less than reasonable in the context of the overall film. Music editors, in general, try to place music in the film whatever they think works best, without regard to any considerations regarding licensing or potential costs. Most editors are not aware of publishers who are difficult to deal with, nor should they be. That is not their job. Because of this practice, however, the lives of producers, directors, and clearance personnel are sometimes thrown into turmoil in trying to clear a song that may not be available on the terms required by the producer or, in some cases, not available at all.

With all due respect to directors and producers, there is no one piece of music that will make or break a film.

The **production companies** must also make sure that they are negotiating with the correct **parties**. Often, I am told that the writer or manager of the artist has given approval for the use. The producer takes this as the song being cleared while I know that the publisher has the exclusive rights to grant this approval, not the manager or artist, so the "approval" is invalid.

Case Study #5

Using master recordings: an example of this type of mistake is the film *Mask*, the story of Rocky Dennis, a boy who was born with a massive facial skull deformity. Peter Bogdanovich, director of the film, had a personal relationship with Bruce Springsteen.

Springsteen apparently gave Bogdanovich approval to use his songs in the film. Bogdanovich edited the songs into the film, to the point of prints of the film being duplicated for release. CBS (now Sony) Records, however, had granted no such approval for the master recordings and wanted a percentage of gross income from the film for the rights, an unheard-of proposal. Needless to say, Universal Pictures forced Bogdanovich to re-edit the film at great expense and delay. So if you see this film today, instead of hearing the music of New Jersey working-class hero Bruce Springsteen, you will hear the music of Detroit working-class hero Bob Seger.

Moral of the story: make sure that the correct parties are contacted for permission. Generally, if the artist has a record or publishing deal, the artist or their manager does not have the authority to grant permission to the production company wishing to use the song.

MUSIC CUE SHEET

Program: Tim McGraw: Reflected
Producer: PROJECT #268866, INC.
Length: 1:00:00
Air Date: April 7, 20__

USAGES
VV = VISUAL VOCAL, VI = VISUAL INSTRUMENTAL, VD = VISUAL DANCE
VB = VOCAL BACKGROUND, IB = INSTRUMENTAL BACKGROUND

CUE NO.	TITLE	COMPOSER(S)	PUBLISHER(S)	SOCIETY	USAGE	TIMING
1	LIVE LIKE YOU WERE DYING	CRAIG WISEMAN TIM NICHOLS	BIG LOUD SHIRT WARNER-TAMERLANE PUBLISHING CORP.	ASCAP BMI	IB/VV	5:09
2	MAKING BELIEVE	JIMMY WORK	SONY/ATV ACUFF ROSE MUSIC	BMI	VV	0:03
3	WITHOUT YOU	TOMMY BARNES	STAGE THREE SONGS TAGUCHI MUSIC	ASCAP ASCAP	VV	0:26
4	WITHOUT YOU	TOMMY BARNES	STAGE THREE SONGS TAGUCHI MUSIC	ASCAP ASCAP	VV	0:10
5	DIXIE		PUBLIC DOMAIN		VV	0:22
6	REAL GOOD MAN	RIVER RUTHERFORD GEORGE TEREN	TEREN IT UP MUSIC ZOMBA SONGS MEMPHISTO MUSIC INC. UNIVERSAL MUSIC PUBLISHING GROUP	BMI BMI ASCAP ASCAP	VV	3:23
7	BEAUTIFUL PEOPLE	KENNY O'DELL	COORS MUSIC INC. EMI LONGITUDE MUSIC	BMI BMI	VV	4:38
8	FAMILY TRADITION	HANK WILLIAMS JR.	BOCEPHUS MUSIC INC.	BMI	VV	1:26
9	LOUISIANA	DALLAS DAVIDSON JIM MCCORMICK HILLARY LINDSEY	BIG BORASSA MUSIC, LLC ALTERNATOR MUSIC RAYLENE MUSIC	BMI BMI ASCAP	VV	4:01
10	THAT'S ALRIGHT	ARTHUR CRUDUP	CRUDUP MUSIC UNICHAPPELL MUSIC	BMI BMI	VV	1:09
11	WHEN THE STARS GO BLUE	RYAN ADAMS	BARLAND MUSIC	BMI	VV	3:26
12	MY LITTLE GIRL	TOM DOUGLAS TIM MCGRAW	TOMDOUGLASMUSIC SONY/ATV TREE PUBLISHING FOX MUSIC L'ILE DES AUTEURS MUSIC	BMI BMI BMI BMI	VV/VB	3:33

MOTION PICTURE SYNCHRONIZATION AND
PERFORMING RIGHTS LICENSE—PRODUCER'S VERSION

1.   The motion picture covered by this license is:
      "_____"

This license is for one production only, not for any other films produced by this Producer, including prequels and sequels to this film. The title may be listed as a tentative title, as the film title may change between the time the license is issued and the film is released.

2.   The musical composition (hereafter referred to as "Composition") covered by this license is: "_____"

3.   Composed by: _____

It is important to list the correct title and composers of the composition so that (a) both parties know that they are licensing the same song and (b) this information is properly listed on the music cue sheet.

4.   The publishers of this Composition are:

      _____

In addition to the publishing company name, the performing rights societies for the publishers should be listed as well for cue sheet purposes. Some publishers list only their own company in this spot, while the preferred method is to list all the publishers of the song, again for accuracy.

5.   The type, maximum duration, and number of uses of the Composition to be recorded are: _____, Timing: _____

The actual timing of the song in the film should be close to the approximate timing given when the quote was requested. Any major variation in increased timing (and this is very subjective) could result in a renegotiation of the fee. For example, if the approximate timing requested was 0:45 and the actual timing is 0:50, this is negligible. If, however, the use is actually 1:45, that is substantial enough to warrant another discussion on the fees.

6.   The administrative interest and territory covered hereby is:
      _____% _____

The percentage and geographic shares controlled by the Publisher are listed here, for example "100% world," or "50%, United States only." This lets the Producer know what rights this Publisher is granting.

7.   IN CONSIDERATION of the sum of _____ dollars ($_____.00), to be paid upon execution and delivery hereof,

The fee listed here is usually the publisher's share of the total fee agreed upon, although some publishers list the total fee with a note as to what their share is.

_____, (hereinafter referred to as "Publisher"), located at _____, hereby grants to _____ (hereinafter referred to as "Producer"), located at _____, the following rights:

The formal names of the parties and their addresses should be listed here.

a.   the non-exclusive right, license, privilege, and authority to fix and record in any manner, medium, form or language, in each country of the territory the aforesaid type and use of the Composition in synchronism or time-relation with the motion picture, and to make copies of such recordings in the form of negatives and prints necessary for distribution, exhibition and exploitation in any and all media, whether now known or hereafter devised, including, without limitation, theatrical or nontheatrical exhibition and broadcast on all forms of television, including network, non-network, local or syndicated broadcasts, "pay television," "cable television," "subscription television," "CATV" and closed circuit television, as hereinafter provided, and to import said recording and/or copies thereof into any country throughout the territory all in accordance with the terms, conditions, and limitations hereinafter set forth;

Here is the language required by most producers. Notwithstanding the "any and all media" language, often the license sets out specific media, as here, where theatrical, non-theatrical, and the various forms of television are specifically listed.

b.   the non-exclusive right to reproduce the Composition, as recorded in the motion picture in copies of the motion picture in any and all media, whether now known or hereinafter devised, manufactured primarily for distribution for the purpose of "home/personal use," including, but not limited to, Video Cassettes and Video Discs (collectively referred to as "Videograms"), and to distribute them by sale or otherwise in each and every country of the territory for any and all purposes now or hereafter known.

This paragraph sets out the home video or "personal" video rights. The use of the word "personal" allows for uses outside the home, such as a DVD played on a laptop computer while on an airplane.

"Videogram" shall include any and all audio-visual devices, such as video discs and video cassettes and all similar devices, via any and all forms of internet/broadband/wireless delivery, and any and all forms of any other methods, systems or devices, whether now known or hereafter devised, via video-downloading or audio-downloading of the Program, so as to allow two way access to originate and receive content.

Language for Internet and wireless uses, including downloading.

This grant shall not, however, extend to or include any so-called "interactive" or "multi-media" product, such as CD-ROM, Compact Disc Interactive (CD-I), video or computer games or other technologies allowing for the non-linear use of the photo-play or Composition.

This excludes interactive product, so that the music cannot be manipulated within the context of the film.

Producer shall not be obligated to make any further or additional payments whatsoever for any of the rights granted hereunder;

Note that this license is a one-time, flat fee buyout payment of fees.

c.   the non-exclusive right and license to publicly perform for profit or non-profit and to authorize others so to perform the Composition in the exhibition of the motion picture to audiences in motion picture theaters and other places of public entertainment where motion pictures are customarily exhibited throughout the world including the right to televise the motion picture into such theaters and other such public places.

> A grant of public performing rights for theaters. Remember that movie theaters in the United States do not have licenses from the PROs, so those rights must be granted directly by the publisher.

d.   Irrespective of any of the foregoing, it is understood that with respect to the public performance of the motion picture by means of theatrical exhibition and by means of any and all forms of television broadcast, clearance by performance rights societies in such portion of the territory as is outside the U.S. will be in accordance with their customary practices and the payment of their customary fees.

> However, since theaters in foreign countries do pay fees to the local PROs on their territory, this language states that local customs and practices will dictate collection and payment of those royalties. This paragraph applies to television broadcasts outside the U.S. as well.

8.   The exhibition of the motion picture in the U.S. by means of Internet streaming or television (other than as described in subparagraph 7(d) hereinabove) including by means of "pay television," "subscription television," "CATV," and "closed circuit into homes television," is subject to the following:

> This is the basic language covering performing rights in the United States.

a.   The motion picture may be exhibited by means of Internet sites and television by networks, non-network, local or syndicated broadcasts, "pay television," "subscription television," "CATV," and "closed circuit" provided that such television stations have valid performance licenses therefore from the American Society of Composers, Authors and Publishers (ASCAP), Broadcast Music, Inc. (BMI) or SESAC.

> Stations and websites must have valid performing rights licenses with the PROs, or . . . (see comment below).

b.   Exhibition of the motion picture by means of Internet sites and television by networks, non-network, local or syndicated broadcasts, "pay television," "subscription television," "CATV," and "closed circuit" station not licensed by ASCAP, BMI or SESAC is subject to clearance of the performing rights either from Publisher or ASCAP, BMI or SESAC or from any other Publisher acting for or on behalf of Publisher, said rights to be negotiated in good faith;

> The stations and websites must negotiate with the PROs or the publisher for said licenses and pay the appropriate fees.

provided, however, that Producer shall have the continued right to distribute and otherwise exploit the motion picture during the course of these negotiations.

> In the event that the stations or websites do not have these licenses, the producer may continue to exhibit the film pending these negotiations. This is decidedly to the producer's advantage, as he does not have to pull the film from distribution pending these negotiations.

9.   This license does not include the right to alter the fundamental character of the music of the Composition, to use of the title or subtitle of the Composition as the title of any motion picture, or to use the story of the Composition.

> The producer may not change the underlying composition, use the story of the song or use the title without prior negotiations.

10.   The recording, fixation and performing rights hereinabove granted include such rights for air, screen, television and audio-visual trailers, commercials, music videos, promotions and advertisements for the promotion or exploitation of the motion picture.

> All producers will want this language but most publishers will not grant it, as it is overly broad. What is common, though, is for "in-context" promo rights to be included if requested. "In-context" means that the music is used in the promo in the same scene in which it appears in the film. "Out-of-context" means that the music is used in different scenes than in the film. Out-of-context promo rights are negotiated and paid separately from the film license.

11.   The recording and performing rights hereinabove granted shall endure in perpetuity without Producer having to pay any additional consideration therefore.

> The buyout fee covers rights in perpetuity.

12.   Publisher represents and warrants that it owns or controls the Composition licensed hereunder and that it has the legal right to grant this license and that Producer shall not be required to pay any additional monies, except as provided in this license, with respect to the rights granted and the exploitation of such rights in this license.

> The publisher's warranties and representations.

13.   Publisher shall indemnify and hold harmless Producer, its successors, assigns and licensees from and against any and all losses, damages, liabilities, reasonable attorneys' fees and costs, actions, suits, or other claims arising out of Producer's exercise of such rights, or any breach or alleged breach, in whole or in part, of the foregoing representations and warranties (**OPTIONAL LANGUAGE: reduced to judgment by a court of competent jurisdiction or settled with Publisher's consent, which consent shall not be unreasonably withheld**).

> Producers will want to be indemnified from breach as well as an alleged breach. If a claim is made but the publisher has not breached this agreement, the publisher should not be held liable for the cost involved to defend. The optional language protects the publisher, making them liable only for an actual breach or a settlement of the claim with their consent.

Publisher shall reimburse Producer upon demand for any payment by Producer at any time with respect to such losses, damages, liabilities, attorneys' fees and costs, actions, suits or other claims to which the foregoing indemnity applies.

> Most publishers try to limit their indemnification to the amount of the consideration (i.e., license fee) paid.

Notwithstanding the foregoing, Producer shall have the right to settle any claim without Publisher's consent thereto upon terms and conditions acceptable to Producer in its sole discretion; provided, however, that in such event, Publisher shall not be obligated to reimburse Producer for any monies paid by Producer to any third party in connection with such settlement.

> Sometimes it is in the producer's best interests to settle the claim instead of having an injunction levied against distribution of the film. With this language, the producer can do just that, but the publisher is no longer liable for the damages.

14.   Publisher reserves all rights not expressly granted to Producer hereunder. All rights granted hereunder are granted on a non-exclusive basis.

15.   Producer shall have the power and authority to assign its rights and obligations under this license to any party whatsoever without Publisher's consent. This license is binding upon and shall inure to the benefit of the respective successors and/or assigns of the parties hereto.

Producers need the right to assign this license to their successors or distributors. That said, in the publisher's version of an agreement, the producer will remain secondarily, if not primarily, liable.

16.   In the event of any breach of any provision of this agreement by Producer, Publisher's sole remedy will be an action at law for damages, if any, and in no event will Publisher be entitled or seek to enjoin, interfere or inhibit the distribution, exhibition or exploitation of the motion picture.

One of the remedies for breach of this agreement by the producer is an action for copyright infringement by the publisher. One of the remedies for infringement is an injunction against distribution. This would be fatal to the producer. One of the keys to getting injunctive relief is that that problem cannot be solved by money damages. Or as a major studio executive once said, "If money solves it, it's not a problem." In most cases, the publisher would settle the case if paid some amount to be determined. Virtually all producers request this language.

17.   All notices hereunder required to be given to the parties hereto and all payments to be made hereunder shall be sent to the parties at their addresses mentioned herein or to such other addresses as each party respectively may hereafter designate by notice in writing to the other.

This determines which state's laws will be used to determine the outcome of any legal actions. Most parties want the jurisdiction to not only be under their state's law, but that the case be heard in their state's courts.

18.   This license shall be governed by and subject to the laws of the State of California applicable to agreements made and wholly performed within California.

IN WITNESS WHEREOF, the parties have caused the foregoing to be

executed as of _____.

_____ (Publisher)

By: _____

_____
Federal Identification Number

In order to be paid the license fees, most payers require a federal tax identification number and a W-9 form. A failure to provide this info requires the producer to withhold almost 30% of the license fee as federal withholding tax. Neither the publisher nor the producer wants this to happen.

MOTION PICTURE SYNCHRONIZATION AND PERFORMING RIGHTS LICENSE— FILM FESTIVALS (WITH STEP DEALS FOR FURTHER RIGHTS) PUBLISHER'S VERSION

Comments below will highlight the differences between this agreement and the previous producer's version.

1.   The motion picture covered by this license is: _____

> This license is for one production only, not for any other films produced by this producer, including prequels and sequels to this film. The title may be listed as a "tentative" title, as the film title may change between the time the license is issued and the film is released.

2.   The musical composition (hereafter referred to as "Composition") covered by this license is: "_____" Composed by: _____

> It is important to list the correct title and composers of the composition so that (a) both parties know that they are licensing the same song and (b) this information is properly listed on the music cue sheet.

3.   The publisher of this Composition is: _____

> In addition to the publishing company name, the performing rights societies for the publishers should be listed as well for cue sheet purposes. Some publishers list only their own company in this spot, while the preferred method is to list all the publishers of the song, again for accuracy.

4.   The type, maximum duration, and number of uses of the Composition to be recorded are: _____, Timing: _____

> The actual timing of the song in the film should be close to the approximate timing given when the quote was requested. Any major variation in increased timing (and this is very subjective) could result in a renegotiation of the fee. For example, if the approximate timing requested was 0:45 and the actual timing is 0:50, this is negligible. If, however, the use is actually 1:45, that is substantial enough to warrant another discussion on the fees.

5.   The administrative interest and territory covered hereby is: _____ % _____

> The percentage and geographic shares controlled by the publisher are listed here, for example "100% world," or "50%, United States only." This lets the producer know what rights this publisher is granting.

6.   IN CONSIDERATION of the sum of _____ dollars ($_____.00),

to be paid upon execution and delivery hereof, _____, (hereinafter referred to as "Licensor") hereby grants to _____ (hereinafter referred to as "Producer"), the following rights:

a.   the non-exclusive right, license, privilege, and authority to fix and record in any manner, medium, form or language, in each country of the territory the aforesaid type and use of the Composition in synchronism or time-relation with the motion picture, and to make copies of such recordings in the form of negatives and prints necessary for distribution, exhibition and exploitation **at film festivals only**, for a period of one (1) year, worldwide.

7.   Producer shall have options for the following rights, said options to be exercised in writing within 12 months of the date of the agreement, accompanied by payment of the license fees for said options:

a.   the non-exclusive right, license, privilege, and authority to fix and record in any manner, medium, form or language, in each country of the territory the aforesaid type and use of the Composition in synchronism or time-relation with the motion picture,

including in-context trailers, advertising and promotions for the motion picture, and to make copies of such recordings in the form of negatives and prints necessary for distribution,

exhibition and exploitation in any and all media, whether now known or hereafter devised, including, without limitation, theatrical or nontheatrical exhibition and broadcast on all forms of television, including network, non-network, local or syndicated broadcasts, "pay television," "cable television," "subscription television," "CATV" and closed circuit television, as hereinafter provided, and to import said recording and/or copies thereof into any country throughout the territory all in accordance with the terms, conditions, and limitations hereinafter set forth;

The fee listed here is usually the publisher's share of the total fee agreed upon, although some publishers list the total fee with a note as to what their share is.

The formal names of the parties and their addresses should be listed here.

The initial grant of rights is for film festivals only. This gives the producer the rights to exhibit the film at festivals in an attempt to secure distribution of the film.

These options allow for further exploitation without further negotiation, as the deals are already set in place prior to wider distribution of the film.

Here is the language required by most producers. Notwithstanding the "any and all media" language, often the license sets out specific media, as here, where theatrical, non-theatrical, and the various forms of television are specifically listed.

In this agreement, in-context trailer rights have been included as part of the broad rights grant.

Traditional "broad rights" for motion pictures.

b.   the non-exclusive right to reproduce the Composition, as recorded in the motion picture in copies of the motion picture in any and all media, whether now known or hereinafter devised, manufactured primarily for distribution for the purpose of "home/personal use," including, but not limited to, Video Cassettes and Video Discs (collectively referred to as "Videograms"), and to distribute them by sale or otherwise in each and every country of the territory for any and all purposes now or hereafter known.

This paragraph sets out the home video or personal video rights. The use of the word "personal" allows for uses outside the home, such as a DVD played on a laptop computer while on an airplane.

"Videogram" shall include any and all audio-visual devices, such as video discs and video cassettes and all similar devices, via any and all forms of internet/broadband/wireless delivery, and any and all forms of any other methods, systems or devices, whether now known or hereafter devised, via video-downloading or audio-downloading of the Program, so as to allow two way access to originate and receive content.

Language for Internet and wireless uses, including downloading.

This grant shall not, however, extend to or include any so-called "interactive" or "multi-media" product, such as CD-ROM, Compact Disc Interactive (CD-I), video or computer games or other technologies allowing for the non-linear use of the photoplay or Composition.

This excludes interactive product, so that the music cannot be manipulated within the context of the film.

Producer shall not be obligated to make any further or additional payments whatsoever for any of the rights granted hereunder;

Note that this license is a one-time, flat fee buyout payment of fees.

c.   the non-exclusive right and license to publicly perform for profit or non-profit and to authorize others so to perform the Composition in the exhibition of the motion picture to audiences in motion picture theaters and other places of public entertainment where motion pictures are customarily exhibited throughout the world including the right to televise the motion picture into such theaters and other such public places.

A grant of public performing rights for theaters. Remember that movie theaters in the United States do not have licenses from the PROs, so those rights must be granted directly by the publisher.

d.   Irrespective of any of the foregoing, it is understood that with respect to the public performance of the motion picture by means of theatrical exhibition and by means of any and all forms of television broadcast, clearance by performance rights societies in such portion of the territory as is outside the U.S. will be in accordance with their customary practices and the payment of their customary fees.

However, since theaters in foreign countries do pay fees to the local PROs on their territory, this language states that local customs and practices will dictate collection and payment of those royalties. This paragraph applies to television broadcasts outside the U.S. as well.

8. As compensation for said option rights, Producer shall pay to Licensor the following fees:

    a. A license fee of $2,500.00 upon the theatrical release or television broadcast of the film, whichever comes first;

    b. When the film earns $2,000,000.00 in box office receipts, an additional fee of $2,500.00;

    c. When the film earns $5,000,000.00 in box office receipts, an additional fee of $2,500.00;

    d. When the film earns $7,500,000.00 in box office receipts, an additional fee of $2,500.00;

    e. When the film earns $10,000,000.00 in box office receipts, an additional fee of $2,500.00;

    f. When the film earns $15,000,000.00 in box office receipts, an additional fee of $2,500.00; and

    g. When the film is released in the "home video" market, an additional fee of $2,500.00.

> Here are the incremental payments, or "steps" that provide for additional compensation to the publisher based upon certain financial or distribution benchmarks being met. These numbers are for demonstration purposes only and are totally negotiable between the parties.

9. All calculations of box office receipts shall be based upon the reportings of the major trade publications, such as "Variety" or "The Hollywood Reporter" and shall include all box office receipts worldwide.

> This allows the box office receipts to be verified for the purposes of paying the "step" fees.

10. The exhibition of the motion picture in the United States by means of Internet sites and television (other than as described in subparagraph 7 C hereinabove) including by means of "pay television," "subscription television," "CATV," and "closed circuit into homes television," is subject to the following:

    a. The motion picture may be exhibited by means of Internet sites and television by networks, non-network, local or syndicated broadcasts, "pay television," "cable television," "subscription television," "CATV," and "closed circuit" provided that such television stations have valid performance licenses therefore from the American Society of Composers, Authors and Publishers (ASCAP), Broadcast Music, Inc. (BMI) or SESAC.

    b. Exhibition of the motion picture by means of Internet sites and television by networks, non-network, local or syndicated broadcasts, "pay television," "cable television," subscription television," "CATV," and "closed circuit" station not licensed by ASCAP or BMI

> Stations and websites must have valid performing rights licenses with the PROs, or . . . (see comment below).

> The stations and websites must negotiate with the PROs or the publisher for said licenses and pay the appropriate fees.

is subject to clearance of the performing rights either from Licensor or ASCAP or BMI or from any other licensor acting for or on behalf of Licensor, said rights to be negotiated in good faith.

In the event that the stations or websites do not have these licenses, the producer may continue to exhibit the film pending these negotiations. This is decidedly to the producer's advantage, as he does not have to pull the film from distribution pending these negotiations.

11. This is a license to record only and does not authorize any use of the aforesaid Composition not expressly set forth herein. By way of illustration but not limitation, this license does not include the right to change or adapt the words, or alter the fundamental character of the music of said musical Composition, or the use of the title thereof as the title or subtitle of said film, or to use the story of said Composition.

The producer may not change the underlying composition, use the story of the song, or use the title without prior negotiations.

12. On or before the first exhibition of said motion picture, Producer agrees to furnish Licensor with a copy of the music cue sheet prepared and distributed in connection therewith.

13. The recording and performing rights hereinabove granted in the option paragraphs shall endure for the worldwide period of all copyrights in and to the Composition, and any and all renewals or extensions thereof that Licensor may now own or control or hereafter own or control without Producer having to pay any additional consideration therefore.

The buyout fee for the option covers rights in perpetuity.

14. No sound records containing the Composition that is the subject of this agreement are to be manufactured, sold or used separately or independently of said film or videotape.

15. Licensor reserves all rights not expressly granted to Producer hereunder. All rights granted hereunder are granted on a non-exclusive basis.

As this is only a sync license for the film, no rights are given for sound recordings, such as a soundtrack album. These rights can be granted and included as part of this agreement but require a specific negotiation.

16. Licensor warrants only that it has the legal right to grant this license and this license is given and accepted without other warranty or recourse. If said warranty shall be breached in whole or in part, Licensor's total liability shall be limited either to repaying the consideration theretofore paid under this license with respect to the Composition to the extent of such breach or to holding Licensee harmless to the extent of the consideration theretofore paid under this license with respect to the Composition to the extent of said breach.

This language limits the amount of the indemnification to the amount of the license fee received by the publisher.

17.   Producer shall indemnify Licensor, its agents and representatives, and save and hold them, and each and all of them, harmless of and from any and all claims, loss, damage, liability and expense, including attorney's fees, arising out of Producer's use of the Composition. Producer further acknowledges that a breach by Producer of any of its representations or warranties hereunder will cause Licensor irreparable damage which cannot be readily remedied in damages in an action at law, and may, in addition thereto, constitute an infringement of Licensor's copyrights, thereby entitling Licensor to equitable remedies and attorney's fees.

This allows all remedies for infringement, including an injunction against distribution. As mentioned in the previous agreement, most production companies will not agree to this provision, although major publishers insist on this provision.

18.   This license shall run to Producer, its successors and assigns, provided it shall remain liable for the performance of all the terms and conditions of this license on its part to be performed and provided further that any disposition of said film or prints thereof shall be subject to all the terms hereof, and Producer agrees that all persons, firms or corporations acquiring any right, title, interest in or possession of said film, or any prints thereof, shall be notified of the terms and conditions of this license and shall agree to be bound thereby.

19.   This license constitutes the entire agreement between the parties and cannot be altered, modified, amended or waived, in whole or in part, except by a written instrument signed by both parties. Should any provision of this agreement be held void, invalid or inoperative, such decision shall not affect any other provision hereof, and the remainder of this agreement shall be effective as though such void, invalid or inoperative provision had not been contained herein.

20.   All notices hereunder required to be given to the parties hereto and all payments to be made hereunder shall be sent to the parties at their addresses mentioned herein or to such other addresses as each party respectively may hereafter designate by notice in writing to the other.

21.   This license has been entered into in the State of California, and the validity, interpretation and legal effect of this license shall be governed by the laws of the State of California applicable to contracts entered into and performed entirely within the State of California with respect to the determination of any claim, dispute or disagreement which may arise out of the interpretation, performance or breach of this license.

IN WITNESS WHEREOF, the parties have caused the foregoing to be executed as of _____, 20___.

_____ (Licensor)

By: _____

_____ (Producer)

By: _____

TELEVISION SYNCHRONIZATION AND PERFORMANCE LICENSE
(WITH OPTIONS)

(see previous agreements for further explanation of "boilerplate" paragraphs)

Agreement between _____, ("Licensor") located at _____ and _____ ("Licensee"), located at _____, dated as of _____, 20_____.

1.   In consideration of the sum of _____ DOLLARS ($_____.00), payable upon the execution here-of, Licensor grants to Licensee the non-exclusive right to record on film or videotape its 100% share of the musical composition entitled "_____", composed by _____, (the "Composition") and published by _____ _____ in synchronization or timed relation with the television pro-gram entitled "_____", Episode # _____, subject to all the terms and conditions herein provided.

> This license is only valid for a single episode of a single television program. There may be provisions for additional episodes, or the use of the music in segments showing "previously on _____." This does not allow, however, for flashback scenes or compilation episodes ("The Best Songs of Glee").

2.   The type of use is to be one (1) BACKGROUND instrumental use for seconds.

3.   The territory covered by this license is the United States and Canada.

> Note that this license only covers the United States and Canada. Other territories are covered in the options below.

4.   This license is for a period of two (2) years commencing on the air date of _____, 20_____.

> This agreement is for two years only, not perpetuity as in the motion picture agreements above.

Upon the expiration of this license, all rights herein granted shall cease and terminate and the right to make or authorize any further use or distribution of any recording made hereunder shall also cease and terminate.

5.   This license is for "Free, Basic Cable and Pay Television (including Video On Demand)" and in-context advertising and promotion only, and specifically prohibits the right to reproduce the Composition out-side the context of the program in advertisements or promotions and, further, prohibits the exhibition of the program in any other media, including, but not limited to, "subscription television," "closed circuit television," theatrical exhibition or any form of audio-visual devices for home use, such as video cassettes or videodiscs.

> Includes in-context advertising and specifically excludes use of the music in out-of-context ads or any other media except as specified in this paragraph.

6.   Licensee shall have the independent rights and options to extend this license to the below-indicated media, by written notice to Licensor within 24 months of the air date listed above accompanied by the pay-ment indicated for the medium for which such option is so exercised:

> Below are the producer's options for additional exploitation, which must be exercised within a certain period of time and accompanied by payment.

A.   To Free, Basic Cable and Pay Television (including Video On Demand) and in-context advertising and promotion only, for a term of three (3) years, in the territory of the World, for an additional payment of $_____;

> This is an expansion of the rights granted above for worldwide use for three years.

B.   To make and distribute videogram copies of the photoplay embodying the fixation of the Composition and to distribute such videogram copies to the general public for "home/personal use" (as such term is understood in the entertainment industry) and in-context advertising and promotion, for a term of perpetuity, in the territory of the world for an additional payment of $_____. "Videogram" shall include any and all audio-visual devices, such as video discs and video cassettes and all similar devices, via any and all forms of internet/broadband/ wireless delivery, and any and all forms of any other methods, systems or devices, whether now known or hereafter devised, via video-downloading or audio-downloading of the Program, so as to allow two way access to originate and receive content. This grant shall not, however, extend to or include any so-called "interactive" or "multi-media" product, such as CD-ROM, Compact Disc Interactive (CD-I), video or computer games or other technologies allowing for the non-linear use of the photoplay or Composition;

> This provides for a videogram buyout, i.e. a one-time payment.

C.   To make and distribute videogram copies of the photoplay embodying the fixation of the Composition and to distribute such videogram copies to the general public for "home/personal use" (as such term is understood in the entertainment industry) and in-context advertising and promotion, for a term of perpetuity, in the territory of the world for an additional payment of $_____, representing a royalty of $_____ per copy for the first 5,000 units sold of the production, with additional payments in the same amount payable in advance as a "rollover payment" for the sale of each of the successive increments of 5,000 units.

> Instead of a buyout as above, this clause sets out the deal for a series of "rollover" payments.

D.   To Free and Basic Cable Television in out-of-context advertising and promotion only, in the territory of the United States and Canada, for an additional payment of $_____ for a term of thirty (30) days or $_____ per week;

> A provision for out-of-context ads and promos. As this is for a television program, promo rights might not be needed in perpetuity but will be needed on a week-to-week basis, leading up to the date of the broadcast.

E.   To all Licensee's official/authorized websites throughout the world, for a term of six (6) months, streaming only, for an additional payment of $_____.

> Many television programs have their own websites, either on their own or through the network on which the program will be aired. This allows for streaming of the program online.

F.   To audio/visual linear downloads on a fee-based, direct to consumer basis via official websites (with a targeted retail price of $1.99 for single audiovisual downloads) to an audiovisual device, such as a personal computer or any other comparable display monitor (handheld or otherwise), for five years, worldwide for clips containing combined total up to one full use, not to exceed 2:30 for the greater of (a) 10% of the actual retail price, or (b) $0.20 per single Audiovisual download with quarterly accounting.

> This provision is often used for "competition"-type programs, like *American Idol* or *So You Think You Can Dance*, and allows downloads of individual performances rather than the entire program.

G.   One year / United States and Canada / The 20____ Live Tour (for clips previously aired on the television Series), $_____;

H.   One year / United States and Canada / educational clinics (for clips previously aired on the television Series), $_____.

> Many of the same type of programs do live tours featuring their performers. This allows the use of the song from clips from the program to be shown in these live tours.

7.   This is a license to record only and does not authorize any use of the aforesaid Composition not expressly set forth herein. By way of illustration but not limitation, this license does not include the right to change or adapt the words, or alter the fundamental character of the music of said Composition or the use of the title thereof as the title or subtitle of said film.

> See agreements above for comments to similar provisions.

8.   Licensor hereby grants to Licensee the non-exclusive license to publicly perform, and to authorize others to publicly perform, said Composition as recorded in said film or videotape, pursuant to the foregoing recording rights license, subject to the terms and conditions of limitation hereinafter contained.

The right to publicly perform said recording of said Composition pursuant to this performing rights license shall be limited and confined to the public performance thereof and the exhibition of said film by means of Internet site and television upon the express condition that at the time of each such performance from, over or through Internet site and television stations such website or television station, either directly or as an affiliated station of a television network, shall theretofore have obtained a valid license separate and apart from this license to so perform the same in exhibition of said film or videotape from the Licensor or from ASCAP, BMI or from any other society, association, agency or entity having the lawful right to issue such license for and on behalf of the Licensor and to collect the license fee for such performance.

In the event that any Internet site or television station does not hold a blanket non-dramatic public performance license from ASCAP, BMI or any other society, association, agency or entity having the lawful right to issue such license for and on behalf of the Licensor, Licensor agrees to negotiate in good faith with said television station or Licensee for the issuance and fee of said performing rights.

9.   Licensee shall supply a copy of the music cue sheet for the program within 30 days of execution of this agreement.

10. No sound records containing the Composition that is the subject of this agreement are to be manufactured, sold or used separately or independently of said film or videotape.

11. All rights not herein specifically granted are reserved by Licensor for its use and disposition anytime, anywhere.

12. Licensor warrants only that it has the legal right to grant this license and this license is given and accepted without other warranty or recourse. If said warranty shall be breached in whole or in part, Licensor's total liability shall be limited either to repaying the consideration theretofore paid under this license, with respect to such Composition, or to holding Licensee harmless to the extent of the consideration theretofore paid under this license with respect to such Composition to the extent of said breach.

13. Licensee shall indemnify Licensor, its agents, employees, representatives, associates, affiliates, parent and subsidiary corporations, and save and hold them, and each and all of them, harmless of and from any and all claims (including claims by labor organizations), loss, cost, damage, liability and expense, including attorney's fees arising out of Licensee's breach of any covenant hereof or Licensee's use of the Composition. In the event of a breach by Licensee, however, Licensor's only remedy shall be monetary damages and Licensor shall not be able to enjoin distribution of the production.

14. This license shall run to Licensee, its successors and assigns, provided it shall remain liable for the performance of all the terms and conditions of this license on its part to be performed and provided further that any disposition of said film or prints thereof shall be subject to all the terms hereof, and Licensee agrees that all persons, firms or corporations acquiring any right, title, interest in or possession of said film, or any prints thereof, shall be notified of the terms and conditions of this license and shall agree to be bound thereby.

15.   Notwithstanding anything to the contrary contained in this agreement, no other licensor of any composition contained in the Program shall be dealt with by Licensee in any respect whatsoever in a manner more favorable than the manner in which Licensor is dealt with herein, including without limitation, the amount of license fees hereunder. In the event more favorable terms are granted to any licensor than are contained herein, this agreement shall be deemed amended to incorporate same as of the date when such higher fees are paid or such more favorable terms are granted to such licensor.

16.   This license constitutes the entire agreement between the parties and cannot be altered, modified, amended or waived, in whole or in part, except by a written instrument signed by both parties. Should any provision of this agreement be held void, invalid or inoperative, such decision shall not affect any other provision hereof, and the remainder of this agreement shall be effective as though such void, invalid or inoperative provision had not been contained herein.

17.   This license has been entered into in the State of California, and the validity, interpretation and legal effect of this license shall be governed by the laws of the State of California applicable to contracts entered into and performed entirely within the State of California with respect to the determination of any claim, dispute or disagreement which may arise out of the interpretation, performance or breach of this license.

AGREED AND ACCEPTED:

_____ (Licensee)

By: _____

_____ (Licensor)

By: _____

Federal Identification Number: _____

For these reality shows, since there is so much music in them, the producers will often offer a specific fee (sometimes based on different types of uses), subject to a Most Favored Nations clause so that each song is treated equally. This makes the licensing process smoother for both sides of the transaction.

CHAPTER 5

PRINT LICENSING

The licensing of printed copies of music is the derivation of the term "music publishing." From the days of monks transcribing copies of music through the invention of the Gutenberg press and until the early 1900s, hard copies were the only method by which music could be reproduced and distributed to the public. Anyone who has ever taken music or voice lessons or sung in a school or church choir has used printed copies of music.

A print license allows for the reproduction of printed copies of music such as sheet music, folios, concert arrangements, and the printing of lyrics in magazines, advertising, and books.

Although not the income producer it once was, print licenses, especially for well-known songs or well-known songwriters, can still generate substantial income. The print music publishers have become very creative in marketing their material, such as a folio containing all the songs on a hit album, or notation on guitar solos from heavy metal songs. Often, this will include name and likeness rights for the artist for an additional royalty.

The most common form of sheet music is "piano copies" or sheet music of a single song. Often, this has the piano part, melody, lyrics, and, for guitarists, the names of the chords and chord diagrams. A royalty to the publisher for this type of use is somewhere between $0.10 and $0.25 per copy sold.

A "folio" is a collection of songs, such *The Greatest Hits of 1980* or songs by a particular artist or album. A third category is music printed for use by school bands and orchestras, in which each instrument has its own part printed separately, with a full score available for the conductor. In a similar fashion, choirs have music from which the singers can read their own parts in the traditional soprano, alto, tenor, and bass ("SATB") format. For these types of licenses, the royalty paid to the publisher is between 10% and 15% of the retail sales price, on a *pro rata* basis with all songs in the folio.

A print license may also be necessary in combination with other kinds of licensing. For example, when granting a mechanical license, the record company may want to print the lyrics on the CD sleeve. Or, when licensing for karaoke, both a synchronization and print license are necessary.

There is still a large market in instructional music books for people taking music lessons and for educational uses, such as choral, marching band, or orchestral scores. For educational uses, it is not uncommon for the original publisher to grant to the print publisher a royalty-free mechanical license for recordings of the arrangement to be made as a promotional tool by the print publisher so that the school band leader can hear what a particular arrangement will sound like.

Royalties have become fairly standardized and are usually granted on a Most Favored Nations basis with other publishers contained in the same arrangement or folio.

The print publisher will engage an arranger to create the printed version of the song and all the parts thereto. A music publisher entering into a print licensing agreement should make sure that the agreement states that the copyright in the new arrangement is owned by the music publisher and that it should be considered a work-for-hire, with the music publisher considered the author of the copyright.

SHEET MUSIC LICENSE
(WITH FOLIO RIGHTS)

Dated:

Gentlemen:

The following shall constitute the understanding and agreement between us:

1.   You hereby grant to us, our successors, assigns, affiliates, subsidiaries and licensees the sole and exclusive (non-exclusive as to mixed folio rights) right during the term hereof, to print, sell and distribute in bound or unbound editions or forms, singly or together with such other compositions and contents as may be selected by us, at our sole cost and expense, your copyrighted musical compositions entitled:

Title:

Composer(s):

(which composition is hereinafter referred to as "Composition") and in any and all arrangements and adaptations thereof as we may elect, in the United States of America, its territories and possessions (including Puerto Rico) and the Dominion of Canada and to sell the same at such prices and on whatever terms, conditions and discounts as we may in our sole discretion determine from time to time.

2.   In full consideration for all rights, licenses and privileges granted to us hereunder and for all warranties, representations and agreements herein made by you, we agree to pay you the following royalties:

(a)   A sum of ___ cents per copy in respect of regular sheet music (piano-vocal) sold and paid for.

(b)   In the event the Composition is included in any folio, songbook or similar publication containing musical compositions or other musical materials in addition to the Composition, a sum equal to that proportionate part of ___ Percent (__ %) of the suggested retail selling price for all copies of such work sold and paid for.

(c)   Said royalties shall be on a Most Favored Nations basis with the co-publishers of this composition as well as all other compositions included in the Folio. In the event that any other publisher receives a higher royalty than stated above, we shall immediately forward the difference in the amounts to your office.

This agreement grants rights for both single sheet (piano) copies as well as for folios. The grant is exclusive for piano copies and non-exclusive for folios.

The print publisher has the right to make arrangements and adaptation of the title(s) listed above and to sell copies in the U.S. and Canada. They have the right to set the prices and terms of distribution as they see fit. Usually, the original publisher would want to know those terms before agreeing to the deal.

Royalty provisions below:

Piano copies are usually paid a certain number of cents per copy instead of a percentage of the sales price, usually between $0.10 and $0.25.

Folios, choral, and band arrangements are usually paid a percentage of the retail sales price, usually between 10% and 15% of the retail sales price, pro rata to the number of songs.

Most print royalties are on a Most Favored Nations basis, with each song receiving a pro rata share of the total royalty, depending on how many songs are contained in the folio.

3.   With respect to all sums which may be received by us in respect of the Composition, we shall account for and pay to you such sums as may be shown due to you, quarterly, within sixty (60) days following the close of each such accounting period. No claim on your part with respect to any statements rendered to you may be maintained unless made in writing (stating the basis thereof) within two (2) years from the date of such statement.

Quarterly accountings.

We agree to keep and maintain full and complete books and records concerning the subject matter hereof; and you shall have the right to examine our books and records at our place of business in Los Angeles, California during normal business hours and upon reasonable notice to verify the correctness of accounting statements rendered hereunder.

Audit provision.

4.   You shall furnish us with all necessary copyright information, an accurate lead sheet and with an original commercial phonograph record of the Composition.

In order for the print publisher to create an accurate arrangement of the song, they want to reference the original publisher's lead sheet, i.e., written copy of the song, as their starting point. As many purchasers of sheet music wish to be able to play their favorite songs just like they have heard them on the radio or TV, it is crucial in many cases that the print publisher be able to have their arranger create an authentic version of the song.

You hereby approve our use of the copyright information as contained on the lead sheet furnished.

The original publisher will want accurate copyright information on the print arrangement. See also paragraph 9, below.

You shall also furnish us with recent photographs of the artist or artists who perform the Composition on such phonograph record and you shall use your best efforts to obtain all necessary consents permitting us to use such photographs in and in connection with the copies of the Composition printed by us.

Many times, the print publisher will want to put the artist's name and picture on the copy of sheet music, to further let people know what they are buying. As the artist may not be the writer and not under contract to the original publisher, the "best efforts" clause is sometimes all they can agree to.

5.   You warrant and represent that you are the sole and exclusive owner of the Composition, the copyright and all rights therein; that you have full right, power and authority to enter into and to perform, this agreement; that no part of the Composition infringes upon any right of any other party;

If the song is co-published, this language would be amended to reflect the original publisher's share of the song.

and that you have not sold, transferred, granted or assigned to any person, firm or corporation any rights herein sold, transferred, granted or assigned to us.

6.   We will print regular sheet music copies of the Composition during the term hereof and will pay all cost of preparation, production, art work, arranging and engraving.

7.   This Agreement shall be in full force and effect for a period of seven (7) years from the date set forth above ("initial period"). You agree that we shall have the right to market any and all copies of said Folio on hand until such inventories thereof shall have been fully exhausted or for a period not to exceed one (1) year from the expiration of the initial period, whichever shall first occur ("sell-off period"). All sales during said sell-off period shall be in the ordinary course of business and shall not be at "close-out" or "distress" prices. We agree during the last six (6) months of the initial period of this Agreement you shall print only reasonable quantities of the Folio authorized hereunder and that during the sell-off period you will not print or reprint any such Folio.

8.   You hereby grant to us a royalty-free mechanical license for the use of the reproduction of the Folio in connection with the manufacture and distribution of phonograph records embodying the musical composition licensed hereunder in order to promote the sale of the Folio for the term hereof; provided, however, no such phonograph records shall be sold by us but shall be employed exclusively for promotion of the Folio.

9.   We agree to forward to you, by mail, five (5) copies of the Folio immediately upon publication thereof. We further agree that we will cause to be printed on every title page of the said Folio printed by you the proper copyright notice(s) as follows):

> "TITLE"
> Written by COMPOSERS
> Copyright (c) _____

Copyright this Folio (c) 2011

Because of the exclusivity for piano copies, the original publisher must represent that they have not granted these rights to anyone else.

The print publisher will absorb all expenses in creating the arrangements and all other costs of preparing the song for printing in the formats chosen.

The term of the agreement is for seven years plus a one-year "sell-off" period. This allows the print publisher to continue to sell any inventory of copies previously produced during the term, but not to reproduce more copies in the last six months than they might reasonably be expected to see and not to manufacture any copies during the sell-off period after the term expires.

This request is usually always granted so that the original publisher has copies for their files.

We further agree to imprint the legend(s) "All Rights Reserved" and "Used by permission" under the aforesaid copyright notices.

Such copyright notice(s) shall be in compliance with formalities of the United States Copyright Act and any international conventions pertaining to the acquisition and/or preservation of copyright in the musical composition, together with a notation that such copy is authorized for sale only in the licensed territory. We understand and agree that all of our rights and licenses hereunder are conditioned upon our compliance with all of said notice provisions and other formalities of all applicable laws, treaties, conventions and the like, and that any publication of the musical composition (in any form, including without limitation, arrangements or versions of the same) without such copyright or like notice, or without compliance with all such notice provisions and other formalities, shall be without the authority of the copyright proprietor, author or owner thereof, and shall not be deemed to be issued pursuant to the license granted hereunder. We shall not do any act or thing or omit the doing of any act or thing which will or might cause the copyright of the musical composition to be dedicated to the public domain.

In the event any of the foregoing is omitted or appears incorrectly on the publication, we shall immediately correct any such errors and/or omissions upon notice of same and we shall indemnify and hold you harmless of and from any and all loss, damage and expense, including attorneys' fees and costs, arising from or connected with the defect.

If the copyright notice is not correct, the print publisher agrees to correct it as soon as possible and is also liable for any damages caused by the incorrect notice.

We further agree that failure on our part to effectuate the aforesaid correction within thirty (30) days of said notice shall automatically terminate all rights granted to us hereunder.

Failure to print the correct copyright notice may result in termination of this agreement.

10. This Agreement shall be deemed made in and is to be construed and interpreted in accordance with the laws of the State of California, U.S.A.

Legal jurisdiction in California.

11. A non-returnable advance against royalties of $_____ is to be paid upon execution of this contract.

Provisions for an advance and bonus advances if the song becomes a hit.

(a) In the event the Subject Composition reaches a Top 10 position in *Billboard*, upon notification by you, we will pay you an additional sum of $_____ as a non-returnable, fully recoupable advance against all royalties due you hereunder.

(b) Should the Subject Composition reach a #1 position in *Billboard*, upon notification by you, we will pay you an additional sum of $_____) as a non-returnable, fully recoupable advance against all royalties due you hereunder.

12.   This Agreement constitutes the full and complete under-standing and agreement of the parties and it shall not be amended, modified or altered in any respect, except by an instrument in writing, executed by both parties hereto.

Please indicate your agreement to the foregoing by signing in the place provided.

Very truly yours,

Agreed to and Accepted

By:

TEXT AND MAGAZINE PRINT LICENSE
(ONE-TIME FEE)

The undersigned grants you a non-exclusive license to reprint:

_____

This material is to be published in: _____	This is a non-exclusive grant to print a portion of the lyrics of the composition in a book, magazine, or website.

This material is to be published in: _____

Where the lyric is being printed.

Proposed Publication Price: _____

Price of the publication or book.

Tentative Publication Date: _____

Date to be published.

Portion of the composition to be printed:

Insert the specific lyrics to be reprinted here.

In consideration of the permission granted herein, you agree to insure that the following copyright notice is printed in each and every copy of the publication concerned:

A requirement that copyright notice must be listed.

"TITLE"
Written by COMPOSERS
Copyright (c) _____

You agree to pay a publication fee of: $ _____ within _____ days after receipt of this License, or License will be deemed void.

These types of grants are usually for a one-time flat fee, not a royalty.

(1)   The rights granted herein apply solely to publication in the English language in the United States, Canada and the Philippines and all territories of the British Empire as constituted on January 1, 1947.

For use in books or magazines published in English only.

(2)   The right to reprint the material described above shall apply only to the issue or edition named in the application, but this permission shall also extend to special editions of the work produced solely for the use of the handicapped by approved non-profit organizations.

An allowance for special editions of the publication.

(3)   This permission does not include any copyrighted matter from other sources that may be incorporated in the material, nor does this license permit quotations therefrom in any other words.

This permission is specific to the works approved by the original publisher only.

(4)   No deletions from, additions to, or changes in the text may be made without the written approval of the undersigned.

No changes permitted to the lyric printed above.

(5)   The title of the material licensed herein shall not be used as the title of the Publication, nor shall the name of the author of such material be given greater prominence than the name of any other author in the Publication.

(6)   In the event payment is not made as specified, or in the event copy right and acknowledgment notices are not printed as specified, then all rights herein granted shall immediately terminate without further notice and without prejudice to any monies that may be due to the author under the terms hereof.

If payment is not received or copyright notice is improper, this license may be terminated.

(7)   Two copies of the work containing the above-licensed material will be sent free of charge to the undersigned on Publication.

Copies for the original publisher's and writer's files.

APPROVED AND ACCEPTED:

_____

CHAPTER 6

SONGWRITER AGREEMENTS

The songwriter agreement establishes the basic relationship between the songwriter and the music publisher. It assigns control of most issues involving the copyrights to the publisher, subject to certain areas of control retained by the songwriter and the songwriter sharing in the royalties earned by the work. As in most agreements, there are certain provisions that are deemed standard boilerplate based upon industry custom and practice, but many points are totally negotiable by the parties depending on the stature of the songwriter, the economic realities, and the flexibility of the publisher.

There are three main types of songwriter agreements with a publisher:

1. A single song agreement, which covers only one song created by the writer;

2. An exclusive songwriter agreement, which is for a particular amount of time (with additional options) and a delivery requirement of a certain number of songs during the term. In this type of agreement, the publisher controls 100% of the copyright in the songs; and

3. An exclusive songwriter/co-publisher agreement, which is similar to the exclusive songwriter agreement except that the writer and publisher share the copyright in the songs.

Each of these types of agreements will be discussed in more detail below and in the sample agreements at the end of this chapter.

Why Would a Songwriter Enter into These Agreements?

For many songwriters, the business of music publishing is a complete mystery to them. While they may be excellent at creating great music, they may lack the knowledge or acumen to understand or handle the business side of things. For successful songwriters, they may be too busy creating or performing to be able to focus on the business side. The primary function of a songwriter should be to write. Any time spent doing other things, whether it be handling business matters or working at a "real" job, reduces the time spent writing.

This is where a publisher can be of great value to a writer. A good publisher understands the music business and knows how to protect and monetize a writer's efforts. In exchange for these services, the publisher acquires an interest in the copyrights and a share of the accompanying revenue stream.

The primary functions of a publisher are to (i) register the songs with the Copyright Office, the performing rights societies, and other royalty organizations, like the Harry Fox Agency, (ii) receive requests for and negotiate licenses for the songs, (iii) collect the royalties from all uses and pay the writer and/or co-publisher their share, (iv) protect the copyrights against infringing uses, including sometimes having to litigate to protect the rights of the publisher and the writer, and (v) engaging publishers in other territories of the world (i.e., sub-publishers) to assist with these same functions in their local territories.

In addition, as discussed below, for some writers, the publisher can offer an advance against future royalties to assist the writer to be able to spend more time writing and less time working on other things. The advance is recoupable but non-returnable, which means that the amount of the advance will be taken and withheld by the publisher from future royalties earned by the writer (i.e., recouped), but the advance is not treated as a "loan" that has to be repaid in the event that the royalties are insufficient to cover the advance.

The following represent some of the major contractual areas of negotiation in most songwriter agreements.

Assignment of Rights

Any assignment of rights between the writer and the publisher must be in writing, showing clearly what is being granted. The assignment may be for 100% of the copyright in the songs or for a lesser percentage as negotiated between the parties.

Term of Services

The initial area of negotiation is the term during which the songwriter must provide their active songwriting services to the music publisher. In most agreements, there is an initial one (1) year contract period with options on the part of the publisher to extend the term for additional one (1) year contract periods. For example, the agreement might provide for a one (1) year period with three (3) to six (6) separate option periods. On occasion, the initial period is for in excess of one (1) year (e.g., a two [2] year initial period made up of two [2] separate one [1] year periods) with additional options or for a set period of years with no options (e.g., the term consisting of a three [3] year contract period with no options).

In the case of writers who are also recording artists, the term is usually tied to the delivery of recorded and released product (e.g., one [1] album with separate options for an additional three [3] albums or two [2] albums containing at least 75% of compositions written by the songwriter) or is co-extensive with the songwriter's recording artist agreement.

Exercising the Options

It is usually the exclusive right of the publisher to exercise the options for additional contract periods. The reason behind this is that, if the writer becomes successful, either due to the efforts of the publisher or through their own means, the publisher will want to renew the agreement to be able to take advantage of the writer's success and, hopefully, build on it for future success. It would be rare, except for the most successful writers, for there not to be option for future terms exercisable solely by the publisher.

The language in certain agreements states that option is automatically exercised unless the publisher gives the writer written notice that it will not be renewed a certain number of days prior to the expiration of the current term. Other provisions might state that the publisher may exercise its option to renew at any time prior to the expiration of the current period, but that the term shall not end until the songwriter notifies the publisher in writing of the publisher's failure to renew prior to the end of the then-current contract period, and gives the publisher an additional ten (10) days to renew. Without such notice from the songwriter, the publisher may continue to operate indefinitely under all terms of the agreement.

Other agreements might call for the publisher to notify the songwriter in writing of its exercise of the option to renew no less than thirty (30) days prior to the expiration of the then-current period. Failure of the publisher to renew in such a manner automatically terminates the agreement at the end of the period. This will allow the songwriter time to make arrangements for future administration of their catalog immediately upon termination.

If the songwriter is a recording artist and the agreement is based on the delivery of albums, the option pickup can either be within a few days after commencement of recording of the new album, delivery to and acceptance by the record company of the new album, or commercial release of the new album.

Copyright Ownership

There are two (2) ways that the publisher can gain ownership of newly created works under this type of agreement: (1) the works are assigned from the songwriter to the publisher; or (2) the songwriter is deemed to be an employee of the publisher, making the new compositions "works-made-for-hire." The distinction is a crucial one.

The term of copyright for works-made-for-hire is 95 years from date of publication or 120 years from creation, whichever comes first. As of this date, the standard term of copyright for works created on or after January 1, 1978, however, is life of the composer plus 70 years. While not only allowing for the possibility of a longer copyright term, the standard term also provides for termination of the assignment to the publisher after 35 years from the date of publication or 40 years from the date of the grant, with the songwriter (or their heirs) gaining control of the copyright.

With established writers, the majority of agreements being entered into are co-publishing agreements whereby the major publisher and the songwriter's publishing company co-own the copyright to all compositions on a 50/50 basis. On occasion, if there are pre-existing recorded and released compositions in the writer's catalogue, these might be only administered by the major publisher (with the songwriter maintaining total copyright ownership) but, in most cases, the back catalogue will be controlled on the same basis as the newly written compositions. As in all areas, however, this is a matter of negotiation and bargaining power.

Exclusivity of Services

Most agreements provide that all songwriting/composing services will be exclusive to the music publisher during the active term of the agreement. This means that everything the writer created during the term is covered under this agreement, even if they exceed their delivery requirement (see below). This does not mean, however, that the songwriter may not co-compose with other writers who are signed to different publishing companies, only that the songwriter's portion of those compositions are controlled by this publisher. In those situations, the publisher could enter into a co-publishing agreement with the other writer or their publishing company.

In addition, some exceptions regarding exclusivity may be negotiated in the area of writing for motion pictures or commercials, when the production company demands all or a portion of the copyright as a condition to the writing assignment. It could be in the best interests of the writer's career, and ultimately their success as a writer, to be able to write a song for an upcoming movie and it would be in the publisher's best interest for their writer to be associated with a song from a hit movie. As such, it is not uncommon for a publisher to waive their exclusivity in situations like this. Sometimes, the publisher can retain a portion of the copyright as a co-publisher with the studio, but the studio will generally retain control over the song.

Minimum Delivery Commitment

Virtually all songwriter agreements contain delivery commitments on the part of the songwriter that must be met before any particular contract period can end. These minimum commitments can either be phrased in terms of delivery of newly written compositions to the publisher (e.g., a minimum of eight [8] newly written compositions) or the delivery and commercial release of a minimum number of compositions (e.g., ten [10] newly written compositions delivered with four [4] being recorded and released in the United States via a record label with national distribution). If the writer is a recording artist, the minimum commitment might relate to a minimum number of compositions recorded and released under the writer's recording artist agreement (e.g., one [1] album per contract period which features the songwriter as a recording artist and contains at least seven [7] compositions written by the songwriter). There are countless variations on this theme; many of which are dictated by the expectations of the parties and the amount of money being paid the writer in advance monies.

The delivery requirement is usually phrased as "100% of X number of songs." This means that if some of the songs have co-writers, only that portion written and credited to this writer will count towards the delivery requirement. For example, look at the songwriting team of Elton John and Bernie Taupin. Elton writes the music and Bernie writes the lyrics. By custom and practice, music and lyrics are each deemed worth 50% of the song, so (hypothetically) if there was a 10 X 100% clause in Elton's agreement, he would have to deliver 20 songs to reach his requirement (20 X 50% = 10 X 100%)

There is usually some language that the songs must be commercially viable to qualify under the delivery requirement. For example, a writer is contractually obligated to deliver 10 songs in a 12-month period. However, at the end of the 10th month, they have only delivered four songs. It would be unreasonable to believe that, if it took the writer 10 months to write four songs, they could write another six songs in the remaining two months of the term. Not impossible, mind you, just improbable. The likelihood is that some of the last six songs will be lousy, i.e., not commercially viable. As such, the songs would not be accepted by the publisher and not count towards fulfilling the requirement.

Also keep in mind that, since this is an exclusive contract for a period of time, *all* songs written during this period fall under the agreement, even if they exceed the delivery requirement. Ethical questions come up for the writer if they have more songs than contractually obligated to deliver:

1. Can they stockpile the extra songs and use them to fulfill the delivery requirement for their next option period? It might seem odd that, one month into a new period, the writer all of a sudden has five songs ready to deliver.

2. If the publisher doesn't pick up the option for another term, can they take these songs and include them in their deal with a new publisher? Technically, these songs belong to the previous publisher, not the next publisher.

Extension of Contract Periods

If the minimum delivery commitment is not met by the songwriter, the then current contract period is usually automatically extended until a certain number of days subsequent to the fulfillment. For example, if the songwriter has a four (4) composition release commitment per contract year, and only three (3) compositions have actually been released, either on CD or digitally, by the end of a contract period, that contract period may be extended until between ten (10) to thirty (30) days after the release of the fourth (4th) composition. The publisher will usually have the right to exercise its option for an additional period during this ten (10) to thirty (30) day post-fulfillment period. During the extension period, the publisher does not have to make any option decisions because an option exercise is predicated upon the songwriter fulfilling the minimum commitment. The songwriter will many times try to limit the extension period to a set period of time (e.g., no longer than three [3] years) regardless of fulfillment or to a recoupment of advances criteria (e.g., if 150% of all advances have been recouped, the suspension will be lifted).

Royalties to the Writer

With one exception, the publisher collects all revenues associated with the works. The income earned by the work will be split 50% to the songwriter and 50% to the publisher, minus certain recoupable expenses incurred by the publisher.

The 50/50 split is not always used for print royalties, which can in many instances be based on a per cent royalty for sheet music and a percentage basis for folios. The exceptions for print royalties are historical in nature and may not be entirely valid in today's marketplace, where it may be more equitable to split these royalties equally as well.

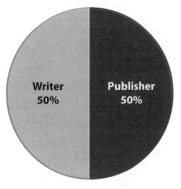

If there is more than one writer of a song, and the second writer has their own publishing deal, the two publishers will each collect 50% of the income and pay the writer one-half of that income.

The exception to the publisher collecting all the revenues is in the area of public performance royalties. ASCAP, BMI, and SESAC are U.S. performing rights organizations ("PROs") that pay writers and publishers directly for the royalties collected. They also collect foreign performance royalties from their counterparts overseas and make direct payments to the composers and, if the publisher does not have a sub-publisher in that territory, the PROs will also collect and pay back the publisher's share.

Given the changing landscape of public performance rights for radio and television, however, provisions should be made for the direct licensing of these rights by the publisher and/or songwriter. While the publisher will want full control over granting of public performance rights directly, there should be some protections for the writer's interests to prevent the possibility that public performance rights could be granted at reduced fees or even a waiver of fees to the detriment of the writer. See Chapter 2: Public Performing Rights Organizations for more detailed information.

While a songwriter, in an attempt to retain as much control as possible, may want to negotiate their share of these rights directly, it is impractical for the songwriter to be involved in every transaction. Therefore, there could be language granting the publisher the right to license both shares of these rights using the standard blanket fees charged by ASCAP or BMI as a guide to "market value" of these rights. For example, there may be language stating that the publisher has the right to grant a direct license but only for fair market value, consistent with industry custom and practice, and that the fees collected are divided 50/50 with the writer.

It should be noted, however, that if a TV or film producer wishes to obtain a source license (i.e., a buyout of performance rights at inception), it is virtually impossible to judge the value since the parties are unable at the time of negotiation to determine how many times and in how many markets the program containing the music will be broadcast. As in most buyout situations, the parties are speculating as to the success (or lack thereof) of a project without any hard facts to rely on.

Nowhere in the agreement is there any guarantee of the amount of royalties that will be earned under the agreement. To the contrary, there is sometimes language whereby the parties recognize that the music publishing business is very speculative and no promises are made regarding potential income. In fact, there is usually no language where the publisher has any obligations to actually exploit the music and attempt to earn money for the compositions. In cases involving well-known writers such as John Mellencamp, it has been held that a publisher has no fiduciary duty to exploit the copyrights, only to pay the writer their share of royalties per the agreement. *John Mellencamp v. Riva Music Ltd.*, No. 87 Civ. 6207 (S.D.N.Y. 1988). In 1983, Mellencamp entered into a publishing agreement with Riva Music, Inc. The written agreement was later amended so that in exchange for the assignment of the copyrights, Mellencamp received a percentage of the royalties earned from the exploitation of his music. Mellencamp claimed that per this agreement Riva became a fiduciary for Mellencamp's interests and said Riva failed to actively promote his songs and to use its best efforts to obtain all the monies rightfully due him from third parties. Mellencamp's complaint suggested that fiduciary obligations attach to the publisher-author relationship as a matter of law and that Riva companies' alleged failure to meet their express or implied contract obligations amounts to a breach of trust. The court held that the "trust elements" in a publisher-author agreement come into play when the publisher tolerates infringing conduct or participates in it, but said that ordinarily, the express and implied obligations assumed by a publisher in an exclusive licensing contract are not, as a matter of law, fiduciary duties. Therefore, Mellencamp's claims concerning Riva's breach of a fiduciary duty were dismissed.

Split Sheets

If there is more than one (1) writer of a song, the royalties may be divided in a number of ways. It is important to determine what percentage each writer is to receive and to document that in the agreement prior to any exploitation of the work. It is general industry practice (not law) that music and lyrics to a song receive equal weight, so if one party writes the music and one party writes the lyrics, they would each generally be entitled to 50% of the composer's share of royalties. Such a division is not always that simple, especially if there are more than two writers. For example, if one person composes the music with two co-writers contributing the lyrics, the split would usually be 50/25/25.

Absent an agreement clearly stating each co-writer's share, however, the default position under the Copyright Act is that all co-writers would share equally, no matter what their actual contribution to the work. In the example above, if there is no agreement, each writer would be entitled to claim a $\frac{1}{3}$ share of the copyright and royalties. With multiple writers, this can get even more complex. A television composer wrote the music for the main title theme for a program. The lyrics were written by the 14 members of the writing staff for the program. In fact, the credits read: *Music by "Composer," Lyrics by A Room Full of Writers*. Without an agreement stating that the music was worth 50%, the composer would have received only $\frac{1}{15}$ (or 6.67%) of the royalties.

If the writer co-writes with other parties, it is in everyone's best interests for the parties to sign a "split sheet." This document, signed after the song is completely written, sets out the agreed upon allocation of ownership and royalties when the contributions of all parties are still fresh and can be discussed but prior to the exploitation of the song. If this agreement is not signed and there is a dispute between the parties as to who owns what shares, the ability to license the song is inhibited and sometimes precluded altogether. If each of the three writers claim a 40% interest in the song, totaling 120% instead of 100%, either a potential licensee will choose another song or, in the case of mechanical royalties from a record company, the record company will just

Case Study #1

An artist who controls their own publishing has a controlled composition clause in their recording agreement calling for mechanical royalties at 75% of the statutory rate. The record company offers the artist a co-publishing deal, which would allow the artist to collect 75% of the income, the record company 25% of the income, and the record company would pay mechanical royalties at 100% of the statutory rate. Is this a good deal for the artist?

NO! Under the controlled composition clause, the record company would "save" 25% of the mechanical royalties paid to the artist's publishing company. But under the co-publishing deal, the record company (as co-publisher) would get 25% of ALL sources of income, not just a 25% discount on mechanical royalties.

hold all the royalties until the splits are resolved. There have been instances of a record selling 6 million copies, but no royalties paid to the writers and publisher because of a split dispute.

There are situations where very tiny shares are given to someone. There is a song recorded by a major artist where a major publisher, on behalf of their writer, owns 0.5% of the song. **Not 5%—0.5%.** One wonders what this person contributed to the song to earn such a small share. Did they suggest a couple of words? Did they add the handclaps? Did they bring the donuts? In this instance, the major publisher administered and controlled their 0.5% share separately, so when a client wished to license this song for a fairly low license fee, the publisher received a check for $3.50. And if that wasn't bad enough, they had to give 50% of that $3.50 to the writer.

Under the usual co-publishing agreement arrangement, in which the songwriter and publisher share copyright ownership in the compositions, the songwriter will receive 75% of the non-performance income received by the publisher from licensing to third parties (i.e, the 50% percent writer's share and one-half of the 50% publisher's share) and 50% of the publisher's share of performance income.

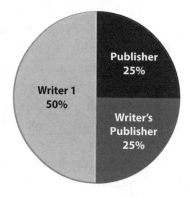

The songwriter usually receives their share of songwriter performance income directly from the performance rights organization.

Songwriting and Band Politics

Whenever there is a band with multiple members, some of whom are prolific writers and some of whom are not, issues can arise as to how publishing ownership and songwriter royalties are split. Obviously, the more songs someone writes that get recorded, played on the radio, and licensed for television and film, the more money that writer earns. In a band setting, however, there are multiple personalities and income streams to consider.

In some bands, there is a member who is the primary writer for most of the music performed and recorded by the artist. Prime examples are Pete Townshend of The Who and Gordon Sumner, aka Sting of The Police, both of whom wrote virtually all the songs recorded by their respective groups. As such, these two writers receive most of the writer's share of income, with the remaining group members not receiving anything unless they also contributed some songs. Consider the theme songs for the television programs *C.S.I.*, *C.S.I.: Miami*, and *C.S.I.: New York*, all of which use songs by The Who and written by Townshend. The band members divide the one-time license fees paid for the master recording, but Townshend gets both the writer and publisher share of the synchronization license fees. More importantly, he also receives writer and publisher shares for public performance of the compositions every time the shows are broadcast anywhere in the world.

In other circumstances, there may be two primary writers who agree to split evenly any songs that either of them writes for the band. Classic examples are John Lennon and Paul McCartney of The Beatles and Don Henley and Glenn Frey of the Eagles. While in their early days, Lennon and McCartney did write together, as their careers progressed, they began to write separately, with the other writer adding a bit here and there. Any student of the music of The Beatles can usually tell who wrote which songs, as the writer usually sang the lead vocals. Nevertheless, all songs were credited to Lennon/McCartney. George Harrison, who also became a fine writer, had to fight to get his songs recorded and usually only got one or two songs per album, with the rest being by Lennon/McCartney.

In the case of The Beatles, the writers assigned their copyrights to a publisher and earned a writer's share only. In some cases of bands with multiple writers, each writer had their own publishing deal as well, so they controlled both the writer and publisher share. An example would be Fleetwood Mac, in which writers Christine McVie, Lindsay Buckingham, and Stevie Nicks each controlled the songs they created.

There are cases, however, where things were done on a more democratic basis. U2, The Doors, and R.E.M. shared writer credit, with all members receiving a portion of the writer's share and each band setting up their own publishing company to collect the publisher's share, which was equally divided among the members. This sounds like a good idea, but it does have its drawbacks. For example, what happens if a band member leaves the band or passes away? If the publishing company is set up so that **all** members must approve any potential licenses, a living or dead departed member can prevent licensing opportunities that the remaining band members might wish to explore.

Accountings

The publisher should make accountings no less than twice a year, issuing detailed statements and paying any royalties that are recouped beyond the outstanding advances, if any. The songwriter should be given a reasonable period of time (the longer the better, from the writer's point of view) to examine and object to said accountings. It may be possible to negotiate a clause whereby if an audit discloses a discrepancy of more than a certain percentage of earnings, the publisher will pay for the cost of the audit.

Advances

Advances can be structured in a number of ways depending on whether the writer is a pure songwriter or songwriter/recording artist. For a young writer, the advance allows them to concentrate on their new job as "songwriter," not their old job as a waiter at Denny's. By taking some financial pressure off the writer, the publisher makes an investment that the money spent will result in better songs and more of them.

In addition, due to the lag time for money to flow through the pipeline to the writer, an additional advance (or an option period being exercised with an advance) will keep the writer solvent until the money gets paid to the writer. For example, assuming all parties are making payments semi-annually, if a writer has a song released on January 1 of year 1, the label will not pay the publisher for royalties earned through June 30 until September of year 1, and the publisher will not pay the writer until March of year 2.

With an established songwriter who controls their own catalog, the previous earnings can be used as an indicator of how the amounts of the advances are determined. As a publisher, you want the advance to be large enough to entice the writer to sign with your company without too much risk that the money might not be recouped. Analyzing previous earnings is one method of determining future earning, but care must be taken to avoid including an unusually high, one-time fee in your calculations.

For example, if in the past year the songwriter has licensed one of their songs for a national commercial for $250,000.00, that large fee would be a spike on the earnings graph that would have to be taken into consideration as an aberration, not the normal earnings pattern. It is better to examine earnings for several years to determine the value of the catalog so that the impact of these large, one-time deals can be minimized.

Among innumerable scenarios, advances can be payable as:

A. One lump sum (e.g., $50,000.00 upon commencement of the agreement) with option advances paid the same way (e.g., the full advance on commencement of each option period). Especially for younger artists, this method would not be favored, due to the risk that a young artist might use the entire advance to make a large purchase (like a new sports car they can drive to their old job at Denny's) and not have enough money to live on for the rest of the year.

B. Monthly intervals (e.g., $4,000.00 at the start of each month of the applicable contract period).

C. A percentage upon commencement of each period with the remainder in monthly or quarterly installments (e.g., $70,000.00 payable $37,000.00 upon commencement of the period with the remaining $33,000.00 payable in eleven (11) pro-rata monthly installments of $3,000.00 each).

D. A portion on commencement of the period with additional portions payable on the fulfillment of specified minimum delivery plateaus (e.g., 50% of the advance payable on commencement of the contract period, 25% of the advance on fulfillment of 50% of the minimum delivery commitment for that contract period, and 25% of the advance on fulfillment of 75% of the minimum delivery commitment).

E. A portion on commencement of the period, a portion on the signing of a recording artist agreement, a portion on acceptance of the album, and a portion upon release of the album (e.g., $200,000.00 in the aggregate payable $50,000.00 upon commencement of the initial period, $50,000.00 upon writer's signing of a recording artist agreement, $50,000.00 upon acceptance of the first album, and $50,000.00 upon release of the first album).

F. Sometimes, part of the advance is spent by the publisher directly on recording equipment for the writer. Previously, a writer would have to go to a recording studio to do a demo of a new song that just popped into their head in the middle of the night. Now, with the superb capabilities of home studio equipment, the writer can just pop out of bed in their "jammies" and lay down a track.

G. In a similar fashion, the publisher might pay for some amplifiers, guitars, keyboards, or a van that would make it easier for a writer/artist to go on the road and tour.

Additionally, there may be advances payable based on chart activity (e.g., an advance paid if a composition reaches the Top 10 on the A-side singles chart) or the achievement of certain sales plateaus (e.g., additional advances due upon the album achieving sales of 500,000 units, 1,000,000 units, etc.).

Option period advances may also be structured on a minimum and maximum basis (e.g., a $100,000.00 minimum and a $250,000.00 maximum) determined by a percentage of the earnings generated in the contract period prior to the commencement of the option period (e.g., 66% of the mechanical income received or credited to the account of the songwriter/co-publisher in the contract period prior to the commencement of the option period). There also may be provisions that reduce an option year advance by any outstanding unrecouped advance balance, many times with a subfloor below which the advance cannot be reduced (e.g., the advance shall be reduced by any outstanding unrecouped advance balance, but in no event shall the advance be reduced to less than $50,000.00).

Foreign Sub-Publishing Fees

With respect to income earned in countries outside the United States, agreements are either on a net receipts basis, an "at source" basis, or a combination of net receipts for certain territories and at source for others. Under a net receipts agreement, the songwriter's 50% of royalties will be computed on the basis of foreign earning less the fee taken by the subpublisher in the foreign territory. Under an at source agreement, the songwriter's 50% of royalties will be computed on the foreign earnings prior to the fee taken by the sub-publisher. The publishing agreement should clearly state what the publisher's deals with their sub-publishers are, sometimes with a ceiling of what the sub-publisher percentages can be.

Retention of Rights

Some agreements are for life of copyright, others provide for a set date on which the compositions will revert to the songwriter (e.g., 20 years after expiration of the term), and others provide for a reversion date which becomes effective upon the later of either a set date or recoupment of all advances plus a percentage of "profit" for the publisher (e.g., 25 years after the expiration of the term or recoupment of 150% of all advances, whichever date is later). In a co-publishing agreement, some agreements will provide that the major publisher will retain its co-ownership in the compositions but that the writer's songwriter and co-publisher share will revert to the songwriter. Irrespective, unless the songs were considered "works-made-for-hire" (see comments on ownership, above), the songwriter (or their heirs) has the right to terminate the publisher's interest in the copyrights between thirty five (35) years and forty (40) years after transfer to the publisher and reclaim one hundred percent (100%) of ownership of the rights in the United States. Termination of this grant may be effected notwithstanding any agreement to the contrary, including an agreement to make a will or to make any future grant.

Reversion of Unexploited Compositions

Regardless of the retention rights on exploited compositions, occasionally the parties will agree that ownership of unexploited compositions will revert to the writer prior to the date specified for exploited compositions. For example, reversion may take place after a set number of years after expiration of the term or after advances have been recouped. If there is an agreement as to reversion of unexploited compositions, the negotiations will then turn to the determination of what definition is to be placed on the word "unexploited."

In a single song agreement, sample language could be as follows:

1. The term of this agreement shall commence on the date first set above and shall continue in full force and effect for the duration of copyright (and all extensions thereof), subject to the following:

    A. Publisher shall, within ten (10) years from the date of this agreement, secure a "use" of the Composition. "Use" shall be defined as:

        i.   The release of a commercial sound recording of the Composition in the customary form and through the customary commercial channels;

        ii. A license authorizing the synchronization of the Composition in a motion picture, television program, home-video release, commercial or any other audio-video synchronization right;

        iii. A license authorizing the right to reproduce the Composition upon electrical transcription for broadcasting purposes.

    B. If, at the end of the period defined above, Publisher has not secured a Use of the Composition, then, subject to the provisions of the next succeeding subdivision, this contract shall terminate.

    C. Upon termination pursuant to paragraph B, all rights of any and every nature in and to the Composition and in and to any and all copyrights secured thereon in the United States and throughout the world shall automatically re-vest in and become the property of Composer and shall be reassigned to Composer by Publisher.

Warranty of Originality

The writer must warrant and represent that the songs being submitted to the publisher are original and capable of copyright protection and rights to the song have not been granted to another party. Without this warranty, the publisher would have no recourse if the writer submitted a song that they did not write, or that they had submitted to another publisher. There are stories of nefarious writers selling the same song to many different publishers, none of whom knew about the other deals.

Indemnity

Some indemnity clauses make the songwriter accountable for any costs related to a claim that is inconsistent with any of their warranties whether or not a breach is established. In my opinion, it would seem unfair for a writer who did not, in fact, breach his agreement to be responsible for the costs of successfully defending an action involving the song. Other clauses would limit indemnification only to a writer-approved settlement or a final adjudicated court judgment. There are many variations in this area and all are subject to negotiation.

Approvals Over Exploitation

The songwriter's right to approve the uses of their compositions represents a major area of negotiation between the music publisher and the songwriter's attorney. The extreme positions are, on the one side, the music publisher having total control over how and to whom compositions are licensed and, on the other, the songwriter having total approval over all uses of their compositions. In most cases, the final resolution of these two disparate positions is somewhere in between the two extremes. For example, a publisher might agree to give a songwriter approval over uses of a composition in an advertising commercial or in an NC-17 or X-rated motion picture and reserve the right to license the composition for use in a television series or in any motion picture which is rated other than NC-17. Although these exceptions might not be in the first draft of a songwriter/publisher agreement, they are an automatic "give" by most publishers if requested.

One well-known example of a writer exercising these rights of approval is the song "(You Make Me Feel Like) A Natural Woman" by Carole King and Gerry Goffin. For many years, Carole's publisher was approached by the makers of feminine hygiene products to use this song in their commercials. Carole, who had rights of approval over this type of use, denied the use every time, despite being offered huge license fees.

For major writers, approval on almost everything is granted by the publisher. But in many cases, young writers seek approval over almost everything, whether they know the business realities or not. In the 1990s, the *Mickey Mouse Club* television program featured, among others, future stars Britney Spears, Justin Timberlake, and Christina Aguilera and the show produced a music video of one of the cast members performing songs that were popular at that time. In many instances, the publishers of those songs had to go to the artists for approval and, in many cases, the artists either didn't approve or never got back to the publisher with a response. In some cases, the artist thought that the *Mickey Mouse Club* wasn't cool enough for their music or they didn't understand the licensing terms, so the use was denied. In many of those situations, had the publishers been given the authority to license without writer approval, the songs could have been licensed, earning both the writer and publisher money not only from the license fee but from the public performance organizations for as long as those programs were broadcast.

These rights of approval are based not only on the desire for control but the practical realities of licensing. For example, most television programs seeking to license music must have a response within 2–3 days. If the songwriter is also an artist, it may not be possible for the publisher to reach the songwriter within the time period necessary to make the deal, thereby losing the revenue opportunity. Some other areas of negotiation on the right of a songwriter to approve uses relate to grand or dramatic rights; interactive media; mechanical licenses at less than a statutory or 75% of statutory rate; certain philosophical, social, or political ideologies (e.g. an animal rights activist prohibiting the use of their song in a commercial for cosmetic companies who experiment on animals); changes in the lyrics and/or music to the composition; and use of the title of a composition. The above list is certainly not inclusive of the exploitation uses included in the negotiation process as, depending on the bargaining power of the various parties, anything under the sun is fair game for discussion.

OWNERSHIP SPLITS—NEW COMPOSITION

A "split sheet" as previously described. This would be used for a new song where all the material is original to the writers listed.

We, the undersigned, have co-written a musical composition entitled "_____
_____" and do hereby agree that each of us shall have the rights to own, control and separately administer our respective shares, as listed below, including the right to assign our shares to our respective music publishing companies.

None of the co-writers listed below may grant permission for the use of the composition, issue licenses for the use of the composition nor collect royalties on behalf of any other party or share beside their own. Each party shall perform the above functions for their share only.

We, the undersigned, have co-written a musical composition entitled "_____
_____" and do hereby agree that each of us shall have the rights to own, control and separately administer our respective shares, as listed below, including the right to assign our shares to our respective music publishing companies.

The song shall be owned in the following shares:

Writer: _____   Share: _____%

Writer: _____   Share: _____%

Writer: _____   Share: _____%

Writer: _____   Share: _____%

AGREED AND ACCEPTED:

Writer: _____   Date: _____

Writer: _____   Date: _____

Writer: _____   Date: _____

Writer: _____   Date: _____

This gives separate administration rights to each party for their respective shares.

This further reinforces the separate administration aspect and sets out what each party can do for their shares or cannot do for any other party's shares.

These percentages clearly spell out what each writer controls.

Although a very simple agreement, once signed this is a binding contract on all parties.

SONGWRITER'S CONTRACT—INDIVIDUAL COMPOSITION

This is a so-called "single song" agreement, covering only one composition.

AGREEMENT made this day of ____, 2____ between _____ (hereinafter called the "Publisher"), and _____ (hereinafter called the "Writer").

If there is more than one writer of this composition, all writers would be listed here, with their shares reflected in paragraph 4, below.

WITNESSETH:

In consideration of the agreement herein contained and of the sum of One Dollar ($1.00), receipt of which is hereby acknowledged, and of an agreement to pay royalties and other good and valuable consideration in hand paid by the Publisher to the Writer, the parties agree as follows:

The fee of $1.00 is a contract formality showing that there has been some consideration for the contract, although I have had clients who wanted to know when they would receive their $1.00.

1. The Writer hereby sells, assigns, transfers and delivers to the Publisher, its successors and assigns, a certain original musical composition (hereinafter called the "Composition") written and composed by the above-named Writer(s), and created in the year, and now entitled: __ _____ including the title, words and music, and all copyrights thereof, along with any registration thereof, including, but not limited to the entire term of copyright

This transfers all rights in the song to the publisher.

under the United States Copyright of 1976 for the entire world, and all rights, claims, and demands in any way relating thereto, and the exclusive right to secure copyright therein throughout the entire world, and to have and to hold the said copyrights and all rights of whatever nature now and hereafter existing thereunder, or under any existing agreements or licenses relating thereto, for and during the full term of said copyright.

This grant is for the life of the copyright throughout the world.

Writer agrees that the above shall constitute a transfer and assignment for the purpose of recordation with the United States Copyright Office and that a separate assignment essentially containing the language in this paragraph may be prepared by Publisher and filed in the United States Copyright Office by Publisher under the authority granted to Publisher in paragraph 6 herein.

This fulfills the requirement that an assignment of copyright must be in writing.

2.   The Writer hereby covenants, represents and warrants that the Composition herein is an original work and that neither said work nor any part thereof infringes upon the title or the literary or musical property or the copyright in any other work, and that the Writer is the sole writer and composer and the sole owner thereof and of all the rights therein, and has not sold, assigned, set over, transferred, hypothecated or mortgaged any right, title, or interest in or to the said Composition or any part thereof, or any of the rights herein conveyed, and that the Writer has not made or entered into any contract or contracts with any other person, firm or corporation whomsoever, affecting the Composition, or any right, title, or interest therein, or in the copyright thereof, and that no person, firm or corporation other than the Writer has or has had any claims, or has claimed any right, title or interest in or to the Composition, or any part thereof, or any use thereof or any use thereof, or any copyright therein, and that said work has never been published, and that the Writer has full right, power and authority to make the present instrument of sale and transfer.

> Warranty of originality, i.e., the work is original by the writer, the writer is sole creator, and this song has not been sold or transferred to any other party previously.

3.   In consideration of this agreement, the publisher agrees to pay the Writer fifty percent (50%) of any and all Net sums actually received by the Publisher from any source for the use of the Composition, except that the Writer shall not be entitled to share in any sum or sums received by the Publisher from any source characterized as performance royalties where corresponding funds are being paid to the Writer directly by public performance rights organizations.

> Defines the royalty splits to the writer—50% of all income except the publisher's share of public performance income, as the writer gets their share of performance income directly from their PRO.

"Net sums" shall mean the actual amounts paid over to Publisher by Publisher's collection agreements and foreign sub-publishers, other than the public performance royalties described in this paragraph.

> Definition of net sums allows for deductions for administration or collection fees retained by third parties, so the writer gets 50% of the money actually received by the publisher.

4.   It is understood and agreed by all the parties hereto that all sums hereunder payable jointly to the Writer shall be paid and divided respectively as follows:

> If there is more than one writer, their shares are listed here.

NAME   SHARE

5.   The Publisher shall render to Writer, as above, within ninety (90) days after June 30th and December 31st, royalty statements accompanied by remittance for any royalties due thereunder. After two (2) years after the date of this agreement, royalty statements shall be rendered solely for periods in which royalties are due.

> Semi-annual accountings from the publisher to the writer.

Said statement and payment, in the absence of written objection hereto shall by Writer within one (1) year from the receipt thereof, shall constitute an account stated as to all royalties due for the period encompassed by such statement and/or payment. Royalties are payable only when received by Publisher in the United States and in dollar equivalent at the rate of exchange at the time Publisher receives payment.

Once per year only, the Writer may appoint a certified public accountant who shall, upon thirty (30) days written notice, have access to all records of Publisher, during business hours, relating to the Composition for the purpose of verifying royalty statements hereunder.

7.   The Writer hereby consents to such changes, adaptations, dramatizations, transpositions, editing and arrangements of said Composition, and the setting of words to the music, and of music to words, and the changes of title as the Publisher deems desirable.

In the event that the Composition covered by this agreement is an instrumental composition, then and in such event the Writer hereby irrevocably grants to the Publisher the sole and exclusive right to and privilege to cause to have lyrics written for such Composition by a writer or writers designated by the Publisher, which lyrics shall require only the approval of the Publisher, whereupon the Writer shall be entitled to only one-half of the aforementioned royalties provided in this agreement.

The Writer hereby waives any and all claims which they have or may have against the Publisher and/or its associates, affiliated and subsidiary corporations by reason of the fact that the title of the Composition may be the same or similar to that of any musical composition or compositions heretofore or hereafter acquired by the Publisher and/or its associated, affiliated, and subsidiary corporations. The Writer consents to the use of their name, likeness, music, folios, recordings, or performances in connection with publicity and advertising concerning the Publisher, its successors, assigns, and licensees, and the Composition, and agrees that the use of such name, likeness, and title may commence prior to publication and may continue as long as Publisher shall own and/or exercise any rights in the Composition.

The writer has one year to review and file an objection to a statement, otherwise all rights to object are waived.

The writer has the right to audit the books and records of the publisher once a year upon 30 days written notice.

The publisher will want a broad grant of rights to be able to allow for changes in the song, translations or adaptations of the lyrics, using the title of the song as the title of a television program or film, or use the story of a song as the plot of a film or television program. In some cases, the writer may retain approval over some or all of these issues.

If the composition is an instrumental, and lyrics are added with consent of the publisher, the lyric writer would be entitled to a share of the writer royalties, so the writer's share of the royalties would be reduced from 100% to 50%.

8.   Any legal action brought by the Publisher against any alleged infringer of the Composition shall be initiated and prosecuted at Publisher's sole expense, and any recovery made by Publisher as a result thereof shall be divided equally after deduction of any and all expense in any way connected with litigation, arbitration, or resolution of a claim.

In the event of an infringement of this copyright, the publisher shall be responsible for bringing any legal action that may be necessary to enforce the copyrights. Any proceeds from such actions will be divided between the publisher and writer after deduction of the publisher's expenses in the matter, such as attorney's fees or court costs.

A.   If a claim is presented against the Publisher in respect of the Composition, and because thereof the Publisher is jeopardized, Publisher shall thereupon serve written notice upon the Writer, containing the details of such claim, and the Publisher shall thereafter hold any monies coming due to the Writer, pending the outcome of such claim or claims. The Publisher shall have the right to settle or otherwise dispose of such claims in any manner as Publisher may, in its sole discretion, determine. In the event of any recovery against the Publisher, either by way of judgment or settlement, all of the costs, charges, disbursements, attorney's fees and the amount of the judgment or settlement may be deducted by the Publisher from any and all royalties or other payments payable to the Writer by the Publisher or by its associates or affiliates, pursuant to this agreement or under any other agreement between said parties.

In the event a claim is brought against the publisher, the publisher shall notify the writer. The publisher may then withhold any royalties that might be due to the writer pending resolution of this dispute. In addition, if the royalties withheld are insufficient to pay the damages or costs of defending the claim, additional money can be withheld from future payments. The theory is that if the publisher has to pay damages to a third party, previously paying the writer their share of disputed income may result in the publisher having to try to collect from the writer and not being able to do so.

9.   "Writer" as used herein shall be deemed to include all authors and composers signing this agreement.

10.   The Publisher shall have the right to sell, assign, transfer, license or otherwise dispose of any of Publisher's rights in whole or in part under this agreement to any person, firm, or corporation, but said disposition shall not affect the right of the Writer to the royalties set forth herein.

As intellectual property, a copyright can be bought and sold, leased, licensed, assigned, or transferred to another party like any other kind of property. The publisher has the rights to do any of these things, but the rights of the writer to be paid royalties from any exploitation remain intact.

11.   This agreement shall be construed under the laws of the State of California. If any part of this agreement shall be invalid or unenforceable, it shall not affect the validity of the balance of the agreement.

12.   This agreement shall be binding upon and shall inure to the benefit of the respective parties hereto, their respective successors-in-interest legal representative and assigns, and represents the entire understanding between the parties.

This establishes California as the jurisdiction for any actions involving this song. It also states that if any provision of this agreement is breached and found invalid, all other portions of the agreement remain in effect.

IN WITNESS HEREOF, the parties have executed this agreement on the day and year first written above.

WRITER

Writer Signature

Address

City, State

Date of Birth

Social Security No.

WRITER

Writer Signature

Address

City, State

Date of Birth

Social Security No.

WRITER

Writer Signature

Address

City, State

Date of Birth

Social Security No.

PUBLISHER

By:

Address

City, State

WRITER

Writer Signature

Address

City, State

Date of Birth

Social Security No.

WRITER

Writer Signature

Address

City, State

Date of Birth

Social Security No.

All the writer information is necessary so that notices and royalties may be sent to the writer at their correct address. The writer's Social Security number is needed by the publisher for tax reporting purposes.

PUBLISHING AGREEMENT

This agreement between a songwriter and publisher assigns 100% of the copyright in the songs to the publisher, with the writer retaining the right to collect their share of royalties only, as specified below. **Please note that this agreement has many terms that are unrealistic and unfair to the writer**, as will be pointed out below, with no co-publishing interest retained by the writer, as shown in the next agreement. Sometimes, you need to see an unfair agreement to recognize a fair one.

This PUBLISHING AGREEMENT (the "Agreement") is made and entered into as of _____ (the "Effective Date"), by and between XYZ Music Publishing (hereinafter referred to as "Publisher"), with offices at _____ and _____(hereinafter "Writer") with an address of _____, with reference to the following facts:

A.   Writer is engaged in the business of creating musical compositions and owns and controls and will own and control during the Term (as defined below) certain musical compositions as hereinafter defined which are and will be available for exploitation and administration throughout the universe.

B.   Publisher is engaged in the business of music publishing and has certain facilities and services available to it for the administration and exploitation of musical compositions.

C.   Writer desires to share with Publisher the ownership of the Compositions

and further desires to appoint Publisher to act as exclusive administrator of the Compositions in the Territory and Publisher is willing to accept such ownership, control, and appointment

NOW, THEREFORE, in consideration of the mutual promises and covenants contained herein, the parties hereto agree as follows:

1.   GRANT OF RIGHTS

1.1.   Writer hereby irrevocably sells, assigns, transfers, and sets over to Publisher during the Term and Retention Period

an undivided one hundred percent (100%) interest in and to all of Writer's right, title and interest in the Compositions throughout the universe including, without limitation, all copyrights, rights to copyrights therein and any other rights relating to the Compositions, now known or which may hereafter be recognized or come into existence,

This language indicates that the writer has existing compositions that will be covered under this agreement in addition to any new compositions created during the term.

The word "share" would seem to indicate a co-publishing agreement, but this agreement is not a co-pub agreement.

Publisher has sole administration and control over the compositions, subject to the terms below.

"Retention period" is defined in paragraph 3.4, below.

Unlike a co-publishing agreement, in which the writer transfers only a percentage of the copyrights (see agreement below), this transfers 100% to the publisher.

and renewals and extensions thereof under applicable laws, treaties, regulations and directives now or hereafter enacted or in effect throughout the world, and all claims and causes of action relating to the Compositions accrued or hereafter accruing at any time. To such effect, Writer shall execute and deliver herewith the Assignment of Copyrights attached hereto.

Although this agreement purports to grant the publisher all rights to the copyrights, including renewals and extensions as part of the retention period, keep in mind that, at least in the U.S., the writer has the right to terminate the grant 35 years after the transfer.

1.2.   Writer grants to Publisher the sole and exclusive right, during the Term and Retention Period, in the Territory, to administer, control, use, exploit, and otherwise deal in and for the Compositions by any manner or method now or hereafter known and collect income in connection therewith whenever earned,

This broad and exclusive grant of rights to the publisher is standard in these types of agreements, but may be somewhat modified, depending on the stature of the writer.

but excluding any so-called "songwriter's" share of public performance income payable to Writer by a performing rights society

This allows the writer to collect his share of public performance income directly from his PRO.

(provided, however, if Publisher collects such income due to a failure to do so by the applicable performing rights society, Publisher shall pay to Writer its applicable songwriter's share of such public performance income), all of which Publisher hereby agrees to do in accordance with business practices generally prevailing in the music publishing industry.

In the event that the publisher collects both the writer and publisher's share of PRO income, they will pay the writer their share.

The foregoing grant includes by way of example but not limitation the following exclusive rights:

The following rights are exclusively granted to the publisher as part of this agreement.

(a)   The right to print, publish, vend, and sell in all forms, printed editions of the Compositions, to authorize others to do so, and to collect all fees and royalties becoming due with respect thereto;

Print rights.

(b)   The right to make or cause to be made, and to license others to make, master records, transcriptions, sound tracks, pressings, and any other mechanical, electrical, or other reproductions of the Compositions, in whole or in part, in such form, manner and frequency as Publisher shall determine in its sole discretion,

Mechanical rights, i.e., records, CDs, and digital downloads.

including the right to synchronize the same with audiovisual works, and the right to manufacture, advertise, license, or sell such reproductions for any and all purposes, including without limitation private performances and public performances, radio broadcast, television, sound motion pictures, wired radio, phonograph records, online or interactive platforms, and any and all other means or devices whether now known or which may hereafter come into existence,

Synchronization rights for audiovisual works like films, television programs, video games, DVDs, and other AV uses.

and to collect all fees and royalties becoming due with respect thereto;

The publisher collects all income from these sources, subject to payment to the writer their share of royalties as described below.

(c)   The right (subject to the rights heretofore granted by Writer to the performing rights societies with which Writer is affiliated) to perform the Compositions publicly, whether for profit or otherwise, by means of public or private performance, radio broadcasting, television, or any and all other means whether now known or which may hereafter come into existence,

The right of public performance.

and to collect all fees and royalties becoming due with respect thereto;

Subject to the writer collecting their share directly, per paragraph 1.2 above.

(d)   The right to substitute a new title or titles for the Compositions or any of them and to make any arrangement, adaptation, translation, dramatization, or transposition of the Compositions or any of them, in whole or in part, and in connection with any other musical, literary, or dramatic material and to add new lyrics to the music of any of the Compositions or new music to the lyrics of any of the Compositions;

This gives the publisher the right to make (or authorize the making of) changes to the composition, such as altering the melody or lyrics as well as allowing for translations and adaptations. This is modified by paragraph 2.1(a) below.

(e)   (i)   The right (subject to sub-paragraph (ii) below) to prosecute, defend and settle any third party action or claim relating to the Compositions and the respective rights of Writer and Publisher therein;

The publisher has the right to pursue any claims involving the compositions, however (see the next page) . . .

(ii) If at any time Publisher, in its sole discretion (due to a conflict of interest or otherwise) decides not to pursue a claim or action relating to any Composition, or maintain a claim or action in progress, Publisher shall give Writer written notice of such decision. If Writer, within fifteen (15) days after the date of such written notice gives Publisher written notice that Writer shall pursue or maintain the claim or action concerned and, with respect to actions in progress, substitutes its own counsel in the action (and, as necessary, moves to intervene as a party), Writer shall have the right to pursue or maintain such claim or action, at Writer's sole expense and in Writer's discretion,

provided that any settlement or recovery arising therefrom shall, after deduction of Writer's and Publisher's reasonable attorney's fees and costs, be turned over to Publisher for treatment as additional Gross Receipts hereunder. Music publishing rights acquired by Writer as a result of such settlement or recovery shall, as applicable, be subject to Publisher's rights hereunder. If Writer fails to provide Publisher the aforesaid written notice within such fifteen (15) day period, Publisher shall have the rights to settle and/or discontinue such claim or action on any terms it deems applicable. No settlement of any claim or action, whether by Publisher or Writer, shall convey any rights in any Composition to any third party or burden any Composition with a lien or other encumbrance or without the prior written consent of Writer or Publisher, as may be applicable, and any attempt to do so in violation of this sub-paragraph 1.2(e)(ii) shall be null and void and of no force or effect;

(f) The right to enter into agreements with related or unrelated third parties for the so-called "sub-publication" of the Compositions throughout the Territory and to collect all fees and royalties becoming due thereunder;

If the publisher declines to pursue said action, they must notify the writer and the writer has the right to take over the claim.

If the writer is successful, all proceeds of the action, after deduction of the writer and publisher's attorney fees, are treated as "gross receipts" and turned over to the publisher. This seems unfair, as the writer now assumes the burden of taking over the action but the publisher still gains by the writer's efforts if successful.

The publisher may enter into sub-publishing agreements and collect all income from said agreements.

(g)   The right to use the names, likenesses and biographies of Writer and any other author(s) and/or composer(s) of the Compositions and the titles of any and all of the Compositions for the purposes of advertising and trade in connection with the use and exploitation of the Compositions and for so-called "institutional advertisements" for Publisher's business and products;

> Rights to use the writer's likeness and biography should be with approval of the writer.

(h)   To secure copyright registration and protection of the Compositions in Publisher's name or otherwise, as Publisher may desire. If any claim to copyright in any Composition or portion thereof, has heretofore been registered in the name of Writer, then Writer shall, upon execution hereof, deliver to Publisher an appropriate assignment of any and all of Writer's interests therein in a form acceptable to Publisher;

> The publisher not only has the right to secure copyright protection, but the obligation to do so as the owner of the copyright.

(i)   Make arrangements, or otherwise adapt, translate, edit, alter or change any Compositions in any manner; and

> This is similar to the rights granted in sub-paragraph (d) above.

(j)   Any and all other rights of every and any nature now or hereafter existing under and by virtue of any common law rights, copyrights or any other rights relating to the Compositions now known or which may hereafter be recognized or come into existence; and renewals and extensions thereof throughout the universe under applicable laws, treaties, regulations and directives now or hereafter enacted or in effect.

> An "umbrella" clause regarding anything not specifically mentioned above.

1.3.   Writer shall exercise all necessary options and take all such other action as may be required to enable Writer to grant, and Publisher to maintain, the rights granted to Publisher under this Agreement.

2.   LIMITATIONS ON GRANT OF RIGHTS

> The following items require approval and consent from the writer.

2.1.   Publisher shall not without Writer's Consent:

(a)   Subject to sub-paragraphs 1.2(d) and 1.2(i) above, make any material change in the music and/or lyrics of any Composition, add new lyrics to the music of any Composition and substitute a new title or titles for any Composition. This sub-paragraph shall not apply to changes permitted by statute or custom, including, without limitation, as needed for translation, in the country concerned; and

> Changes to the compositions.

(b)   Issue mechanical copyright licenses for any Composition, with respect to the initial release of top-line records, at a rate less than seventy-five percent (75%) of the then-current minimum statutory rate in the United States and Canada (without regard to playing time).

This paragraph shall not apply to any reduced-price records or other records or sales customarily subject to discounted mechanical copyright royalty rates in the record industry, such as, without limitation, club sales, TV/radio or key outlet sales, free goods, and other non-normal retail channel sales.

2.2.   Publisher shall not, during the Term, without Writer's Consent license the Compositions for use in the United States and Canada (and Publisher shall instruct its sub-publishers in all other countries in the Territory that such Consent is necessary) in commercial advertisements or endorsements for feminine hygiene products, weapons, or tobacco;

provided that, if Writer fails or refuses to provide Consent, which for the purposes of this paragraph 2.2 shall mean within five (5) calendar days after Publisher provides notice to Writer requesting Writer's approval to license any Compositions for any use set forth in this paragraph, it shall be conclusively deemed that Writer has given such Consent.

2.3.   Writer may produce a reasonable number of Demos, which number shall not exceed _____ (__) during the Term. Writer must obtain Publisher's written approval of the budget for each such Demo prior to commencing any work in connection therewith, which budget shall be determined and paid by Publisher on a case-by-case basis in consultation with Writer but shall not exceed $500.00 for each such Demo. Publisher shall exclusively own all rights in and to any and all such Demos.

2.4.   If, during the Term, Writer is engaged by a third party (the "Third Party") to write new music and/or lyrics for any live or recorded program or project [such as, but not limited to, live stage performances, legitimate theatrical productions, radio programs, television programs, theatrical motion pictures, inter-active projects (electronic games, etc.)] (the "Score")

The writer must approve the granting of mechanical licenses for less than 75% of the statutory rate. Note that the publisher has the right to reduce to 75% without the consent of the writer.

These types of sales traditionally sell for less than normal retail price, so reductions in mechanical royalties are fairly standard.

Writer approvals are needed for certain types of commercials. As mentioned previously, these approvals are automatically granted if requested. Many writers, however, request approval of all types of commercials.

The writer has five days to consent or deny these approvals. However, if no response is received within five days, the approval is deemed granted.

The writer may produce a limited number of demos and be compensated for them at no more than $500 per demo. Two issues: (1) the agreement states in paragraph 5.1 that the demo fees are deemed an advance against the writer's future royalties and (2) the publisher owns the demos, which means that they have the right to license these recordings, despite the fact that no mention is made as to whether the writer would participate in the license fees for the demo recordings.

This paragraph addresses the possibility that the writer may be engaged to write music for a television program, motion picture, stage show, or video game. Many moving parts here for the writer and publisher to navigate.

then the Score shall be deemed Compositions hereunder but shall not count as part of any Minimum Delivery Commitment hereunder and

Music is considered owned by the publisher under the terms of this agreement (subject to the exceptions below) but does not count towards the minimum delivery requirement.

Publisher shall be free to negotiate in good faith ownership and licenses with the Third Party for the use of the Score.

The publisher can negotiate with the third party for licensing the score to that party.

Writer shall cause any such Third Party, prior to Writer entering into any agreements and/or rendering any services in connection with such Score, to negotiate with Publisher in good faith ownership and licenses with the Third Party for the use of the Score.

The writer must cause the third party to negotiate with the publisher for licenses and/or ownership of the score.

If the Third Party requires, as a condition of the engagement or employment, ownership and control of all or a portion of the Score, then subject to the following, Publisher shall give up its rights to that portion of the Score required by the Third Party:

If the third party requires ownership of the score, the publisher will agree based on the conditions listed below.

(a)   Writer is not then in breach of this Agreement;

(b)   Advances payable to Writer under this Agreement are not then in suspension;

(c)   The term of any Contract Period of this Agreement is not then in suspension by reason of Writer's failure to deliver the Minimum Delivery Commitment for such Contract Period;

The writer must be current with their delivery requirements.

(d)   Writer shall, prior to accepting any such engagement or offer of employment, require the Third Party to first negotiate with Publisher regarding the ownership and control of the Score; and

Since the writer's services are exclusive to the publisher, this requires the writer to attempt to get the third party to negotiate with the publisher for ownership of the score. As stated above and below, however, the publisher will give up their claim if all other conditions are met.

(e)   Not more than one Score per Contract Period (on a non-cumulative basis) will be subject to the provisions of the third sentence of this paragraph 2.4.

The writer may only accept one "outside" project in each contract period. This protects the publisher's position as exclusive rights holder to the writer's work as well as allows the writer to focus on their obligations to the publisher without the interference of outside projects.

(f)   Should Publisher be unable to retain ownership or control of the Score without requiring Writer to accept a service fee below competitive rates for a writer of Writer's standing and reputation,

then Publisher shall waive its and Writer's rights to that portion of the Score required by the Third Party as a condition of the engagement or employment of Writer provided Publisher shall, in consideration of such waiver, be hereby authorized by Writer to collect from the Third Party all service fees, royalties and other consideration payable to Writer by the Third Party for the Score and remit to Writer one-half (1/2) thereof (or Publisher may, in its discretion, direct the Third Party to pay such amount directly to Writer) without regard to recoupment of any advance hereunder and the balance of such service fees, royalties and other consideration shall be retained by Publisher. Publisher shall consult with Writer regarding Publisher's negotiations with such Third Party under this sub-paragraph 2.4(f) but a failure to consult shall not be deemed a breach of this Agreement by Publisher.

3.   TERM AND RETENTION PERIOD

3.1.   The term of this Agreement (the "Term") shall begin as of the Effective Date, and will continue, unless extended or sooner terminated as provided herein, for an initial period (the "Initial Period") ending thirty (30) days after the date when Publisher receives written notice from Writer of fulfillment of the Minimum Delivery Commitment for the Initial Period, together with copies of the Released recordings of the Compositions required to satisfy the Minimum Delivery Commitment for the Initial Period. In no event shall the Initial Period subsist for less than one (1) year from the date of execution of this Agreement by Writer.

3.2.   Writer hereby grants to Publisher two (2) separate and irrevocable options to extend the Term for two (2) additional Contract Periods ("Option Periods"), on the same terms and conditions as the Initial Period except and unless as otherwise provided hereunder.

The publisher wants to maintain the writer's financial standing so they will not insist on ownership in exchange for a lower fee to the writer.

The publisher waives their exclusive rights on the condition that the writer's fee for this project is paid to the publisher. The publisher will then pay the writer 50% of the fee whether the writer's royalty account is recouped or not. This arrangement protects the publisher's financial interest in the writer while allowing the writer to benefit without regard to the recoupment status of any advance. In some agreements, the writer may retain 100% of the outside fee, but this is a negotiable point for the parties.

Term of the agreement shall be no less than one year, subject to the writer notifying the publisher that the minimum delivery commitment (see paragraph 4, below) has been met together with copies of the released recordings required under the delivery commitment. The term would end 30 days after said notice, unless the publisher exercises the options below.

The publisher has options for two additional terms, on the same conditions as the initial term.

Publisher may exercise each of such options by sending Writer a notice not later than the expiration date of the Contract Period which is then currently in effect. Each Option Period will begin immediately after the end of the current Contract Period, and will continue for a period ending thirty (30) days after the date when Writer sends written notice to Publisher of fulfillment of the Minimum Delivery Commitment for then current Option Period, together with copies of the Released recordings of the Compositions required to satisfy the Minimum Delivery commitment for such Option Period;

except that the last Option Period will continue for a period ending three (3) months after Writer's fulfillment of the Minimum Delivery Commitment for such last Option Period. No Option Period (other than the last Option Period) shall subsist for less than one (1) year.

3.3.   If Publisher fails to exercise its rights for an Option Period within the thirty (30) day period concerned, subject to paragraph 10.10 below, the Term will terminate as of the end of that thirty (30) day period (or three (3) month period with respect to the last Option Period). Publisher shall have no rights in the Compositions delivered in connection with any succeeding Contract Period for which Publisher did not exercise an option, but Publisher shall retain all other rights acquired during the Term.

3.4.   Notwithstanding the expiration of the Term, Publisher shall retain all rights acquired by it under this Agreement for the life of copyright in each Composition in each respective country of the Territory and all renewals and extensions thereof (the "Retention Period").

The option must be exercised in writing prior to the expiration of the current term and will terminate on the same conditions as above, i.e. fulfillment of the minimum delivery commitment for that option period. Note that the option is at the publisher's discretion, not the writer's. Under these conditions, the writer cannot terminate the agreement unless the publisher declines to exercise the option. This is standard practice so that the publisher can benefit from their investment in the writer and keep a writer under contract if they are having some success.

Note that the last option period does not expire until three months after delivery, not 30 days as in the previous periods.

Even after expiration of the agreement, the publisher retains all rights to the compositions delivered during the term for life of copyright, including all songs created prior to the term that are covered under this agreement. Although this agreement purports to grant the publisher all rights for life of copyright, keep in mind that, at least in the U.S., the writer has the right to terminate the grant 35 years after the transfer.

4.   MINIMUM DELIVERY COMMITMENT

4.1.   During each Contract Period Writer shall deliver to Publisher newly written and entirely original whole or partial Compositions suitable for commercial recording by established recording artists written and composed by Writer, not previously recorded and acceptable to Publisher as satisfactory for commercial exploitation, and constituting, in the aggregate, not less than ten (10) one-hundred percent (100%) original controlled Compositions (i.e., Compositions, of which of one-hundred percent (100%) the music and/or lyrics to which are written and composed by Writer),

all of which shall have been recorded for and Released by a Major Label and licensed at not less than one hundred percent (100%) of the minimum statutory rate (a "Commitment Album") while constituting not less than $.91 in collectable aggregate mechanical royalties, or proportionately higher as and when the statutory rate escalates beyond $.091 (collectively the "Minimum Delivery Commitment").

Musical compositions that are not Released by a Major Label shall be Compositions hereunder but shall not count as part of the Minimum Delivery Commitment.

For the reasons explained below, this is one of the most onerous delivery requirements I've ever encountered. Even though I advised against signing the agreement, the client needed the advance being offered and signed. The client was never able to fulfill the requirements and had to negotiate her way out of the agreement.

Ten original compositions—so far not so bad.

All of which have been recorded and released on a major label? And all at the full statutory rate? Even the most successful writers don't get *all* of their songs recorded, much less released on a major label. This requirement is virtually impossible to meet, thereby making satisfaction of the delivery requirement unrealistic. The failure to meet this requirement could mean that the writer is tied to this publisher for an initial term of far longer than one year. This impacts the writer's ability to leave the publisher or to earn any future advances (see below).

Even if the songs are not released, they count as compositions under the agreement and the publisher owns them 100%, but they are not counted towards the minimum delivery requirement. So if the writer creates 15 songs and only 10 are recorded and released, the publisher still controls the remaining 5 songs.

Notwithstanding the foregoing to the contrary, musical compositions of which Writer writes and composes less than one-hundred percent (100%), but under no circumstances less than thirty-three and one-third percent (33-1/3%) of any such musical composition(s), and are Released by a Major Label shall count in the aggregate toward the Minimum Delivery Commitment to the extent of Writer's share thereof (e.g., if Writer shall deliver four (4) musical compositions for which he wrote and composed fifty percent (50%) each, which are Released by a Major Label, then it shall be deemed that Composer delivered two (2) one-hundred percent controlled Compositions to Publisher which counts toward the Minimum Delivery Commitment).

Musical compositions of which Writer does not write or compose at least thirty-three and one-third percent (33-1/3%) thereof shall be deemed Compositions hereunder but shall not count as part of the Minimum Delivery Commitment and no advance(s) shall be payable to Writer therefore.

For any Compositions for which Writer does not write and have at least a one-hundred percent (100%) ownership interest, Writer must deliver to Publisher at the time of delivery of said partially written Compositions a document confirming Writer's writer and ownership percentage interest confirming Writer's writer and ownership percentage interest in any such Compositions signed by all the writers of and by those who have an ownership interest in any such Compositions.

Compositions for which Writer does not deliver the aforementioned document, or otherwise violates any other restrictions set forth herein, shall be deemed Compositions hereunder but shall not count as part of the Minimum Delivery Commitment.

In each Contract Period the Compositions required to be recorded for and Released on a Major Label to satisfy the Minimum Delivery Commitment shall be contained on two (2) or more albums. Compositions so recorded and Released in violation of such restriction shall not count towards the Minimum Delivery Commitment but shall be deemed Compositions hereunder.

Songs partially written by the writer and released by a major label shall count towards the delivery requirement in the percentage that the writer has contributed. So if the writer composes, but does not write lyrics, each song would be worth 50% towards the delivery commitment.

The writer's share of the song must be at least 33⅓% to count towards the delivery requirement. If the share is less than 33⅓%, it still counts as a composition (and is subject to publisher control) but does not count towards delivery. Again, this is grossly unfair to the writer.

The writer must deliver "split sheets" for any co-written songs.

If the writer fails to deliver a split sheet, the song will still be deemed a composition under this agreement but will not count towards the delivery requirement.

The 10 songs must be released on two separate albums, so if the writer is an artist releasing their own material, the songs in one term under this agreement must be spread out over more than one album. This further extends the term of the agreement by making it more difficult for the writer to meet the delivery requirements.

5.   ADVANCES

5.1.   All monies paid to Writer during the Term, and any monies paid by Publisher on Writer's behalf, or at Writer's direction, other than royalties paid pursuant to this Agreement, shall be deemed advances. During the Term, Publisher shall pay to Writer the following advances, subject to sub-paragraph 5.1(d) below, recoupable from all Net Income payable hereunder:

(a)   For the Initial Period: Forty-eight Thousand Dollars ($48,000.00) payable in twelve (12) monthly install-ments of Four Thousand Dollars ($4,000.00) each, the first installment of which shall begin after the first (1st) day of the first (1st) month following complete execu-tion of this Agreement and shall thereafter be paid after the first (1st) day of the succeeding eleven (11) months.

All payments to Writer under this Agreement shall be made and payable to: _____, Social Security #_____.

(b)   For each Option Period(s): Forty-eight Thousand Dollars ($48,000.00) payable in twelve (12) monthly installments of Four Thousand Dollars ($4,000.00) each, the first installment of which shall begin after the first (1st) day of the first (1st) month following com-mencement of the applicable Option Period and shall thereafter be paid after the first (1st) day of the suc-ceeding eleven (11) months.

(c)   Notwithstanding anything herein to the contrary, ad-vances to Writer shall be recoupable from any and all Net Income and royalties owing Writer, except for so-called "songwriter" public performance royalties which shall be payable to Writer directly from Writer's public performance society.

(d)   If Writer does not fulfill any portion of the Minimum Delivery Commitment within the time prescribed here-in, Publisher will have the option to require Writer to repay to Publisher the amount, not then recouped, of any advance previously paid to Writer by Publisher, it being understood and agreed that if Writer fails to make such repayment Publisher shall have the right to deduct such unpaid amount from any and all payments otherwise payable to Writer hereunder; provided, however, that any amounts so repaid shall not be recoupable.

This would include the demo fees listed above.

Advance paid in monthly installments for 12 months. Keep in mind that, if the writer does not meet the delivery requirement listed above, they are still under contract and obligated to fulfill the terms, even though they may not receive any further advances.

Additional advances for each option period.

Advances recoupable from all sources owed to the writer except the writer's share of performing rights.

This goes against the basic principle that advances are recoupable but non-returnable. Repayment from future earnings is standard, but not repayment by the writer.

6.   <u>ROYALTIES AND ACCOUNTINGS</u>

6.1.   Publisher shall credit to Writer's account royalties in an amount equal to the following percentage of Publisher's Net Income:

(a)   With respect to uses of the Compositions in the United States:

(i)   0% of the Publisher's share of public performance income

(ii)   50% of the Publisher's share of synchronization license income which shall not be less than eighty-seven and one-half percent (87-1/2%) of synchronization license income received by Publisher's administrator)

(iii)   50% of Other Income (which shall not be less than eighty-seven and one-half percent (87-1/2%) of other income received by Publisher's administrator)

(b)   With respect to uses of the Compositions outside the United States:

(i)   0% of the Publisher's share of public performance income:

(ii)   50% of the Publisher's share of synchronization license income (which shall not be less than eighty percent (80%) of synchronization license income received by Publisher's sub-publisher)

(iii)   50% of the Publisher's share of mechanical royalty income derived from local Cover Records (which shall be not less than sixty percent (60%) of the mechanical royalty income received by Publisher's sub-publisher)

Notice the language "credit to Writer's account," not "pay to Writer." If the writer is unrecouped, no additional money shall be paid out until recoupment.

The writer is already getting their share of performance income from their PRO, so the publisher gets to retain 100% of the publisher's share of this income. Sometimes there is language added that, if the publisher collects the writer's share also, 50% of that income will go to the writer.

50% of all sync income, less a 12½% commission for the publisher's administrator..

50% of all other income, less a 12½% commission for the publisher's administrator.

This would indicate an 80/20 sub-publishing deal.

For a cover recording, the foreign sub-publisher would get to retain 40% instead of the usual 20%.

(iv)   50% of the Publisher's share of other income (which shall not be less than eighty percent (80%) of other income received by Publisher's sub-publishers)

6.2.   The amounts provided as payable to Writer by Publisher as royalties in paragraph 6.1 above are inclusive of all fees and royalties becoming due to any other authors or composers, it being the parties' express intention that Publisher shall have no obligation to account for or to pay any royalties to any other authors or composers, such obligation to be solely and exclusively that of Writer.

Although co-writers would usually be covered under a separate agreement, this clearly states that the publisher is not responsible for any co-writers that might be involved with this agreement and that the responsibility of paying any other writers falls on the writer.

Publisher shall in no event have any songwriter royalty obligation to Writer or any other authors or composers with respect to income on which a songwriter share is paid directly to such authors and composers. Without limiting the foregoing, Publisher shall not be required to make any payments of any nature for, or in connection with, the acquisition, exercise or exploitation of any rights by Publisher pursuant to this Agreement, except as specifically provided in this Agreement.

This refers to the writer's share of income paid by the PROs.

6.3.   Publisher will compute Writer's royalties as of each June 30th and December 31st for the prior six (6) months. (Publisher reserves the right to alter such accounting periods without notice, but in no event shall Publisher account less frequently than every six (6) months). On the next September 30th or March 31st (or if Publisher alters the accounting periods, on the date ninety (90) days following the period concerned) Publisher will send Writer a statement covering those royalties and will pay Writer any net royalties which are due after deducting unrecouped advances or other recoupable and/or deductible amounts hereunder.

Semi-annual accountings.

Publisher will not be required to send Writer a royalty payment or statement for any period in which the royalties payable to Writer will be $50.00 or less; such royalties shall be held and paid along with the next statement requiring payment in excess of $50.00.

Payment will be made only if advances are recouped and amount actually owed is over $50.00.

Publisher shall only hold reserves against Writer's royalties in instances where there is a possibility of a charge, credit or return (e.g., if Publisher enters the business of distributing printed editions). Such reserves shall be reasonable and shall be liquidated by the end of the fourth (4th) accounting period after they are taken. If Publisher makes any overpayment to Writer, Writer will reimburse Publisher for it; to the extent not immediately reimbursed, Publisher may also deduct it from any payments due or becoming due to Writer under this Agreement; and/or any agreement entered into between Writer and Publisher, or any of its affiliates.

> As most payments to the publisher are net after reserves are held, such as mechanical royalties, most agreements don't allow for reserves to be held by the publisher. Here, however, there is an allowance made in the event that the publisher is involved in the print music industry, where there might be returns of product.

6.4.   Net Income for the exploitation of Compositions outside the United States shall be converted from the national currency concerned (on the date actually credited to Publisher's account) at the same rate of exchange that Publisher uses to convert accountings from its sub-publishers and shall be computed and paid in U.S. Dollars.

> In the event of payments from outside the U.S., the money will be converted to U.S. dollars at the exchange rate in effect at time of the conversion.

Such royalties shall not be due and payable by Publisher until payment therefore has been received by Publisher, or credited to Publisher's account, in the United States in United States Dollars. If Publisher shall not receive payment in the United States, or in United States Dollars, and shall be required to accept payment in a foreign country or in foreign currency, Publisher shall deposit to the credit of Writer (at Writer's written request and expense), in such currency in a depository designated by Writer in the country in which Publisher is required to accept payment, Writer's share of royalties due and payable to Writer with respect to such exploitations. Deposit as aforesaid shall fulfill all the obligations of Publisher as to exploitations to which such royalty payments are applicable. Such royalties shall be subject to any taxes applicable to royalties remitted by or received from foreign sources. Further, if any law, government ruling or any other restriction affects the amount of the payments which Publisher's licensee can remit to Publisher, Publisher may deduct from Writer's royalties an amount proportionate to the reduction in such licensees' remittances to Publisher.

> Foreign royalties are not payable to the writer until the money is actually received by publisher in the U.S. In the event that foreign monies cannot be sent to the U.S., the publisher agrees to deposit the money in an account of the writer's choosing in that country. This doesn't happen very often but can change depending on the political climate in a foreign country.

6.5.   Publisher will maintain books and records which report exploitation of Compositions for which royalties are payable to Writer. Writer may, at Writer's own expense, examine those books and records, as provided in this paragraph only. Writer may make those examinations only for the purpose of verifying the accuracy of the statements sent to Writer under paragraph 6.3. Writer may make such an examination for a particular statement only once, and only within two (2) years after the date when Publisher is required to send Writer such statement under paragraph 6.3. For the purpose of this Article 6 such statement shall be deemed to have been sent to Writer on the due date prescribed in paragraph 6.3 unless Writer gives Publisher written notice of non-receipt within thirty (30) days after such due date. Writer may make such examinations only during Publisher's usual business hours, and only at the place where it keeps the books and records to be examined. If Writer wishes to make an examination Writer will be required to notify Publisher at least sixty (60) days before the date when Writer plans to begin it, and to make an appointment with Publisher at a time reasonably convenient to Publisher. Writer will not be entitled to examine any records that do not specifically report exploitation of Compositions as to which royalties are payable to Writer. Only an independent certified public accountant experienced in music publishing audits may make such an examination for Writer, but not a particular accountant if he or his firm has begun an examination of Publisher's books and records for any person or entity except Writer, unless the examination has been concluded and any applicable audit issues have been resolved. Such accountant must execute a confidentiality agreement relating to Publisher's books and records before proceeding with any audit.

The writer has the right to audit the books and records of the publisher with regard to the accuracy of statements and income, but each statement only once within two years of sending by the publisher.

6.6.   If Writer has any objections to a royalty statement, Writer will give Publisher specific notice of that objection and Writer's reasons for it within two (2) years after the date when Publisher is required to send Writer that statement under paragraph 6.3. Each royalty statement will become conclusively binding on Writer at the end of that two (2) year period, and Writer will have no further right to make any other objections to it. Writer will have no right to sue Publisher in accordance with any accounting, or to sue Publisher for Net Income derived from exploitation of Compositions during the period an accounting covers, unless Writer commences the suit within that two (2) year period and Writer hereby waives any longer statute of limitations that may be permitted by law. If Writer commences suit on any controversy or claim concerning accountings rendered to Writer under this Agreement, the scope of the proceeding will be limited to determination of the amount of the Net Income due, if any, for the account periods concerned; and the court will have no authority to consider any other issues or award any relief except recovery of any royalties found owing.

Writer's recovery of any such Net Income will be the sole remedy available to Writer or any other authors or composers by reason of any claim related to Publisher's accountings. Without limiting the generality of the preceding sentence, neither Writer nor any applicable authors or composers will have any right to seek termination of this Agreement or avoid the performance of Writer's obligations under it by reason of any such claim.

7.   REPRESENTATIONS, WARRANTIES AND INDEMNITIES

7.1.   Writer represents and warrants to Publisher that:

(a)   It has the right, power and authority to enter into this Agreement, to fully perform hereunder, to grant to Publisher all of the rights purported to be granted to Publisher hereunder, and that neither this Agreement nor the fulfillment hereof by any party infringes upon the rights of any person or entity;

(b)   The Compositions will be originally composed and created by Writer, and any other authors and composers, and protectable by copyright in the Territory, and the administration, control, use and exploitation thereof by Publisher hereunder will not subject Publisher to liability of any kind to any third party (including, without limitation, such authors and composers);

The writer must file written objections to any statement and bring a lawsuit within the same two-year period as above. Many agreements allow for an additional period to file objections or file suit, as using the same two-year period actually shortens the amount of time the writer has to examine the statements.

Recovery of any unpaid funds is the only remedy available to the writer, i.e., no punitive damages or termination of the agreement in the event of a breach regarding unpaid royalties.

Compositions must be original and capable of copyright protection without infringing the rights of others.

(c)   Without limitation of anything contained herein, there are and will be no liens or encumbrances upon the Compositions and Writer has not heretofore solicited or accepted and will not hereafter solicit or accept any advance from any third party which would in any manner diminish the monies available to Publisher in connection with the use, administration or exploitation of the Compositions;

> There are no outstanding liabilities against the compositions that would inhibit the right of the publisher to collect all sources of income.

nor are the Compositions subject to any "controlled composition" clause or other agreement which purports to fix the compensation payable with respect to any uses of the Compositions for less than the minimum statutory rate (except as and unless provided for herein);

> No previous controlled composition clauses that would reduce the publisher's income.

(d)   Writer has and will have valid and enforceable written exclusive songwriter agreements with any applicable other authors and composers under which the Compositions are and will be the property of Writer;

> If there are other writers covered under this agreement, the writer has valid agreements with those writers.

(e)   During the Term hereof Writer shall conscientiously pursue and continue its songwriting efforts, shall do so exclusively for Publisher and shall not materially alter Writer's professional status in effect as of the commencement of this Agreement. Without limitation of Publisher's other remedies hereunder, any material change in such status and/or performance shall allow Publisher the right to terminate this Agreement;

> The writer agrees that they will continue to be a songwriter, shall be exclusive to the publisher, and that any change in that status will allow the publisher to terminate the agreement.

(f)   Writer is, and at all times during the Term shall be, a member in good standing of ASCAP, BMI, or SESAC, and Writer hereby represents and warrants that it is a member of good standing of SESAC pursuant to an affiliation agreement entered into as of _____.
In the event that Writer is not affiliated with such society and/or such affiliation lapses during the Term, Publisher shall have the right to register a one hundred percent (100%) interest in the Compositions with such society in Publisher's name, subject to the payment of Net Income to Writer hereunder;

> The writer is a member of a PRO.

(g)   Writer has not previously issued any licenses to use or otherwise exploit the Schedule "A" Compositions to any third party, nor has Writer itself commercially exploited such Schedule "A" Compositions, anywhere in the Territory;

(h)   Writer is not under any disability, restriction or prohibition respecting any of the Compositions provided or to be provided to Publisher;

(i)   Neither Writer nor any person or other entity deriving any rights from Writer shall at any time, do or authorize any person or other entity to do, anything inconsistent with, or which might diminish, impair or interfere with any of Publisher's rights hereunder or the full and prompt performances of Writer's obligations hereunder. Without limiting the foregoing, Writer agrees to perform its obligations hereunder to the best of its ability;

(j)   Writer is above the legal age of majority pursuant to the laws governing this Agreement and the performance hereunder; and

(k)   There have been no, nor shall there be, during the Term or the Retention Period, advances made by ASCAP, BMI, SESAC or any other third parties which are recoupable from income (other than the songwriter's share of non-dramatic public performance royalties) derived from any use of the Compositions. Writer is, and shall during the Term and the Retention Period continue to be, entitled to be paid and to collect on all such income in accordance with this Agreement. Without limiting the generality of the foregoing or any other remedy available to Publisher with respect to a breach of this Agreement by Writer, to the extent such advances are made, Publisher shall have the right to: (i) terminate the Term; (ii) reduce any payments to Writer hereunder by the amount of such advances; and/or (iii) require Writer to repay any advance previously made hereunder by the amount of such advance.

For existing songs, there might be some previous exploitation, so this clause would need to be amended to reflect those uses.

If the writer is a minor, this agreement could be voided by the writer upon turning 18 years old. If an adult, the writer is held to the terms of the agreement.

The writer warrants that there are no publishing advances from the PROs or any other third parties that would inhibit the publisher's ability to earn and collect royalties. If so, then the publisher can terminate the agreement or reduce payments to the writer in that amount.

7.2. Publisher represents and warrants to Writer:

(a) Publisher is, and will be during the Term, active in the United States and, through sub-publishers, licensees or collection agents or societies elsewhere in the Territory, in the business of music publishing; and

(b) Publisher has the full right, power and authority to enter into this Agreement and to grant to Writer all of the rights purported to be granted to Writer hereunder.

7.3. Writer represents, warrants, covenants and agrees that Writer will write exclusively for Publisher during the Term of this Agreement.

7.4. Publisher may elect to pursue a claim or action against any third party or parties (Publisher being under no obligation to take such action) relating to the Compositions or to refrain therefrom. If Publisher elects not to pursue a claim or action it shall notify Writer in writing of such decision. Writer shall, after receipt of such notice from Publisher, have sixty (60) days to institute an action against said third party, at Writer's sole expense.

If such action is instituted, any settlement arising after all pleadings have been served by the plaintiff and defendant(s) or any recovery arising from the successful prosecution of such action, shall, after deduction of Writer's and Publisher's out-of-pocket reasonable attorney's fees and costs ("Net Recovery") be divided equally between Writer and Publisher.

If any settlement is made by Writer prior to the service of all pleadings, as aforesaid, or on terms less advantageous to Writer and Publisher than the then current market license fee or any other fee proposed by Publisher, the Net Recovery shall be paid to Publisher as Gross Receipts hereunder. Further, any music publishing rights acquired by Writer as a result of such settlement or recovery, shall be subject to Publisher's rights hereunder and governed by this Agreement without any additional advance being payable.

Note the lack of language whereby the publisher makes any representations about what they will do to exploit the compositions or money they might earn.

This reaffirms the exclusive nature of the writer's services to the publisher.

If there is a potential infringement of the copyright of one of the compositions covered under this agreement, the publisher has the right (but not the obligation) to pursue action against a third party. If the publisher fails to do so, the writer may step in at their own expense.

For any recovery after litigation has commenced, the writer and publisher agree to split the proceeds 50/50 after payment of their attorney fees.

If the action is settled prior to litigation, all proceeds are paid to the publisher and distributed per the terms of the agreement.

7.5   (a)   If any claim shall be lodged with Publisher or any action commenced having as its basis a claim which, if proved, would constitute a breach by Writer of any of Writer's representations, warranties, or covenants contained herein, Publisher, in addition to any other right or remedy otherwise available, may withhold from any payments otherwise due to Writer hereunder an amount equivalent to that claimed or sued for plus reasonable costs and attorney's fees relating thereto. Any amount so withheld shall be held by Publisher in an interest bearing account for the benefit of Writer and shall be released to Writer (after deduction of any amounts Publisher may retain under sub-paragraph 7.5(b) below) when Publisher shall have received reasonable assurances that the claim or action has been finally settled or fully adjudicated and the judgment satisfied, or that the statute of limitations on such claim has run, or when reasonable and adequate security for the claim has been provided by Writer to Publisher or if no suit is instituted by the claimant within twelve (12) months after the claim is asserted in writing; and

(b)   Writer agrees to indemnify and hold Publisher and its parent, affiliates, divisions, successors and assigns and the officers, directors, and employees of the foregoing harmless from and against any liability, damage, cost or expense (including costs and reasonable attorneys' fees) occasioned by or arising out of any breach or alleged breach of this Agreement or any claim, demand or action which is inconsistent with any warranty, representation, agreement or grant of rights made or assumed by Writer hereunder. Publisher agrees to give Writer notice of any claim, demand or action to which the foregoing indemnity applies, and Writer may participate in the defense of same at its sole expense, through counsel of its choice; provided, that the final control and disposition of same (by settlement, compromise or otherwise) shall remain with Publisher. Writer agrees to pay Publisher on demand any amount for which Writer may be responsible under the foregoing indemnity and, without limiting any of Publisher's other rights or remedies, upon the making or filing of any claim, demand or action subject hereto, Publisher shall be entitled to withhold sums payable under this Agreement in an amount reasonably related to the potential liability, plus costs and reasonable attorneys' fees. Writer shall, at Publisher's request, cooperate fully with Publisher in any controversy which may arise with third parties or litigation which may be brought by third parties concerning this Agreement or any of Publisher's rights hereunder.

If there is a claim brought against the publisher based on one of these songs, the publisher may hold payment of royalties pending resolution, but money will be disbursed if no litigation is commenced within 12 months. This protects the publisher from paying money to the writer that might be owed to a third party.

The writer agrees to pay the publisher for any costs resulting from a breach or alleged breach of this agreement. When representing writers, I try to strike the words "alleged breach" from the agreement, as the writer should not be held liable if they didn't actually breach the agreement.

7.6   It is expressly understood and agreed that any remedies that Writer may have against Publisher in connection with a breach or purported breach of this Agreement for any reason shall be limited to the right to recover monetary damages in a sum not greater than the advance paid by Publisher to Writer under the applicable Contract Period during which the breach has occurred, in an action at law, and Writer hereby waives any right or remedy in equity, including, without limitation, any right (a) to terminate this Agreement, (b) to rescind Publisher's right, title and interest in and to the Compositions, or (c) to enjoin, restrain or otherwise impair in any manner the distribution, advertising, sale and/or exploitation of the Compositions, including any parts thereof, or any other rights granted to Publisher hereunder.

> The writer's only remedy in the event of a breach by the publisher is an action at law for damages, limited to the amount of the advance paid during that contract period. No injunctive relief or termination of the agreement is available to the writer, only monetary damages.

7.7.   Writer expressly acknowledges and agrees that Publisher is part of a diversified, multi-faceted national or international group of companies, whose affiliates include, or in the future may include, among others, broadcasters, distributors, exhibitors, programming services, video device distributors, television and radio stations and networks, Internet and e-commerce companies and services, publishers and wholesale and retail outlets (each, an "Affiliated Company"). Publisher hereby informs Writer that Publisher may at any time or times, in its sole discretion, make use of Affiliated Companies in connection with the distribution and exploitation of the Compositions or any other material hereunder where it determines it appropriate to do so and Writer hereby expressly waives any right to object to any such distribution or exploitation, or to assert any claim, whether at law or in equity, that Publisher should have offered the applicable distribution and/or exploitation rights to unaffiliated third parties in lieu of, or in addition to, offering the same rights to Affiliated Companies and, in consideration thereof, Publisher agrees that its transactions with Affiliated Companies shall be on monetary terms comparable to the monetary terms on which Publisher enters into similar transactions with third parties that are not Affiliated Companies.

> In this case, the publisher is the music division of an entertainment company that has interests in the record, radio, film, and television industries. The writer waives an objection that the publisher attempts to exploit the compositions through its sister companies to the exclusion of others. In exchange, the publisher agrees that transactions with its sister companies shall be on comparable terms to outside companies, i.e., arms-length deals.

7.8.   All of the parties' respective warranties, representations, and indemnities under this Agreement, and the limitations set forth in paragraph 7.6 above, shall survive the end of the Term and Retention Period, as applicable.

8.   ADDITIONAL REMEDIES

8.1.   Writer acknowledges that the rights granted to Publisher and the services to be rendered hereunder are of a special, unique, unusual, intellectual, and extraordinary character involving skill of the highest order which gives them peculiar value, the loss of which cannot be reasonably or adequately compensated in damages in an action at law, and that in the event of a breach or threatened breach by Writer, or conduct by Writer which could result in such breach, of any term or condition hereof, Publisher will be caused immediate irreparable injury and damage. Accordingly, Publisher shall be entitled to injunctive and other equitable relief to prevent such breach and to prevent Writer from performing services for any third party other than Publisher, or on Writer's own behalf. Publisher's resort to any such equitable relief shall not be deemed as a waiver of any other rights or remedies to which Publisher may be entitled.

8.2.   The rights and remedies of Publisher set forth in this Agreement are not to the exclusion of each other or of any other rights or remedies which may be available to Publisher at law or in equity. Publisher's decision to exercise or refrain from exercising any of its rights or remedies shall not affect any other rights or remedies of Publisher. All of Publisher's rights and remedies in connection with this Agreement shall survive the expiration of the Term. Notwithstanding anything in this Agreement, Publisher may at any time exercise any right which it now or at any time hereafter may be entitled to as a member of the public as though this Agreement were not in existence.

9.   DEFINITIONS

9.1   "Affiliate Company" shall have the meaning set forth in paragraph 7.7 above.

9.2   "Annual Period" shall mean each successive one (1) year calendar period of the Term (as defined below), beginning upon the Effective Date of this Agreement.

9.3.   "Commitment Album" shall have the meaning set forth in paragraph 4.1 above.

This language, always taken as a compliment by writers, actually sets up the basis for a personal services contracts, for which the publisher can get an injunction against the writer to prevent the writer from performing services for anyone else. It is also often found in composer agreements for TV and film productions.

9.4.   "Composition(s)" shall mean (a) all musical compositions presently owned or controlled, in whole or in part, directly or indirectly, by Writer (to the full extent of Writer's interest therein) a complete and exhaustive list of which Writer represents and warrants are set forth and identified in Schedule "A" attached hereto and incorporated herewith, and (b) all musical compositions written, created, owned or controlled, in whole or in part, directly or indirectly, by Writer during the Term hereof (to the full extent of Writer's interest therein) regardless of the method of acquisition of such ownership or control, including, without limitation, the musical compositions listed in Schedule "A" attached hereto.

9.5.   "Consent" shall mean (a) Writer's written approval which shall be sent to Publisher within ten (10) calendar days following Publisher's request, and if Writer does not respond within such time period, the request shall be deemed approved; and (b) which approval shall not be unreasonably withheld. This right is personal to Writer and may not be exercised on his behalf by any third party including his estate, heirs, legatees, administrators or personal representatives.

9.6.   "Contract Period" shall mean the Initial Period (as defined below) or any Option Period (as defined below) of the Term (as such periods may be suspended or extended as provided herein).

9.7.   "Cover Record" shall mean (a) a phonorecord and/or audio-visual work (as such terms are defined in the U.S. Copyright Act) recorded and initially released or distributed in the Territory embodying a Composition or portion thereof, other than recordings embodying featured performances of the Writer or any other author(s) and/or composer(s) who wrote the Composition concerned, and (b) a phonorecord of any Composition co-written by Writer with a writer introduced to Writer by Publisher.

9.8.   "Demos" shall mean the demonstration recordings produced by Writer during the Term in accordance with paragraph 2.3 above.

9.9.   "Grand Rights" shall have the meaning set forth in sub-paragraph 2.1(c) above.

9.10. "Gross Receipts" shall mean all monies directly and identifiably attributable by title to the use and exploitation of the Compositions in the Territory computed "at source" but subject to the sub-publishing fees set forth in paragraph 6.1(b) below, which monies are actually received, or credited against a prior advance, by Publisher in the United States (whether from publishing licensees affiliated with Publisher or otherwise). If at any time Publisher enters the business of manufacturing and/or distributing printed editions of musical compositions, Gross Receipts with respect to printed editions of the Compositions shall be deemed to be an amount equal to an industry standard royalty payable by a third party print licensee for the use concerned.

9.11. "Initial Period" shall have the meaning set forth in paragraph 3.1 above.

9.12. "Major Label" shall mean any record label owned or distributed by Sony Music, Warner Music Group or Universal Music Group, through the distribution system principally utilized by such record companies for their wholly owned labels.

9.13. "Minimum Delivery Commitment" shall have the meaning set forth in sub-paragraph 2.1(c) above.

9.14. "Net Income" shall mean Gross Receipts less: (a) Publisher's direct actual costs of administration including, without limitation, costs of transcribing lead sheets, advertising and promotion expenses, costs of producing and disseminating demonstration recordings, copyright registration fees, legal fees and costs protecting the Compositions or defending claims against such Compositions; and (b) reasonable attorney's fees and accountant's fees, if any, actually paid by Publisher for any agreements (other than this Agreement) affecting the Compositions.

9.15. "Net Recovery" shall have the meaning set forth in paragraph 7.4 above.

9.16. "Option Period" shall mean an option period exercised by Publisher to extend the Term, as further defined in paragraph 3.2 above.

9.17. "Pipeline Monies" shall mean Publisher's good faith estimate of the Writer's share of the Net Income generated by the exploitation of the Compositions in the United States through the last day of the month preceding the delivery of the Commitment Album for which an advance is payable hereunder, but for which Writer has not yet been accounted to on a royalty statement hereunder.

9.18. "Release" or "Released" shall mean the later of (a) general commercial release in the United States on a Major Label, (b) Publisher's issuance of a mechanical license for the use of a Composition embodied on a recording hereunder, or (c) clearance of all Samples

9.19. "Retention Period" shall have the meaning set forth in paragraph 3.4 above.

9.20. "Sample" shall mean any recording, composition (including, without limitation, a Composition), or portion(s) thereof, interpolated by a third party in a recording or composition (including, without limitation, a Composition), other than in which it was originally embodied.

9.21. "Score" shall have the meaning set forth in paragraph 2.4 above.

9.22. "Term" shall mean the period beginning upon the Effective Date and continuing as set forth in Article 3 above.

9.23. "Territory" shall mean the universe.

9.24. "Third Party" shall have the meaning set forth in paragraph 2.4 above.

10.   <u>MISCELLANEOUS</u>

    10.1. This Agreement is personal to Writer and may not be assigned or transferred in whole or in part by Writer to any third party except Writer may assign this Agreement to a "Loan-Out" company or corporation wholly owned or controlled by Writer, provided that the Loan-Out company executes a written agreement satisfactory to Publisher agreeing to furnish the services of Writer hereunder and to be bound by this Agreement and Writer executes a standard inducement letter satisfactory to Publisher. Notwithstanding the foregoing, Writer shall remain liable for its obligations set forth herein under such an assignment. Writer shall not sell, transfer, assign, or otherwise dispose of or encumber any of its interest under this Agreement, its earnings therefrom, or its interests in the Compositions without first offering the same in each instance to Publisher in writing at the same price and on the same terms as any such contemplated sale, transfer, assignment, or encumbrance. If Publisher accepts such offer within thirty (30) days after receipt of a copy of the proposed third party offer, then the transaction shall be concluded between Writer and Publisher. If Publisher does not accept such offer within such time, Writer shall be free to sell or assign the interest(s) offered to Publisher upon the same terms and conditions as offered to Publisher to third parties within two (2) months thereafter. Should such sale or assignment not be made within such time, the foregoing first-offer-to-Publisher procedure shall again be applicable to such sale or assignment as well as any new or different contemplated sale, transfer, assignment, or encumbrance of the offered interest; and

        (b)   Publisher may sell, assign or license the rights set forth under this Agreement in whole or in part only to any subsidiary, affiliated or controlling corporation, to any entity owning or acquiring a substantial portion of the stock or assets of Publisher or to any partnership or other venture in which Publisher participates, and such rights may be assigned by any assignee.

10.2.   Notices which either party desires or is required to give to the other hereunder shall be in writing, sent postage prepaid, certified or registered mail (return receipt requested), personal delivery, or by overnight air express (or courier shipment if outside the United States) if such service actually provides proof of mailing, facsimile (with transmission report indicating receipt and copy concurrently sent by first class mail) and the day of mailing (or transmission in the case of facsimiles) of any such notice shall be deemed the date of the giving thereof (except notices of change of address, the date of which shall be the date of receipt by the receiving party). Any such notices shall be addressed as follows:

TO WRITER: At the address set forth on the first page hereof.

TO PUBLISHER: At the address set forth on the first page hereof
Attention: Vice President Business Affairs

or to such other address(e) as to which the noticing party shall have theretofore received written notice.

10.3.   This Agreement constitutes the entire agreement of the parties hereto with respect to the subject matter hereof and supersedes all prior agreements and understandings, both written and oral, with respect to the subject matter hereof.

10.4.   This Agreement shall be governed by, and construed in accordance with, the laws of the State of California, applicable to contracts executed in and to be performed entirely within that State.

10.5.   This Agreement may not be amended or modified except by an instrument in writing signed by, or on behalf of, Publisher and Writer. Either party to this Agreement may (a) extend the time for the performance of any of the obligations or other acts of the other party or (b) waive compliance with any of the agreements or conditions of the other party contained herein. Any such extension or waiver shall be valid only if set forth in an instrument in writing signed by the party to be bound thereby. Any waiver of any term or condition shall not be construed as a waiver of any subsequent breach or a subsequent waiver of the same term of condition, or a waiver of any other term or condition, of this Agreement. The failure of any party to assert any of its rights hereunder shall not constitute a waiver of any such rights.

10.6.   The parties hereto agree that all actions or proceedings initiated by either party hereto and arising directly or indirectly out of this Agreement which are brought pursuant to judicial proceedings shall be litigated in a Federal or state court located in the State of California, County of Los Angeles. The parties hereto expressly submit and consent in advance to such jurisdiction and agree that service of summons and complaint or other process or papers may be made by registered or certified mail addressed to the relevant party at the address to which notices are to be sent hereunder. The parties hereto waive any claim that a Federal or state court located in the State of California, County of Los Angeles, is an inconvenient forum or an improper forum based on lack of venue.

10.7.   If any provision of this Agreement as applied to any party or any circumstance shall be adjudged by a Court to be unlawful, void, or for any reason unenforceable, such provision shall be deemed separable from the remainder of this Agreement and the same shall in no way affect the validity or enforceability of any other provision of this Agreement, the applicability of such provision to other parties or circumstances, or the validity or enforceability of this Agreement as a whole.

10.8.   Each party shall execute and deliver to the other and to third parties such other and further instruments and correspondence as shall be reasonably required to effectuate the intents and purposes hereof.

10.9.   In the event of litigation between Writer and Publisher hereon the prevailing party shall be entitled to recover from the other reasonable attorney's fees in addition to any and all other reasonable costs and awards.

10.10.   Publisher shall not be in default of any term, condition, or provision of this Agreement unless and until Writer shall give written notice specifying such default in detail and such default, if curable, shall not have been cured within thirty (30) days after receipt of such notice.

10.11. If because of: act of God, unavoidable accident, fire, lockout, strike or other labor dispute, riot or civil commotion, act of public enemy; enactment, rule, order or act of any government or governmental instrumentality (whether federal, state, local or foreign); failure of computer facilities, loss of books or records; or other causes of a similar or different nature not reasonably within Publisher's control, Publisher is materially hampered in the exploitation or administration of musical compositions and/or its normal business operations become commercially impracticable, then, without limiting Publisher's rights, Publisher shall have the option by giving Writer notice to suspend the then current Contract Period for the duration of any such contingency and Publisher shall be excused of its obligations hereunder during such suspension, including its obligation to account and pay royalties. No such suspension shall exceed twelve (12) months.

> A "force majeure" clause, allowing for suspension of the term in the event of some natural disaster, war or riot, or other disturbances that impair the writer and publisher's ability to do business.

10.12. Writer hereby grants Publisher the benefits of all warranties and representations now possessed and hereafter obtained under all agreements affecting the Compositions.

10.13. Nothing contained herein shall be construed or interpreted as constituting a partnership, joint venture, agency, or employer/employee relationship between the parties. No third party is intended to be a third party beneficiary hereof.

10.14. Writer does hereby irrevocably constitute, authorize, empower, and appoint Publisher (acting through any of its officers) Writer's true and lawful attorney-in-fact (with full power of substitution and delegation), in Writer's name, and in Writer's place and stead, or in Publisher's name, to take and do such action, and to make, sign, execute, acknowledge, and deliver any and all instruments or documents, which Publisher from time to time may deem necessary to vest in Publisher, or its designees, successors, assigns, and licensees, all of the rights or interests granted by Writer hereunder. Writer acknowledges that Publisher's agency and power granted in this paragraph 10.14 are coupled with an interest.

10.15. Any rule of construction disfavoring the drafting party shall not apply in the construction of any provision of this Agreement. All of the parties hereto acknowledge and agree that each party has been, or has had the opportunity to be, represented by legal counsel of their own choice throughout all negotiations which preceded the execution of this Agreement, and that the parties have executed this Agreement after consulting with their own legal counsel.

10.16. Any and all of the riders, exhibits or schedules annexed hereto, together with this document, shall collectively constitute this Agreement.

10.17. This Agreement shall not be binding upon Publisher until signed by Writer and countersigned by a duly authorized officer of Publisher.

AGREED AND ACCEPTED:
XYZ MUSIC PUBLISHING

By: _____
   President & CEO

AGREED AND ACCEPTED:

_____
(Writer)

Social Security No. _____

Date of Birth: _____

Date of Signature: _____

All the writer information is necessary so that notices and royalties may be sent to the writer at their correct address. The writer's Social Security number is needed by the publisher for tax reporting purposes.

ASSIGNMENT OF COPYRIGHTS

The undersigned ("Assignor"), for good and valuable consideration, receipt of which is hereby acknowledged, hereby sells, conveys and assigns to XYZ Music Publishing, its successors and assigns, an undivided one hundred percent (100%) interest in the entire right, title and interest throughout the universe which is derived from Assignor, in and to the musical composition(s) listed on the attached Schedule, including, without limitation, the copyrights and any other rights relating to such musical compositions, now known or which may hereafter be recognized or come into existence, and any and all renewals and extensions of such copyrights and other rights under applicable laws, treaties, regulations and directives now or hereafter enacted or in effect, together with the exclusive right in perpetuity to administer and license such assigned interest throughout the universe.

IN WITNESS WHEREOF, Assignor has executed this instrument on this _____ day of _____, 20__

_____

ACKNOWLEDGMENT

STATE OF California   )
_____)
COUNTY OF Los Angeles)

On _____, 20__, before me personally came, known to me to be the individual described in and who executed the foregoing instrument, and acknowledged to me that they executed it.

_____

Notary Public

An assignment of the copyrights, which must be in writing.

SCHEDULE "A"

EXISTING COMPOSITIONS

Name of Songwriter(s) and Share(s) (Include Writers, if any, and Their Shares)	Name of Publisher(s) and Share(s) (Include Third Party Co-Writers, if any, and Their Shares)	Title	Copyright Regis. No.	Date

LETTER OF DIRECTION

Letters of direction are needed to advise another party that the publisher has the right to collect income on behalf of the co-publisher. Separate letters should be sent to the PRO, Harry Fox, sub-publishers, and any other party who might be making payments to the writer's publishing company, such as record companies or TV/film producers.

As of: _____

American Society of Composers, Authors and Publishers
1 Lincoln Plaza
New York, New York 10023

Dear Sir/Madam:

Please be advised that I, the undersigned, have entered into an agreement with XYZ Music Publishing ("Publisher") dated as of _____, pursuant to which Publisher has the sole and exclusive right as of the date of my agreement with Publisher to collect and receive the publisher's share of all royalties and other sums which are or may become payable to me pursuant to my agreement with you.

I hereby authorize and direct you to pay the publisher's share of all royalties and other sums which are or may become payable to me on and after the date of this letter directly to XYZ Music Publishing, _____ _____.

This letter of direction may not be revoked, modified or terminated except by a written instrument signed by Publisher and me.

Very truly yours,

_____
(Writer)

As of: _____

Publisher Relations Department
 Broadcast Music, Inc.
7 World Trade Center
250 Greenwich Street
New York, NY 10007-00309

Dear Sir/Madam:

Please be advised that I, the undersigned, have entered into an agreement with XYZ Music Publishing ("Publisher") dated as of _____, pursuant to which Publisher has the sole and exclusive right as of the date of my agreement with Publisher to collect and receive the publisher's share of all royalties and other sums which are or may become payable to me pursuant to my agreement with you.

I hereby authorize and direct you to pay the publisher's share of all royalties and other sums which are or may become payable to me on and after the date of this letter directly to XYZ Music Publishing, _____.

This letter of direction may not be revoked, modified or terminated except by a written instrument signed by Publisher and me.

    Very truly yours,

    _____
    (Writer)

As of: _____

SESAC
152 West 57th St
57th Floor
New York, NY 10019

Dear Sir/Madam:

Please be advised that I, the undersigned, have entered into an agreement with XYZ Music Publishing ("Publisher") dated as of _____, pursuant to which Publisher has the sole and exclusive right as of the date of my agreement with Publisher to collect and receive the publisher's share of all royalties and other sums which are or may become payable to me pursuant to my agreement with you.

I hereby authorize and direct you to pay the publisher's share of all royalties and other sums which are or may become payable to me on and after the date of this letter directly to XYZ Music Publishing, _____.

This letter of direction may not be revoked, modified or terminated except by a written instrument signed by Publisher and me.

Very truly yours,

_____
(Writer)

As of: _____

The Harry Fox Agency, Inc
601 West 26th Street Suite 500
New York, NY 10001

Dear Sir/Madam:

Please be advised that I, the undersigned, have entered into an agreement with XYZ Music Publishing ("Publisher") dated as of _____, pursuant to which Publisher has the sole and exclusive right to administer all copyrights owned or controlled by me and act as the publisher thereof, including, without limitation, the copyrights that are subject to the agreement between Publisher and me. Publisher also has the sole and exclusive right as of the date of my agreement with Publisher to collect and receive all royalties and other sums which are or may become payable to me pursuant to the aforesaid agreement, to license and cause others to license any such copyrights, and to publish and sell sheet music and/or folios of such copyrights.

I hereby authorize and direct you to pay all royalties and other sums which are or may become payable to me on and after the date of this letter directly to XYZ Music Publishing, _____.

This letter of direction may not be revoked, modified or terminated except by a written instrument signed by Publisher and me.

Very truly yours,

_____
(Writer)

As of: _____

Canadian Musical Reproduction Rights Agency Limited (CMRRA)
56 Wellesley St. West
Suite 320
Toronto, Ontario M5S 2S3
Canada

Dear Sir/Madam:

Please be advised that I, the undersigned, have entered into an agreement with XYZ Music Publishing ("Publisher") dated as of _____, pursuant to which Publisher has the sole and exclusive right to administer all copyrights owned or controlled by me, including, without limitation, the copyrights that are subject to the agreement between Publisher and me. Publisher also has the sole and exclusive right as of the date of my agreement with Publisher to collect and receive all royalties and other sums which are or may become payable to me pursuant to the aforesaid agreement.

I hereby authorize and direct you to pay all royalties and other sums which are or may become payable to me on and after the date of this letter directly to XYZ Music Publishing, _____.

This letter of direction may not be revoked, modified or terminated except by a written instrument signed by Publisher and me.

Very truly yours,

_____
(Writer)

As of: _____

Society of Composers, Authors and Music Publishers of Canada (SOCAN)
41 Valleybrook Drive
Don Mills, Ontario M3B 2S6
Canada

Dear Sir/Madam:

Please be advised that I, the undersigned have entered into an agreement with XYZ Music Publishing, ("Publisher") dated as of _____, pursuant to which Publisher has the sole and exclusive right as of the date of my agreement with Publisher to collect and receive the publisher's share of all royalties and other sums which are or may become payable to me pursuant to my agreement with you.

I hereby authorize and direct you to pay publisher's share of all royalties and other sums which are or may become payable to me on and after the date of this letter directly to XYZ Music Publishing, _____.

This letter of direction may not be revoked, modified or terminated except by a written instrument signed by Publisher and me.

Very truly yours,

_____
(Writer)

Dated: as of _____

To: Whom It May Concern

Re: Notice of Appointment of Co-publisher and Administrator

Dear Sir/Madam:

1. Please be advised that, effective immediately, XYZ Music Publishing ("Publisher") is appointed my irrevocable exclusive administrator with respect to all musical compositions that I own or control or that I hereafter acquire (the "Compositions"), throughout the universe, including, without limitation, the compositions listed on the Schedule annexed hereto.

2. Effective immediately, I authorize and irrevocably direct you to pay to Publisher all royalties payable and become payable by you to me, regardless of when earned.

3. All statements, checks and correspondence relevant to the foregoing Compositions are to be directed to:

    XYZ Music Publishing

    _____

    _____

    _____

4. Please mark your records accordingly, and I would appreciate your acknowledging receipt of this notification by signing the enclosed copy and returning it to the Publisher address above.

    Very truly yours,

    _____
    (Writer)

Acknowledged By Recipient:

_____

SONGWRITER/CO-PUBLISHING AGREEMENT

This is an agreement in which the writer and publisher co-own the copyrights in the songs delivered. While many of the terms are similar to the songwriter agreement above, the delivery requirements in this agreement are far more reasonable (and realistic) than in the agreement above and should be used as a model of an agreement fair to both sides.

[PUBLISHER'S NAME]
[PUBLISHER'S ADDRESS]

[DATE]

[WRITER'S NAME]
[WRITER'S ADDRESS]

Dear [WRITER]:

The following, when signed by [Writer] ("you") and [Publisher] ("us"), will constitute the terms and conditions of the exclusive co-publishing (i.e. participation) agreement between you and us.

1.   Term:

    1. 1.   The term of this Agreement shall commence as of the above date and shall consist of an initial period of one (1) "Contract Year" (as defined below) and three (3) options to renew such Term for a period of one Contract Year in each instance (such options being consecutive and successive).

        1.1.1.   A "Contract Year" shall continue for twelve months or, if later, until 30 days following completion of your "Delivery Commitment" (as defined below) for such Contract Year.

        1.1.2.   Your "Delivery Commitment" for each Contract Year shall consist of the delivery to us at our offices in accordance with paragraph 7.1 below of a minimum of eight (8) 100% newly-written compositions

---

Term of one year, plus three one year renewal options.

This gives separate administration rights to each party for their respective shares.

A "contract year" is the later of one calendar year or 30 days following delivery of all songs required.

Note that the requirement is eight times 100% of the compositions, so if the writer co-writes with another, only that portion attributed to the writer is credited towards the delivery requirement.

(or the equivalent in compositions only partly written by you) of which a minimum of one and one half (1.5) compositions (or the equivalent in compositions only partly written by you) which have been recorded and released in the U.S. by a "Major U.S. Record Company" (herein defined as "Sony/BMG, Warner Music Group/WMG or Universal"), or a company then regularly distributed by one of them together with notice to us of the completion of delivery of the requisite number of compositions and released compositions (with titles, names of co-writers and percentages subject to this Agreement, as well as the name(s) of any co-writer(s) and/or co-publisher(s) and the respective share(s) of each such third party and in respect to the released compositions, two commercial copies of the recordings together with written notice of the release date in the U.S.).

A secondary requirement is that a certain number of songs be recorded and released in the U.S. (or at least distributed) by one of the major record companies. With digital distribution available to almost everyone, a physical release is still required under many agreements.

1.2.   The options are exercisable in each instance by notice (all notices referred to herein shall be given in the manner prescribed by paragraph 9 below) within thirty (30) days following the completion of delivery of your Delivery Commitment for the then-current Contract Year, provided, that we shall in no event be required to exercise an option prior to the end of the eleventh month of the then-current Contract Year.

The option may be exercised within 30 days of the completion of the delivery requirement but not before the 11th month of the term.

2.   Territory: The Universe

As James Bond would say, "The World Is Not Enough."

3.   Scope of Agreement:

3 .1.   Subject Compositions:

3.1.1.   (A)   Subject to those requirements and/or restrictions set forth in paragraph 3.3., below, we will own an undivided 50% share of;

"An undivided 50% share" means that the publisher owns 50% and the writer maintains 50% ownership, i.e., co-publishing, with the writer also retaining his share of writer royalties, as shown below.

i)   your interest in all songs written or co-written by you prior to the Term which are not subject to prior publishing contracts, including but not limited to all songs included on the attached Schedule ("Existing Compositions"), plus

This agreement also covers the writer's share of existing songs that are not already published by another party.

ii)   your interest in any songs written or co-written by you prior to the Term which are presently subject to prior publishing contracts, but which will become available during the Term, plus

This addresses songs currently controlled by another publisher that may become available during the term, such as if a previous deal terminates and the rights to the songs revert to the writer.

iii)   your interest in all songs written or co-written by you during the Term.

Songs written during the term.

Subject to the provisions of paragraph 3.1.2., below, in the case of co-written compositions (collectively referred to below as "Subject Compositions" or "SCs"). We will have exclusive worldwide life-of-copyright administration of the SCs.

Life of copyright administration does not equal ownership for the same period. Keep in mind that, at least for U.S. rights, writers may terminate a transfer to a publisher (such as this) between 35 and 40 years after the transfer. A reading of this paragraph indicates that the publisher would still have administration rights in the U.S., even if they only own the copyrights outside the U.S.

(B)   A composition first recorded and/or released during the Term or within three months following the expiration of the Term shall be deemed to have been written and composed during the term.

This addresses the issue of a writer not delivering all songs written during the term and having a "new" song released right after the agreement ends.

3.1.2. In the case of co-written compositions, such co-ownership and administration shall only extend to your fractional interest, calculated (at a minimum) by multiplying 100% by a fraction, the numerator of which is 1 and the denominator of which is the total number of contributing writers.

This presumes that all co-writers have an equal share of the song, which is not necessarily the case. See section on split sheets, above.

3.2.   Administrative Requirements and Restrictions:

3.2.1. It is intended that we and our foreign subsidiaries, affiliates and licensees have the fullest possible rights to administer and exploit SCs, to utilize your name and likeness in connection therewith and to execute PA forms, and other routine copyright documents, in your name and on your behalf as your attorney-in-fact (which appointment is coupled with an interest and is therefore irrevocable).

This paragraph covers a lot of points. (1) It clarifies that the publisher (and their sub-publishers) have total administrative rights in the songs, (2) that they have the rights to use the writer's name and likeness in connection with the songs (I usually try to get approval over likeness and any biographical material), and (3) grants a limited power of attorney to execute any documents that involve the songs.

3.2.2. It is understood that we will have the right to issue mechanical licenses to our affiliated record companies at 3/4 rate, with a 10-song cap (1/2 rate on budget lines, television, advertised and premium goods sales).

This is like a controlled compositions clause (see Chapter 3: Mechanical Licensing for Audio-Only Product) between the publisher and their affiliated record company. Although the publisher is already getting 25% of the income (i.e., half of the publisher's 50% share), they now want to give an additional 25% discount to their sister record company, along with a 10 song cap on total royalties. This could significantly cut into the writer's share of income, both as writer and co-publisher.

3.3.   Reassignment Provisions

This section describes the process whereby the writer may regain ownership of an unexploited composition.

3.3.1. Unexploited Material

(A)   Notwithstanding anything to the contrary contained in this Agreement, you shall be entitled to a reassignment of any SC as to which a recording or other exploitation has not been secured as of the later of (1) Three (3) years following the end of the Term or (2) the end of the accounting period during which all advances hereunder are finally recouped, provided that you, in your sole discretion, shall have the right, at any time on or after the third anniversary of the end of the Term, to repay us one-hundred and twenty five percent (125%) of the then-unrecouped balance and to receive such reassignment in accordance with paragraph 3.3.2, below.

If a song has not been exploited by the later of three years after the term or when the advances have been recouped, the writer may have the copyright reassigned. In the alternative, they can "buy" back the unexploited songs by paying 125% of the unrecouped balance.

(B)   For the purposes of this subparagraph, a recording or other exploitation shall be deemed to have been "secured" if a recording of the SC shall have been distributed in the United States by a Major U.S. Record Company ("Major U.S. Record Company") or an established independent record company or an independent record company released through a major record company, or by any established active record company outside of the U.S. or such SC shall have been included (A) in a film release theatrically or on a video cassette or other video format, (B) as a use in a television production exhibited on a free, pay or basic cable television network, or (C) in any commercial, and released or exhibited (as applicable) commercially in the U.S., during the applicable period or scheduled during the applicable period for release or exhibition (as appropriate) within three months thereafter.

This paragraph defines "secured" as released or distributed by a major U.S. label, included in a film or video production, used in a television production broadcast on a network, or contained in a commercial. On the television use, note that this requirement is for broadcast on a free, pay, or basic cable network. This prevents a minor use on local television from triggering a "secured" use.

3.3.2. Reassignment Procedure

(A)   In the event you become entitled to reassignment of the SCs pursuant to the preceding provisions of this paragraph 3.3., above, we shall execute and deliver an assignment of copyright to you (which shall include all licenses the terms of which continue in effect subsequent to such reassignment) within 15 days following our receipt of notice requesting such reassignment.

The publisher will execute a written assignment of their share of the copyright.

(B)   In the event that we fail to execute and deliver such assignment within such fifteen-day period, you shall have the right to do so in our name and on our behalf as our attorney-in-fact, which appointment is coupled with an interest and is therefore irrevocable.

If they fail to deliver the assignment, the writer has the right to do so in their name.

4.   Collection and Division of Income

4.1.   We will be entitled to collect (and shall employ best efforts consistent with our reasonable business judgment to collect) all writer/publisher income (except the writer's share of public performances collected by societies and any other amount paid normally directly to songwriters by disbursing agent) generated by each SC (including pre-Term earnings on Existing Compositions not subject to collection by third parties under presently-existing agreements listed on Schedule A).

The publisher shall collect all sources of income except the writer's share of public performance income, including money earned prior to the term if not previously collected.

4.2.   Royalties/Net Income Share:

4.2.1.   We shall pay you songwriter royalties with respect to monies received by us from our exploitation of SCs in accordance with the annexed Schedule A, all such royalties (except for royalties with respect to printed editions) to be based upon "Gross Receipts" (as defined below).

4.2.2.   (A)   In addition to your songwriter royalties, we shall pay you 50% of the "Net Income" (as defined below) from SCs.

(B)   As used herein, "Net Income" shall mean all amounts received by us, or credited to our account in reduction of an advance, from licensees and performing and mechanical rights societies ("Gross Receipts") after deduction of writer royalties as per annexed Schedule A and (1) actual and reasonable out-of-pocket collection costs (including subpublisher fees or income shares) (2) out-of-pocket copyright registration costs; (3) costs of demo recordings and of lead sheets; and (4) an administration fee of ten percent (10%) of Gross Receipts from SCs to be retained by us solely for our account.

4.2.3.   As used herein, "Gross Receipts" shall include the following:

(A)   Amounts received by us in the United States (Or credited to our account in reduction of an advance previously received by us in the United States) in respect of the use of exploitation of SCs, it being understood and agreed that our share of amounts collected by our foreign music publishing subpublishers, which shall be calculated on a receipts basis (i.e., with the U.S. share of foreign income being monies received by us, or credited to our account against advances from our subpublishers and licensees). We hereby agree that all sub-publishing agreements will be no less favorable than 75%/25% of mechanical royalties on original recordings and 50%/50% on local territory cover recordings, synchronization license and commercials.

Royalties paid as a songwriter are described in Schedule "A."

This section describes the royalties paid as a co-publisher as basically 50% of net income less certain expenses and the writer royalties. This also deducts a 10% administration fee of gross revenue that is added to the publisher's share of this income. This clause is contained in some, but not all, agreements, on the theory that the publisher is doing all the work and is entitled to be compensated for that work in addition to their 25% share of all net income.

This definition of gross receipts is basically all money received by the publisher in the U.S., including actual payments forwarded by their foreign sub-publishers after the sub-publisher takes their commissions. Although it does not state what the sub-publisher commissions are in general, it does put a ceiling on split for mechanical income for cover recordings and synchronization income.

5.   Advances: We shall make the following nonrefundable payments, which shall be recoupable from your songwriter royalties and from your Net Income share of royalties hereunder:

During The First Contract Year:

5.1. $_____ ("initial advance") on execution. This initial advance shall be payable upon release of the first album produced by you containing SCs hereunder, released during the initial period by a Major Record Company, payable as follows:

5.2   In the event that we exercise a renewal option, an amount (Payable in twelve (12) equal monthly installments) equal to 66-2/3% of your combined writer/publisher royalties and Net Income share hereunder (as reported on your royalty statements for the first four quarters of the immediately preceding contract year), but not less than nor more than the following:

Contract Year	Minimum	Maximum
Year 2 (option)	-	
Year 3 (option)	-	
Year 4 (option)	-	

Advances are recoupable but non-refundable and taken from both the writer and publisher's share of net income.

Based on the requirement that an album be released to receive the advance, this agreement appears to be with a writer/artist, rather than a non-artist writer. This makes the "released on a major label" portion of the delivery requirement above much easier to fulfill.

If an option is renewed, this paragraph sets out the structure of the succeeding year's advances, with a minimum and maximum payment based on the previous year's income. One pitfall in this is that, due to the length of time it takes for money to pass through the pipeline to the publisher, and even longer to the writer and his publisher, it is very difficult to earn enough in the first year to exceed the minimum advance threshold. For example, royalties earned in the first six months of a record release would not be paid by the record company to the publisher until the second six months. The publisher would then pay the writer and co-publisher in the third six-month period, after the exercise of the option has already taken place. Assuming the writer has some success, the pipeline then should flow on a regular basis and the "minimum/maximum" system will be more equitable.

5.3   Upon our receipt of notice (which notice shall include the title of the SC, co-writers, if any, the percentages subject to this Agreement, and a commercial copy of the single in its CD Format) in each instance during the Term that an SC has been recorded and is embodied in a "A Side" single recording embodying a pop performance that initially attains a position on the Billboard Magazines "Hot Singles" chart, (prorated where your interest in the SC is less than 100%), we shall pay you additional advances as follows:

Chart Position	Advance
Top 25	$
Top 10	$
Top 5	$

The foregoing advances will be paid only once, after our receipt of notice that the SC first reaches the particular chart positions (i.e., not if the SC reaches a chart position, falls off and re-enters the chart).

6.   Accounting and Payment:

6.1.   We will account to you (and make payment where appropriate) within 90 days following the end of each semi-annual calendar period. However, if the amount due for a specific statement is less than $, payment and statements may be deferred until the aggregate amount due to you exceeds $. The exchange rates used by third parties in accounting to us shall be used by us in accountings hereunder.

6.2.   We will only be required to account and pay with respect to amounts actually received by us in the U.S. (or credited to our account in reduction of a previous advance received by us in the U.S.)

Additional advances are paid upon songs achieving success on the Billboard charts, even though the initial advance has not been recouped. This allows the writer to benefit from the initial success without waiting for total recoupment and pipeline earnings to flow through and, based on the potential earnings from a hit song, the publisher feels secure that the advances will be recouped.

These advances are only paid once for each song, based on the highest chart position.

Accountings are semi-annual, with a minimum amount of earnings necessary for actual payment to be made. Of course, if the writer has not recouped their advances, statements will still be issued but no additional payments will be made until recoupment.

Again, only payments actually received (or credited) in the U.S. will be included on the statements.

6.3.   Audit and Suit:

6.3.1.   You (or a certified public accountant on your behalf) shall have the right to audit our books and records as to each statement for a period of Two (2) years after such statement is received (or deemed received as provided below). Legal action with respect to a specific accounting statement or the accounting period to which such statement relates shall be barred if not commenced in a court of competent jurisdiction within Two (2) years after such statement is received (or deemed received as provided below), except for Fraud.

> Writer has the right to audit the publisher within two years after a statement is received and bring suit if necessary by the end of that same two years. Sometimes, a writer is given an additional period of time after the right to audit to bring suit.

6.3.2.   For the purposes of calculating such time periods, you shall be deemed to have received a statement when due unless we receive notice of non-receipt from you (in the manner prescribed in paragraph 9, below) within 60 days thereafter. However, your failure to give such notice shall not affect your right to receive such statement (and, if applicable, your royalty and/or net income payment) after such sixty-day period.

> For the purpose of the time period in which to bring an audit, this does not require actual receipt of a statement but a presumption that it was received unless the writer notifies the publisher.

6.4.   In "blocked currency" situations, we shall not be required to pay you until the blockage shall have been removed, but if requested to do so, we shall deposit blocked currency royalties in the local currency in a depository of your choice.

> In the event that foreign royalties are blocked from being received in the U.S., the publisher will deposit the money in a foreign account of the writer's choosing.

6.5.   All payments hereunder shall be subject to all applicable taxation statutes, regulations and treaties.

7.   Warranties and Representations:

7.1.   By your signature below, and in each instance in which SCs are delivered to us ("delivery" to include a CD or digital audio file (i.e., MP3, AIFF, etc.), and lyric sheet, delivered to the attention of _____ at our offices, together with complete writer and publisher splits and society affiliations and satisfactory written clearance of any and all so-called "samples" embodied in any SC) you warrant and represent (1) that you have the right to do so,

> This requires the writer to clear any samples used in the song, a requirement that most writers are unable to fulfill due to their lack of knowledge about the sample-clearance process.

(2) that such SC does not infringe any third party's rights or violate any applicable criminal statute, including but not limited to such third party's copyright, trademark, service mark, or right of privacy or publicity,

> This is not only a warranty of originality but a declaration by the writer that the song does not infringe any copyright, trademark, or service mark of a third party.

(3) that the SC is not defamatory and

> This is very subjective and difficult to enforce.

(4) that you and your music publishing designee are and will remain affiliated with ASCAP, BMI or another recognized performing rights society (and in the event of your failure to so affiliate and for the purpose of preventing loss of income due to such failure, we shall be entitled to claim 100% of the publisher's share with the performing rights society and account to you for income derived therefrom per paragraph 4.2.1 until such time as you formally affiliate and notify us of such affiliation).

Membership shall be maintained with one of the performing rights organizations, or the publisher has the right to collect all of the publisher's share of performance income instead of the co-publisher collecting directly.

7.2.   Additional Warranties and Representations

7.2.1. You warrant and represent that you have full right, power and authority to enter into and perform this Agreement in accordance with its terms, and that you will adhere to all of the terms and conditions set forth herein.

7.2.2. Except as set forth in the annexed Schedule B, neither you nor your music publishing designee, nor anyone acting on your and/or your music publishing designee's behalf or deriving rights from or through you or your music publishing designee:

(A)   has received or will receive an advance, loan or other payment from a performing rights society, record company or other third party which is or may be recoupable from (or otherwise subject to offset against) monies which would otherwise be collectible by us hereunder,

Any outstanding loans or advances will inhibit the publisher from collecting royalties to satisfy the advances paid under this agreement.

(B)   is presently subject to any so-called "controlled compositions" clause under a recording agreement or

Note the word "presently." This would indicate that the writer has not yet signed a recording agreement. But see paragraph D below.

(C)   is presently subject to any provision of a recording agreement which would allow a record company to charge any amount against mechanical royalties,

This prevents cross-collateralization of recording artist advances against any music publishing royalties.

(D)   Notwithstanding the foregoing, we shall comply with the licensing requirements of the "controlled compositions" clause of any recording agreement into which you (or an entity furnishing your services) may enter subsequent to the date of this Agreement, and your and/or such entity's acceptable of such clause shall not constitute a breach of this Agreement, provided:

*Here, the publisher accepts the terms of any controlled composition clause entered into **after** the date of this agreement.*

(a)   the applicable mechanical rate in the United States is not less than 3/4ths of the statutory compulsory mechanical license rate in effect on the date of initial U.S. release of the first record embodying a specific SC, and the rate in Canada is the full rate in effect on the comparable Canadian release date;

> This sets out the terms of the controlled composition clause that the publisher is willing to accept. This may or may not conform to the language in the artist agreement with their record company. See Chapter 3: Mechanical Licensing for Audio-Only Product for more info.

(b)   the per-record maximums are not less than 10 times such rate in the case of full-length records (LPS, cassettes, CDs) (with payment on 50% of LP-length "free goods"), 3 times such rate in the case of 12" singles, and 2 times such rate in the in the case of 7" singles or cassette singles; and

(c)   no advances or other charts under the recording agreement are recoupable from, or capable of being offset against, mechanical royalties in respect of SCs.

8.   Indemnities; Cure of Breaches; Waiver:

8.1.   You shall defend and indemnify and otherwise hold us and our successors, licensees and assignees free and harmless from and against any and all liabilities, claims, demands, damages, costs, penalties, and expenses (including, without limitation, reasonable attorneys' fees and court costs) arising out of or resulting from any breach or claim of breach of this Agreement or any representation or warranty hereunder. Such indemnity shall extend to the "deductible" under any errors-and-omissions policy we may have.

> This holds the writer liable for a breach or **claim of breach**. Some agreements would limit indemnification only to an actual breach, or a writer-approved settlement, or a final adjudicated court judgment.

You shall notify us of any such claim, demand or action after you have been formally advised thereof, and you shall have the right, at your sole expense, to participate in the defense thereof with counsel of your choice, provided that we shall have the right at all times, in our sole discretion, to retain control, or resume control, of the conduct of said defense. You shall reimburse us, on demand, for any payment made by us at any time with respect to such damage, liability, cost, loss or expense to which the foregoing applies.

> The writer must notify the publisher of any claims and has the right to participate in the defense of said claims, but the publisher controls the defense of the claim.

8.2. If a claim, demand, action or proceeding is made against us, we may withhold an amount reasonably related to the amount of the claim (together with reasonable anticipated court costs and outside counsel fees) from monies due or to become due to you. If (and to the extent that) suit is not brought with respect to that sum within 1 year thereafter, then you may post a bond with a firm acceptable to us and in an amount consistent with the claim and anticipated cost of the defense thereof and we shall release the sums being withheld pursuant to the preceding sentence.

> The publisher may withhold any royalties that might be due to the writer pending resolution of this dispute. In addition, if the royalties withheld are insufficient to pay the damages or costs of defending the claim, additional money can be withheld from future payments. The theory is that if the publisher has to pay damages to a third party, previously paying the writer their share of disputed income may result in the publisher having to try to collect from the writer and not being able to do so. The publisher may only hold these amounts for one year unless litigation is filed. If not, then the money is disbursed to the writer.

8.3. We will not be deemed in breech unless you give notice and we fail to cure within 30 days after receiving notice; provided, that if the alleged breach does not involve a payment of money and is of such a nature that it cannot be completely cured within 30 days, we will not be deemed to be in breach if we commence the curing of the alleged breach within such thirty-day period and proceed to complete the curing thereof with due diligence within a reasonable time thereafter.

> In the event of a breach by the publisher, the writer must give notice and the publisher has 30 days to cure the breach, or if the breach cannot be cured in 30 days, the publisher must at least commence an attempt to cure with 30 days.

8.3.1. Your rights and remedies in the event of any breach by us of this Agreement shall be limited to your right to recover damages, if any, in an action at law, and you hereby waive any right or remedy in equity, including any right to terminate this agreement or to rescind our right, title and interest in and to the SCs or any other right granted to us, or to enjoin or restrain any exercise of the rights acquired by us hereunder.

> The writer may only sue for monetary damages, not injunctive relief or termination of the agreement.

8.3.2. Our remedies provided herein shall be cumulative and the exercise of one shall not preclude the exercise of any remedy for the same or any other disability or default, nor shall the specification of our remedies herein exclude any rights or remedies at law, or in equity, including any of our rights to damages or to seek injunctive relief. You and we agree that your services pursuant to this Agreement are of a special, unique, unusual, extraordinary and intellectual character giving them peculiar value, the loss of which cannot be reasonably or adequately compensated in damages in an action at law. You and we expressly agree that we shall be entitled to seek the remedies of injunction and other equitable relief to prevent a breach of this Agreement by you, which relief shall be in addition to any other remedies which may be available to us.

> As a personal services contract, the publisher may sue for injunctive relief. The language sounds like it is flattering to the writer but, in reality, it sets up the premise of the writer's unique talent, the loss of which cannot be compensated for through monetary damages alone. The injunctive relief sought could include a prohibition against the writer signing with another company without fulfilling their obligations to the publisher.

8.4.   Our waiver of the applicability of any provision of this Agreement or of any default hereunder in a specific instance shall not affect our rights thereafter to enforce such provision or to exercise any right or remedy in the event of any other default, whether or not similar.

> Even if the publisher breaches one section of the agreement, all other sections remain in full force and effect.

9.   Notices/Statements/Consents:

9.1.   Notices shall be sent by certified (return receipt requested) or registered mail or telex to you (with a courtesy copy to:) and us (to the attention of with a courtesy copy to ___ at our address) at the above addresses or any other addresses the parties designate by notice in like manner. Statements (and payments, [if applicable] shall be sent by ordinary mail).

If the party's consent is required, it shall not be unreasonably withheld (unless expressly provided otherwise herein) and shall be deemed given unless the notified party gives notice of non-consent within five (5) days after receipt of notice requesting consent.

> If consent is not denied within five days, it is deemed granted.

10. Law and Forum

10.1. This Agreement has been entered into in, and is to be interpreted in accordance with the laws of, the State of California. All actions or proceedings seeking the interpretation and/or enforcement of this Agreement shall be brought only in the State or Federal Courts located in Los Angeles County, all parties hereby submitting themselves to the jurisdiction of such courts for such purpose.

10.2. Service of Process

10.2.1. Service of process in any action between the parties may be made by registered or certified mail addressed to the parties' then-current addresses for notice as prescribed in paragraph 9, above.

10.2.2. Service shall become effective 30 days following the date of receipt by the party served (unless delivery is refused, in which event service shall become effective 30 days following the date of such refusal).

Very truly yours,

[Publisher]

AGREED AND ACCEPTED:

_____

[Writer]

Social Security #: _____

Although a very simple agreement, once signed this is a binding contract on all parties.

Schedule A

WRITER ROYALTIES

(1)   U.S. and Canada

Print: (all on net paid sales):

Piano/vocal sheet: __ cents

Folios (other than "fake books" or "educational editions"): 50% of our Gross Receipts from print licensees (prorated in the case of "mixed" folios to reflect number of royalty-bearing compositions);

"Fake books" and "educational editions" 50% of our Gross Receipts from print licensees (subject to same pro-ration);

During the Term, no other writer of similar stature to Writer will be granted a royalty rate on printed editions at the rate(s) higher than those prescribed above. In the event that during the Term we grant to any other writer of similar stature to Writer royalties and/or other forms of compensation whose combined value with respect to a specific category of printed materials is in excess of that granted hereunder, we shall pay such higher royalties and/or other compensation on all copies of material in the same category sold subsequent to the effective date of such higher third-party royalty or other compensation, except with respect to (1) pedagogical editions and/or "methods"; (2) "special arrangements," that is, arrangements upon which an additional royalty is payable to the arranger; and (3) musical compositions written or composed for use in instrumental books or books of arrangements by individuals well known as arrangers or instrumentalists.

Above royalties to be prorated where only part of a composition is subject to this agreement.

(2)   Mechanical Royalties: 50% of Gross Receipts

(3)   Performance Royalties if collected directly by us and not through a society: 50% of Gross Receipts

(4)   Foreign Income: 50% of Gross Receipts

A reminder that these are the writer's share of royalties. As a co-publisher, the writer also shares in the publisher's share.

This is one instance in which the writer does not receive 50% of the publisher's net income.

This is a modified Most Favored Nations clause, giving the writer equal royalties to writers of similar stature.

This is for direct performing rights only, in which the publisher also collects the writer's share.

(5)   Other Income: 50% of Gross Receipts; provided, that Writer shall not be entitled to receive any portion of any amount received by us from a source which pays Writer an equivalent amount directly (including but not limited to distributions from a performing rights society and direct payments or portions of any blank tape tax or charge which may be enacted by Congress if writers and publishers are paid separately.

Above royalties to be prorated where only part of a composition is subject to this agreement.

(6)   Demo Costs: All of a pro rata share (corresponding to writer's percentage of a SC) (of demo recording costs paid by us) shall be deemed additional advances to Writer hereunder. Writer will not incur any such demo costs without prior written approval in each instance.

EXISTING COMPOSITIONS

Including but not limited to . . .

Title	Writers	% Controlled	Received By

The release of the above songs in the first year in the USA on major labels will count towards the first year's minimum release commitment.

EXISTING THIRD-PARTY AGREEMENTS

None

SCHEDULE B

(Pursuant to subparagraph 7.2.2.)

None

The writer does not get a share of the publisher's share of public performance royalties as a writer, but does as a co-publisher.

If there are multiple publishers besides these parties, the fees will be prorated among them.

If the publisher pays for a demo to be created, the costs are deemed an additional advance against the writer's account. Some agreements only charge 50% of the demo costs against the writer.

This is a list of existing compositions at the time of signing this agreement and all songs listed are covered under this agreement.

If any of these songs are released in the first year, even though written prior to the agreement, they will count towards the delivery requirement and release commitment.

ASSIGNMENT

ASSIGNORS(S):

ASSIGNEE(S):   _____ (50%), and _____ d/b/a

_____(writer's publishing designee) (50%)

PORTION CONVEYED: One Hundred Percent of Assignor(s) interest

For valuable consideration, ASSIGNOR hereby assigns, transfers, sets over and conveys to ASSIGNEE and its successors and assigns that portion of all right, title and interest set forth above in and to the following musical composition(s)

Title   Co-Authors (Co-Publishers)   % Controlled

Assignor's Interest in all SCs listed in Schedule A attached.

Including copyrights and proprietary rights therein and in all versions of said musical composition(s), and any renewals and extensions thereof (whether available or subsequently available as the result of intervening legislation) in the United States of America and elsewhere throughout the world, and further including any and all causes of action for infringement of the same, past, present and future, and all proceeds from the foregoing accrued and unpaid and hereafter accruing.

This Assignment includes the exclusive, worldwide right to administer and exploit 100% of said compositions (or fractional interests) in accordance with the terms and conditions of the Co-publishing Agreement between parties of even date herewith.

As stated previously, an assignment of copyright must be in writing.

This would be the writer.

These are the publisher and the writer's publisher.

ASSIGNOR agrees to sign any all other papers which may be required to effectuate the purpose and intent of this Assignment and hereby irrevocably authorizes and appoints ASSIGNEE his attorney and representative in its name or in his name as his true and lawful attorney-in-fact to take such actions and make, sign, execute, acknowledge and deliver all such documents as may from time to time be necessary to convey to ASSIGNEE, its successors and assigns, all rights granted herein.

IN WITNESS WHEREOF, the undersigned has (have) executed the foregoing Assignment as of this _____th day of _____, 2___.

"ASSIGNOR"

_____

"ASSIGNEE"

LETTER OF DIRECTION TO ASCAP

Letters of direction are needed to advise another party that the publisher has the right to collect income on behalf of the co-publisher. Separate letters should be sent to the PRO, Harry Fox, sub-publishers, and any other party who might be making payments to the writer's publishing company, such as record companies or TV/film producers.

Date: _____

American Society of Composers,
Authors and Publishers
One Lincoln Plaza
New York, NY 10023

Gentleman:

You are hereby authorized to pay to our administrator, _____ ("Administrator"), at _____ and we hereby assign to Administrator, all monies payable from and after the date thereof (regardless of when earned) as the publisher's share of performance royalties with respect to the compositions described below:

Each and every musical composition co-owned by the undersigned and Administrator.

Copies of all statements shall be sent to Administrator and to us.

The foregoing authorization and direction shall remain in full force and effect until modified or terminated by both the undersigned and Administrator.

Very truly yours,

By: _____

LETTER OF DIRECTION TO BMI

Date: _____

Publisher Relations Department
 Broadcast Music, Inc.
7 World Trade Center
250 Greenwich Street
New York, NY 10007-0030

Gentlemen:

 This is to advise BMI that we have entered into an agreement with another BMI publisher for the administration of our catalog, and that BMI's records should be marked to reflect the agreement as follows:

    1. Name of BMI Publisher acting as our administrator:

    _____

    2. Effective date of agreement: Effective with the performances on and after _____, 20__. (Must be as of the beginning of a calendar quarter; i.e. January 1, April 1, July 1, or October 1.)

    3. Checks for all our BMI royalties, both domestic and foreign, should be made payable to the administrator and should be sent together with statements and all other correspondence to the administrator at its address on BMI's records.

 We understand that BMI cannot mark its records at this time so as to indicate the termination date of the administration agreement and that, therefore, the above information will continue to be reflected on BMI's records until such time as we or the administrator notifies BMI that the administration agreement is about to terminate.

                Very truly yours,

                (Publisher)

                By: _____
                   (Name)

WORK FOR HIRE CLAUSES

1.   Writer acknowledges and expressly agrees that the work entitled "_____" is prepared within the scope of Company's engagement of Writer's personal services and is a work made for hire.

[or]

1.   Writer acknowledges and expressly agrees that Writer's contribution to Company's work entitled "_____" is specially ordered or commissioned for use as a contribution to a collective work or compilation, as a part of a motion picture or other audiovisual, or as a translation, and that Writer's contribution to "_____" is a work made for hire.

[and]

2.   Writer further acknowledges that Company is considered the author of the work and Company is the exclusive owner of copyright in each work made for hire, and of all rights comprised in copyright, and that Company shall have the right to exercise all rights of copyright owner with respect thereto, including but not limited to, all exclusive rights specified in 17 U.S.C. § 106.

DELIVERY COMMITMENT/EXTENSION CLAUSE

Notwithstanding the foregoing, however, it is understood and agreed that you shall be required to deliver at least 10 newly-written compositions 50% written and/or composed by you (or the equivalent in compositions only partially written and/or composed by you) during each contract year of the Term, 5 of which shall have been recorded and released in the U.S. during such contract year by a major U.S. label (i.e., Sony, Warner Music Group, EMI-Capitol or Universal, or a company then regularly distributed by one of them), or recorded and scheduled for final release in the U.S. by such label within three months following the applicable contract year, (your "Delivery Commitment") in respect of such contract year.

A "contract year" shall continue for twelve months or, if later, until the completion of such Delivery Commitment for such contract year. In the event that your Delivery Commitment for a specific contract year shall not have been fulfilled (and notice of such fulfillment delivered to us in accordance with para. B).

CHAPTER 7

PUBLISHING ADMINISTRATION

Administering their publishing and the collection of royalties is one of the most complicated issues facing songwriters and publishers today. Many writers and artists do not have the time or background necessary to properly protect their intellectual property or to maximize its exploitation. Having an administrator or publisher look after the business aspects allows creative people the freedom to do what they do best—create—while someone else takes care of the details.

Administration Agreements

Administration of a copyright involves handling the business functions of a music publisher. This may involve only the collection and distribution of royalties and license fees or may include all the same activities as a music publisher, such as registering the copyright, issuing licenses, and actively seeking exploitation of the work. An administrator may be an existing publishing company, a co-publisher, or a separate, stand-alone company that handles administration for their clients. Companies of this last type do not own a portion of the copyright but, in exchange for these services, will charge a fee, usually a negotiated percentage of the gross revenues (usually between 10% and 20% but excluding the writer's share of performance income), but sometimes working on an hourly basis, plus reimbursable expenses. Since this a service provided and not ownership, the length of the administration agreement is for a period of years and may be renewed or terminated upon conclusion of the term of the agreement.

Several instances of the rationale behind administration are discussed above, but the most valid reason for assigning the administration of a copyright to another party is because that party has the expertise and resources to properly exploit the work and the ability to enforce the rights of the copyright owner, both with regard to use of the copyright and the collection of royalties.

In acquiring full administration of a copyright, the administrator acts in the place of the copyright owner, making all business decisions on behalf of the owner and handling all legal and financial matters, which may include paying the composer's share of royalties. When acquiring administration rights, the administrator must notify the applicable performing rights society of the agreement between the parties so that royalties are paid directly to the administrator. This requires a letter of direction, sample copies of which are included as addendums to the songwriter agreements in the previous chapter.

Like a songwriter agreement, it is possible to negotiate for an advance against future earnings in an administration agreement. Generally speaking, the larger the advance, the larger the percentage of the commission taken by the administrator. And, like a songwriter agreement, if the advances are not recouped by the end of the term, the term extends for additional periods until recoupment.

A good administration agreement (including a sub-publishing agreement) negotiated from a favorable position would probably contain the following:

+ No advance, or if anything, a token advance in exchange for a smaller commission of gross revenues. Consider the short-term gain vs. the long-term loss.

+ A term of usually no more than three years, which is often the minimum term permitted by foreign societies for registration for foreign-owned copyrights by a local representative. On a practical level, it takes some time for registrations and notices of changes in payment to be processed in the various systems. A shorter period would only cause confusion with respect to the catalog.

+ These deals can provide that when the term expires, collection rights to income earned during the term also expire, but the more common provision is the continuance of collecting royalties earned during the term for at least an additional year or until fully collected, i.e. a post-term collection period.

+ Accounting and payment procedures, approvals of translations and other types of uses, copyright and society registrations, etc., would be similar to the usual provisions of a songwriter agreement previously discussed.

Foreign Sub-Publishing Agreements

One form of administration is a foreign sub-publishing agreement. This may involve only the collection and distribution of royalties and license fees or may include all the same activities as a music publisher, such as registering the copyright with the local performance and mechanical societies, issuing licenses, and actively seeking exploitation of the work. Having sub-publishers is important because the policies and activities in each country are very different, and having local representation acting on behalf of the publisher can make a big difference in the timeliness and amount of royalties collected, as well as the protection and enforcement of the copyright in that territory. A sub-publisher does not, however, own a portion of the copyright, only an administrative interest.

To this day, sub-publishing is unquestionably the most common arrangement a music publishing company makes for the representation of its catalog overseas. This grants a sub-publisher the right to administer a copyright (or a catalog) in their country and to collect the royalties earned in that territory.

Generally, United States music publishers have foreign music publishing companies around the world represent them to collect income, promote the songs, get foreign local language recordings and other forms of uses for the rights the U.S publishers own on their song titles.

The U.S. music publisher enters into agreements ("sub-publishing agreements") with sub-publishers in the individual countries (or with a multi-national publishing company for more than one country [or the world]) outside the U.S., granting most or all rights owned by the U.S. music publisher ("owner") for one or more countries ("territories") for a specific term and on certain financial conditions. These conditions divide the income from the local territories between the owner and sub-publisher.

The key points in sub-publishing deals are:

(1) a limited term of three to five years;

(2) the territory covered by this agreement, usually a specific country or contiguous countries (such as Spain and Portugal, or the "GAS" territories of Germany, Austria, and Switzerland);

(3) the royalty split, i.e., the percentages of collected monies to be divided between the sub-publisher and the U.S. publisher;

(4) a possible advance against monies to become due the U.S. publisher; and, finally,

(5) a provision for covers, that is, a new use of a sub-published composition originating within a sub-publishing territory, such as a new recording by a local artist in the local language.

Other terms in a sub-publishing agreement apply to semi-annual accountings and payment to the U.S. publisher, auditing rights, print rights, the right of the sub-publisher to collect and distribute income earned during the contract term, which may or may not include the right to collect income earned during the term but paid post termination.

In acquiring foreign administration of a copyright, the sub-publisher acts in the place of the copyright owner, making business decisions in consultation with and on behalf of the owner and handling all legal and financial matters in their territory. For these services, the sub-publisher will usually charge a fee (a negotiated percentage of the publisher's share of gross revenues, usually from 10% to 25%, depending on the size of any advances—the higher the advance, the higher the administration fee) plus reimbursable expenses.

When acquiring these administration rights, the sub-publisher must notify the applicable performing and mechanical rights societies of the agreement between the parties so that royalties are paid directly to the sub-publisher. This is done, in part, through the use of the *fiche internationale*, a database link between the foreign societies for the titles that they each control.

Sub-publishers perform many of the same functions as domestic administrators. They register copyrights with the local performing and mechanical rights societies, issue licenses for uses originating within their territories, collect royalties, and monitor the use of the owner's copyrights. It is important to notify them whenever a license is issued for any type of use so that if the product is distributed or broadcast in their territory, they can be sure to collect the royalties earned. Copies of music cue sheets for movies and television programs (with translated program titles and distribution schedules, if possible) should be supplied to sub-publishers so that they may advise the local performing rights societies of the use of the copyright.

Sub-publishing administration can be handled by one of the multi-national companies for the entire world (or world excluding the U.S. and Canada) *or* deals can be made in each territory (or group of territories) with different parties, including the local office of one of the multi-nationals. There are advantages and disadvantages to both methods.

The advantage of dealing with one multi-national company for the entire world is that the larger companies may be in a position to pay a substantial advance against recoupment of future royalties. Also, there is only one (large) royalty statement to review. The disadvantage of dealing with a large company is that interests of a small publishing company may get lost in the shuffle and not get the attention that the publisher thinks it deserves.

Conversely, dealing on a territory-by-territory basis, a publisher can pick the administrator in each country that best suits the needs of the publisher and their catalog, even if it is the local office of one of the multi-nationals. But there will be many royalty statements to review, each with a different structure and format, with varying administration fees being deducted.

When dealing with a sub-publisher for administration for more than one territory, or for a territory that is not the sub-publisher's home country, there should be language that royalties are paid "at source," which means that the monies paid to the publisher are subject only to deduction of the administrator's fees per the agreement, not also deducting any fees imposed by the sub-publisher of the administrator (sometimes called a "sub sub-publisher"). For example, if an administration deal is entered into with one of the multi-national companies, their local offices should not able to deduct an administration fee and then have the home office deduct their fees as well. This "double dipping" is a common practice unless contractually prohibited.

It is also possible to get advances from the individual publisher that can be larger or on more favorable terms than that received from a multi-national company. Assume for purposes of this analysis that a multi-national company is willing to pay an advance of $500,000 to cover five territories. At the end of the term, the earnings and recoupment from the five countries looks like this:

TERRITORY	EARNINGS	RECOUPMENT BALANCE
#1	$ 100,000.00	
#2	$ 50,000.00	
#3	$ 75,000.00	
#4	$ 125,000.00	
#5	$ 150,000.00	
TOTAL	$ 500,000.00	$ -0-

At this point, the advance would be fully recouped and the sub-publisher would not be obligated to pay any further money under the agreement.

In contrast, assume that the publisher does territory-by-territory deals with five different sub-publishers, each of whom offers an advance of $100,000, or $500,000 total. This seems like the same deal, unless the recoupment in each territory is taken into account, as follows:

TERRITORY	EARNINGS	RECOUPMENT BALANCE
#1	$ 100,000.00	$ -0-
#2	$ 50,000.00	$ (50,000.00)
#3	$ 75,000.00	$ (25,000.00)
#4	$ 125,000.00	$ 25,000.00
#5	$ 150,000.00	$ 50,000.00
TOTAL	$ 500,000.00	**$ 75,000.00**

In this example, while territories #2 and #3 would be unrecouped, and the term of the agreements in those territories extended until recoupment, territories #4 and #5 would owe the publisher a combined additional payment of $75,000.

It is crucial that the arrangement be made with an experienced and reputable foreign firm. A large advance from a firm that a publisher might not ordinarily deal with will get exactly what is bargained for—trouble. If a publisher does not know if a foreign company they are about to deal with is reputable or efficient, it is incumbent on that publisher to find out. This can be accomplished by checking with other U.S. publishers or with a lawyer knowledgeable in this field. The international music publishing community lives in its own glass house. Any overseas publisher previously dealt with and whom there is some rapport with will often know the reputation (or lack of one) of publishers in other countries. Naturally, consensus is better than one opinion.

How Foreign Royalty Streams Are Paid and Distributed

Mechanical royalties (for the sales of audio-only product, such as vinyl records, audio tapes, CDs, and digital downloads) are paid by the record companies to the local mechanical collection society. Unlike the United States, where the record companies pay the publishers or the Harry Fox Agency, most foreign countries have mechanical collection societies similar to the performing rights societies, who collect all the royalties from the record companies. The society then pays the royalties to the local sub-publisher. If music is being distributed for sale in foreign countries, a sub-publisher can more easily monitor the sales and royalties generated in their territory. In today's sub-publishing agreements, the sub-publisher collects 100% of the mechanicals in their territories.

The mechanical licensing fees paid by the record companies outside the U.S. are calculated differently from the method used in the U.S., where the copyright law determines the amount paid per song on a "fixed" number of cents per copy sold (the "statutory rate"), or a negotiated percentage thereof. In Europe, the rate is covered by an agreement by the European part of the International Federation of the Phonographic Industries (IFPI) and the European association of the copyright collection societies (BIEM). The mechanical rate is a percentage of the record company's sales price to the record retailers.

This price to the record retailers is generally referred to as the published price to dealers ("PPD"), and is approximately what we would term the wholesale price. PPD is not the actual price to the dealers but includes individual various addons (yearend bonuses to dealers, etc.) and deductions (taxes, packaging, etc.). The current rate is around 9% of PPD and does not allow for reductions in the rate that are common in the U.S., even if the songwriter/artist is bound by a controlled composition clause in their agreement with the record company calling for a reduced mechanical rate for songs they control. The PPD royalty is then divided equally among all the songs on the album, regardless of their length.

For digital phonorecord delivery, or downloads, the same concepts apply. The downloads are treated as a physical sale, the same way they are by the U.S. record companies, and a percentage of PPD is paid to the publisher as a mechanical royalty for each song downloaded.

The sub-publisher, after receiving 100% of mechanical royalties, will deduct its share of the mechanicals for a particular song "off the top" (usually between 10%–25% commission). The sub-publisher then accounts to the owner for the remaining share (90%–75%) in the form of a royalty statement and the respective payment(s) thereof, usually on semiannual basis. The owner will then pay the writer(s) their share of the income received according to the agreement between the writer(s) and the owner.

Sub-publishers may also try to get "cover" recordings done by artists in their native language. This would generally entitle the sub-publisher to retain a higher percentage of royalties (25%–40%), since it was their direct efforts that resulted in additional income. If a foreign lyric is created, most of the foreign countries have standards whereby the foreign lyricist participates in a share of all royalties earned by the foreign version. For mechanicals, the foreign writer takes a part of the sub-publisher's increased percentage but for performances, the foreign lyricist receives a portion of the writer's share of income.

In general, the sub-publisher's share of the above 100% income includes other foreign local participants such as local lyric writer(s), adapters, and other possible local income participants. All additional local participants are paid directly through the local performing and mechanical rights societies and their percentage of the income is defined by the rules of the local societies.

This means that the royalties payable to local participants other than the sub-publisher are deducted from the sub-publisher's shares. The local lyric writer receives 16.66% (or $^2/_{12}$) "off the top" out of the sub-publisher's share for any use of his version only.

For U.S. publishers who have no foreign sub-publishers, if they are affiliated with The Harry Fox Agency, HFA does have some reciprocal representation agreements with over 30 foreign societies whereby the foreign societies will pay mechanical royalties earned for HFA members in their territories to HFA for distribution to HFA publisher members. The U.S. publisher must file with HFA a Notification of Foreign Activity form so that HFA can notify their foreign counterparts of the uses in their territory and that the foreign societies should forward the royalties to HFA.

The foreign society will take their standard commission, as will HFA, so there are some costs involved. An important note is that HFA does not undertake royalty examinations in foreign territories, so the U.S. publisher must rely on the information and payments made to HFA by the foreign society without the ability to audit their books and records. This is where a foreign sub-publisher has a distinct advantage over HFA, in that they have the right to monitor the sales figures and audit the foreign societies of which they are members.

In the event that HFA does not have an agreement with a particular territory, or if the U.S. publisher is not represented by a local sub-publisher, the mechanical royalties owned to the U.S. publisher are unpaid and retained by the foreign society in their "black box" income (see below).

Synchronization licensing works differently in some foreign territories than it does in the U.S. The procedure for licensing sync rights for motion pictures, commercials, and DVDs is the same, where the sub-publisher negotiates a license fee, collects 100% of the fee, and pays to the U.S. publisher their agreed upon share, with the U.S. publisher then paying the writer.

In some countries, however, television rights are included in the licenses issued by the performing rights organization ("PRO") and there is no negotiation or payment of fees for those uses. This frequently confuses U.S. publishers, who are used to a one-on-one negotiation for sync rights. Conversely, TV producers from overseas don't understand that they need to obtain permission and negotiate a fee for sync rights for music on U.S. television.

Public performance royalties are collected through performance rights societies in each territory. Much as ASCAP, BMI, and SESAC collect these royalties in the United States, most major territories have their own PROs. These PROs are almost like quasi-governmental bodies and license performing rights to the radio stations, television stations, and (unlike the United States) motion picture theaters in their territory.

These foreign PROs monitor the broadcasts in their territories and calculate the value of the performances, much like the U.S. PROs. They conduct surveys (i.e., a statistical sampling instead of a census) of local television and some cable stations, but many foreign PROs are able to provide a virtual census for the main terrestrial stations, which is certainly preferable to a sample survey. In addition, in most foreign countries, there is monitoring of live music in concert halls, clubs, and sports stadiums, providing more detailed and accurate accountings of music performed in the territories.

Unlike the 50/50 division between writers and publishers in the U.S., the foreign royalties are divided into $^{12}/_{12}$ outside the United States. $^{6}/_{12}$ (or, in some cases, $^{8}/_{12}$) are paid by the local performing rights society directly to the U.S. performance rights societies (ASCAP, BMI and SESAC) as the writer's share of these royalties, and the U.S. societies pay the writers directly as they do for domestic income. The remaining $^{6}/_{12}$ (or $^{4}/_{12}$) represent the owner and sub-publisher's share of the performance income, which is paid 100% to the sub-publisher.

Other than in mechanicals, the local adapter's (local lyric writer[s], arrangers, and other) share(s) of performance royalties are automatically deducted by the local societies out of the U.S. writer's share of performance royalties before payment is made to the U.S. performance rights societies (ASCAP, BMI and SESAC). This is usually equal to $^{2}/_{12}$ of the writer's share.

Music Created for Television and Film

In many cases, the music created for television and motion pictures is done as a work-made-for-hire, with the production company being the owner/publisher of the music, and the composer a passive participant in the writer's share of the royalty stream. In these cases, it is up to the publisher to make sure that all the necessary paperwork is properly filed and that the info sent around the world as the program is distributed is accurate.

In some instances, the writers are able to retain ownership of the copyright and are, in fact, the music publishers. It is then their responsibility to handle the business aspects of worldwide collection and tracking, as with any copyright owner/publisher.

For most writers of original music for television and motion pictures, the greatest source of income is their public performance royalties. The greatest challenge here is that, in order for the foreign PROs to accurately track a particular program, there must be a cue sheet filed with that PRO. Having the cue sheet filed with the U.S. PRO will usually take care of that, as the PROs have reciprocal agreements with each other and exchange data as well as income, but there are potential issues that composers and production companies need to be aware of. For example, the cue sheet has the English title of the program and the episode title. But does the cue sheet filed in France have these titles in French? In the age of computers, if the computer is looking for the French title, it will not recognize the English title and the royalties for that program may not be accurately accounted to the writers and publishers. While it is in the producers' and publishers' best interests to make sure that they supply the correct info, as they would usually receive the publisher's share of this income equal to the writer's share, many producers do not understand this aspect of the business at all and fail to follow through, to the detriment of themselves and the composers. Also, there are many producers who create a domestic U.S. version of the show with certain music and then change some or all of the music to fit the needs of the foreign market. A TV or film composer needs make sure that *they* receive cue sheets for all versions of the program.

The U.S. PROs do not actively monitor foreign broadcasts, relying on the foreign societies to perform that function. The foreign societies utilize services of Mediametrie/Eurodata TV, which is the equivalent of Nielsen and/or *TV Guide* here in the U.S. Foreign broadcast information is regularly provided to the foreign PROs under a standing agreement. For writers, their share of income from these royalties is sent back to their U.S. PRO, which makes distributions for foreign income a few times a year. Foreign societies as a whole pay less frequently than the U.S. PROs. For example, the BUMA/STEMRA (Netherlands) distribution occurs in October representing payment for the previous year's performances: 2011 performances will be paid in October 2012. Most societies pay for their domestic performances on a semester basis. For publishers, payment is made either through the U.S. PRO if the publisher is not represented by a sub-publisher, or to the publishers' sub-publishers in that territory. That is why copies of music cue sheets for movies and television programs (with translated program titles and distribution, sales and/or airdate schedules, if possible) should be supplied to a sub-publisher so that they may advise the local performing rights societies of the use of your copyright, and collect all royalties due.

One of the interesting differences between U.S. royalties and foreign royalties in some of the major territories is the concept of a " **broadcast mechanical** " (or sometimes called a "performance mechanical") royalty, which does not exist in the U.S. Historically, the royalty developed when radio stations would record artists or orchestras in one city, then would reproduce the music on record or tape copies to be sent to other stations for rebroadcast. This "mechanical" reproduction triggered a new royalty, as if it were pressed on a record. While the need to reproduce and transport physical copies no longer exists, as the music can be transmitted digitally or by satellite, the royalty has become an important source of income for parties whose music is played on radio and television, sometimes equaling about $1/3$ of the performance income.

However, since this is not strictly considered a performance royalty, but a mechanical right, the payments are not made to the publishers and writers separately, as performance royalties are, but paid 100% to the publisher (or sub-publisher). As with other sources of mechanical income, such as CD or digital downloads, it is the publishers' responsibility (usually by contract) to pay the writers their 50% share. The U.S. PROs cannot collect broadcast mechanicals, therefore the publisher (through their sub-publisher in the territory) is the only entity that can collect 100% of the broadcast mechanicals and pay to the writer their 50% share of this income. This revenue needs to be provided for in the composer's agreement, where it should specifically state that the composer has the right to 50% of any such broadcast mechanical royalties collected by the production company (or their publishing designee) for the performance of these copyrights. If the composer owns the copyright to your music, having a direct relationship with a knowledgeable sub-publisher is essential.

One of the issues here is that, since in some territories the performing rights organization and mechanical rights organization is the same (such as SACEM in France or GEMA in Germany), a U.S. publisher receiving a statement from their sub-publishers that shows a distribution from these parties might not recognize that there is money credited as a broadcast mechanical and think that they are entitled to keep 100% of the money as the publisher's share. If composers are getting performing rights income from the territories that have this broadcast mechanical right, they should check with their publishers to make sure that the publisher is making the proper distributions.

"Black Box" Income

In many territories, income that is not distributed for various reasons (not being able to identify the publisher, the publisher not being represented in the territory, a mistitled music cue sheet, or other local customs and practices) is deposited into an account called a "black box" and saved for a period of time. At some point, the local societies decide to distribute this income to their local members only.

If a U.S. publisher is represented by a local publisher in that territory, it is possible for the U.S. publisher to be paid a share of that income, but it must be covered in their agreement with the local sub-publisher. For example, there could be language stating that the local publisher will pay to the U.S. publisher a share of this income proportionate to the share of income the U.S. publisher is paid compared to the overall earnings of the local publisher. In other words, if the U.S. publisher generates 2% of the local publisher's income, the U.S. publisher would be entitled to 2% of the black box income.

This can sometimes be a significant amount of income, whether from undistributed royalties or settlements between the societies and the broadcasters or record companies. As this income is paid without any information as to the source of the income, the U.S. publisher, upon receiving this income, then must make a determination of how to pay to its writers and co-publishers (if any) their share of the black box income. It would not be uncommon to use the same methodology to determine the U.S. publishers' highest earners and pay them a share of the black box income.

PUBLISHING ADMINISTRATION AGREEMENT

This agreement can be used either with a domestic administrator for the U.S. only, for worldwide administration by a multi-national company, or with a foreign sub-publisher for their territory only.

AGREEMENT made _____ by and between _____ with offices at _____ _____ (Publisher) and _____, with a principal place of business at _____ (Administrator).

WITNESSETH:

WHEREAS, Publisher wishes to grant to Administrator certain rights in and to the "Compositions" (as that term is defined in subparagraph 1(a) hereof), and Administrator wishes to obtain such rights, on the terms and conditions hereinafter set forth.

NOW, THEREFORE, in consideration of the foregoing premises and the mutual covenants hereinafter contained, the parties hereto hereby agree as follows:

1.   Definitions. As used herein the following terms shall have the following meanings:

a)   "Composition(s)" shall mean Publisher's fractional share of the compositions owned or controlled by Publisher for and in the Territory: (i) as of the date of this agreement, some but not all of which are specified on Exhibit "A" annexed to and made part hereof and (ii) during the term of this agreement.

Since the publisher may not own 100% of the songs listed or not control the entire territory, this states that the songs listed on exhibit "A" are controlled by the publisher in the shares listed.

b)   "Cover Record" shall mean a new phonorecord embodying a Composition that is originally produced, recorded and released in the Licensed Territory during the term of this agreement. Such new phonorecord must be initially procured through Administrator's direct efforts. Administrator shall submit written documentation, adequate in Publisher's good faith judgment, to establish Administrator's efforts in procuring such new phonorecord. If a dispute arises with respect to Administrator's direct efforts in procuring such new phonorecord, Publisher's decision shall be final and binding on the parties.

This would be a new recording of a composition generated through the efforts of the administrator, which would earn the administrator a higher percentage of royalties, per paragraph 10.

c)   "Income" shall mean any and all gross payments, royalties, fees, receipts, revenues, collections, monies and other consideration of any kind and nature derived from, or payable by reason of, any and all Sales and Uses of any and all of the Compositions after deducting customary service charges, if any, of the respective mechanical rights and performing rights societies in the Licensed Territory and sales, excise or similar taxes; provided, however, that such deductions shall be made only in the event that similar deductions are made with respect to Administrator's own music catalog and all other music catalogs administered by the Administrator.

> This defines how the royalties and license fees are treated with respect to any deductions for fees for service charges taken by the performing rights or mechanical licensing agencies, but only if the administrator's own catalogs are charged the same fees.

All Income shall be calculated on one hundred percent (100%) of monies payable from the source. No deductions shall be made for percentage of monies payable to Administrator's subpublishers, agents or designees.

> Income is calculated "at source," i.e., as earned in the territory from which they are received, without any deductions for the administrator's sub-publishers or agents. In administration agreements covering more than a single territory, or in foreign sub-publishing agreements, this is especially important to avoid more than one commission being taken, i.e., double dipping.

d)   "Licensed Territory" shall mean _____.

> The territory covered by this agreement and for which rights are being granted to the administrator.

e)   "Mechanical Rights" shall mean the right to (i) manufacture parts which are used to produce and/or reproduce the Compositions, (ii) manufacture, sell or distribute mechanical, electrical or magnetic reproductions of the Compositions on records,

> All audio-only product.

compact discs, prerecorded tapes, tape cassettes and digital phonorecord delivery ("DPD") or digital download (iii) manufacture, sell or distribute reproductions of the Compositions by any other method or on any other media now known or hereafter devised including reproductions of the Compositions embodied on Videograms.

> In some foreign territories, DVDs generate a mechanical royalty per unit sold or rented.

The term "Mechanical Rights" shall also mean and include so-called "broadcast mechanical" or "mechanical performing" rights.

> See description of "broadcast mechanical" or "mechanical performing" rights above.

f)   "Motion Picture Synchronization Rights" shall mean the right to record, reproduce, perform, present, synchronize and exhibit the Compositions in, or in connection with, motion picture productions, screen trailers and related publicity.

(g)   "New Media Rights" shall mean a digital transmission of a (i) download of a sound recording of a single musical work to the local storage device (e.g. the hard drive of the user's computer or a portable device) using technology designed to cause the downloaded file to be available for listening that is not time limited or other use limited, and (ii) digitally "streamed" performances, digital interactive uses, ringtones and any other digitized use that results in reproduction or performance of a Composition currently known.

This includes downloading, streaming, interactive uses, ringtones, and other digital uses.

(h)   "Performing Rights" shall mean the right to perform the Compositions non-dramatically by live performance, radio or television broadcast or otherwise.

"Or otherwise" would include Internet streaming and other types of public performances.

(i)   "Printed Music" shall mean written reproductions of the Compositions whether such reproductions are copied, printed, lithographed, photo-offset or otherwise reproduced by xerography, thermal processing or by any and all other means of written reproduction now known or hereafter devised.

(j)   "Sales and Uses" shall mean any and all uses or exploitation of the Compositions and any and all of the rights related thereto.

(k)   "Similar Rights" shall mean any and all rights which are substantially similar to copyright with respect to those areas in the world in which copyright protection shall not be obtainable.

(l)   "Television Synchronization Rights" shall mean the right to record, reproduce, perform, present, synchronize and exhibit the Compositions in, or in connection with, television productions broadcast for private home use.

(m)   "Videogram" shall mean DVDs, videocassettes, videodiscs, digital audio-visual downloads and similar or future audio-visual devices intended for sale, lease or rental for private viewing in the home.

The term "videogram" has been expanded to include audio-visual digital downloads.

(n)   "Videogram Synchronization Rights" shall mean the right to record, perform and synchronize the Compositions in synchronization or timed relation with Videograms.

2.   <u>Term</u>.

(a)   Subject to the terms and provisions of subparagraphs 12(c)-(e) hereof, the term of this agreement shall commence on _____ and shall terminate on _____.

The term is generally no less than 3 years. Some agreements have language calling for automatic renewal of the agreement unless terminated by one of the parties.

Administrator shall retain the rights herein granted with respect to each Composition until the expiration of the term of this agreement, at which time such rights shall terminate, absolutely, and revert to Publisher free of any claim thereto by Administrator, or any persons or firms claiming rights through or under Administrator. Administrator shall have the right to collect all Income earned during the term within the Licensed Territory for a period of one (1) year after expiration of the term (Post-Term Collection Period) and shall pay same to Publisher pursuant to the terms hereof.

A post-term collection period of one year. This means the administrator has the right to collect and take commissions on any royalties earned during the term but paid within one year of the termination date. For example, since the PROs are generally 6–9 months behind in their payments, the administrator has the right to collect for any period during which they had administration rights even though paid after termination. This applies to all other types of income as well.

Upon expiration of the Post-Term Collection Period, Publisher or its designees shall have the sole and exclusive right to collect all Income earned in the Licensed Territory, regardless of when paid or payable.

Once the post-term collection period is over, the publisher has the right to collect all money, even if earned during the term.

During the Post-Term Collection Period, Publisher or its designees shall have the sole and exclusive right to collect all Income <u>earned</u> <u>after</u> expiration of the term. If Administrator receives either any Income earned during the term after expiration of the Post-Term Collection Period, or any Income earned after expiration of the term during the Post-Term Collection Period, Administrator shall remit one hundred percent (100%) of such Income to Publisher or its designees.

For any royalties earned after the term has ended, the publisher has the sole right to collect (or to assign administration to another party).

(b)   Within thirty (30) days after expiration of the term Administrator shall deliver to Publisher or to Publisher's designee any and all information with respect to the Compositions, including, without limiting the generality of the foregoing any and all copyrights, correspondence, statistical and financial information together with a copy of Administrator's database on a CD-Rom disc.

If the publisher is going to change administrators, they need all the information from the current administrator in order for a smooth transition. As many publishing database programs combine all data for all clients into one file, it may not be possible for the administrator to deliver all data in a digital format.

(c)   With respect to Printed Music distributed by Administrator or its licensees during the term of this agreement, Administrator shall, at Publisher's request:

(i)   Destroy any and all plates, negatives, and other material relating to such publication and shall deliver to Publisher a certificate of destruction therefore; or

(ii)   Deliver to Publisher or its designee such plates, negatives, other material upon payment to Administrator of the actual scrap value of such plates, negatives, other material and Printed Music, together with shipping costs in respect thereof.

(iii)   Administrator shall furnish to Publisher or its designee an accurate inventory of such plates, negatives, other materials within thirty (30) days after termination of this agreement, and, within sixty (60) days after termination of this agreement, Publisher shall notify Administrator whether it wishes to exercise the option set forth in subparagraph (i) or (ii) above with respect to all or any portion of such plates, negatives, other material or Printed Music.

(iv)   Administrator and its licensees shall have a period of six (6) months after expiration of the term to sell-off its inventory of Printed Music existing on expiration of the term. On expiration of such six (6) month period, Administrator and its licensees shall cease selling any Printed Music and shall thereupon immediately notify Publisher of the then remaining inventory. Publisher shall have the right to either purchase the existing inventory at Administrator's actual cost of printing or to cause Administrator to destroy same.

> A six-month "sell off period" allows a publisher to continue to sell remaining inventory for a period after the term expires. If any inventory remains, the publisher has the option to purchase the inventory to sell after the term and sell-off period expire.

3.   <u>Collection of Income</u>. Subject to the terms and conditions of this agreement, Administrator shall collect, on behalf of Publisher, one hundred percent (100%) of all Income which,

> The administrator collects all income except the writer's share of performance income.

during the term of this agreement, shall become payable in connection with any and all Sales and Uses of the Compositions in the Licensed Territory including without limitation the share of Income derived from Performing Rights allocated by the performing rights society in the Licensed Territory as the so-called "publisher share" of Performing Rights referred to in paragraph 10(a)(i)(C)(iii) below (but excluding the so-called "writer share" of Performing Rights paid directly to writers through their performing rights societies).

In the U.S., the publisher's share is 50% of the total income. In foreign territories, due to the differences in how the shares are allocated, this is usually shown as $^{6}/_{12}$.

Administrator shall also have the right to collect any Income earned in the Licensed Territory prior to commencement of the term of this agreement which Income is not otherwise collected or collectable by Publisher's previous representative in the Licensed Territory. All Income shall be calculated and payable from the country of sale, regardless of the country of manufacture.

In addition to post-term collection rights, the administrator has the right to collect any royalties not previously collected by the publisher in their territory. This is subject, of course, to any prior administration agreements in effect, including any post-term collection clauses in those agreements.

4.   Rights Granted. Subject to paragraph 5, Publisher grants to Administrator, and Administrator hereby accepts, for the term of this agreement and in the Licensed Territory, the following rights with respect to the Compositions:

Note that some of these rights are exclusive, some non-exclusive.

(a)   The non-exclusive right to print, publish, sell or lease Printed Music and to authorize others to print, publish, sell or lease Printed Music.

(b)   The exclusive right to license Performing Rights.

The performing rights would be licensed to the PRO in the territory only.

(c)   The exclusive right to license non-exclusive Mechanical Rights.

Due to compulsory licensing, all mechanical licenses are non-exclusive.

(d)   The exclusive right to grant non-exclusive licenses for the use of Television Synchronization Rights relating to a television production

Note the language "the exclusive right to grant non-exclusive licenses" here and in the paragraphs below. With rare exceptions, most TV and film sync licenses are also non-exclusive. Exceptions would be theme songs or category exclusivity for commercials.

originally produced within the Licensed Territory;

In a worldwide administration deal, this language is unnecessary. But in a deal for a particular territory, the administrator only has the right to issue licenses for productions that originate in their territory. This prevents a publisher in Italy licensing to a French production company.

provided that Administrator shall not exercise such right without Publisher's express, prior, written consent.

(e)   The exclusive right to grant non-exclusive licenses for the use of Motion Picture Synchronization Rights for a theatrical motion picture originally produced within the Licensed Territory; provided that Administrator shall not exercise such right without Publisher's express, prior, written consent.

(f)   The exclusive right to grant non-exclusive licenses for the use of Videogram Synchronization Rights for a Videogram that is originally manufactured in the Licensed Territory; provided that Administrator shall not exercise such right without Publisher's express, prior, written consent.

(g)   The non-exclusive right to grant non-exclusive licenses for the use of New Media Rights that originate in the Licensed Territory; provided that Administrator shall not exercise such right without Publisher's express, prior, written consent.

(h)   The right to make, or have others make translations of the lyrics or new lyric versions of the Compositions in the language or languages,

but only if the principal language or languages of the Licensed Territory is not English, subject to Publisher's express prior written consent.

Administrator shall use its best efforts to cause all local lyric versions of the Compositions to bear local language titles; provided that if a local language title is not possible, then Administrator shall not make or have others make a local lyric version without Publisher's express, prior, written consent.

In many administration agreements, approval is needed from the publisher. Sometimes there is language that consent shall not be unreasonably withheld or some time frame is given for consent which, if not denied within that period, is deemed approved.

Sometimes, a new lyric is called an adaptation, not a translation, as the new lyrics are very different than the existing lyrics. An example is the song "My Way," which is based on a French song *"Comme d'habitude"* but has new lyrics in English by Paul Anka.

For a song that originates in English, another English lyric would not be a translation, but a derivative work, subject to express approval from the publisher, sometimes with no credit to the new additional writer. Only a song translated into another language would possibly allow the foreign writer a portion of the writer's share of income.

In order to avoid confusion and maintain separate royalty streams, a version in a foreign language should have a title in that language to distinguish between the original song and original writers and the foreign version that will have an additional foreign writer.

All translations of the Compositions shall be made at Administrator's sole cost and expense and shall be faithful to the fundamental character of the original lyrics to the extent permitted by the local language. Administrator shall provide that the local lyric writers' share of Performing Rights and Mechanical Rights Income shall be limited to local lyric versions only. If the local lyric writer's share of such Income is not so limited, Administrator, prior to authorizing the making of such local lyric version, shall so advise Publisher in writing and the authorization of the making of such local lyric version shall be subject to the express written approval of Publisher.

See notes above about local writer shares.

If Administrator breaches this agreement by failing to obtain Publisher's written approval pursuant to the immediately preceding sentence, then in addition to Publisher's other rights and remedies, Administrator shall credit Publisher's account the amount paid to the local lyric writer and Administrator shall bear the amount paid to the local lyric writer out of Administrator's share of Income. If Publisher expressly approves a local lyric version pursuant to this subparagraph, then Administrator shall not be obligated to compensate or reimburse Publisher as provided above.

The administrator is held financially liable for not obtaining the publisher's permission by having the local writer's share of income paid from the administrator's share of revenue.

(i)   Notwithstanding anything to the contrary contained in this agreement, the rights granted to Administrator in this agreement are and shall be subject to all limitations, restrictions and conditions imposed on Publisher pursuant to any agreement by which Publisher acquired rights to any Composition(s) including without limitation any termination or expiration of Publisher's rights during the term of this agreement.

As it would be unusual for an administrator to be aware of all contractual restrictions in a songwriter or publishing administrations agreement, this clause shows why there are so many consents from the publisher necessarily built into this agreement.

5.   Reservation of Rights. Publisher hereby reserves any and all rights of every kind and nature not specifically granted to the Administrator herein, and the right to any and all fees, payments or other monies derived from such reserved rights. Without in any way limiting the generality of the foregoing, the following rights and any fees, payments or other monies derived therefrom, except as herein provided, shall be reserved to Publisher:

Certain rights are retained by the publisher only, as follows.

(a)   Any and all copyrights in the Compositions and in any adaptations, arrangements, translations and new lyric versions thereof, throughout the world, and any and all rights existing under such copyrights in the Licensed Territory. In any area in the world where copyright law does not exist, Publisher hereby reserves all Similar Rights.

Any agreements must state that the publisher is the owner of all copyrights in any translations or adaptations.

(b)   The exclusive right, throughout the world, to dramatize the Compositions and to license the use of "grand rights" on the live stage and to public performance of such dramatic versions.

These are rights that are granted for the use of music in stage plays or musicals. They are licensed directly from the publisher and are different from the "small performing rights" that are granted by the PROs.

(c)   The exclusive right, throughout the world, to make cartoon, literary and other subsidiary versions of the Compositions and to print, publish and sell such cartoon, literary and other subsidiary versions.

These would be derivative works, which would require approval from the publisher.

(d)   The exclusive right, throughout the world, to use or to license the use of the titles of the Compositions separate and apart from the Compositions.

Generally, titles, in and of themselves, are not protectable. However, when a song is used in a production and the title of the song becomes the title of the production, additional permissions and fees are involved. The classic example is the film "Ode to Billy Jo," which used not only the title of the song, but the story as well.

(e)   The exclusive right, throughout the world, to grant licenses for any use, whether now known or hereafter devised, of the Compositions, or any part thereof, for or in connection with commercials, advertising or merchandising tie ins for any goods, products, wares or services of any and all kinds.

This agreement calls for the publisher to have the sole right to license for commercials and other merchandise. In many agreements the administrator has the rights to do this for their territory, but only with the publisher's approval.

(f)   The exclusive right to grant licenses for Videograms, the manufacture of which originates outside the Licensed Territory, provided, however, that Administrator shall have the right to collect Income derived from the Sales and Uses of the Compositions embodied on Videograms sold or distributed within the Licensed Territory, pursuant to the provisions of the licenses issued by Publisher or Publisher's authorized designees or agents. Administrator shall account to and pay the Publisher with respect to such Income pursuant to the provisions of this agreement.

In some foreign territories, there is a payment similar to a mechanical royalty paid for videograms. Despite the fact that the publisher might have granted a buyout of all video rights to the producers of the video, the local customs and practices will dictate payment of any other royalties. This clause gives a sub-publisher the right to collect these royalties on behalf of the publisher.

(g)   The exclusive right to grant licenses for Motion Picture Synchronization Rights or Television Synchronization Rights for productions originally produced outside the Licensed Territory.

Since the administrator is only granted the rights to issue synchronization licenses for productions that originate within the licensed territory (see above), the rights for productions outside their territory are retained by the publisher, who might grant them to other administrators for other territories.

6.   Obligations of Publisher. Publisher shall provide Administrator with all necessary information concerning each Composition, such as the title, the names of the writers, and the date of first publication.

The administrator cannot properly register or monitor the compositions without all this information.

7.   Warranties of Publisher. Publisher hereby represents and warrants to Administrator that it owns or controls the rights in the Compositions granted herein and has full right power and authority to enter into this agreement and grant Administrator the rights herein granted.

This solidifies the grant of rights from the publisher to administrator.

8.   Obligations of Administrator.

An umbrella clause covering money received for all exploitation of the compositions in the administrator's territory.

(a)   Payments to Publisher hereunder shall be based upon all Sales and Uses of the Compositions in the Licensed Territory.

(b)   Administrator shall pay to all local adaptors, composers, arrangers, translators and lyricists, any and all royalties, fees or other compensation due to such persons; provided, however, that Administrator shall not agree to pay royalties, fees or other compensation to such persons for a period extending beyond the term of this agreement without Publisher's express written consent.

The administrator is responsible to pay all local contributors out of their share of royalties. Note the limitation on paying after termination of the administrator's agreement.

(c)   Administrator shall not make any Sales and Uses of the Compositions outside of the Licensed Territory nor shall it authorize others to do so.

Further prohibits any licensing outside the administrator's territory.

(d)   Administrator shall print at the bottom of the first page of any and all Printed Music published and distributed in the Licensed Territory an inscription bearing the proper copyright notice of the copyright owner. If Administrator fails to print or cause to be printed a proper copyright notice, then such edition of Printed Music shall be deemed unauthorized.

This gives proper attribution to the publisher on any printed music, dispelling confusion as to who the correct copyright owner is.

(e)   Without Publisher's express written consent, Administrator shall not print or otherwise indicate the names of any persons on Printed Music other than such names as Publisher designates or as may appear on the copies of Printed Music printed by or for Publisher, and the name of Administrator as the selling agent of Publisher in the Licensed Territory; provided, however, that Administrator may give the local lyric writer of any version of the Composition such credit as is customarily given local lyric writers.

This grants permission for the administrator to also be listed on printed music as well as the names of any local writers.

(f) (i)   Not later than thirty (30) days after the publication of Printed Music of any Composition, or release of a Cover Record in the Territory, Administrator shall so notify Publisher in writing and shall deliver to Publisher four (4) copies of each such edition of Printed Music or Cover Record.

> If the administrator licenses a printed version of the composition or secures a cover recording, copies must be sent to the publisher for their files.

(ii) Not later than thirty (30) days after initial telecast in the Territory of a television commercial that includes an approved Composition, Administrator shall deliver a copy of the commercial to Publisher via Internet transmission, VHS videocassette or DVD for Publisher's archives.

> While the publisher also wants a copy of any commercials, it might not be possible to secure from the sponsor until after the advertising campaign is finished, if at all.

(g) Administrator shall promptly register after delivery any and all of the Compositions with any and all of the mechanical rights societies and performing rights societies in the Licensed Territory.

> Clearly, one of the administrator's prime obligations.

(h) Administrator shall, to the extent necessary to protect Publisher's rights in the Compositions, the copyrights therein and any and all Similar Rights, in full compliance with all of the formalities of any applicable copyright law, the Berne Convention, the Universal Copyright Convention and any and all other applicable laws, treaties and conventions, in the name of Publisher or in such other name or names as Publisher may from time to time direct, imprint, or cause to be imprinted, on any and all copies of Printed Music, proper copyright and other notices and do all other acts necessary to obtain, preserve and protect Publisher's copyrights and Similar Rights in and to the Compositions. Administrator hereby acknowledges and agrees that any and all of its rights and licenses hereunder are subject to, and conditioned upon, its compliance with the notice provisions and other formalities of all applicable copyright laws, treaties and conventions or Similar Rights and that any act or omission by Administrator not in compliance therewith shall be without the authority of Publisher.

> It is part of an administrator's function to protect the copyrights under all relevant laws, treaties, etc. A failure to do so jeopardizes the owner's right in the copyright and the ability to enforce those rights in any territory.

(i) Arrangements of music and translations of lyrics of the Compositions shall be copyrighted in the name of the copyright owner (whose name Publisher shall supply) and shall be its sole and exclusive property free and clear of any and all royalty obligations or other restrictions.

(j) (i) Administrator shall have the right but not the obligation to enforce and protect, at its sole cost and expense, any and all rights in and to the Compositions in the Licensed Territory. If required by Publisher and subject to satisfactory agreement between the parties regarding expenses or other charges to be negotiated in good faith, Administrator shall take any appropriate legal or other proceedings in the Licensed Territory reasonably necessary to enforce and protect the copyright in the Compositions and Publisher agrees that it will give all reasonable assistance to Administrator in this respect.

To enforce the copyright, the administrator has the right, but not the obligation, to take whatever legal action they deem necessary and the publisher agrees to assist.

Administrator hereby acknowledges that it may not settle any such suit or proceeding without the express written consent of Publisher.

The administrator may not settle a matter without the publisher's consent, as any such settlement could potentially affect the publisher's rights in the compositions.

_____ percent (__%) of any sums recovered with respect to any such suit or proceeding, less reasonable legal fees and expenses (receipts for which such expenses shall be made available to the Publisher), shall be payable by Administrator to Publisher.

In the event of a successful settlement or legal proceeding, the administrator will be entitled to a share of the proceeds plus any reasonable legal fees they may have expended in the action.

If at any time Publisher shall require Administrator to institute any legal or other proceedings to enforce and protect any and all of the aforesaid rights and Administrator does not believe such proceedings are reasonably necessary to enforce and protect such rights and shall submit to Publisher documentation as Publisher may require supporting Administrator's position, then Publisher shall have the right to institute, at Publisher's sole expense, legal or other proceedings in Publisher's name and shall have the right to retain one hundred percent (100%) of all sums recovered with respect to any such proceeding. In such event, Administrator shall have no duty to institute such legal proceedings.

If the publisher wants the administrator to institute proceedings and the administrator declines to do so, the publisher may, at their expense, assume control over the action, but the administrator will not share in the proceeds.

(ii) Administrator shall give Publisher notice of any claim or action of a third party against Administrator and/or Publisher relating to a breach or alleged breach of Publisher's warranties, representations or agreements made under this agreement. Publisher shall have the right to defend such claim or action at its expense and with counsel of its choice. Administrator shall have the right to participate in the defense of such claim or action with counsel of its choice and at its expense.

This is the reverse of the paragraphs above. In this instance, a claim is being made **against** the composition, not on behalf of the composition, and the publisher and administrator have to defend against the claim.

(l)   Administrator shall collect and be responsible for the collection of all Income due and owing to Publisher from any and all Sales and Uses whatsoever of the Compositions in the Licensed Territory earned during the term or prior to commencement of the term, if available, as provided in this agreement

and shall use its best efforts to promote and procure Sales and Uses of the Compositions in the Licensed Territory and shall obtain the maximum payments for such Sales and Uses.

> It is the administrator's responsibility to collect all monies earned by the compositions, both before and during the term.

> The administrator shall use best efforts to exploit the compositions and to maximize the income from them.

9.   Warranties of Administrator. Administrator hereby represents and warrants to Publisher that:

> There are no impediments to the administrator conducting business.

(a)   It has not made, and shall not during the term of this agreement make, any assignment for the benefit of creditors; no bankruptcy or other proceeding based upon insolvency is pending or threatened against it; and it knows of no charges, actions, suits, proceedings, agreements or other impediments, actual or threatened, which would prevent or impair it from performing its duties hereunder.

(b)   It now is and shall remain during the term of this agreement a member in good standing of any and all performing rights societies and mechanical rights societies in the Licensed Territory; it is, and shall remain during the term of this agreement, entitled to the highest benefits available to a music publisher in the Licensed Territory from such performing rights societies and mechanical rights societies, and it knows no charge, actions, suits, proceedings or other impediments, actual or threatened, against it with respect to said societies which may prevent or otherwise impair it from performing its duties hereunder.

> It is crucial that the administrator be a member of the performing and mechanical rights societies and remain a member in good standing in order to collect the publisher's royalties.

(c)   It now is, and shall remain during the term of this agreement, an active music publisher as that term is commonly understood in the music publishing industry, and shall use its best efforts to exploit the rights granted to it hereunder and to collect the Income earned as a result of any and all Sales and Uses of the Compositions.

> The administrator is an active member of the music publishing community and shall perform all the functions of a music publisher in their territory.

10.   Percentages of Income Payable to Publisher.

(a)   Administrator shall pay to Publisher the following percentages of Income:

(i)   As the Publisher's share of Printed Music:

> Based on the wording ("Administrator shall pay to Publisher"), these percentages are the shares of income the publisher will receive, with the administrator retaining the balance. If the publisher is paid 80%, the administrator's fee is then 20%, or an "80/20" deal.

(A)   ____percent (__%) of the marked retail selling price of any copy of Printed Music in any and every form sold or otherwise distributed by Administrator, except that no payment shall be made by Administrator on a reasonable number of professional copies distributed without charge for promotional or professional exploitation.

This is for single sheet or "piano copies" of songs sold individually. The second part of the language is somewhat standard and allows the administrator to distribute a reasonable number of copies for promotional purposes without paying a royalty to the publisher.

(B)   A fraction of __percent (__%) of the marked retail selling price of each songbook or folio sold or otherwise distributed by Administrator, the numerator of which shall be the number of Compositions in such songbook or folio and the denominator of which shall be the total number of copyrighted compositions in such songbook or folio.

Songbooks and folios are collections of songs with multiple compositions. Here, the basis for payment is a *pro rata* share of the overall royalty, divided amongst all compositions in the folio. So if the royalty paid by the administrator is 10% of retail, and there are 10 songs, the effective rate for each of the publisher's songs is 1% of retail.

(C)   _____ percent (__%) of all other Income in connection with Printed Music.

(ii)   As Publisher's share of Mechanical Rights: _____ percent (__%) of all Income derived from any source whatever in connection with Sales and Uses of Mechanical Rights, except _____(%) in connection with Sales and Uses of Cover Records. Administrator shall pay shall pay the local lyric writer's share of mechanical income derived in respect of such a Cover Record solely from its _____ percent (__%) share of such Income.

For mechanical income from cover records (as defined above), the administrator would retain a higher share due to the extra work of the administrator to secure the cover, so the publisher's percentage would be lower. In the event that there is a payment to the local writer, the administrator makes that payment out of their share of the royalties.

(iii)   As Publisher's share which share shall be not less than 6/12 of the total performing fees of Performing Rights: _____ percent (__%) of the "publisher share" of all Income, including without limitation, Performing Rights with respect to Cover Records, derived from any source whatever in connection with Sales and Uses of Performing Rights.

For a U.S. administrator, this would be listed as 50%. In some countries, the publisher's share of performing rights is less than 6/12, so this language would need to be adjusted for that territory.

(iv)   As Publisher's share of Television Synchronization Rights: ____percent (__%) of all Income derived from any source whatever in connection with Sales and Uses of Television Synchronization Rights.

(v)   As Publisher's share of Motion Picture Synchronization Rights: ____percent (__%) of all Income derived from any source whatever in connection with Sales and Uses of Motion Picture Synchronization Rights.

(vi)   As Publisher's share of Videogram Synchronization Rights: _____percent (__%) of all Income derived from any source whatever in connection with Sales and Uses of Videogram Synchronization Rights.

(vii)   As Publisher's share of New Media Rights: _____percent (__%) of all Income derived from any source whatever in connection with Sales and Uses of New Media Rights.

(viii) (A)   If Administrator receives during or after the term of this agreement, from any source whatever, including local mechanical rights and/or performing rights societies, or record companies, a payment or other distribution of funds, special or regular, including without limiting the generality of the foregoing, increased royalty rates, bonus payments or rebates based upon or related, directly or indirectly, to the Sales and Uses of Performing or Mechanical Rights with respect to any of the Compositions, _____ percent (__%) of such payment or other distribution of funds.

> If there are special payments, bonus payments, or settlement payments made to the administrator that relate to the compositions under this agreement, the administrator will pay to the publisher the share listed here.

        (B)   If Administrator receives during or after the term of this agreement, from any source whatever, including local mechanical rights and/or performing rights societies, or record companies, a payment or other distribution of funds, special or regular, including without limiting the generality of the foregoing, increased royalty rates, bonus payments or rebates based upon or related, directly or indirectly, to unidentified or general funds, a fraction of _____percent (__%) of such payment or other distribution, the numerator of which shall be the Income received by Administrator from the source of such payment or other distribution which shall be attributable to the Compositions and the denominator of which shall be the total Income received by Administrator from the source of such payment or other distribution.

> The phrase "unidentified or general funds" refers to so-called "black box" income. If the administrator receives any unallocated income, they are required under this clause to allocate to the publisher a share of black box income in the ratio that the publisher's catalog compares with the total collected by the administrator. In other words, if the publisher's catalog generates 5% of the administrator's total earnings, they would receive 5% of the black box income, less the administrator's percentage of the fees under this agreement.

(b)   If Administrator (i) performs all the services required to be performed by it pursuant to the terms and provisions of this agreement and (ii) is not otherwise in default of any of the terms and provisions of this agreement, Administrator shall be entitled to retain the balance of the Income received by it for its services during the term of this agreement and for any and all other costs and expenses incurred by it.

If the administrator does everything required by the agreement, it gets to keep the percentage of income not given to the publisher.

11.   <u>Statements and Accountings.</u>

Semi-annual accountings, within 90 days of the end of each period.

(a)   Administrator hereby agrees to render accountings to Publisher on or before the first day of April for the period ending the immediately preceding December 31 and on or before the first day of October for the period ending the immediately preceding June 30th, together with payment of accrued royalties, if any, earned and due to Publisher during such preceding half-year. The parties hereby agree that time is of the essence with respect to the rendering of such statements and payments. All payments to be made hereunder shall be made by demand draft on a bank designated by Publisher; provided, however, that Publisher shall have the right, at any time or from time to time, to notify Administrator that it requires, subject to local law, the whole or any part of any payment due it to be paid in another manner, form or currency.

The rate of exchange shall be the rate in effect on the date such payment is due or the date such payment is made, whichever shall be more favorable to Publisher, if such payment is made after the due date.

Foreign publishers collect royalties in their local currencies, which then must be converted to U.S. dollars. This is called the "exchange rate," which can change on a daily basis. Therefore, the date of the exchange rate can alter the amount of money received by the publisher.

The parties hereby agree that taxes required to be withheld or to be paid upon earned Income in accordance with local law shall not be deducted from the amounts payable to Publisher unless Administrator shall deliver to Publisher a certificate of deduction and withholding, or some like certificate, and a copy of the governmental receipts establishing that such payments were made.

The administrator must prove that taxes are being withheld in order to deduct them from the publisher's income.

Publisher agrees to submit to Administrator all forms and declarations that are required to avoid double taxation, as permitted by treaty.

Similarly, there are forms that a U.S. publisher can obtain from the Internal Revenue Service that will reduce or eliminate foreign taxes.

If a local government shall not permit a payment to be made to Publisher, Administrator shall so notify Publisher immediately and Administrator shall, when so instructed by Publisher, deposit such payment to the account of Publisher in a local bank designated by Publisher.

Administrator shall pay Publisher simple interest at the rate of ten percent (10%) per annum with respect to Publisher's share of any Income, undisputed as to time and date due, which is not timely paid to Publisher hereunder, provided however that payments shall not be deemed late if delay is caused by exchange control or other governmental, legal or fiscal regulations or authorities, provided Administrator shall have timely requested all necessary consents. Publisher shall do all things reasonably necessary to assist Administrator in gaining such consents. Publisher shall not be barred or otherwise limited in any claim, action or proceeding against Administrator from claiming interest on any disputed portion of Publisher's share of Income.

Without limiting the generality of the foregoing, Publisher shall be entitled to claim interest at the rate of five percent (5%) per annum on any Income due Publisher resulting from any audit of Administrator's books and records.

(b)   All such statements and payments shall, if there shall be more than one country in the Licensed Territory, reflect Income separately for each such country. All such statements shall contain at least the following information:

(i)   the title of the Composition;

(ii)   the number of copies of Printed Music of each Composition sold;

(iii)   the identification number and number of copies of each phonorecord or DVD/videodisc/videocassette embodying a Composition sold;

(iv)   the source and amount of Income;

(v)   Publisher's share of Income;

(vi)   the period during which Income was earned.

If, for some reason, it is illegal to transfer money out of a country, the publisher may instruct the administrator to deposit any royalties owed into a local bank of the publisher's choosing.

If the administrator's payments are late, there is a 10% penalty charge unless caused by some legitimate local laws or regulations.

In the event of an audit (see paragraph (c) below), the administrator will pay the publisher 5% interest on any funds discovered and not previously paid as a result of the audit.

This paragraph states the requirements for the information required on each statement.

(c)   Publisher or its designated representative shall have the right during the term of this agreement and for a period of three (3) years thereafter to appoint an independent chartered accountant or a certified public accountant to audit the books and records of Administrator at any time and from time to time during the reasonable business hours of Administrator, but not more than once during any twelve (12) month period. The costs of any such audit shall be borne by Publisher; provided, however, that, if it is determined that Publisher shall have been underpaid by a sum equal to or exceeding five percent (5%) of the amount paid to Publisher for the audited period, any and all reasonable auditors' professional fees and expenses related to the audit shall be borne by Administrator.

Fairly standard audit language. Note that if the publisher finds a discrepancy of over 5% of the total money paid, the administrator is responsible for the costs of the audit.

12.   Termination.

(a)   If, during the term of this agreement, (i) any application, petition, suit or proceeding is filed or instituted by or against Administrator involving, concerning or relating to the general property rights of the Administrator or, (ii) a petition or proceeding in bankruptcy or insolvency or for the reorganization or liquidation is filed or instituted by or against Administrator, or (iii) a receiver, liquidator, assignee, or anyone occupying a like or similar position, is designated or appointed for, or takes charge of, the business or any of the assets of Administrator, or (iv) a deed of assignment of its property is executed by Administrator, or (v) any steps or proceedings are taken by or against Administrator, for, on behalf of, in the interest of or for the benefit of creditors or (vi) any right, interest, property or asset of Administrator is levied upon and sold in any action or proceeding or under any judgment, lien, order or decree, then, Publisher shall have the right to terminate this agreement.

The publisher may terminate this agreement upon events that negatively affect the administrator's ability to conduct business.

(b)   If, during the term of this agreement Publisher for any reason Publisher no longer owns and controls a Composition or Compositions, then Publisher shall have the right to terminate this agreement either in its entirety or only with respect to such Composition or Compositions.

Partial termination can occur with respect to any composition to which the publisher no longer has an interest.

(c)   If Publisher terminates this agreement, then with respect to Printed Music distributed by Administrator during the term of this agreement, Administrator shall, at Publisher's request:

(i)   Destroy any and all plates, negatives, and other material relating to such publication and all of Administrator's inventory of Printed Music and shall deliver to Publisher a certificate of destruction therefore; or

(ii)   Deliver to Publisher or its designee such plates, negatives, other material and Printed Music upon payment to Administrator of the actual scrap value of such plates, negatives, other material and Printed Music, together with shipping costs in respect thereof.

(iii)   Administrator shall furnish to Publisher or its designee an accurate inventory of such plates, negatives, other materials and Printed Music within thirty (30) days after termination of this agreement, and, within sixty (60) days after termination of this agreement, Publisher shall notify Administrator whether it wishes to exercise the option set forth in subparagraph (i) or (ii) above with respect to all or any portion of such plates, negatives, other material or Printed Music.

(d)   In addition to any and all of its other rights and remedies, in the event of a default by Administrator: (i) in making any payment as and when such payment shall become due or (ii) in keeping any accounts or in rendering any statement with respect to such accounts or (iii) in duly carrying out or otherwise performing or failing to perform any of the duties and obligations required to be performed by it pursuant to the terms and provisions of this agreement, then Publisher shall have the right to terminate this agreement if, on written notice to Administrator, Administrator shall not cure such default within thirty (30) days from receipt of the notice.

(e)   If _____ ceases active involvement in the management of Administrator for any reason, Publisher shall have the right to terminate this agreement.

This paragraph (c) applies to printed music distributed by the administrator, calling for destruction or delivery of elements needed for reproduction of the printed music.

In event of breach by the administrator, after giving the administrator a 30-day notice to cure, the publisher may terminate the agreement.

This is what is known as a "key man" clause. As many agreements of this type are based upon a relationship with a particular individual, if that individual leaves the company, the publisher has the right to terminate the agreement.

(f)   Publisher shall effect termination of this agreement by notice to Administrator, (the "Termination Notice") effective thirty (30) days after the date of the Termination Notice. If Publisher terminates this agreement, any and all rights and interests whatever acquired by Administrator and/or by other party by or through Administrator shall automatically cease, terminate and revert to Publisher. After the effective date of termination, Publisher or its designees solely and exclusively shall be entitled to receive and collect any and all monies thereafter accruing from any and all Sales and Uses of the Compositions in the Licensed Territory regardless of when earned,

Termination is valid 30 days after the publisher gives notice to the administrator, at which point the administrator no longer has any rights as previously granted under the agreement, including the right to collect any monies due to the publisher, with no post-term collection period.

provided however that such termination shall not affect the obligation of Administrator to make any payment to Publisher that Administrator may be obligated to make pursuant to this agreement.

The administrator still has the obligation to pay the publisher for any monies previously collected and undistributed.

Within thirty (30) days after the date of the Termination Notice Administrator shall deliver to Publisher or to Publisher's designee any and all information regarding the Compositions, including, without limiting the generality of the foregoing any and all copyrights, correspondence, statistical and financial information together with a copy of Administrator's database on a CD-Rom disc.

The administrator may not be able to supply the publisher's info from their database, as many programs do not segregate an administrator's multiple clients into separate databases.

13.   Miscellaneous.

(a)   All notices, statements and other communications hereunder shall be in writing and shall be sent by cablegram (or similar means of communication) or first class air-mail to the address first set forth above; if intended for Publisher, shall be addressed to it at the address first set forth above, attention _____, or to such other address of which Publisher shall have given notice to Administrator in the manner herein provided; if intended for Administrator shall be addressed to it, attention Managing Director or to such other address of which Administrator shall have given notice to Publisher in a manner herein provided.

(b)   This agreement shall be binding upon and inure to the benefit of the parties hereto, their respective heirs, administrators, executors, successors and assigns; provided,

Any assignees or successors to the parties are bound by the terms of this agreement.

however, that, without the express written consent of Publisher, the rights and obligations of Administrator may not be transferred, assigned, licensed, delegated or otherwise conveyed to any person, firm or corporation.

The administrator may not assign this agreement with the consent of the publisher, except …

Notwithstanding the foregoing, Administrator shall have the right, without Publisher's prior, written consent to license rights hereunder to agents, licensees or subpublishers within the Licensed Territory in the normal course of business, subject to all the terms and conditions herein contained; provided, however, that:

(i)   Publisher's share of fees and royalties shall be calculated and payable on Income earned at the source in each separate country or territory of the Licensed Territory, (ii) Administrator shall be entitled to its share of Income only on Income earned at the source and shall not be entitled to any additional Income, deductions, commissions or other payments for so-called "sub-subpublishing" and (iii) Administrator shall remain primarily liable to Publisher for all its obligations to Publisher hereunder, including without limitation all payments due Publisher.

No transfer or license of any of Administrator's rights, as provided in the immediately preceding sentence, shall relieve Administrator of any liability for failure by Administrator or by any of its subpublishers, agents or licensees to comply with all of the duties and obligations to be performed by Administrator hereunder.

However, Publisher shall have the right to initiate claims or actions directly against any of Administrator's subpublishers, agents or licensees that exercise rights granted to Administrator hereunder from, through or under Administrator, as provided in subparagraph 13(c), in addition to all its rights and remedies against Administrator.

(c)   This agreement shall be governed by, and construed in accordance with, the laws of the State of California, United States of America as though it were to be performed entirely therein. The parties hereby agree to submit any disputes, claims or actions arising under this agreement exclusively to the jurisdiction of the appropriate state or federal courts of California, and hereby grant exclusive jurisdiction to such courts. Both parties agree that service of process may among other methods be made by delivering or mailing the same via registered or certified mail, return receipt requested, addressed to the other party at its last known address and that time to respond to such process shall be thirty (30) days from the date of receipt of process. Any such delivery or mail service shall be deemed to have the same effect as personal service within the State of California.

The administrator may assign certain rights in the normal course of business to third parties (like PROs, mechanical rights societies, or sub-publishers) without consent, and they shall be subject to the terms of this agreement.

The publisher's income shall be calculated "at source" without additional administration fees being deducted other than what is stated in this agreement. No "double dipping" by sub-publishers of the administrator in addition to the administrator's fees.

The administrator is primarily liable for any actions by its licensees, agents, or assigns.

The publisher may also bring actions directly against said licensees, agents, or assigns.

This establishes which courts have jurisdiction and which laws shall be applied in the event of litigation. For a U.S. publisher, jurisdiction in the U.S. is always preferred.

(d)   No waiver by either party of any breach of this agreement shall be deemed to be a waiver of any preceding or succeeding breach thereof whether similar or dissimilar.

(e)   The rights herein granted to Administrator are granted subject to the rights, if any, now or hereafter granted, authorized or permitted by or through the Publisher, or any successor in interest to ASCAP, BMI, SESAC or any other bona fide third party organization in the United States of America that exercises or licenses rights of Performing Rights in musical compositions, numbers or works

(f)   In any suit, action or proceeding between the parties hereto arising out of or in connection with this agreement which results in final adjudication, the party which shall prevail shall be entitled to recover reasonable attorney's fees and reasonable travel costs and any other costs permitted by law.

> In the event of a lawsuit, the party that loses has to pay the winner's attorney fees and costs. This is often a major deterrent to litigation but is not contained in all agreements. Some agreements have language calling for binding arbitration in the event of a dispute, rather than bringing suit in a court of law.

(g)   All prior or contemporaneous agreements, contracts, promises, representations and statements, if any, between the parties hereto or their predecessors-in-interest or their representatives are merged into and superseded by this agreement and this agreement shall constitute the entire agreement between them.

> This agreement takes the place of any previous oral or written agreements between the parties.

This agreement constitutes the entire understanding between the parties and the terms hereof cannot be modified, amended, extended or waived except by an instrument in writing signed by the party to be charged and only to the extent therein set forth.

> Any changes in the terms of this agreement must be in writing and signed by the parties.

If any provision hereof shall for any reason be illegal or unenforceable, then such illegality or unenforceability shall not affect the validity of the remaining provisions hereof and the illegal or unenforceable provision shall be deemed modified to the minimum extent necessary to render it legal and enforceable.

> If any portion of the agreement is found invalid, the remaining portions remain in full force and effect.

IN WITNESS WHEREOF, the parties hereto have executed this agreement the day and year first above written.

(Publisher)

By: _____

Name: _____

Its: _____
An authorized signatory

(Administration)

By: _____

Name: _____

Its: _____
An authorized signatory

CHAPTER 8

COMPOSER AGREEMENTS

The agreement between an audio-visual production company and a composer sets out the basic relationship, duties and obligations of each party. Similar to a songwriter/publisher agreement, but with some key differences (as discussed below), it usually assigns complete ownership and control of the music created to the producer, subject to the composer sharing in the royalties earned from exploitation of the music. These royalties would come from the music used within the context of the production and by exploitation of the music by the producer licensing it to others.

Basic Terms

The services to be provided by the composer should be spelled out completely. In some cases, the composer will only create the music for the production and leave it to others to orchestrate, conduct, produce, and record the music. Usually, however, the composer will perform all of these functions, under the direction of and in consultation with the producer. Included in these services may be producing the soundtrack album from a motion picture.

As music is usually done in post-production, the composer's services generally begin after the principal photography is complete unless there are scenes in the production where the music is an integral part, such as a concert or nightclub scene in which singers or musicians are on camera. As such, the term can usually be clearly defined from the date of "spotting" the picture (reviewing the production with the producer and director to determine where and what kind of music will be used) until the music is dubbed in to the final edited version. In cases where music must be pre-recorded for use in the film, the term may be designated to cover both situations.

Compensation for a composer is determined by the budget of the film and the composer's stature in the industry. Fees range from zero to $1,000,000.00, depending on the situation. This is merely a creative fee and does not cover the costs of recording, such as studio time, engineers and mixers, rental of recording equipment, and recording media. The costs of third party musicians, orchestrators, instrument cartage, and copyists as well as studio time and engineers are paid by the producer. Payments to the composer are usually staggered and triggered by certain events in the composing and recording process.

Sometimes, however, a composer will be asked to deliver a "package deal," in which the composer assumes all responsibility for payments to musicians, copyists, orchestrators, studio time, instrument cartage and rentals, and recording media. Any overages are the responsibility of the composer and any money not spent is their compensation. This is more common with electronic scores consisting primarily of synthesizers, since many composers have their own equipment and recording facilities.

If the composer is required by the producer to travel outside their local area in order to record the music, they are usually given no less than business class airfare, hotel and ground transportation, and a weekly per diem to cover their expenses. Payment for travel days, "off" days, and overtime are usually the subject of negotiation.

Whatever the nature of compensation, the composer's fees include any payments they might receive as a result of their services being under the jurisdiction of the American Federation of Musicians (AFM). It is important to note that composers are not unionized, but may fall under AFM jurisdiction if they participate as an orchestrator, arranger, or instrumental performer on their compositions.

Upon completion of the composer's duties, the producer's only responsibility is to make the appropriate payments. He is under no obligation to actually utilize the music in the production and has the complete right to edit or cut the music without the consent of the composer. More than one music score has been dumped by the producer and a new one created instead.

Perhaps the most important part of the typical composer agreement is the section whereby the parties agree that the music created is deemed to be a work made for hire. Section 101 of the Copyright Act of 1976 (17 U.S.C. 101) defines a "work made for hire" as:

(1) a work prepared by an employee within the scope of his or her employment; or

(2) a work specially ordered or commissioned for use as a contribution to a collective work, **as a part of a motion picture or other audiovisual work** . . . if the parties expressly agree in a **written instrument** signed by them that the work shall be considered a work made for hire.

Note that a work made for hire must be in writing. This gives the producer complete control and ownership of the music and recordings created and all associated elements, such as musical scores, instrumental parts, outtakes, etc. This allows the producer to use the music in any way he sees fit, including exploiting the music in the production in any and all media now known or hereafter devised, including trailers, advertisements, and other types of promotions. It also eliminates the reversion of any ownership rights to the composer, as might be the situation in the case of a typical songwriter agreement. In addition, the producer may employ others to change, modify, or re-write the music to meet his needs in the event that the composer fails to do so. In many cases, the producer will require language allowing him to use the music in prequels, sequels, television programs based upon the film, or in any other production produced by this producer at no additional fee for the composer.

The producer has all the powers of a music publisher, such as licensing of the music to third parties and collecting most types of royalties. He may also assign his rights to an actual music publishing company to administer, subject to the composer receiving their share of royalties.

There may be occasions, however, in which the producer will allow the composer to keep all or part of the publishing of the music. This is usually done on a low-budget project in lieu of compensation to the composer. This allows the composer to receive all or part of the publisher's share of royalties from all sources and to exploit the music in other ways. In cases where the composer retains one hundred percent (100%) of the copyright in the music, the agreement may be in the form of a broadly worded license from composer to producer, giving the producer the right to use the music in the film in any and all media, now known or hereafter devised, including all promotional aspects of the film. In this situation, however, the producer may not use the music for any other project.

Certain restrictions may be placed on the future use of the music so as not to compete with the producer's film. Irrespective, however, the composer is entitled to collect the "writer's share" of public performance royalties from their performing rights organizations (ASCAP, BMI or SESAC) directly, without any interference by the producer. **Please note that the right of the composer to collect from their PRO is by custom and practice and must be stated in the contract, as it is not a right guaranteed by copyright and there is no mention of a composer's share of royalties in The Copyright Act.**

If a soundtrack album from the film is released, the composer would normally be entitled to mechanical royalties (usually at a controlled composition rate) for the use of their music or their services in connection with creating the music. If his underscore is included, the composer is considered the artist and record producer and would additionally receive a royalty based upon the retail sales price of the album as well as mechanical royalties from the publisher. If there is another artist on a track produced by the composer, only a record producer royalty would be payable.

The composer's soundtrack royalties would be subject to the same terms and deductions that the producer receives from the record company. In addition, no royalties would be payable to the composer until a negotiated portion of the recording costs and "conversion" costs are recouped. Conversion costs are those incurred in transforming the music recorded for the production into a format suitable for release on the soundtrack album. This usually involves editing, remixing, any studio costs for either, and any additional talent payments.

The composer must warrant that the music created for the film is original and indemnify the producer against any costs incurred by the use of the music, including any claims based upon a breach by the composer of these warranties. See the section below for a more detailed discussion on warranties and indemnification.

If the composer has a loanout company—i.e., a composer-owned corporation that employs them for these types of services—the agreement is actually between the producer and the lending company. As such, it is important to have a letter of inducement directly from the composer to the producer. This letter states that the composer agrees to abide by all conditions of the composer agreement, will look solely to the lender for compensation, and that if the lender should cease to exist, the composer will become personally responsible for all obligations.

The agreement also includes a provision that, in the event of a breach by the producer, the composer's remedies are limited to damages at law and not equitable relief in the form of an injunction inhibiting or preventing the exhibition or distribution of the project. This clause is crucial because it would be disastrous to the producer for a composer paid $200,000.00 to be able to enjoin the release of a $50,000,000.00 movie.

The Certificate of Authorship reiterates the "work made for hire" language and also waives all moral rights.

Lastly, there should be a schedule of royalties to be paid to the composer in the event that the music is exploited by licensing its use to a third party. These royalty provisions are similar in nature to those between a songwriter and a music publisher and define the various types of exploitation and the composer's share of each source of income. Since the producer/publisher collects all license fees and royalties (except the composer's share of public performance royalties, which are paid directly to the composer by their performing rights society), there is also an accounting provision that states how these royalties are to be paid and an audit provision on the composer's behalf.

Composer agreements can range from 4 to 20 pages but, for the protection of both parties, all of them should contain the basic terms listed above. As these are legally binding agreements, the parties are encouraged to engage competent legal counsel before entering into this type of agreement.

Warranties and Indemnification

One of the most glossed over, but legally important, clauses in a composer agreement for television or film is the warranty and indemnification clause. In layman's terms, the most crucial parts of this clause are that this is a guarantee by the composer to the producer that the music is original and that the composer will compensate the producer against any claims that it isn't. It makes sense for the producer to get protection for any acts by the composer that result in claims against the producer, but whether the composer should be liable if they don't actually do anything wrong is the focus of most negotiations regarding this clause.

While some agreements are better and some worse, a typical clause reads like this:

> "Composer hereby warrants, covenants and represents to Producer that it is the sole writer, creator and composer of the Score submitted to Producer hereunder, that the Score is original and does not (in whole or in part) infringe upon the copyrights, proprietary rights or any other rights of any third party or entity; that Composer has the full right, power and authority to enter into this Agreement and shall at all times have the full right, power and authority to transfer to Producer all rights to the Score, free and clear of any claim, lien or encumbrance by any third party; that Composer knows of no adverse claim or litigation by any third party; and that Composer has not made and will not make any use (or allow any use) of the Score which violate the terms of this Agreement or infringes upon Producer's exclusive rights to exploit the Score. Composer agrees to hold Producer (and its parent, subsidiary and/or affiliated companies) harmless from all liability for any breach or alleged breach of the representations and warranties herein and to fully indemnify Producer, its shareholders, officers, directors and employees and its parent subsidiary and/or affiliated companies, successors and licensees and assignees, from any and all losses, penalties, damages and/or expense, including attorney's fees, incurred as a result thereof."

While this boilerplate language taken as a whole can be quite complicated, when broken down, it clearly states what the responsibilities of the composer are to the producer and how the composer is financially responsible in the event of certain types of problems. Let's look at this clause phrase by phrase:

"Composer hereby warrants, covenants and represents to Producer" — this sets out the basic guarantees from the composer to the producer of all that follows in this paragraph;

"that it is the sole writer, creator and composer of the Score submitted to Producer hereunder" — the producer is hiring a particular composer and wants to make sure that the person hired is the person actually writing the score. If there is more than one composer that is a formal party to the agreement, they are listed at the top of the agreement with the language "Party A and Party B, (hereafter jointly known as 'Composer')". Although, in reality, the composer may hire others (credited or uncredited) to assist them in the writing, this makes the composer responsible for the actions of others under his direction. Often, if a composer does hire others, having the other composers sign a Certificate of Authorship will usually comply with this clause;

"that the Score is original and does not (in whole or in part) infringe upon the copyrights, proprietary rights or any other rights of any third party or entity;" — the desire of the producer to have an original score is based upon several things. First, one of the reasons for hiring a composer in the first place is to have a score that is original and unique to their film—that's why the composer gets the big bucks! Second, they want to be able to collect the revenue generated by the score. Third, and most important, they want to make sure that the music in their film is not already owned by some third party, which would require permission and a fee to that third party and would probably also include some restrictions on how the producer can use the music. Using music owned by third parties can be not only expensive, but using it without permission can cause the distribution or broadcast of the film to be stopped. Sometimes, a modification of this clause excludes from this representation music in the public domain and/or music specifically requested by the producer;

"that Composer has the full right, power and authority to enter into this Agreement" — this means that the composer has no other legal obligations (such as an exclusive publishing or recording agreement, where his services are already promised to another party) that would prevent him from performing the terms of the agreement;

"and shall at all times have the full right, power and authority to transfer to Producer all rights to the Score, free and clear of any claim, lien or encumbrance by any third party; that Composer knows of no adverse claim or litigation by any third party;" — since most scores are works made for hire with the producer owning all rights to the music, the producer wants to make sure that he is actually getting all rights, without the possibility of any claims by an unknown third party. And, since most producers are not musicologists, it is the composer who is in the best position to know if any of the music delivered isn't original and would infringe on someone else's copyright;

"and that Composer has not made and will not make any use (or allow any use) of the Score which violate the terms of this Agreement, or infringes upon Producer's exclusive rights to exploit the Score." — since the producer will exclusively own the score (both compositions and recordings), they want to make sure that the composer has not granted any rights to any third parties in violation of this exclusive ownership;

"Composer agrees to hold Producer (and its parent, subsidiary and/or affiliated companies) harmless" — the composer not only makes these guarantees to the producer who hired him, but to all their affiliated companies, such as the studio, network, other broadcasters, etc. who might be sued in the event of a problem. Remember, those whose pockets are deeper are more likely the target of any claims;

"from all liability for any breach or alleged breach of the representations and warranties herein" — this is one of the most dangerous clauses for composers. It not only makes the composer liable for an actual breach of the agreement but for an alleged breach, which means that even if the composer didn't do anything wrong to breach the agreement, in the event of a claim, the composer is still liable for the costs listed in the next phrase;

"and to fully indemnify Producer, its shareholders, officers, directors and employees and its parent subsidiary and/or affiliated companies, successors and licensees and assignees," – there are those deep pockets again, basically everyone in the potential chain of infringement;

"from any and all losses, penalties, damages and/or expense, including attorney's fees, incurred as a result thereof." — a composer could be liable for a potentially long list of costs, most of which are out of his control.

The liability for an alleged breach is the main sticking point of these clauses. If, in fact, a composer breaches his warranty of originality, he should be responsible for the consequences. But what about when a claim of infringement is made that is ultimately defeated? The composer has lived up to the terms of his warranty but still may be responsible for the costs of defending the claim.

In some agreements, the burden of defending the claim falls on the composer and makes him hire an attorney to argue on behalf of the producer's copyright at his own expense. Given the relative financial backing of the parties, this would seem to be inappropriate. Other clauses give the composer the opportunity (but not the obligation) to participate in the defense of the claim at his own expense.

When representing composers, an effort should be made to eliminate the "alleged breach" portion of the agreement, making the composer liable only if there is an actual breach of the agreement. Sometimes, if this isn't possible, the composer can try to modify the agreement so that the composer is liable for costs incurred for any breach or claim of breach "adjudicated by a court of competent jurisdiction or settled with the composer's consent, not to be unreasonably withheld." This allows the composer to have a say in whether a frivolous claim might be settled at a lesser cost than having to litigate it.

Common Misconceptions in Composer Agreements

In negotiating composer agreements for motion picture and television projects, there are several areas that are frequently misunderstood by both sides to the transaction. While there are many clauses in a composer agreement that can be interpreted incorrectly by someone not familiar with the language, the areas to be discussed in this article are more conceptual in nature.

The first of these areas is the legal and practical significance of a work made for hire.

Note the language in section (2) of Section 101 of the Copyright Act (cited above) that requires that there be something signed by the parties expressly stating the work-made-for-hire status of the material. Some production companies issue a document solely for this purpose called a Certificate of Authorship, expressly stating that the material is created by the composer pursuant to an employment agreement and that the work is specially ordered by the producer. This language, when signed by the parties, meets the requirements of the statute, even without a long-form composer agreement.

Under this clause, the employer is technically considered the "author" for purposes of copyright. In most composer agreements, the Certificate of Authorship states exactly that, language that frequently upsets composers because they don't understand the legal significance of it. This does not mean to imply that the employer's name will be listed on the music cue sheet or in the credits of the film (which have nothing to do with ownership or legal authorship) but that, since copyright protection commences upon creation and fixing in a tangible form, the producer wants to be considered the originator of the work.

This is important to the producer because the form of authorship has bearing on the ownership of the copyright in terms of length of the protection granted and any potential terminations or reversions. For example, the general term of copyright in the United States for works created after 1978 is life of the author plus 70 years (thank you, Congress!). The author has the right to terminate an assignment of rights to a third party (such as a songwriter agreement with a publisher) between 35 and 40 years from creation and regain their rights in the work.

For works made for hire, however, the term is now 95 years from publication and there is **no right of termination**. The employer has the ownership rights for the full term of copyright.

The reason that the terms contained in the Certificate of Authorship are created as part of a separate document is that the copyright owner, when registering the copyright, has to indicate how they acquired ownership of the material. Rather than filing the entire composer agreement, they can merely attach the (usually) one page Certificate of Authorship as evidence.

Ownership by the producer does not mean, however, that there may not be continuing obligations to the composer. By industry custom and practice, the composer shares in any revenues earned from the music, even if created as a work made for hire. While there are a few companies who do not follow this custom due to a conscious business practice (a subject too expansive to discuss in this book), many producers mistakenly believe that, just because the music is a work made for hire, their ownership means that the composer is not entitled to any future revenue.

In conversations with these producers, the dialogue usually goes something like this:

SW: "The contract needs to have a clause for standard composer royalties."

PROD: "What royalties? We own the music."

SW: "Yes, but the composer shares in the revenue generated by the music."

PROD: "What revenue? We own the music."

This goes on for some time, until the producers can be convinced that ownership means control over the use of the music, not an exclusion of royalties to the composer. Some producers, although familiar with the terms "ASCAP" and "BMI," don't really know what they are and are unaware of the various sources of income that the music in their programs can generate. All they seem to know is that they need to own the music.

Sometimes, composers want to believe that the music they create for a particular project can only be used in connection with that project. Generally speaking, however, the owners of the music can use it any way they choose without any further compensation to the composer. This includes the use of the music in other productions created by the producer. While the composer would still be entitled to the writer's share of any performance income generated from these other productions, there would generally not be any out-of-pocket payments from the producer to the composer. As with many other aspects of these agreements, this point is a negotiable one but an area in which most composers, unless they have some leverage, will not succeed.

The use of the words "piece of the publishing" is another widespread misconception. Sometimes, as part of the negotiation, especially for low-budget films where there is not much money (if any) for composing a score, the composer will ask for a "piece of the publishing." What does this really mean? To knowledgeable parties, this means that, in addition to the traditional writer's share of music publishing income, the composer will also share in the publisher's share of the income stream. This might mean co-ownership of the material or merely being a participant in the publisher's royalty stream without any ownership. In either case, the composer will earn more than the usual 50% writer's share of income.

Unfortunately, often a producer will misinterpret this as the composer receiving a portion of any music publishing income, including the traditional 50% writer's share. So when a composer asks for

50% of the publishing, the producer may believe that this only represents the writer's share of any royalties. In fact, however, what is meant by the composer is that he gets the writer's share plus 50% of the publisher's share, for a total of 75% of the revenue.

Too often, there are no written agreements, or even deal memos, until the project is finished. It is at this time, unfortunately, that the parties find that there are substantial differences in their understandings of the deal in question. At this point, crucial negotiating leverage has been lost by both sides and business concerns might interfere with the relationship developed in the creative phase of the project.

Another area that requires clarity is the desires of the producer to have the composer re-score portions of the picture because of some creative or technical problem. Often, there will be language stating that the producer shall have the right to require the composer to make such changes, modifications, or additions to the score. Obviously, this is open to potential abuse, so there should be some language limiting the amount of re-scoring covered under the original or provisions specifying how to compensate the composer for the additional work. This is especially important when the composer is working on a package deal, in which he is responsible for all costs associated with production of the music.

For low-budget projects, it may be possible for the composer to retain ownership of the copyright in the score in exchange for the reduced fees that most low-budget films can offer. In this case, the composer **licenses** the score to the producer for use in the film and all uses related to the film, such as trailers and promos. The composer is then free to license this music to another party and earn additional income from the score, although the producer may want to restrict licensing to a third party for a period of time.

While all of these issues allow for the "Attorney's Full Employment Act," a basic understanding of the potential pitfalls can eliminate a host of problems for both sides to the transaction. And, as an attorney, I am sure I am not alone when I say that I would rather be able to navigate around these land mines for my clients before they blow up in everyone's faces and turn a flourishing creative relationship into a bad working situation for all involved.

SHORT FORM COMPOSER AGREEMENT

This is a short agreement that can be used by composers or production companies that has most of the key deal points but is not as extensive as the long form agreement shown later in this chapter.

AGREEMENT BETWEEN _____ ("Producer") AND _____ ("Composer") RE: THE MUSIC UNDERSCORE FOR THE MOTION PICTURE _____ ("Film")

> Recitals of the parties and the name of the project.

1.   SERVICES: Composer shall compose, record, produce and deliver approximately _____ minutes of Original Music Score for the Film (the "Score"), subject to the creative decisions of the Producer and Composer during the scoring process.

> This language would usually be used for an electronic score, in which the composer performs most of the services themselves. It sets out the requirement of how much music is expected to be delivered for the film.

Composer shall also attend the Film's mix, as required by Producer.

> The composer is often required to attend the final mix of the film in order to make sure that all the audio elements he delivers match the visuals of the film. Last-minute adjustments may also be required at this time.

Composer's services shall be rendered on a non-exclusive basis, provided that the Producer and Composer agree that the Composer's services for third parties will not materially interfere with the Composer's services for Producer.

> As it is not uncommon for a composer to be working on more than one project at a time, their services are non-exclusive to this producer. However, the agreement states that services for another project will not interfere with the composer's services on this project.

It is the intent hereof that the Composer will begin composing the Score as soon as the locked and final video version is delivered to him, and that the completed Score for the Film will be delivered, in the format specified by Producer, within _____ days of obtaining the locked and final video version.

> The composer needs a final "locked" cut of the film to match the music to the picture. This clause specifies how much time after receipt of a locked picture the composer has to deliver the score.

2.   PACKAGE FEE: $_____. The Package Fee shall include all costs for writing, recording and delivering the Score, including all costs for the electronic score.

> In an agreement for a package fee, all costs (except those listed below) are the responsibility of the composer. Any money not spent is theirs to keep, any overages come out of their pocket. For beginning composers, a package fee can be a challenge, as they might not have the experience to manage costs properly.

However, the following costs are in addition to, and excluded from, the Package Fee:

> Exclusions from the package fee, to be paid by the producers of the film.

a. Third-party live musicians specifically requested by Producer in writing and costs related thereto, including, but not limited to new use, re-use and residuals, if any;

> If the producer wants specific musicians other than the electronic and acoustic instruments played by the composer, the producer should be responsible for the costs. In some cases, the agreement will state that the composer is responsible for up to X number of live musicians as part of the package but in most cases, if the producer wants (hypothetically) a marching band, the composer should not have to absorb these costs.

b. Licensing and clearance of music not composed by Composer

> The costs of clearing and licensing outside music not created by the composer should be the responsibility of the producer, as they have control over the use of these outside songs, not the composer.

c. Actual rescoring and rerecording costs (i.e., re-recording required for creative reasons outside the control of Composer and after delivery and acceptance of the Score by the Producer);

> If the producer wants some re-scoring for either creative or technical reasons after acceptance of the score, the composer should not have to rescore or re-record at their own expense.

d. Music editor and music editing costs; and

> Usually, a music editor will be engaged by the producer to make sure that the music matches up with the picture or edit it to match. For very low-budget films, the composer may be asked to deliver a fully edited score that syncs up to the picture, thereby functioning as the *de facto* music editor.

e. Vocalists and lyricists

> If the producer wishes to have songs written and performed for the film, there are extra costs for a lyricist or vocalist(s) that the producer should be willing to pay for, as the use of these parties is entirely at the producer's discretion.

3. PAYMENT SCHEDULE: 50% due immediately upon execution of this contract; 50% due upon Composer's delivery, and Producers approval, of the finished Score on or about _____. Time is of the essence to the delivery of the Score.

> Payment is made to the composer one-half up front and one-half upon delivery and acceptance of the score.

4.   SCREEN CREDIT: If the Composer's Score is used, the Composer shall receive screen credit in the main titles of the Film, to read: Original Score by _____.

For young composers, as well as established writers, a screen credit is very important to their career. Here, the credit will be listed in the main titles of the film, along with the stars, the writer, and the director. Sometimes there is language stating that the credit will read "substantially as follows" so as not to cause a breach of the agreement by the producer for minor changes in the wording.

5.   SOUNDTRACK ALBUM: In the event that any of the Composer's Score is included on a Soundtrack Album from the Film, the Composer and Producer shall negotiate in good faith for any artist and/or producer royalties to be paid to Composer from said Soundtrack Album.

Although soundtrack albums of underscore are rare, it is possible that a score album could be created, or that a portion of the score could be included in a soundtrack album that features mostly songs from the film. This clause provides for good faith negotiations between the parties for royalties to be paid to the composer for his services as artist and producer of the tracks containing their music.

If fifty percent (50%) or more of the Score is on a Soundtrack Album from the Film, Composer shall receive credit on the front cover, to read: Music by _____, Produced by _____.

Credit to the composer is also important on a soundtrack album.

6.   PAID ADVERTISING: Composer to receive credit in any advertising that includes the so-called "billing block". Composer understands that there will be no injunctive relief if there is any error in the accorded credit, and that Producer has the final decision as to all other credit matters. However, Producer shall employ best efforts to remedy such an error on a prospective basis.

The "billing block" is the list of credits usually found in newspaper ads or on posters for the film and lists all the key contributors to the film. The second sentence states that a failure to accord such credit will not be breach subject to injunctive relief and that the producer will attempt to rectify the error.

7.   OWNERSHIP OF SCORE: Composer hereby acknowledges and agrees that the Score and all other results and proceeds of Composer's services (collectively, "Work") hereunder have been specially ordered or commissioned by Producer for use as part of the Picture, that the Score shall constitute a "work-made-for-hire" as defined in the United States Copyright Act of 1976, that Producer shall be the author of said work-made-for-hire and the owner of all rights in and to the Work, in accordance with the terms and conditions herein contained, including, without limitation, the copyrights therein and thereto, throughout the universe in perpetuity.

The language regarding ownership meets the requirements of the Copyright Act for work made for hire—i.e., requested by the producer as part of a collective work, and that the producer is deemed the author under copyright—so there can be no termination of the producer's ownership by composer.

8.   RIGHTS OF PRODUCER: Producer to have the perpetual, irrevocable right to use the Score in connection with any and all exploitation of the Film in all media, including advertising and promotion of the Film.

Even though the producer is the owner of the score, this clarifies his rights to use the score in any way in connection with the film. In all media, including any promotion of the film.

9.   MUSIC PUBLISHING ROYALTIES:

a.   Composer shall be entitled to collect the "writer's share" of public performance royalties (as that term is commonly used in the music industry) directly from a public performance society that makes a separate distribution of said royalties to composers and publishers. In order to effectuate this, Producer shall prepare a music cue sheet (with a copy to Composer) and Composer's name shall be listed on the music cue sheet for the program as "composer".

This grants to the composer the right to collect the writer's share of income from their PRO. Remember that this right is mentioned in the Copyright Act and must be spelled out in the agreement.

b.   In addition, on a semi-annual basis, Producer, or its music publishing designee, shall pay to Composer the following songwriter royalties:

i.   Ten cents ($0.10) per copy for each piano copy of the Score;

ii.   Twelve and one-half percent (12 1/2%) of the wholesale selling price for each printed copy of the Score printed, published and sold in the United States & Canada by Producer or its licensees;

iii.   Fifty percent (50%) of all net sums received from exploitation in the United States & Canada by Producer or its licensees;

iv.   Fifty percent (50%) of all net sums received from exploitation outside the United States & Canada by Producer or its licensees; and

v.   In the event that Producer receives a distribution of public performance income that includes both the writer's and publisher's share, 50% of all net sums received.

Similar to a songwriter agreement, this clause sets out the share of music publishing income to be paid by the producer (or their designee) to the composer. Sometimes, there is an umbrella clause stating that composer gets 50% of everything received by producer from all sources except for the publisher's share of performance royalties.

10.   PERFORMING RIGHTS SOCIETY: Composer hereby acknowledges that he is a member of _____.

In order for the producer to register the cues and prepare a music cue sheet, the composer must list their performing rights organization. The producer must have a publishing company set up with the same PRO as the composer.

11.   NOTICES AND PAYMENTS: All Composer's monies and correspondence to be directed to:

_____

_____

_____

A simple notice provision with contact information for the composer.

12.   WARRANTIES AND REPRESENTATIONS: Composer hereby
makes customary representations and warranties as to the originality
of the Score, that the Score violates no rights of any third party, that
there will be no liens or encumbrances on the Score, and that the
Producer will be free to use the Score in the Film and the exploitation
thereof.

A simplified version of a complicated clause.

If the above is correct, please sign below. Once fully signed, this will constitute our agreement.

APPROVED AND ACCEPTED:

_____
Composer

Dated: _____

The agreement must be signed by both parties to be an effective contract.

_____
Producer

Dated: _____

COMPOSER LICENSING AGREEMENT

This agreement is slightly different from the previous agreement, as in this case, the composer retains ownership of the music and licenses it to the producer for all uses connected to the film.

AGREEMENT   BETWEEN   _____
("Producer")   AND   _____   ("Composer")
RE: THE MUSIC UNDERSCORE FOR THE MOTION PICTURE
_____ ("Film")

Recitals of the parties and the name of the project.

1.   SERVICES: Composer shall compose, record, produce and deliver approximately _____ minutes of Original Music Score for the Film (the Score), subject to the creative decisions of the Producer and Composer during the scoring process.

This language would usually be used for an electronic score, in which the composer performs most of the services themselves. It sets out the requirement of how much music is expected to be delivered for the film.

Composer shall also attend the Film's mix, as required by Producer.

The composer is often required to attend the final mix of the film in order to make sure that all the audio elements he delivers match the visuals of the film. Last minute adjustments may also be required at this time.

Composer's services shall be rendered on a non-exclusive basis, provided that the Producer and Composer agree that the Composer's services for third parties will not materially interfere with the Composer's services for Producer.

As it is not uncommon for a composer to be working on more than one project at a time, their services are non-exclusive to this producer. However, the agreement states that services for another project will not interfere with the composer's services on this project.

It is the intent hereof that the Composer will begin composing the Score as soon as the locked and final video version is delivered to him, and that the completed Score for the Film will be delivered, in the format specified by Producer, within _____ days of obtaining the locked and final video version.

The composer needs a final "locked" cut of the film to match the music to the picture. This clause specifies how much time after receipt of a locked picture the composer has to deliver the score.

2.   PACKAGE FEE: $_____. The Package Fee shall include all costs for writing, recording and delivering the Score, including all costs for the electronic score.

In an agreement for a package fee, all costs (except those listed below) are the responsibility of the composer. Any money not spent is theirs to keep, any overages come out of their pocket. For beginning composers, a package fee can be a challenge, as they might not have the experience to manage costs properly.

However, the following costs are in addition to, and excluded from, the Package Fee:

Exclusions from the package fee, to be paid by the producers of the film.

a.   Thirdparty live musicians specifically requested by Producer in writing and costs related thereto, including, but not limited to new use, re-use and residuals, if any;

If the producer wants specific musicians other than the electronic and acoustic instruments played by the composer, the producer should be responsible for the costs. In some cases, the agreement will state that the composer is responsible for up to X number of live musicians as part of the package but in most cases, if the producer wants (hypothetically) a marching band, the composer should not have to absorb these costs.

b.   Licensing and clearance of music not composed by Composer

The costs of clearing and licensing outside music not created by the composer should be the responsibility of the producer, as they have control over the use of these outside songs, not the composer.

c.   Actual rescoring and rerecording costs (i.e., re-recording required for creative reasons outside the control of Composer and after delivery and acceptance of the Score by the Producer);

If the producer wants some re-scoring for either creative or technical reasons after acceptance of the score, the composer should not have to rescore or re-record at their own expense.

d.   Music editor and music editing costs; and

Usually, a music editor will be engaged by the producer to make sure that the music matches up with the picture or edit it to match. For very low-budget films, the composer may be asked to deliver a fully edited score that syncs up to the picture, thereby functioning as the *de facto* music editor.

e.   Vocalists and lyricists

If the producer wishes to have songs written and performed for the film, there are extra costs for a lyricist or vocalist(s) that the producer should be willing to pay for, as the use of these parties is entirely at producer's discretion.

3.   PAYMENT SCHEDULE: 50% due immediately upon execution of this contract; 50% due upon Composer's delivery, and Producers approval, of the finished Score on or about _____. Time is of the essence to the delivery of the Score.

Payment is made to the composer one-half up front and one-half upon delivery and acceptance of the score.

4.   SCREEN CREDIT: If the Composer's Score is used, the Composer shall receive screen credit in the main titles of the Film, to read: Original Score by _____.

For young composers, as well as established writers, a screen credit is very important to their career. Here, the credit will be listed in the main titles of the film, along with the stars, the writer, and the director. Sometimes there is language stating that the credit will read "substantially as follows" so as not to cause a breach of the agreement by the producer for minor changes in the wording.

5.   SOUNDTRACK ALBUM: In the event that any of the Composer's Score is included on a Soundtrack Album from the Film, the Composer and Producer shall negotiate in good faith for any artist and/or producer royalties to be paid to Composer from said Soundtrack Album.

Although soundtrack albums of underscore are rare, it is possible that a score album could be created, or that a portion of the score could be included in a soundtrack album that features mostly songs from the film. This clause provides for good faith negotiations between the parties for royalties to be paid to the composer for his services as artist and producer of the tracks containing their music.

If fifty percent (50%) or more of the Score is on a Soundtrack Album from the Film, Composer shall receive credit on the front cover, to read: Music by _____, Produced by _____.

Credit to the composer is also important on a soundtrack album.

6.   PAID ADVERTISING: Composer to receive credit in any advertising that includes the so-called "billing block". Composer understands that there will be no injunctive relief if there is any error in the accorded credit, and that Producer has the final decision as to all other credit matters. However, Producer shall employ best efforts to remedy such an error on a prospective basis.

The "billing block" is the list of credits usually found in newspaper ads or on posters for the film and lists all the key contributors to the film. The second sentence states that a failure to accord such credit will not be breach subject to injunctive relief and that the producer will attempt to rectify the error.

7.   PUBLISHING ROYALTIES: Artist's publishing company, _____, shall retain 100% of the copyright in both the Score and the master recordings thereof and all publishing income in connection with the Score.

This clause is the key difference between this agreement and the short form composer agreement, as the language here indicates that the composer retains the copyright to the music, not the producer. As such, the composer is entitled to receive all royalties, both the writer and publisher's shares, generated by the score.

8. RIGHTS OF PRODUCER: Producer to have the perpetual, irrevocable right to use the Score in connection with any and all exploitation of the Film in all media, including advertising and promotion of the Film. All rights in this agreement are assignable by Producer to a distributor, however Producer shall remain primarily liable for any obligations under this agreement.

Even though the producer is not the owner of the score, this clarifies his rights to use the score in any way in connection with the film. In all media, including any promotion of the film. It also allows the producer to assign the rights from this license to a distributor, with the producer remaining primarily liable for all terms.

9. PERFORMING RIGHTS SOCIETY: Composer hereby acknowledges that he is a member of _____.

In order for the producer to register the cues and prepare a music cue sheet, the composer must list their performing rights organization. The producer must have a publishing company set up with the same PRO as the composer.

10. NOTICES AND PAYMENTS: All Composer's monies and correspondence to be directed to:

_____

_____

_____

A simple notice provision with contact information for the composer.

11. WARRANTIES AND REPRESENTATIONS: Composer hereby makes customary representations and warranties as to the originality of the Score, that the Score violates no rights of any third party, that there will be no liens or encumbrances on the Score, and that the Producer will be free to use the Score in the Film and the exploitation thereof.

A simplified version of a complicated clause.

If the above is correct, please sign below. Once fully signed, this will constitute our agreement.

Must be signed by both parties to be an effective contract.

APPROVED AND ACCEPTED:

_____

Composer

Dated: _____

_____

Producer

Dated: _____

LONG FORM COMPOSER LOANOUT AGREEMENT

This is an agreement that is more typical of that used by a major production company and is far more detailed and complicated than the previous agreements. It is an agreement for creative services only, i.e., not a package, so many of the terms regarding services and compensation are different than the previous agreements.

Dated as of _____

_____

_____

_____

_____

Re: _____

The following will summarize the basic terms of the agreement between _____ ("Lender") for the services of _____ ("Composer") and _____ ("Producer") in connection with an original musical score ("Score") for the featurelength motion picture tentatively entitled "_____" (the "Picture").

1.   Services: Lender shall lend the services of Composer to Producer and shall cause Composer to compose, arrange, orchestrate and conduct the Score for the Picture

(and, if requested by Producer, arrange, orchestrate, conduct and integrate preexisting musical compositions into the musical score for the Picture) as may be required and requested by Producer,

and at Producer's election, to produce a soundtrack album derived therefrom (the "Album"), if any, as requested by Producer.

During the term hereof, Lender shall cause Composer to render, exclusively to Producer, all services customarily rendered in connection with such services and in connection with composing original musical scores for motion pictures.

As you will see, this is a loanout agreement between the production company and the composer's corporation, who is "lending" the services of the composer. Technically, the composer is the employee of the lender, not the production company. The agreement will be addressed to the loanout company (or "lender") regarding the services of the composer.

These recitals identify the parties and the project. Note that the lender is providing the services of the composer via the loanout company.

The composer shall write the score, arrange the instruments (i.e., decide what instruments will play which notes), create the orchestrations (i.e., write out the parts for the different instruments), and conduct the orchestra needed to record the score.

Composer will provide similar services as above for any pre-existing music requested by the producer.

If requested by the producer, the composer will also produce a soundtrack album comprised of music from the picture.

Unlike the previous agreements, this calls for the services of the composer to be exclusive to this project. Sometimes, this exclusivity is restricted to the actual recording and mixing periods.

2.   <u>Term:</u> The term hereof shall commence upon the date Composer commences spotting the Picture (which date shall be designated by Producer) and expire upon the date of the completion of services deemed satisfactory by Producer. Composer must deliver the completed Score, satisfactory to Producer, by the date designated by Producer. In the event that Producer requires Composer to produce the Album, Composer shall complete such services in a manner satisfactory to Producer by the date designated by Producer. The parties agree that time is of the essence of this Agreement.

> "Spotting" the picture is when the composer, producer, director, and music editor view a rough cut of the film to determine where the underscore will go in the film and approximately how long each cue will last. This is probably the first time that the composer will have seen the film and when his work officially begins. The term ends when all of the composer's work on the film is complete and deemed satisfactory to the producer.

3.   <u>Compensation:</u>

a.   Provided that Composer and Lender fully perform their obligations and Composer's services hereunder, Producer shall pay to Lender for providing Composer's services to Producer hereunder, the sum of _____ Dollars ($_____.00).

> This is the total creative fee being paid to the composer. As this is not a package deal, and the composer is not responsible for any of the costs of musicians, recording studios, etc., this is the actual amount the composer gets to put into his pocket.

Lender agrees that to the extent the services to be rendered by Composer hereunder are subject to the provisions of any collective bargaining agreements between Producer and any guild, union or labor organization having jurisdiction, including, without limitation, services rendered by Composer in connection with trailers, commercials, or other promotional materials for the Picture, the compensation herein provided shall be deemed to include compensation for such services in the minimum amount specified for such services in the applicable collective bargaining agreements (including any residual or reuse payments specified in such agreements), and the excess shall be deemed to be compensation for such services as are not subject to the provisions of any such collective bargaining agreements.

> If this is a major motion picture, there is a good chance it will be recorded under the jurisdiction of the American Federation of Musicians (AFM). If so, the composer's services that might fall under AFM rules are deemed to have been paid pursuant to AFM scale, with the balance retained by the composer.

4.   <u>Credit</u>

a.   Provided that Composer's score is substantially embodied in the Picture as theatrically released, Composer shall receive:

> In order to receive a credit, the composer's score must be the primary source of the music for the film. In the event that the composer's music is replaced by the score of another composer, but a small portion of it remains, this composer would not receive the credits listed below.

Notwithstanding the foregoing, any applicable union fees for Composer's orchestration services hereunder shall be paid at minimum union scale in addition to said compensation.

> There are different AFM scales for musicians, arrangers, orchestrators, and conductors. This clause states that the composer's orchestration services, if any, shall be paid at AFM minimum scale.

Producer shall pay said compensation as follows:

i.   One-third (1/3) upon the later of the date of the complete execution of this agreement or the date Composer commences spotting the Picture;

ii.   One-third (1/3) upon the later of the date of the complete execution of this agreement or the date Composer commences recording the Score;

iii.   One-third (1/3) upon the later of the date of the complete execution of this agreement or the date of delivery to and acceptance by Producer of the complete recorded score.

b.   In the event that Producer requires Composer to render services at a destination outside of the Los Angeles area, Producer shall provide first-class air travel between Los Angeles and such destination for Composer on a reasonable basis. Composer shall also receive _____ Dollars ($_____) per week (prorated, as appropriate, on a seven [7] day basis) while rendering services at such destination, which sum shall be deemed inclusive of all travel related expenses incurred by Composer, including, without limitation, all hotel, transportation, telephone and meal expenses. Except as provided in this subparagraph 3(b), Producer shall have no obligation to reimburse Composer for such expenses.

i.   a single card main title credit on release prints of the Picture in substantially the following form:

"Original Music by _____"

The composer's compensation will be paid in three parts: upon commencement of spotting; commencement of recording the score; and upon completion, delivery, and acceptance by the producer. All of these payments are contingent upon there being a signed agreement between the parties. Sometimes, there are long delays in having the agreements generated or the language negotiated to the mutual satisfaction of the parties. This can cause issues with the composer's ability to engage third parties without having received any payments with which to pay these third parties.

Sometimes a composer has to travel to a location far from where they live, sometimes to one of the major European cities, to score the film. In that situation, the producer pays for all travel expenses. Here, first-class airfare is included, although it is not uncommon for business class to be substituted. Also included are the costs of ground transportation, hotels, and meals. In this paragraph, all those costs are lumped together into a weekly fee to composer, but sometimes the hotel and transportation costs are paid directly by the producer, with a *per diem* payment to cover meals and other incidental expenses.

This is the preferred credit by most composers and is listed in the opening titles of the film with the main actors, director, and writer.

ii.   with respect only to paid advertising for the Picture prepared by Producer after the date Composer's score is physically embodied on release prints of the Picture, Composer shall receive a credit to read substantially as follows:

   "Music by _____"

The size, placement, prominence, etc. of said credit shall be at Producer's sole and absolute discretion. Said credit shall be subject to all customary exclusions and exceptions.

c.   In the event that the Album is commercially released and a majority of the musical compositions contained thereon are composed and produced by Composer hereunder, Composer shall receive:

i.   Back cover credit, with size, placement, prominence, etc. to be at Producer's sole and absolute discretion, in substantially the following form:

   "Music composed by _____"

ii.   An appropriate producer's credit on the Album cover and/or label with size, placement, prominence, etc. to be at Producer's sole and absolute discretion.

d.   Producer's failure to comply with any of the foregoing credit provisions shall not be deemed a breach of this agreement; however, Producer shall use its best efforts to prospectively cure such failure on materials prepared by Producer after its receipt of written notice from Lender of such failure. In no event shall Composer or Lender be entitled to injunctive relief in connection with these provisions.

This credit is for the "billing block," i.e., the credits listed in the print ads and posters for the film. The producer has total discretion as to how this credit is listed. An example of "customary exclusions and exceptions" would be ads for Academy Award consideration for an actor or best picture, which is unique to the aspect being advertised instead of the entire picture.

As mentioned previously, soundtrack albums consisting primarily of score are rare these days, although there are a few small labels that specialize in these types of recordings. If most of the music on the album is from the composer's score, the credit below would be appropriate.

As there are likely to be other artists whose recordings are included on the soundtrack album, the producer will need to balance the contractual requirements of those artists (and their labels) with the credit listed for the composer.

As the composer may be asked to produce the soundtrack album, an additional credit for these services is appropriate.

A producer's error in listing the credits above are not to be deemed a material breach of the agreement and the producer agrees to try to correct on a prospective basis. Unfortunately, once prints of the film are made, it is unlikely that any future prints will be created and errors corrected.

5.   <u>Copyrights:</u> Producer and Lender acknowledge and agree that all works, scores, compositions, recordings, and all other results and proceeds of Lender's and Composer's services hereunder (hereinafter collectively referred to as the "Work") constitute and will constitute a work specially ordered or commissioned by Producer for use as part of a motion picture or other audiovisual work; that the Work is and shall be deemed a "workmadeforhire" within the meaning of the United States Copyright Act of 1976; and that Producer is and shall be considered for all purposes the author, composer, and first proprietor of the Work. Producer shall own all rights (whether now or hereafter existing) throughout the universe in and to the Work, including, without limitation, the title, words, music, and sound recordings thereof, and all copyrights therein and extensions thereof, and the right to secure copyright registration and protection of the Work or of any arrangement, adaptation, derivative work, or other versions thereof, and any other rights relating to the Work which Lender or Composer now have, may hereafter have, or could have had if this Agreement had not been entered into. Producer in its absolute and sole discretion shall have the exclusive right to administer and exploit the Work, to print, publish, sell, and use and license the use of the Work throughout the universe, and to execute in its own name any and all licenses and agreements affecting or respecting the Work, including, but not limited to licenses for mechanical reproduction, public performance, synchronization, sub-publication, merchandising, and advertising, and to assign or license such rights to others without limitation. Without limiting the generality of the foregoing, Lender and Composer expressly agree that Producer shall have the right to exploit the Work in synchronization with the Picture or otherwise in any and all media now known or hereafter devised (including, without limitation, audiovisual devices) and in trailers, advertisements, and other promotions and ancillary uses of the Picture or other photoplay, with no additional payment to Lender or Composer other than that specifically provided herein. The decision as to whether the Score shall be embodied in the Picture shall be made by Producer in its sole discretion.

6.   <u>Music Publishing:</u> Producer, _____, and/or any other music publisher designated by Producer shall pay music publishing royalties to Lender f/s/o Composer in accordance with the rates, terms and conditions set forth on Exhibit "C" attached hereto. The term "Publisher" as used in said Exhibit shall mean Producer, or its music publishing designee, as applicable. The term "Composition(s)" as used in said Exhibit shall mean the musical Composition(s) written and composed by Composer and delivered to Producer hereunder.

This is standard work-made-for-hire language, giving all rights in the copyright in the score (both the compositions and recordings thereof) to the producer, including the right to register the copyright, administer the publishing of the score (with all accompanying powers, such as licensing, collecting royalties, etc.), and utilize the score in connection with the film and all promotions thereof without any additional compensation to the composer.

This paragraph references an exhibit that spells out the composer's share of music publishing royalties. It also indicates that the producer may assign his publishing rights to a third party designee to administer the copyrights and make these payments, if any.

7.   <u>Soundtrack Album:</u>

a.   In connection with the Album, if any, containing music composed by Composer hereunder and/or produced by Composer hereunder, Producer or its record distributor shall pay to Lender royalties for Composer's services as follows:

In the event that there is a soundtrack album, additional royalties will be paid to the composer, as described below. Note the language that the payments will be made either by the producer or the record distributor. If paid by the distributor, the composer will receive their royalties faster. The producer will have to sign a letter of direction advising the distributor to pay the composer directly.

i.   As a recording artist:

Remember that the composer performs two separate and distinct services for the soundtrack album: artist and producer. This paragraph addresses the royalties paid as an artist.

On records sold in the United States through normal retail channels, _____ percent (_____%) of one hundred percent (100%) of the suggested retail selling price, multiplied by a fraction, the numerator of which shall be the number of Artist Masters (as hereinafter defined) and the denominator of which shall be the total number of Masters (as hereinafter defined).

The artist royalty is a percentage of the retail sales price, *pro rata* by the number of tracks that contain the composer's music in relation to the total number of tracks. A range of the artist royalty is between 5% and 8% of retail, depending on the negotiating leverage of the parties.

With respect to records sold in Canada and other foreign countries, said royalty shall be reduced by the same percentage as Producer's royalty for such records is reduced as set forth in the agreement between Producer and the applicable record company.

Outside the United States, the film producer's royalty is reduced, so the composer's royalty base (i.e., sales price) is equally reduced.

ii.   As producer:

On records sold in the United States through normal retail channels, _____ percent (_____%) of one hundred percent (100%) of the suggested retail selling price, multiplied by a fraction, the numerator of which shall be the number of Produced Masters (as hereinafter defined) and the denominator of which shall be the total number of Masters (as hereinafter defined). With respect to records sold in Canada and other foreign countries, said royalty shall be reduced by the same percentage as Producer's royalty for such records is reduced as set forth in the agreement between Producer and the applicable record company.

The composer may be the producer on tracks for which he is not the artist, so a separate royalty is set out for those services, also on a *pro rata* basis. A producer royalty will range between 2% and 5% of retail.

b. Notwithstanding anything to the contrary contained in this Paragraph 7, no royalties shall be payable to Lender for Composer's services as recording artist or producer unless and until _____ percent (_____%) of Recording Costs (as hereinafter defined) and onehundred percent (100%) of Conversion Costs (as hereinafter defined) attributable to the Masters (as hereinafter defined) have been recouped from the royalties payable to Lender pursuant to subparagraph 7, A, (i) and 7, A, (ii). After such recoupment, Lender's royalties for Composer's services as recording artist and producer shall be paid prospectively, commencing with the next record sold after such recoupment.

> The film producer will want to recoup certain costs before paying any royalties to the composer for the soundtrack album. This language calls for the costs of recording the score and the conversion costs (to be discussed below) being recouped from the composer's royalties prior to any further payments. It would seem unfair for the recording costs to have to be recouped, as they are a production expense, not a soundtrack expense, and would have been paid with or without a soundtrack album. Sometimes the royalty for the composer as the producer of the soundtrack would be paid retroactively to the first unit sold once recoupment is achieved.

c. i. "Master" as used herein shall mean any master recording embodying a single musical composition contained on the Album.

> Each individual track on the album.

ii. " Artist Master" as used herein shall mean any Master composed and conducted by Composer for which no other recording artist receives an artist's royalty.

> A track containing only music created by the composer, with no other artist receiving a royalty. Sometimes, if there is another royalty artist on the track, the composer's royalty is reduced by the amount of the other artist's royalty.

iii. "Produced Master" as used herein shall mean an Artist Master produced by Composer.

> A track produced by the composer.

iv. "Recording Costs" as used herein shall mean direct costs incurred in the production of the Masters, including, without limitation, payments to persons rendering services in connection with the recording of the Masters; payments to a union or guild trustee or fund based on services at recording sessions; studio or rehearsal hall rental payments; payments to sound engineers, and for tape, editing, mixing, and other similar functions; and costs for rental and cartage of instruments, musical equipment and transportation thereof, and all other costs which are now or hereafter recognized as recording costs in the motion picture and record industries.

> This list of recording costs would need to be recouped from the composer's royalties prior to any further payments to composer. As mentioned above, these are properly designated as production costs for the film, not the soundtrack.

v.   "Conversion Costs" as used herein shall mean the cost of converting the Masters from use in the Picture to use in phonograph records, including, without limitation, rerecording costs, reuse or newuse fees, editing, mastering, equalizing, reference dubs, etc.

In order to convert score cues to full-blown tracks for the album, several cues might have to be edited together to create a longer piece of music. The audio requirements for the film and the soundtrack album would be different, so often there are remixing costs as well. In addition, any AFM musicians (or SAG singers) would require some additional "new use" payments, as their work is being transformed from a film to a soundtrack. These conversion costs are legitimate amounts to be recouped prior to any additional royalties paid out.

d.   The decision as to whether the Album shall be released, the selection of the musical compositions to be contained thereon and the producers thereof, shall be made by Producer in its sole discretion.

The film producer (and the record distributor) will require final approval over all aspects of the soundtrack album.

8.   Recordings: With respect to the Score and master recordings produced hereunder, Lender agrees that Composer shall:

Here, the lender, on behalf of the composer, agrees to the following.

a.   produce and record in recording studios designated by Producer;

As the decision maker on all creative elements of the film, and the party paying the bills, the producer will want to determine where the music will be recorded.

b.   work within the framework of a recording budget approved by Producer;

As the party responsible for the budget of the film, the producer will require that the composer adhere to the parameters set for the creation of the score.

c.   submit to Producer in writing a fully detailed recording authorization, including, but not limited to, specification of the proposed budget setting forth, without limitation, all costs or fees paid to individuals, including, but not limited to, recording artists, sidemen, arranging and copying fees, etc., all studio charges, all union contributions and payments to be made and the applicable copyright royalty rates due for any compositions recorded. Said recording authorization must be submitted to Producer prior to the applicable recording session and must be approved by Producer in writing;

The composer is required to provide to the producer a detailed report showing which parties are going to be paid and how much so that the producer can make sure that the budget requirements are being met **prior** to the commencement of scoring. A composer should always allow for some contingencies, such as delay, overtime, re-scoring of some cues, etc.

d.   abide by all appropriate union regulations;

The AFM has strict policies about the booking or cancellation of recording sessions, the length of sessions overtime, meal breaks, wages and benefits (such as health & welfare and pension) that need to be adhered to in order not to violate the union rules, which could cause penalties to be levied against the production company.

e.   maintain and submit all applicable job sheets and obtain appropriate title clearances for any compositions used;

"Job sheets" are records kept for AFM purposes.

f.   make timely delivery to Producer of documents, information and other materials, if any, required by Producer to make payment, when due, of unionscale compensation, or to effect timely compliance with any other obligations under any applicable agreement with any union or labor organization with reference to such master recordings; and to pay and reimburse Producer, upon demand, for any penalties, fines, lateness charges or other costs incurred by reason of Composer's failure to do so. Any such amount paid by Producer, and not properly reimbursed by Lender may, at Producer's election, be applied by Producer in reduction of any sums due or becoming due under this Agreement.

The composer must files AFM documents in a timely manner or risk penalties to the producer. Penalty amounts will be deducted from the composer's compensation.

g.   upon Producer's request, perform as liaison between recording artists and Producer in all necessary or appropriate matters;

The composer will work with any artists brought in to record for the score or songs for the film.

h.   mix down and edit the recordings and obtain Producer's approval of the same; and

Mixing down and editing the score are usually the responsibility of the music editors and sound engineers, not the composer. Nevertheless, the composer would be involved in supervising these functions.

i.   deliver to Producer fully edited master recordings in the configurations required by Producer.

While scores used to be delivered in two-channel stereo, now they are delivered in 5.1 surround sound.

9.   Music Video: Producer will have the right to make an MTVtype music video embodying the works created hereunder, and to use and exploit the same, as well as to exploit Composer's name and likeness in such video, in all media and for any purposes whatever; provided however, that in the event that the provisions of any collective bargaining agreement between Producer and any guild, union or labor organization having jurisdiction requires additional compensation to Composer in connection with any such music video, the compensation otherwise provided in this Agreement shall be deemed to include such compensation in the minimum amount specified in the applicable collective bargaining agreements (including any residual or reuse payments specified in such agreements), pursuant to paragraph 3 above.

For some films, the producer will want to create a music video with the composer's music for promotional purposes. In such a case, the composer agrees to have his name and likeness used, and agrees that the compensation paid for the film will cover any possible union payment that might arise from the creation of the video.

10.   Name and Likeness: Lender hereby grants to Producer the nonexclusive right to use, and to designate others to use, Composer's name, likeness and biographical material concerning Composer solely in connection with the publicity, promotion, distribution, exhibition, and other exploitation and ancillary uses of the Picture and Album. Lender shall, upon Producer's request, promptly submit to Producer photographs and biographies of Composer for use by Producer in connection therewith.

The right of the producer to use the composer's name and likeness is non-exclusive, as the composer (or others) may be using them or wish to use them in connection with other projects the composer is working on. The use of likeness and biographical material should be with the composer's approval, as they will want to have some control over the information or pictures given out about them, hence the language that the lender shall supply this info.

11.   Warranties: Lender warrants and represents that it is free and able to enter into and fully perform this agreement and to grant all the rights granted hereunder;

Standard language that a party entering into an agreement has the right to do so.

that it has the right to furnish Composer's services to Producer upon the terms and conditions set forth herein at no additional cost to Producer;

Lender warrants that they have an agreement with the composer for the lending of the composer's services and that any payments to the lender satisfy all payments to the composer.

that all works and compositions created, produced or delivered by Composer and/or Lender to Producer hereunder shall be original works and compositions by and of Composer and shall not infringe on any copyright or any other right (whether statutory, common law or contractual) held or owned by any other person or entity, or be subject to any claims by third parties, nor require Producer to make any additional payment for the use or exploitation thereof other than as set forth in this agreement;

Warranty that all compositions are original and do not infringe on the rights of any third parties.

that neither Lender nor Composer are subject to any rerecording restriction in connection with the works or recordings composed or produced hereunder

A re-recording restriction is usually in a recording artist agreement prohibiting the recording artist from making new versions of previously recorded material.

and that neither Lender nor Composer shall record or produce such works or compositions, or any parts thereof, for any third party prior to the date which is five (5) years after the date hereof;

This prohibits the composer from making new versions of any music created for this film for a period of five years.

that during the term hereof, Composer shall be, at Lender's expense, a member in good standing of any labor organization or organizations as may have jurisdiction pursuant to applicable law;

If the music for this film is recorded under AFM jurisdiction, this requires the composer to be an AFM member.

and that Lender shall cause Composer to execute the attached Exhibit "A" "Composer's Guarantee and Inducement" and the attached Exhibit "B" "Certificate of Authorship" contemporaneously with Lender's execution of this Agreement. Said Exhibits are hereby incorporated herein by this reference.

The inducement letter and Certificate of Authorship must be signed by the composer to satisfy copyright and liability requirements, as will be discussed below.

12.   Indemnities: Lender agrees to hold Producer, its subsidiaries, affiliates, assigns, agents, officers, employees, designees and licensees harmless from any and all costs, losses, damages, expenses, judgments and reasonable attorneys' fees arising from any use of the music or other works created hereunder and/or the breach or claim of breach of any of Lender's warranties, representations or obligations hereunder.

Lender agrees to indemnify the producer (and their affiliated parties) for any breaches or claims of breach of this agreement. In many cases, the words "claim of breach" are deleted or modified by other language requiring final adjudication or settlement with the composer's consent, not to be unreasonably withheld.

13.   Miscellaneous:

a.   No failure by Producer to perform any of its obligations hereunder shall be deemed a breach hereof, unless Lender has given written notice of such failure to Producer and Producer does not cure such nonperformance within thirty (30) days after receipt of such notice.

Notice provision for potential cure of breach by the producer.

Lender and/or Composer shall obtain permission from any third party, if applicable, necessary to enable Producer and its designees to exercise the rights granted to Producer hereunder, with no additional payment.

If the lender or composer engage any third parties, they are responsible for making payments to and obtaining any documents necessary for the producer to exploit the work of said third parties.

This agreement sets forth the entire understanding between the parties and supersedes all prior and contemporaneous negotiations and understandings, and cannot be terminated or modified except by a writing signed by all parties hereto.

Unless there is another document signed by all parties, this agreement shall be deemed the final terms between the parties.

This Agreement shall be governed by the laws of the State of California applicable to contracts made and to be wholly performed therein.

This sets California as the jurisdiction for adjudication of any disputes under this agreement.

All notices hereunder shall be sent by personal delivery or by telex, email or Certified Mail, Return Receipt Requested, to the applicable address below:

Procedure of each party giving formal notice to the other.

    If to Lender:

        _____

        _____

        _____

        _____

    If to Producer:

        _____

        _____

        _____

        _____

Very truly yours,

Signature lines for both parties.

_____

By _____

AGREED AND ACCEPTED:

_____

By _____

Fed. Taxpayer I.D. #: _____

EXHIBIT "A"

INDUCEMENT

Date: _____

_____

_____

_____

_____

Gentlemen:

I have read the Composer Loanout Agreement ("hereinafter referred to as Agreement") to which this Inducement is attached and, as an inducement to you to enter into the Agreement, I hereby consent to the execution thereof. I shall perform and comply as an individual, even if the employment agreement between _____ ("Lender") and myself should hereafter expire, terminate or be suspended. I, as an individual, hereby join in and confirm all grants, representations, warranties and agreements made by Lender under this Agreement.

I will look solely to Lender for all compensation for my services under the Agreement and you shall have no obligation to compensate me for any services to be performed by me or for any rights granted to you hereunder.

I agree that you shall be entitled to apply for equitable relief, by injunction or otherwise, to prevent a breach of the agreement between Lender and myself or of the Agreement.

The inducement letter is signed by the composer and verifies the relationship between the composer and the lender for composer's services and recognizes that, if the agreement between the lender and composer should come to an end, the composer will still be responsible for all obligations under the composer loanout agreement.

The composer will be paid by the lender only and will not seek compensation from the producer.

Equitable relief is available only when irreparable harm will be caused and monetary damages are insufficient. In this case, from the producer's perspective, no amount of money can cure a breach of the agreement between the composer and lender if the composer refuses to provide services under the agreement.

In the event of a failure or omission by Lender or by you or by others to give me the credit to which I am entitled pursuant to the Agreement and in the event such failure or omission constitutes a breach of the obligations of Lender to me to give me appropriate credit, then I agree my rights and remedies shall be limited to the right, if any, to obtain damages at law and I shall have no right in such event to rescind the agreement between Lender and myself nor cause Lender to rescind the Agreement

nor shall I have the right to rescind any of the rights assigned by me to Lender and by Lender to you or to enjoin or restrain the distribution or exhibition or any motion picture or any advertising, publicity, or promotion in connection therewith.

Yours truly,

_____

> The composer shall not be entitled to injunctive relief for a breach of the credit provisions, only monetary damages at law.

> The composer may not rescind any rights to the producer or prevent the picture from being distributed via the equitable relief of an injunction. Signed by the composer.

EXHIBIT "B"

CERTIFICATE OF AUTHORSHIP

I hereby certify that for good and valuable consideration I am writing or have written original _____ (the "Music") for possible use in the _____ production tentatively entitled "_____" (the "Production") at the request of _____ ("Producer"), pursuant to a contract of employment between Producer and me dated _____ (the "Agreement"). I hereby acknowledge that the Music and all other results and proceeds of my services under the Agreement ("Additional Material") were specially ordered or commissioned by Producer for use in the Production; that the Music and Additional Material constitute and shall constitute works made for hire as defined in the United States Copyright Act of 1976; that Producer is and shall be the author of said works made for hire and the owner of all rights in and to the Music and Additional Material including, without limitation, the copyrights therein and thereto for the universe for the initial term and any and all extensions and renewals thereof; and that Producer shall have the right to make such changes therein and such uses thereof as it may deem necessary or desirable.

> This sets out the formal requirements for a work made for hire: specifically ordered by the producer for use in a collective work, with the producer being acknowledged as the "author" under the Copyright Act.

I hereby waive all rights of droit moral or "moral rights of authors" or any similar rights or principles of law which I may now or later have in the Music and Additional Material.

> *Droit moral* is a concept whereby creators have certain controls over the use of their works, despite ownership by the copyright owner. Largely a European concept, this language expressly waives any moral rights of the composer in the music.

I warrant and represent that I have the right to execute this certificate, that the Music and Additional Material is and shall be new and original with me and not an imitation or copy of any other material, and that the Music and Additional Material shall be capable of copyright protection throughout the universe, does not and shall not violate or infringe upon any common law or statutory right of any party including, without limitation, contractual rights, copyrights and rights of privacy.

> Another warranty of originality by the composer.

By: _____

Address: _____

Date: _____

> Signature by the composer.

SCHEDULE C

Music Publishing Royalties

1. _____ ("Producer") shall pay the applicable Composer the following royalties under the following terms:

a)   Ten cents ($.10) per copy for regular piano copies sold and paid for in the United States and Canada, after deduction of returns.

For exploitation of the music outside the context of the film, these clauses are similar in nature to the royalty provisions of a songwriter agreement.

b)   Ten percent (10%) of the wholesale selling price (after trade discounts, if any) of each copy sold and paid for in the United States and Canada of orchestrations, band arrangements, octavos, quartets, arrangements for combinations of voices and/or instruments, and/or other copies of the Music (other than regular piano copies), after deduction of returns, except that in the event the Music shall be used in whole or in part in conjunction with one or more other compositions in a folio, album or other publication, Composer shall be entitled to receive that proportion of said royalty which the Music shall bear to the total number of compositions contained in such folio, album or other publication.

Print royalties are the exception to the general rule that the writer gets 50% of the publishing income. Instead, the composer will get a certain number of cents per copy for each piano copy sold and a percentage of the wholesale sales price (*pro rata*) for other types of printed music.

c)   Fifty percent (50%) of all net sums actually received by Producer in the United States (after deduction of returns, if any), for regular piano copies, orchestrations, band arrangements, octavos, quartets, arrangements for combinations of voices and/or instruments and/or other copies of the Music sold in any country other than the United States and Canada, and not covered under paragraphs A. and B. hereof.

Although this is also a provision for royalties on sheet music, because it addresses sales outside the United States and Canada, the composer will be paid 50% of the net income received in the U.S. by the publisher.

d)   Fifty percent (50%) of all net sums actually received by Producer in the United States for (a) any licenses authorizing the manufacture of parts of instruments serving to mechanically reproduce the Music; (b) any licenses authorizing the use of the Music in synchronization or in timed relation with sound motion pictures produced by anyone other than: (i) the Producer, its parent, subsidiary and affiliated companies; (ii) any company using the Music in a motion picture financed substantially by or to be distributed by Producer; and (iii) producer for whom the Music was originally composed, and its parent, subsidiary and affiliated companies; (c) any licenses authorizing the right to reproduce the Composition upon electrical transcription for broadcasting purposes; or (d) from any other source or right now known or which may hereafter come into existence.

The composer receives 50% of net sums from mechanicals, synchronization (except for projects produced by this producer or any affiliated companies), and all other sources.

Notwithstanding the above, Composer shall not be entitled to any share of the monies distributed to the Producer by any performing rights society anywhere in the world, or other source, which makes a distribution to composers directly or through another performing rights society or other person, company, society, association or organization.

If the Producer administers such licenses through an agent, trustee or other administrator acting for a substantial part of the industry and not under the exclusive control of the Producer (hereinafter sometimes referred to as a licensing agent), the Producer in determining its receipts shall be entitled to deduct from gross license fees paid by the licensees a sum equal to the charges paid by the Producer to said licensing agent.

e)   No royalty shall be payable for "professional or complimentary material" nor sold or resold or for any copies or mechanical derivatives thereof distributed gratuitously for purposes of advertising, promotion or exploitation.

f)   The foregoing rates shall apply only in cases in which all of the music and lyrics of the Music have been composed by one composer, or in cases in which a musical composition has been composed for which no lyrics have been written. As to songs, if one person composes the music and another the lyrics, the foregoing rates shall apply, but onehalf (2) shall be allocated to the composer of the music and onehalf (2) to the author of the lyrics (no allowance being made for the title). If there shall be more than one composer or more than one lyricist (including those employed by Producer to add to, change or translate the words or to revise or change the Music), then they shall agree among themselves upon the division of their respective royalties, but in the absence of such agreement, their royalties shall be divided in a manner to be fixed by Producer based upon a good faith determination by Producer as to the relative contributions of each party.

The royalties hereinabove provided for shall be payable only in connection with the Music originally created by Composer, it being agreed that no royalties shall be payable with reference to arrangements, orchestrations, translations or other adaptations or modifications of compositions written by others.

Excluded from the sources above is the publisher share of public performance income, which the producer/publisher retains since the composer receives their share directly from their PRO.

If the producer has their publishing administered by another company, the fees charged by the administration company are deducted prior to a determination of net receipts.

No royalties are to be paid for demo or promo copies.

If there are co-writers of the compositions, the royalties above will be split between the parties. In determining the splits, music and lyrics shall each be given 50% weight. If there are multiple parties within those two categories, the co-writers shall determine the splits between themselves. If they are unable to agree on the split, the producer shall have the right to make that determination in good faith.

These royalties only apply to music originally written by the composer, and shall not apply to any third-party music despite the composer having written arrangements, orchestrations, etc.

OPTIONAL LANGUAGE

Lender and Composer acknowledge that Producer may, if required by the Album Distributor, with respect to phonorecords, if any, sold through normal retail channels, grant a mechanical license at no less than three-fourths (3/4) of the then current minimum statutory rate for portions of the Music embodied thereon, or at such other mechanical license rate as may be required in connection with the sale of phonorecords other than through normal retail channels in the United States (e.g. record clubs, budget lines, mail order or key outlet sales). No mechanical royalties shall be payable with respect to copies of any phonorecord (including the Album) for which no royalties are payable to Producer pursuant to Producer's agreement with the applicable Album Distributor.

Lender and Composer acknowledge that Producer's agreement with the applicable Album Distributor may include a mechanical license provision limiting the maximum aggregate copyright royalty rate payable by the Album Distributor in respect of the Album. As used in this paragraph, the term "Maximum Aggregate Album Rate" shall mean the maximum aggregate mechanical copyright royalty rate payable by the applicable Album Distributor in respect of the Album, which the parties hereby acknowledge may be no greater than eight (8) selections multiplied by the applicable statutory mechanical rate. Notwithstanding anything to the contrary contained herein, with respect to net sales of the Album in the United States, in the event that eight (8) or more selections are contained on the Album and the actual aggregate mechanical copyright royalty rate which would otherwise be required to be paid in respect of the Album exceeds the Maximum Aggregate Album Rate, then Producer shall have the right to reduce the mechanical license rate for the Music to the extent necessary for the actual aggregate mechanical copyright royalty rate in respect of the Album to equal the Maximum Aggregate Album Rate.

No royalties shall be payable for any uses made by the Producer or by the independent producer for whom the Music was originally composed (or by its or their associated, affiliated, parent or subsidiary corporations or by any persons, firms, corporations or other entities with whom or which any of said corporations, etc., may have contracts or arrangements for the production, performance, televising, exhibition or distribution of motion pictures) in motion pictures (theatrical or television) or in connection with any advertising, publicizing or exploitation thereof.

This language is similar to a controlled composition clause found in an artist agreement (as discussed in Chapter 3: Mechanical Licensing for Audio-Only Product), in that it sets a reduced fee for mechanical royalties with a ceiling on the total amount of royalties payable on the soundtrack album.

No further royalties shall be paid for the use of the music in connection with the film or trailers/promotions for the film.

g) If for any reason exportation of money to the United States of America from any foreign country, territory or place should be prohibited, prevented, or rendered commercially impracticable, the amount received by Producer (if Producer's share thereof is actually paid to Producer in such foreign country, territory or place) shall not be considered gross receipts hereunder unless and until the same shall have actually been received in the United States of America in United States currency, less any discounts, losses, costs, or expenses suffered by or imposed upon Producer with respect to transmittal of such money to the United States of America and the conversion thereof to United States currency; provided, however, that, if Composer so requests in writing, that portion of such blocked or frozen funds which would represent Composer's share of net proceeds of such gross receipts but for being blocked or frozen shall be deposited in Composer's name at Composer's sole expense in any bank or depository designated by Composer in such country wherein such funds are blocked or frozen, subject to the laws of such country with respect to such deposits and withdrawals by Composer therefrom.

> This clause addresses potential issues with foreign currency not being able to be sent to the U.S. This is a rare occurrence but, given the political instability in certain parts of the world, currency can be blocked for foreign governments. This language sets out an alternative method of the composer receiving their money from foreign territories.

h) If Producer assigns or licenses any of the rights hereunder to any third party and if Producer authorizes such third party to account directly to Composer with respect to royalties payable to Composer by reason of such uses of such right, then Composer agrees that during the term of any such assignment or license, Composer shall look only to such assignee or licensee for payment of such royalties, it being agreed that Producer shall be relieved of any obligation or liability with respect thereto. If said assignee or licensee has offices in any country other than the United States then with respect to provisions such as "sums actually received" and the "exportation of money," as referenced for example in subparagraphs C., D. and F. above, such provisions shall be deemed amended to apply to the territory in which said assignee or licensee has its principal place of business and not the United States.

> If the producer enters into agreements directing a third party (like a publishing administrator) to pay royalties to the composer, then the composer shall look to the administrator for payment and not to the producer.

i) Composer acknowledges that Producer has not made and is not hereby making any representation or warranty with respect to the amount of royalties, if any, which may be derived from uses of the Music hereunder, it being understood that nothing herein shall be deemed to impose any obligation on Producer to use or authorize the use of the Music and/or any rights derived therefrom.

> As there are no guarantees as to the amount of potential income, if any, this clause clarifies that no promises have been made to the composer as to any income amounts that might be forthcoming.

j)   Except as herein expressly provided no other royalties or monies shall be paid to Composer. In no event shall Composer be entitled to share in any advance payments, guarantee payments or minimum royalty payments which Producer may receive in connection with any subpublishing agreement, collection agreement, licensing agreement or other agreement covering the Music.

As the composer is entitled to a share of the money earned only, they are not entitled to any portion of any publishing advance until earnings accrue from the use of the music. Payment will come after royalties have been earned, whether or not the advances have been recouped, as the publisher has had the money all along.

2.   Within ninety (90) days after the last days of June and December in each year, Producer will prepare and furnish semiannual statements to Composer hereunder whenever royalties and fees are payable, and each such statement shall be accompanied by payment of any and all sums shown to be due thereby, after deduction of any and all advances. Producer shall have the right to retain as a reserve against returns such portion of payable royalties and fees as shall be necessary in its best business judgment. Composer shall notify Producer in writing of any specific objection to such statements no later than one (1) year after the receipt thereof by Composer. Any and all objections, questions or disputes concerning any such statement shall be waived by Composer unless such written objection is received by Producer within such one (1) year period. Composer or a certified public accountant on Composer's behalf may, at Composer's expense and not more than once during each one (1) year period, examine Producer's books insofar as the same concern Composer, during Producer's usual business hours and upon reasonable written notice, for the purpose of verifying the accuracy of any statements rendered to Composer hereunder. Producer's books relating to activities during any accounting period may only be examined as aforesaid during the one (1) year period following receipt by Composer of the statement for said accounting period.

Semi-annual accountings with audit provisions.

Furthermore and notwithstanding anything contained in this Agreement to the contrary, with respect to any royalties and/or fees to be paid to Composer hereunder, Producer shall have the right to deduct from said royalties and/or fees Composer's proportionate share of the following expenses incurred by Producer with respect to the Music:

a.   all direct outofpocket expenses with respect to copyright, copyright registration and related costs;

b.   all costs allocable to transcribing and duplicating lead sheets;

c.   all costs relating to advertising, promotion and exploitation of the Music including, but not limited to, the costs of producing demonstration records;

d.   all costs associated with collection and/or foreign taxes;

e.   all costs associated with preparing, printing, engraving, arranging, editing and/or insuring printed editions of the Music as well as packaging, mailing and related shipping expenses;

f.   reasonable attorneys' fees and other legal expenses, if any, in collecting sums due, protecting rights held under this Agreement, and issuing, preparing, reviewing and/or otherwise dealing with agreements (other than this Agreement).

For purposes hereof, "Composer's proportionate share" shall be that percentage of the royalties and/or fees that Composer receives of the total received by Producer and Composer. For example, if Composer receives ten cents ($.10) for each regular piano copy sold in the United States and Producer receives forty cents ($.40), "Composer's proportionate share" (of expenses) shall be ten-fiftieths (10/50) or twenty percent (20%) thereof.

Certain expenses are deductible from gross earnings before "net sums" are calculated. The items listed below are fairly standard deductions as out-of-pocket costs to a publisher.

CHAPTER 9

PITCHING AND PLACEMENT AGREEMENTS

Introduction

With the decline of the recording industry and diminishing revenues from the sale of recorded music, many publishers, record companies and independent artists are looking for placements in television programs, motion pictures, and commercials as a way of replacing some of the lost income.

"Television is the new radio" is the cry you hear, as placement in a television show not only generates income, it can stimulate record sales, touring income, and merchandise sales if licensed properly. Getting music into these programs is harder than it looks and there are companies set up to provide services to music licensors specifically for this purpose.

"Pitching" or "placement" companies acquire certain limited rights from the owners of musical content in order to solicit the decision makers in film and TV. Often, those making the decisions are the music supervisors, who consult with the producers and directors to select the music for a particular project.

In exchange for these services, the companies may be compensated with a combination of a commission on license fees and/or "back end" income or an ownership percentage in the copyrights of the songs placed. (Note: there are some pitching companies who charge the artists for their services, whether any music is placed or not. Although there are a few companies that are legitimate, most of the companies that follow this business practice should not be used.) This chapter will discuss how these companies work, what the fee structures look like and discuss a sample agreement from the perspectives of both the company and the artist.

What Does a Placement Company Do?

Once an agreement is signed with an artist, the company attempts to get the music used by the various production companies it does business with. Those attempts may take the following forms:

1. Review the music and categorize it based upon genre, tempo, male or female vocal, and assign key words to the song to be included in the metadata attached to the song. The "metadata" is information that is either included on a list or embedded digitally on the song file itself that includes all of the above information, as well as the title, composer, and publishers of the song. This allows the song to be included in a searchable database and supplies needed information for licensing and payment;

2. Develop a website where the music can reside to be searched by the company's clients. Usually, this is an FTP site where music can be streamed for review purposes or where low-quality files can be downloaded, subject to broadcast-quality files being sent when a song is actually going to be used in the program;

3. Send the music directly to the music supervisor for a specific use in a specific project. This is where the company's relationships really come into play, as the staff of the company reviews programs to see what kind of music they might use that fits the genre of the program. Sometimes, the supervisors will call the company asking for a particular type of song to see if the company can offer something that matches the criteria;

4. Enter into agreements with studios and supervisors to supply hard drives of music for consideration. Sometimes, the companies work out the deal terms prior to sending of the music, so it is "pre-cleared," or the music is subject to negotiation on a case-by-case basis.

The Placement Agreement

For writers and/or artists signed to record companies or publishing deals, both of those companies usually have to be consulted for approvals and negotiation of fees. If there are multiple writers and, therefore, multiple publishers, the number of parties expands accordingly.

However, as we shall see, with many independent artists, both of these copyrights may be controlled by the same party. This is what is known as a "one stop," which greatly simplifies the licensing process and is favored by the placement companies and music supervisors as it greatly speeds up any approval process called for in the agreement.

The key terms of the placement agreement are as follows:

1. **Exclusive vs. non-exclusive grant:** Many placement companies attempt to get the exclusive rights to pitch the music covered under the agreement. Having multiple parties pitch the same music is confusing to the music supervisors and can lead to disputes over which company actually secured the placement. In addition, the company will want to continue to be thought of as the representative for that artist if the supervisor wants to license another of their songs;

2. **Term of the agreement:** As it takes some time for the company to distribute the music effectively and for the supervisors to listen and become aware of it, most companies request a term of 2–3 years, plus some post-term language for deals that have commenced but not reached completion. In many agreements, the term automatically renews for additional one-year periods unless the artist gives notice no less than 60–90 days prior to the end of the current terms, including renewal terms;

3. **Music covered under the agreement:** In this instance, both the musical compositions and master recording by the artist are included in the grant of rights. It is not necessary for the artist to grant rights for their entire catalog, so there is usually a schedule of titles that are covered under the agreement, with more titles added as the artists continue to create more music;

4. **Grant of rights:** The artist grants to the company the rights to pitch their music and to license the music on behalf of the artist with the potential audio-visual production companies who wish to use it. The company gets a **limited power of attorney** in order to execute the agreements and **letter of direction** allowing them to collect the license fees and distribute according to the terms of the agreement. Generally, the agreement does not allow the company to license the music for audio-only product, with the exception of a soundtrack album derived from a production to which the music is being licensed.

   The artist retains all copyrights in their compositions and master recordings and has the full right to release, sell, and distribute audio-only product, either physically or digitally, without the company participating in the income stream. This may change, however, depending on the nature of compensation to the company.

5. **Compensation:** In virtually all agreements of this type, the company will collect the license fees and retain a portion (or all) of the fees as compensation for their efforts. It is not uncommon for the company to retain up to 50% of the license fees as the reward for their efforts. In addition, some companies require that a percentage of the copyright in the musical composition be assigned to the company to allow them to participate in the public performance royalty stream derived from the broadcasts of the production.

   Keep in mind that this co-ownership **only** applies to the songs for which a placement has been secured, not a co-publishing deal for the artist's entire catalog or all songs listed on the schedule to the agreement.

   As the company is now a co-copyright owner, the company (or their publishing designee) is registered with the PRO as a co-publisher and is able to collect their percentage of the publisher's share of performance income directly from the PRO. This is important to the company as it is not uncommon, for a program that is very popular and gets wide distribution, for the performance income to exceed the license fee and, since the placement was a direct effect of the company's efforts, the company should be allowed to participate in the downstream income. The percentage assigned to the company ranges from 25% to 75%, with a 50% share not being uncommon. Note that no ownership of the master recording is taken under this arrangement.

Often, the company will also request the right to administer the publishing (for an additional percentage, as is standard for publishing administrators) in order to better control the flow of income and to make sure that the writers and co-publishers get paid properly. As many independent artists are unfamiliar with how to register their songs with the PROs or how to collect their income streams, this additional service can benefit both parties.

This business model may seem weighed heavily in favor of the company, but it should be remembered that their efforts and any associated costs are at the company's sole expense, without cost to the artist and with no guarantees that those efforts and costs will be repaid. The company is working "on spec," if you will, and absorbing all the risk associated with these costs. In exchange for that risk, their reward is the compensation listed above.

There are certain companies that charge an up-front fee to the artist for the company's efforts to secure placements, but there are no guarantees that placements will actually be secured, so artists should consider whether these types of deals are to their benefit.

6. **Approvals and restrictions:** In some agreements, the company is given free reign to license the music in any way they see fit. However, in many agreements, there are restrictions about certain types of licenses requiring artist approvals. Usually, these contractual approvals are for films rated X or NC-17, political announcements, or commercials. Sometimes, with artists who have more leverage, all licenses must be approved by the artist, but there is usually language allowing a certain period for the artist to approve or deny the proposed use and if that response is not received, the request is deemed approved. Especially in television, the time allowed for clearance and approvals is very short, so the approval period to the artist could be as short as 48 hours from receipt of notice from the company.

7. **Warranties and indemnifications:** The artist warrants that they have the right to convey to the company the rights contained in the agreement, including that there are no other third parties who might have an interest in the songs, that there are no samples contained in the songs, and that they will indemnify the company from any third-party claims. Often, it isn't until a song gets placed that someone comes out of the woodwork to say that they were a co-writer on a song, at which point the company is liable to the party that they licensed it to, and the artist (who probably has no money) is liable to the company.

Benefits to the Artist

The most obvious benefit to the artist is income from the license fees and resulting public performance income. For independent artists, even a few thousand dollars is the difference between them surviving or folding. Consider that many indie artists make their living on the road and that $2,500 as their share of the license fee or performance income could keep them on the road for an additional couple of weeks, resulting in additional touring, merchandise, and CD sales income.

In addition, the exposure of having a song on a television program drives all of the revenue sources listed immediately above. It is not uncommon for the company to be able to negotiate for non-monetary benefits for the artist, such as the band name or website on a chyron or in a crawl at the bottom of the screen. In some cases, programs have their own websites that list the music contained in episodes of the program and it is possible to get a link on the program sites to the artist's website or iTunes page, thereby driving up sales.

Being able to say "as seen on program X" also aids in the artist marketing themselves to club and concert promoters and bringing more fans to their appearances, also driving sales of CDs and merchandise on site.

Potential Pitfalls for the Company

The whole idea behind the one-stop clearance is for the company to have all the rights necessary to give a quotation and issue a license on behalf of the entire song. It is essential that the artist is able to convey 100% of the rights needed, which would include all co-writers, co-publishers, and band members.

Too often, the artist "forgets" that someone they knew contributed to the song, or that one of the band members on the track is no longer a member. This can be a disaster for the company, as their license agreement with the producers contains language that the company warrants and represents that they have 100% of the right and will indemnify the producers from any such third-party claims. Although the agreement between company and artist has similar language, it is the company who is more likely to have the resources to pay the indemnification costs, not the artist.

In addition, if the company finds itself in this situation, it is likely that the production company will not accept more material from the company and no further placements can be obtained from that producer.

Conclusion

As with any successful negotiation, relationships like these can benefit both parties. The artist gets their music exposed to decision makers at the highest levels at no cost to the artist, and both parties can earn income from the initial placement and a continuing revenue stream that could last for years.

EXCLUSIVE REPRESENTATION AGREEMENT

This Agreement is made and entered into as of _____, by and between _____ (ASCAP) and/or _____ (BMI) and/or _____ (SESAC) ("Publisher"), located at ___ _____, on the one part, and _____, demo/master owner, and _____ (BMI) (collectively, "Licensor"), _____, on the other part. Publisher and Licensor agree as follows:

1. Licensor seeks Publisher's services to exclusively administer and procure placements of some of Licensor's musical works, compositions and Master recordings, as are detailed on Schedule "A", and such other compositions and Master recordings as Licensor may designate in writing during the Term hereof ("referred to hereinafter individually as the "Composition", and collectively as the "Compositions", "Works", or "Recordings").

2. If and when a placement of one of Licensor's Compositions is procured directly by Publisher,

    subject to Licensor's approval, not to be unreasonably withheld,

    for either: (a) synchronization in a theatrical motion picture; (b) synchronization in a television program for broadcast to the public; (c) synchronization in a home video program for sale to the public; or (d) any audio-visual production (including, but not limited to, productions released on video cassette, video disc or DVD, audio soundtracks derived from said placements, commercials, promotional film or television trailers, Internet sites, computer programs and/or games, karaoke or any similar media), Licensor hereby irrevocably transfers, grants and assigns exclusively to Publisher, its successors and assignees the right to collect or receive revenues derived from all commercial activities above and resulting from such placement of the Composition(s) throughout the world (Territory"), including but not limited to, the following:

    (A) Publisher shall receive and collect one hundred percent (100%) of all license and option fees obtained in procuring placements of Licensor's Recordings, and Publisher shall remit to Licensor fifty percent (50%) of all said licensing fees and option fees pursuant to this paragraph within thirty (30) days of receipt by Publisher. Publisher shall be compensated with an amount equal to fifty (50%) of all said front-end Gross placement fees and option fees generated per placed Composition, as its commission ("Commission"), and

"Licensor" is usually an independent artist who controls the rights to both the publishing and master recordings of the songs covered under this agreement.

Most placement companies will want exclusivity to avoid multiple parties pitching the same music.

Sets up the criteria for compensation to Publisher.

Allows for reasonable rights of approval by the licensor.

Although this agreement is for placement primarily in audio-visual works, it makes sense that if the publisher places a song in a film that then generates a soundtrack album, the publisher should be able to license that use as well as a natural extension of the rights already granted.

The publisher collects 100% of the license fee for both publishing and master rights and pays 50% to the licensor.

(B)   fifty percent (50%) of Licensor's entire right, title and interest throughout the world and universe, including without limitation, the copyright (so-called Publisher's share), the right to secure copyright registration, and any and all copyright renewal rights, in and to the specific Composition ("Co-Published Composition").

The publisher becomes 50% co-publisher of the composition and, therefore, is entitled to 50% of the publisher's share of all ancillary income, such as performing rights, generated by that composition. No interest in the master is transferred to the publisher.

(C)   Licensor agrees that if and when Publisher procures an approved use of Licensor's music for a specific television, film production, or with a specific advertising agency, that Publisher shall then become Licensor's exclusive representative for music placements in that specific television, film production, or with such advertising agency, according to the terms of this Agreement, during the Term hereof, and for the duration of that specific production or show.

Since the publisher made the contact with the production company, music supervisor, or agency, the publisher is now the exclusive representative for the licensor with that party.

(D)   Upon expiration of the term, Publisher shall have the right to collect all license fees earned for the placement of the Compositions during the term for a period six (6) months after expiration of the term (the "Collection Period"). License fees received during the Collection Period shall be deemed to have been received by Publisher during the term and shall be subject to all terms and conditions of this agreement.

A post-term collection period of six months for any deal **completed** during the term but not paid until after the term has expired.

(E)   In addition, Publisher shall have the right to collect all license fees for any negotiations commenced during the Term, even if completed after expiration of the Term and all provisions of this paragraph 2 shall come into effect regarding division of fees and assignment of copyright.

A post-term collection period for any deal **commenced** during the term but not paid until after the term has expired.

3.   This Agreement shall come into effect as of _____ and remain in effect for a period of __ years until _____ ("Term"). Upon expiration of the initial Term, this agreement shall automatically renew for successive one-year periods, unless terminated by either party upon sixty (60) days written notice prior to the expiration of any term.

The term is usually no less than two years, with automatic renewals unless notice is sent by the licensor.

If and when a placement of one of Licensor's Compositions and Masters is procured directly by Publisher (per paragraph 2, above), Publisher's right to administer said Composition (an "Admin Composition") shall remain in effect for a term of two years ("Admin Term"), commencing as of the date of the License for the placement.

If a song gets placed, the publisher remains the exclusive administrator of the song for an additional two years after the date of the placement (see paragraph 4, below).

4.   Licensor hereby assigns to Publisher the right to administer any Placed Composition (per paragraph 2, above), ("Admin Composition"), and exploit the Admin Compositions in any manner or media now known or unknown, to enter into and execute any and all licenses and agreements regarding the reproduction and other exploitations of the Admin Compositions, as well as the right to receive and collect and all gross sums (except for Writer's share of the "songwriter's share" of small performing rights payments hereunder, which if received by Publisher shall be promptly forwarded to Licensor without deductions or offset), together with accounting statements as received by Publisher derived from the use and exploitation of the Admin Compositions. Licensor, _____ (SS# : _____) agrees to be the fiduciary recipient of one hundred percent (100%) of all net distributable royalties, fees, and income pursuant to this Agreement, for and on behalf of itself and its co-Licensors, co-writers, and co-publishers herein, and that Licensor shall be responsible to distribute and account for said fees and income according to its agreements with its co-Licensors.

(A)   Licensor shall compensate Publisher with an administration fee of ten (10%) percent of all of Licensor's "back-end" royalties received in the U.S., which were generated by and attributed to any placement (as described in paragraph 2 above) procured by Publisher pursuant to this Agreement. Publisher shall pay to Licensor 100% of any income received in the United States after deduction by Publisher of the ten percent (10%) Administration Fee, as set forth herein, such payments to be made quarterly, within forty-five (45) days following March 31, June 30, September 30, and December 31 of each year.

5.   In consideration of the above undertakings on the part of Publisher, the Licensor hereby agrees:

(A)   Publisher shall have the right to deduct from any amounts payable to Licensor hereunder such portion thereof as may be required to be deducted under the applicable provision of any applicable statute, regulation, treaty or other law under any applicable union or guild agreement.

(B)   Licensor, or its designee, shall collect Licensor's share of the "songwriter's share" of public performance royalties directly from the performing rights organization to which Licensor belongs.

In addition to becoming a co-owner/co-publisher, the publisher becomes the administrator of the song, collecting all revenues except the writer's share of performing rights. The publisher pays the licensor their share of income, including any portion that might need to be paid out to any other third parties.

The publisher will deduct a 10% administration fee for the services provided in the paragraph above and pay the balance to the licensor quarterly.

This codifies that the licensor may collect the writer's share of performing rights.

(C)   Publisher may substitute a new title or titles for the Composition, make changes, arrangements, adaptations, translations, dramatizations, and transpositions of the Composition, in whole or in part, subject to Licensor's approval.

> The issue of re-titling a song is very controversial as, due to digital recognition technologies not being able to distinguish between the original title and the work with a new title. See Chapter 10: Production Music Libraries for more detailed information.

(D)   Publisher shall not, without Licensor's consent, exploit grand performing rights, exploit or grant licenses for x-rated or NC-17 rated films.

> Certain rights of approval granted to the licensor. As discussed in the section on synchronization licensing, more detailed consents may be granted if requested.

6.   During the Term, the Licensor hereby authorizes Publisher in the Licensed Territory the worldwide license and right to:

(A)   use, perform, and reproduce (and grant to others the right to use, perform, and reproduce)

> Note the language in these paragraphs that grants certain rights to the publisher but also authorizes the publisher the right to grant those rights to others.

the master recordings and musical compositions indicated on Schedule "A"

> This agreement covers only the specific titles listed on the schedule, not everything in the licensor's catalog.

in connection with live and recorded audio visual programs and productions, for purposes of exploitation pursuant to the terms of this Agreement.

> Rights are being granted for specific uses in live and recorded audio-visual productions. In this context, "exploitation" is a good thing.

Licensor acknowledges that Publisher and its licensees are not signatories to any music labor unions or guilds (collectively "Guilds") and that Licensor's works were not recorded pursuant to any such Guilds.

> Due to additional payments having to be made for music created under union jurisdiction, for music of this nature, most productions will require that the music is free of any continuing union obligations or payments. For most independent artists, this is not an issue.

(B)   record (and grant the right to others to record on film, videotape, computer disk and/or any other medium, whether known or hereafter devised, Licensor's works in synchronization or timed-relation to audio visual productions, and to issue synchronization licenses for the reproduction and/or synchronization or timed-relation of the Recordings on any visual, audio or audio-visual sound carrier now known or hereafter devised including but not limited to videocassette, DVD, CD-ROM, Internet and all other new media now known or hereinafter developed.

> Basic sync rights language.

(C)   broadcast, telecast, syndicate, license, distribute, and otherwise exploit (and grant to others the right to broadcast, telecast, syndicate, license, distribute, and otherwise exploit) the Recordings contained in Schedule "A", and

Grants rights for exhibition and distribution of the programs into which the music has been licensed.

to manufacture, if necessary, on compact disc, copies of the Recordings in sufficient numbers as may be required by Publisher solely for the promotion of continuing exploitation of the Recordings in the Licensed Territory as authorized hereunder. The costs of design, editing, mixing, production, manufacture and packaging of those discs and related artwork shall be borne solely by Publisher.

Allows the publisher to reproduce copies of the music for promotion of the licensor's songs, such as making CDs or DPD files to send to music supervisors.

(D)   issue performance licenses in the Licensed Territory as deemed necessary in the normal course of business;

In the event that the end user does not have licenses from the PROs, the publisher can grant direct performing rights licenses.

(E)   the right to use the name, photograph, likeness, and or biographical material as submitted or approved by the Licensor of any and all composers of the original recordings, for the purpose of the trade or otherwise in connection with the Recordings;

Grants the use of the licensor's name, likeness, and bio for promotional purposes.

(F)   all rights to license, assign, and enter into agreements to or with any person or entity with respect to all or any rights or part of the rights granted hereunder;

(G)   all rights not expressly set forth herein as a licensed right are reserved by Licensor.

As this is a limited grant of rights, any rights not covered in this agreement are retained by the licensor.

7. Licensor hereby warrants and represents that _____ has the right to enter into this agreement and to grant to Publisher all of the rights granted herein, and that the exercise by Publisher of any and all of the rights granted to Publisher in this agreement will not violate or infringe upon any common law or statutory rights of any person, firm or corporation, including, without limitation, contractual rights, copyrights and rights of privacy. All elements within the Composition and Master are either original with the Licensor, or are fully cleared by the Licensor. No Composition shall, in whole or in part, be an imitation or copy of, or infringe upon, any other material, or violate or infringe upon any common law or statutory rights of any person, firm or corporation, including, without limitation, musical samples, contractual rights, copyrights and rights of privacy. Licensor further represents and warrants that the rights granted herein are free and clear of any claims, demands, liens or encumbrances from any other party or musician or Guild, and that Licensor owns and controls all Master and Composition rights, together with co-writers, to the works and performances contained in Schedule "A", and that such use authorized herein will not give rise to any claims of infringement, invasion of privacy or publicity or claims for payment of re-use fees or residuals (any and all third party payments shall be Licensor's responsibility).

> As these are not newly created works, as in an exclusive songwriter agreement, it is essential to the publisher that the licensor warrant and represent that they have all rights in the music being delivered, especially that there are no other parties who might have a claim on the music.

8. Licensor hereby indemnifies, saves and holds Publisher, its assigns, licensees and its directors, officers, shareholders, agents and employees harmless from any and all liability, claims, demands, loss and damage (including reasonable counsel fees and court costs) arising out of or connected with or resulting from any breach of any of the warranties, representations or agreements made by Licensor in this agreement and resulting in a final, non-appealable adverse judgment to Licensor, or a settlement entered into with Licensor's prior written consent which consent shall not be unreasonably withheld.

> Standard indemnification language.

9. Licensor empowers and appoints Publisher, or any of Publisher's officers, Licensor's true and lawful attorney (with full power of substitution and delegation) in Licensor's name, and in Licensor's place and stead, or in Publisher's name, to take such action, and to make, sign, execute, acknowledge, deliver and record any and all instruments or documents which Publisher, from time to time, deems necessary to vest in Publisher and Licensor, their successors, assigns and licensees, any of the rights granted by Licensor hereunder, and which pertain to the Compositions included in Schedule "A", including, without limitation, the securing of copyright in the Composition by Publisher in the names of those parties entitled to such copyright interest as set forth herein.

> This is a limited power of attorney. As the publisher is not the copyright owner, the publisher needs the ability to sign agreements on behalf of the song and the licensor in order to issue quotes and execute license agreements.

10.   This agreement sets forth the entire understanding between the parties and cannot be changed, modified or canceled except by an instrument signed by both parties. This agreement shall be governed by and construed under the laws of the state of California applicable to agreements wholly performed therein.

11.   In the event of legal proceedings between the parties, the parties agree to resolve such disputes through binding Arbitration in the County of Los Angeles. The prevailing party in any action brought to enforce or interpret the terms of this agreement shall be entitled to recover from the other its reasonable attorney's fees and court costs, in addition to any damages or other remedies awarded by the court.

12.   If any provision of this contract shall be held void, voidable, invalid, inoperative or otherwise unenforceable, no other provision of this contract shall be affected as a result thereof, and accordingly, the remaining provision of this contract shall remain in full force and effect as though such void, voidable, invalid, inoperative or unenforceable provision had not been contained herein, provided, however, that such provision was not clearly a material element of the consideration for this Agreement.

13.   All notices, statements, payments or other written communications desired or required to either party under this Agreement shall be sent to Licensor at the addresses set forth below, or to such other addresses as the parties may designate to each other in the future. All notices shall be in writing and shall be sent by U.S. post or by personal delivery by means of a nationally recognized delivery service (e.g. FedEx or UPS).

14.   Licensor acknowledges and agrees that Licensor has been represented by independent legal counsel or has had the opportunity to be represented by independent legal counsel of Licensor's own choice for purposes of advising Licensor in connection with the negotiation, preparation and execution of this Agreement.

Establishes California as the jurisdiction for resolution of any disputes.

In addition to establishing arbitration as an alternative to dispute resolution, this also states that the party that wins gets to collect their attorney fees from the losing party.

IN WITNESS WHEREOF, the parties hereto have this day signed below to confirm the agreement reached.

Dated as of: _____

_____
Publisher

_____
Licensor

social security #:

and on behalf of _____

_____
Publishing Designee, (Licensor)

CHAPTER 10

PRODUCTION MUSIC LIBRARIES

Introduction

One of the most misunderstood and maligned types of music is "library" music or "production" music, terms used to describe music that is usually generic in nature and not readily known to the public. It is comprised mainly of instrumental compositions and recordings (although there is also a market for songs with vocals) that evoke a certain style of music without being recognized by the listeners.

For example, if there is a scene in a film that takes place in a nightclub, but the scene focuses on the dialog between two characters, what is important to the scene is the style of music being played in the club, not necessarily the specific song. As most songs have vocals that would interfere with the dialog, the director might wish to use an instrumental composition in a style that would be played in the club but does not have to be by a known artist. The production music acts as ambiance to the scene without dominating or distracting from the dialog.

Up until recently, production music was generated by cheap-sounding synthesizers or small combinations of instruments to try to replicate a larger sounding orchestra. While the compositions were good, the recordings were usually not up to the quality of commercially available music.

With the revolution in digital recording equipment, the advances in digital samplers of instruments, and other technological improvements, production music today can sound as good, if not better, than any other music being produced. Because the music is generally unknown and not created by artists signed to publishers or labels, the costs of licensing this music is usually much lower than commercially available music. That is the reason that producers will seek out production music for their programs, a market that the production music libraries are exploiting with great success.

Because of these opportunities, many of the major music companies have opened library divisions to service this market by buying smaller libraries or engaging their own composers directly.

In order to maximize their licensing possibilities, many libraries enter into agreements to have other libraries in foreign territories also represent the U.S. library's catalog in their territory. Similar to a subpublishing agreement, the foreign library usually retains 50% of the license fees and the publisher's share of performance income generated in their territory, sending the remainder to the U.S. library. While this 50% "commission" is significantly larger than the usual sub-publishing deal, the foreign libraries, like their U.S. counterparts, deal with different clients and on a different level than the traditional publishers in their market.

Library Composer Agreements

Libraries will engage composers to create original compositions and master recordings that the library will then license to its clients. Usually, the composer is also the artist, so all rights necessary can be granted to the library in a single agreement. Sometimes the composer will create music in any style that they choose; other times the library will request music of a certain genre. The composer will create a number of "tracks" or "cues" in varying tempos, keys, and moods, including versions in different lengths so that the end users can use the version that fits their production's needs.

The composer will be required to deliver fully produced stereo master recordings of the compositions, along with versions in varying lengths. Sometimes the composer will also be asked to deliver the "stems," which are the tracks of the individual instruments used to create a multi-track recording, so that the library or their clients can remix the cue to fit their individual needs.

It is possible, although rare, that the library composer will be asked to create a new recording of an existing popular composition. In this case, the library's client will still have to negotiate with the original publisher for the rights necessary for their production, but the client can license the library's master recording instead of the original artist's, almost always at a lower fee. The composer may create a version that has a completely different sound than the recording by the original artist, but sometimes they are asked to have the new recording sound similar (if not identical) to the original. This is called a "sound-a-like," as it sounds like the original artist's recording. Although legal to use in television programs and motion pictures, it is not permissible to use a sound-a-like in commercials, due to lawsuits brought and won by artists such as Bette Midler and Tom Waits, who claimed that these recordings appropriated their aural "image" in the same way that a photograph would have appropriated their visual image. See Chapter 4: Synchronization Licensing for Audio-Visual Productions for more information.

There are occasions when the composer will be specifically asked to create an original piece that emulates a particular popular piece of music. For example, if the client wants a song that sounds like Bonnie Raitt, the composer needs to create an original composition and engage a singer that sounds like Raitt. A casual listener may think they are listening to a Bonnie Raitt song, but the composition and recording are original. This is sometimes called a "sounds-like" (not a "sound-a-like," as discussed above), as the new recording may sound like another artist even though all elements are original. In these cases, the composer must make sure that the cue they create does not infringe the original composition. This is a fine line for the composers and libraries to tread, as the clients want the music to sound a certain way but the composer and library don't want to get too close to the original and risk legal action.

In a typical library agreement, the composer will be allowed to retain the writer's share of royalties paid by their performing rights organization. The publisher's share will either be retained by the library or, in some cases, divided with the composer. In a similar fashion, the license fee charged by the library may either be kept 100% by the library, divided 50/50 with the composer, or the composer could be paid up to 75% of the license fee, as if it were a co-publishing agreement. These splits are negotiable but each library usually has a business model in mind when they engage a composer, so the composer may be locked into accepting whatever splits the library typically uses.

One of the unique aspects of composer royalties in a production music library agreement is how license fees for "blanket" or "bulk" licenses are treated. These are agreements in which the library has offered an "all you can eat" license for a flat fee, so that the client can use anything in the library, all covered under the one-time payment. There are two basic methods of how composer royalties can be paid from the license fee:

1. If the client reports the actual uses of each piece of music to the library, the library can use that information to allocate the royalties amongst the composers whose music is actually being used. Hypothetically, if the client uses 1,000 pieces of music and a composer has written 100 of those pieces, he would receive 10% of the writer's 50% share of income.

2. If, however, the client does not report (or is not obligated to report), another method is to measure the amount of music a composer has in the library against the total size of the library. Again, hypothetically, if the library is comprised of 1,000 CDs worth of music, and the composer has 10 CDs of music in the library, the composer would receive 1% of the 50% allocated to writers, irrespective of how much his music was used. This is a less equitable system that the first example, but might be the only way to allocate if there are no client reports of actual uses.

As in a songwriter agreement, the library composer will be required to warrant that, except for arrangements of public domain material or "sound-a-likes," all compositions are original and capable of copyright protection and registration with the PROs.

Re-titling Agreements

Some libraries will offer artists the opportunity to market their music as part of the library. In these cases, the artist is already attempting to market or sell their music to the public but wants to take advantage of the library's contacts and established relationships with the production community. In order to retain as much of their rights as possible, including the rights to sell copies of their own music, some artists will enter into a re-titling agreement with the library.

In this type of agreement, the library is given the right to take existing compositions, written and published by the artist, and re-title the composition and re-register the new title with the PROs. This is necessary because it would be confusing (and probably not accepted by the PROs) to have the same title, same writer, and different publishers.

An example of the listings for a re-titled work looks like this:

ORIGINAL TITLE	RE-TITLED WORK
Written by Composer	Written by Composer
Published by Composer's Pub. Co.	Published by Library's Pub Co

This creates a derivative work under a new title or "shadow copyright," so that the income streams created by the artist are separated from the income streams created by the library. Although it is improper to have a single work registered as two separate copyrights, this is a standard practice in the music library industry.

These types of agreements can be either exclusive for the music library business or non-exclusive, meaning that the artists can enter into agreements with multiple parties for the same underlying music. This raises several issues that can cause confusion and, sometimes, litigation regarding the multiple titles created by the different libraries based on the same recording. The use of digital recognition technologies to identify music only adds to these types of problems. For example:

A. An artist or composer enters into multiple agreements for the same tracks with different libraries, each of whom re-titles the songs. A music editor, who has access to more than one library with the same music, includes the music in a production that they are working on. From what library did he get the music and which library gets paid?

B. Using digital recognition technology, a music library (Library #1) identifies one of its tracks in a program that does not have a license with it. Library #1 contacts the production company, claiming copyright infringement for an unlicensed composition. The production company determines that they actually used a track from Library #2, with whom they have a valid license.

   If the composer's agreements were non-exclusive with both libraries, the production company is not liable for copyright infringement. In order to avoid future claims, however, they decide not to use any of Library #2's music in the future unless Library #2 will warrant that they have the exclusive rights to the music supplied to the production company.

C. Same factual situation as above, except that the composer's agreement with Library #2 was exclusive. Now the composer has breached their contract and can be held liable for any damages caused to the production company or Library #2, which could include loss of revenue if the production company cancels their license with Library #2.

For writers entering into non-exclusive agreements, the different libraries may each re-title the same pieces of music, so that there are multiple versions of the same composition being distributed and licensed to production companies. This only increases the likelihood that the issues above will occur and the writers and libraries expose themselves to greater liability.

The concept of re-titling has come under fire due to the problems listed above, but it is still used by many libraries in order to add to their catalogs. Writers entering into these types of agreements need to be aware of the issues involved and protect themselves by not granting exclusive rights to one party while licensing the same catalog to another party.

Library Licensing Agreements

With production music libraries having music that is not song- and artist-specific, and their fees being lower than traditional music publishers and record companies, the libraries have business relationships with elements of the production community that many publishers and labels do not have. For example, there are many uses of music that are generally unseen by the public and used by companies internally, at conventions and conferences or on their intranet site when the business desires music but does not need (or cannot afford) popular music. Production music can be used as background score to the video productions created by these companies to enhance the visuals created for their particular needs.

In addition, some libraries feature what can be termed "sound design," such as tracks for different percussion sounds (drums or cymbal sounds) or short bursts of instruments, called "hits," that offer a producer the chance to add an audio impact to their visual components.

Many of the agreements libraries have with their clients are similar to the agreements traditional music publishers have with their licensees, with synchronization licenses being the most prevalent. One form of these agreements is sometimes referred to as a "needledrop" agreement, a term that relates back to the times when the libraries were distributed on vinyl and the stylus (or "needle") of a record player was placed on the record. Each use of a track was considered a separate use and generated a separate fee.

As with most synchronization licenses, the term, territory, and media come into play in setting the fees for the various cues being used. Many libraries have "rate cards" that potential users can utilize to determine what their costs will be before using the tracks. Each library sets its own fees, based on the various criteria they deem important.

Another type of agreement is a "production agreement," in which a particular program or film can use anything in the library for a one-time flat fee payment. Similar to this is the "blanket agreement," which allows a particular production company or post-production facility to include the production music into any production on which they are working. Both of these types of agreements raise issues about how the composers would be paid their share of the license fees, as discussed above.

With the explosion of reality-based programming, which is usually produced with very low budgets, there are television programs that make extensive use of production agreements by using library music as a substitute for original underscore and use very little original music in their programs.

These agreements are usually for a short period of time, such as one or two years, so that the end users have a limited period during which they can use the library's music in their productions. However, despite the term being for a short period, the libraries can grant rights in perpetuity to their clients, as long as the music is included in the productions during the term of their agreement with the library.

All of the agreements above usually have provisions that the production companies must prepare and submit music cue sheets to the PROs so that the library and composers can collect their public performance royalties for any uses of the music in which a royalty would be generated under the PROs' systems of monitoring.

NON-EXCLUSIVE LIBRARY PLACEMENT AGREEMENT

This type of agreement is used by independent artists or composers who wish to have their music exploited in the music library market while still being able to exploit the music on their own. No ownership is granted as is done in a publishing agreement and the library has limited rights as to how it can license the music.

Non-Exclusive Library Placement Agreement

This Agreement is made and entered into as of the 1st day of _____, 2012, by and between _____, ("Library"), d/b/a _____ Music, (ASCAP), _____ Music Publishing (BMI), and _____ Publishing (SESAC), located at _____, on the one part,

and _____ (ASCAP), master owner and composer ("Composer"), and _____ Publishing Designee, (ASCAP), (collectively referred to as "Company"), _____, on the other part. Library, Composer, and Company agree as follows:

1.   Subject to the terms, conditions, and limitations hereinafter mentioned, the Composer and Company hereby licenses to Library, and appoints Library his non-exclusive agent for the World (hereinafter referred to as the "Licensed Territory") for the introduction and exploitation as hereinafter mentioned of wholly-owned and controlled original and

re-titled compositions ("Derivative Works") and recordings, as listed on Schedule A ("Sample Library"), based on original compositions and master recordings (hereinafter known as the "_____ Catalogue"), into the music library marketplace ("Market").

Additional compositions may be determined to be included by both parties upon mutual consent during the Term of this Agreement, and would then be added to Schedule A, and would be subject to the terms and conditions herein.

Although a non-exclusive agreement on some levels, this does have certain elements of exclusivity—see below in paragraph 1.

As most libraries contain music by composers from all three performing rights organizations, the library usually has publishing companies with each PRO as well.

In most cases, the composer owns the music and, therefore, is the party licensing it to the library.

This grants the library the rights to exploit the music under the original titles as well as under a re-title in the music library market.

See paragraph 2 below for more details about re-titles and derivative works.

Attached to this agreement is a schedule of titles covered. This paragraph also allows for additional titles to be added.

As to Derivative Works that may be created under the terms of this Agreement, Composer and Company hereby appoint Library as the exclusive agent for the Licensed Territory under the same terms and conditions. Hereinafter, unless otherwise set forth, "Recordings" shall mean the Derivative Works which are intended to be disseminated and otherwise distributed.

For the derivative works created under this agreement, the library is the exclusive agent for the composer. Some agreements state that the library would be the exclusive agent for the composer in the market, not only for the derivative works, but for all music listed on Schedule A. This would prevent the composer from licensing the same compositions and master recordings to several different libraries, all under different titles. This could cause confusion in the marketplace as well as difficulties in identification of the source of any particular track using digital recognition technologies (see discussion in the article above).

2.   To facilitate tracking and royalty distributions, Composer and Company agree that all previously-released songs submitted for inclusion in the Sample Library shall be re-titled ("Derivative Works"), and that Composer and Company assign and grant the one hundred percent (100%) Library's administration right and "publisher's share" of revenue of the Company's Derivative Works to Library, and that Company shall (A) retain one hundred percent (100%) of the "writer's share" of said Derivative Works. In the event a Composition or Master Recording listed on Schedule A has been licensed or otherwise exploited prior to the date hereof, the Composition and the related Master will be re-titled by Library in an effort to differentiate uses procured by Library and its designees hereunder from any other of Composer and Company's licenses or exploitations.

By re-titling the existing songs, a second version is created to separate the revenue streams of exploitation by the composer and exploitation by the library, with the composer still listed as the writer but the library listed as publisher for the derivative works and collecting the publisher's share of income from the PROs, per paragraph 5 below.

Accordingly, it is understood and agreed that Library shall not be entitled to participate in the proceeds of any license under the original title of the Composition or recording.

Due to the separation of income streams, the library will not be entitled to share in the proceeds of any licenses issued by the composer under the original titles.

Needle-drop payments for use of Company's works in the Library shall be distributed equally, fifty percent (50%) to Company, and fifty percent (50%) to Library.

A "needle drop" is a term derived from the days when vinyl records were used and a "needle" was used for playback (see the section on the early days of mechanical licensing on page 28). While many agreements between the library and potential users will be a blanket license, there may be times when the end user wants to license only a particular track (or tracks) and not use the blanket agreement. Unlike a blanket or "bulk" license (see paragraph 3h, below), the fees are split with the composer.

3.   During the Term, the Composer and Company hereby authorize Library in the Licensed Territory the worldwide license and right to:

a)   use, perform, and reproduce (and license others to use, perform and reproduce) the master recordings and musical compositions indicated on Schedule "A" in connection with live and recorded audio visual programs and productions, for purposes of exploitation pursuant to the terms of this Agreement.

Company acknowledges that Library and its licensees are not signatories to any music labor unions or guilds (collectively "Guilds") and that Company's works were not recorded pursuant to any such Guilds.

b)   record (and license others to record) on film, videotape, computer disk and/or any other medium, whether known or hereafter devised, Company's works in synchronization or timed-relation to audio visual productions, and to issue synchronization licenses for the reproduction and/or synchronization or timed-relation of the Recordings on any visual, audio or audio-visual sound carrier now known or hereafter devised including but not limited to videocassette, DVD, CD-ROM, Internet and all other new media now known or hereinafter developed.

c)   broadcast, telecast, syndicate, license, distribute, and otherwise exploit (and license others to similarly exploit) the Recordings contained in Schedule "A", and to manufacture, if necessary, on compact disc, copies of the Recordings in sufficient numbers as may be required by Library solely for the promotion of continuing exploitation of the Recordings in the Licensed Territory as authorized hereunder. The costs of design, editing, mixing, production, manufacture and packaging of those discs and related artwork shall be borne solely by Library.

d)   transpose, revise, add to, take from, substitute, and to prepare and re-title the original compositions and Recordings;

e)   issue performance licenses in the Licensed Territory as deemed necessary in the normal course of business;

The rights granted below are similar to those granted by songwriters to a publishing company as applied to audio-visual productions, such as television, motion pictures, videos, and games.

Most library music is not recorded under union contract, so there are no additional payments made under union rules. This is crucial to the end users, who want to pay a fee to the library without any further obligations.

The library is granted the right to license for synchronization to audio-visual works.

A limited right to reproduce CDs or other audio-only files for promoting the music to potential end users.

This grants the library the rights to make changes and modifications to the compositions, including the right to re-title.

The library has the right to issue direct performing licenses if necessary. Optional language would be that the composer is entitled to 50% of any such license fee.

f)   the right to use the name, photograph, likeness, and or biographical material as submitted or approved by the Composer and Company of any and all Composers of the original recordings, for the purpose of the trade or otherwise in connection with the Recordings;

g)   all rights to license, assign, and enter into agreements to or with any person or entity with respect to all or any rights or part of the rights granted hereunder;

h)   collect and retain bulk Library Market license fees, if any, on contracts and licenses entered into by Library under and during the Term of this Agreement;

> In this context, "bulk Library Market license fees" are fees paid to the library for access to its entire catalog, not just the compositions covered under this agreement. In such a case, it is difficult, if not impossible, to determine which songs in the library are being used and, therefore, difficult to allocate a portion of the fees to any particular song or composer. There are methods for allocating these types of fees (see discussion above) but they are based on various formulae, not actual use.

4.   In consideration of the above authorization granted by the Composer and Company, Library hereby undertakes:

a)   to register with ASCAP, BMI or SESAC all necessary details in respect to the Recordings and compositions therein.

> Since the library is re-titling the compositions, with their own publishing companies listed, it is the library's responsibility to register the new titles with the PROs.

b)   to exploit the Recordings and compositions therein within the Licensed Territory;

c)   to supply the Recordings and compositions therein or copies thereof, at its own expense, to its clients for audition, selection, and use at their own place of business.

5.   In consideration of the above undertakings on the part of Library, the Composer and Company hereby agree:

> The composer gets 100% of writer's share of PRO income from uses licensed by the library.

a)   that Composer shall be entitled to collect and retain one hundred percent (100%) of the Composer's pro rata share of performing rights fees accrued in the Licensed Territory generated from uses of the Derivative Works issued by Library in accordance with the provision of Paragraph 2;

b)   that Library shall be entitled to collect and retain one hundred percent (100%) of Library's administration right and revenue of the Company's Derivative Works to Library, as administrator, and that Company shall retain (A) one hundred percent (100%) of the Composer's pro rata share of said Derivative Works, accrued in the Licensed Territory generated from uses of the Derivative Works issued by Library in accordance with the provision of Paragraph 2.

The library gets 100% of the publisher's share of PRO income for uses licensed by the library.

c)   that Library shall collect and retain one hundred percent (100%) of all license fees, if any, derived from licensing the Library works in the bulk Library Market. Said license fees, if any, shall offset costs and expenses incurred in reproducing, manufacturing, and promoting the Library. Composer and Company shall retain the ownership and rights to license fees from any non-Library, individual placement of the works, pursuant to paragraph 6, below;

The library retains 100% of fees from the bulk library market but the composer retains fees from placements of individual works, subject to paragraph 6.

d)   all rights not expressly set forth herein as a licensed right are reserved by Composer and Company.

6.   If and when a non-Library, individual placement of one of Company's and Composer's Compositions is procured by Library for either: (a) release for sale to the public on records, tapes, compact discs, soundtrack releases, compilations, or other recorded products; (b) synchronization in a theatrical motion picture; (c) synchronization in a television program for broadcast to the public; (d) synchronization in a home video program for sale to the public; or (e) any audiovisual production (including, but not limited to, productions released on video cassette, video disc or DVD, commercials, promotional film or television trailers, Internet sites, computer programs and/or games, karaoke or any similar media), Composer and Company shall be compensated according to any previously negotiated and current placement Agreement with Winogradsky/Sobel, or upon an equal, fifty-fifty (50% – 50%) split of front-end licensing fess, and an equal, fifty-fifty (50% – 50%) co-publishing grant to Library, for any specific individual song placement, in the absence of such a placement agreement.

If the library secures a placement of an individual composition (as opposed to a bulk license), the library and composer split the license fee 50/50 and the library becomes a 50% co-publisher of the compositions. This is similar to the deal for representation in paragraph 2a and 2b in the sample contract in Chapter 9: Pitching and Placement Agreements.

7.   This Agreement shall come into force as of _____ 1, 2012 and remain in force for a term of three years ("Term"), it being understood and agreed that Library's licensees shall retain, in perpetuity, the rights to exploit Company's and Composer's Derivative Works, as set forth in this Agreement, in connection with any Production created and embodying music from Library during the Term.

These types of deals are usually at least two to three years, as it takes time for the music to get into the systems of the end users and for uses to begin. Note that, although the term in this agreement is three years, the rights being granted by the library to end users may be in perpetuity.

Said three-year term shall automatically roll over into successive three-year terms, and may be terminated by either party upon 3 months written notice prior to the end of any such term.

The term automatically extends unless 90 days' notice is given by either party.

At no time does Library have or maintain any rights (other than specifically set forth herein) in the original Compositions, works or Recordings, as differentiated from the Derivative Works subsequently created.

The composer retains all rights ownership, licensing, and royalty rights in the original compositions.

8.   Library shall not be liable to Composer or Company for the payment of any sums with respect to the performance rights income of the Derivative Works (or any parts thereof); provided however, that in the event and to the extent that the performing rights society inadvertently pays the entire performance fee revenue (Composer and Library share) to Library, then Library shall retain fifty percent (50%) of all performing fees accruing in the Licensed Territory generated from uses of the Library, according to paragraph 2, above, and shall account and pay the one hundred percent (100%) pro-rata Composer's share to the Composer (or designated entity).

Unless the PRO pays both the writer and publisher shares to the library, the library is not liable to the composer for performance fees. See comment to 3e above.

9.   Notwithstanding any provision to the contrary contained herein, if at any time any entity, television network, television station, radio station or other company licensed to broadcast, incorporate or otherwise utilize the Recordings or any parts thereof, does not or may not hold a valid performing license from ASCAP, BMI, SESAC or any other applicable performing rights society covering the non-theatrical performance of the Recordings, Library, or its publishing designee, shall automatically have the right to grant to each such network, station, or other entity the non-dramatic performing rights in and to the Recordings (or any number thereof) for use in connection with the license obtained through Library. In the absence of said performance rights Agreements, the parties herein agree to negotiate the distribution and payment of collected performance rights income in good faith.

This further clarifies the library's right to issue direct performance licenses but also has language that the parties agree to negotiate in good faith for an allocation of these fees.

10.   Nothing herein shall be construed in any manner to mean that any license and/or right granted herein to Library shall allow Library to sell, license or otherwise take Recordings, in whole or in part, directly into the non-Library market, without the specific permission of Composer and Company, and according to paragraph 6, above.

This grant of rights to the library is for the library market only. All other rights remain with the composer.

11. Composer and Company hereby warrants and represents that they have the right to enter into this agreement and to grant to Library all of the rights granted herein, and that the exercise by Library of any and all of the rights granted to Library in this agreement will not violate or infringe upon any common law or statutory rights of any person, firm or corporation, including, without limitation, contractual rights, copyrights and rights of privacy. All elements within the Composition and Master are either original with the Company, or are fully cleared by the Company. No Composition shall, in whole or in part, be an imitation or copy of, or infringe upon, any other material, or violate or infringe upon any common law or statutory rights of any person, firm or corporation, including, without limitation, musical samples, contractual rights, copyrights and rights of privacy. Company further represents and warrants that the rights granted herein are free and clear of any claims, demands, liens or encumbrances from any other party or musician or Guild, and that Company owns and controls all Master and Composition rights to the "_____ Catalogue" granted to Library herein, together with co-writers, to the works contained in Schedule "A", and that such use authorized herein will not give rise to any claims of infringement, invasion of privacy or publicity or claims for payment of re-use fees or residuals (any and all third party payments shall be Company's responsibility). Company shall secure any appropriate and necessary release and authorization from any other performers or rights-holders in the compositions and Recordings.

> These are standard warranties and representations about the (1) right to enter into this agreement; (2) the compositions do not violate any copyrights or other rights; (3) the grant is free of any claims by any third parties (including co-writers); and (4) the composer has secured any rights necessary from any third parties.

12. Composer and Company hereby indemnify, save and hold Library, its assigns, licensees and its and their directors, officers, shareholders, agents and employees harmless from any and all liability, claims, demands, loss and damage (including reasonable counsel fees and court costs) arising out of or connected with or resulting from any breach of any of the warranties, representations or agreements made by Composer and Company in this agreement and resulting in a final, non-appealable adverse judgment to Composer and Company, or a settlement entered into with Composer and Company's prior written consent which consent shall not be unreasonably withheld, or incurred in connection with any claim, action or proceeding brought at Composer and Company's request.

> The composer indemnifies the library against breach, as determined by a court, or settled with the composer's consent, not to be unreasonably withheld.

13. This agreement sets forth the entire understanding between the parties and cannot be changed, modified or canceled except by an instrument signed by both parties. This agreement shall be governed by and construed under the laws of the state of California applicable to agreements wholly performed therein.

14. In the event of legal proceedings between the parties, the parties agree to resolve such disputes through binding Arbitration in the county of Los Angeles.

15.   If any provision of this contract shall be held void, voidable, invalid, inoperative or otherwise unenforceable, no other provision of this contract shall be affected as a result thereof, and accordingly, the remaining provision of this contract shall remain in full force and effect as though such void, voidable, invalid, inoperative or unenforceable provision had not been contained herein, provided, however, that such provision was not clearly a material element of the consideration for this Agreement.

16.   Composer and Company acknowledge and agree that Composer and Company have been represented by independent legal counsel or have had the opportunity to be represented by independent legal counsel of Composer and Company's own choice for purposes of advising Composer and Company in connection with the negotiation, preparation and execution of this Agreement. Additionally, Composer and Company acknowledge and agree that, if Composer and Company have not been represented by legal counsel of Composer and Company's own choice for purposes of advising Composer and Company in connection with the negotiation, preparation and execution of this Agreement, Composer and Company's failure to be represented by independent legal counsel in connection with this Agreement was determined solely by Composer and Company, without any interference by Library or any person, firm or corporation affiliated with or related to Library.

> The composer has either been represented by an attorney or waives that right.

IN WITNESS WHEREOF, the parties hereto have this day signed below to confirm the agreement reached.

Dated as of: _____ 1, 20___

_____   _____
Library Composer   Company

- -

SCHEDULE A

For purposes of this agreement, the term "Compositions" shall be deemed to mean Company's undivided copyright interest in and to the musical compositions and Recordings, written in whole or in part by _____, as set forth below:

ORIGINAL TITLE	NEW LIBRARY TITLE	COMPOSERS	SHARE

_____
Writer

_____
Company

REPRESENTATION AND ADMINISTRATION AGREEMENT

This agreement is between a composer who has an existing library catalog (not a collection of songs and cues that they are marketing themselves as an independent artist) and another library that will now have the rights to administer and license the composer's works.

Dated as of _____ between:

_____   _____

_____   _____

_____   _____

(hereinafter "Composer")   (hereinafter "Library")

The library has the exclusive rights to market and administer the composer's library.

Scope of Agreement: Composer hereby engages Library, and Library hereby accepts such engagement, to act as the exclusive licensing representative and administrator of Composer's Music & Sound Design Library as provided herein below throughout the Term and Territory.

"Composer's Music & Sound Design Library" shall mean, individually and collectively, the musical compositions and sound recordings listed and specified in <u>Exhibit A</u> attached hereto and such sound recordings and musical compositions created, composed and/or owned by Composer (collectively, the "Works") over the Term of this Agreement which are to be delivered exclusively to Library (except as otherwise provided for herein). All sound recordings to be delivered to Library shall be fully mastered.

Schedule A will define the list of compositions and master recordings being supplied by the composer to the library for exploitation. Note that this agreement does not allow for re-titling the music, as was stated in the previous agreement.

1.　Term: "Term" shall be for ___ years, commencing as of _____ and expiring _____.

The term is for a period of years. Often, there will be language about automatic renewals or options to renew.

2.　Territory: "Territory" is defined as the United States of America.

The territory of the library's exclusive rights is the U.S., but that does not preclude them from issue a worldwide license. Many libraries have different representatives in each country, like a sub-publisher, so that their music can be marketed in the local territories by local libraries.

3.　Post-Term: Library, and Composer, as appropriate, shall collect and remit to Composer and Library, respectively (as provided for below), all license fees and royalties generated hereunder during the Term for a period of one (1) year following the end of the Term.

One-year post-term collection period.

4. Duties of Library: Library agrees to act in good faith and to use its best efforts in the performance of the following duties during the Term:

> "Good faith" and "best efforts" are legal terms that don't have a strict definition, so it can be hard to determine if the standards of conduct are met. It is easier to identify "bad faith."

a) Library will promote Composer's Music & Sound Design Library throughout the Territory to secure offers from third parties and negotiate license agreements for use of the Works in all forms of media now known or hereafter devised.

> The library will promote, offer to third parties, and negotiate for uses of the composer's material.

Library shall be responsible for Library's "overhead" costs including but not limited to the costs of issuing licenses; the design of CD and DVD packages (if such design was performed by Library); ancillary materials (such as stationery, mailing labels, buck slips, etc.); and employee costs. During the Term, Library shall also send regular emails promoting Composer to current and potential Library clients, continuously feature Composer on the Library website and promote Composer in no less favorable fashion than any other libraries administered or controlled by Library.

> The library will pay all costs of promoting the composer's material, promote on their own website, and treat the composer no less favorably than other composers signed to the library.

b) Library will not enter into any so-called "direct licenses" of public performance rights for the Works without first securing Composer's written approval. In the event that any direct performance licenses are issued, Composer shall receive seventy five percent (75%) of the license fee collected by Library for said license (i.e., fifty percent [50%] as writer's share and twenty-five percent [25%] as Composer's share of publisher's share).

> Composer approval must be sought for the library to issue and direct performing rights licenses and money is split 75/25 in the composer's favor. This follows the royalty division discussed in paragraph 6a, below.

c) Library will work closely with Composer and secure Composer's approval in connection with (i) the preparation of all promotional materials to be used and disseminated hereunder and (ii) the packaging used to distribute copies of the Works to prospective licensees of the Works. Notwithstanding anything to the contrary contained herein, the allocation of costs in connection with materials to be prepared hereunder will be subject to the mutual approval of the parties.

> This regards cooperation between the parties about promotional material. To many successful library composers, this is crucial, as they have been marketing their library for many years and have a sense of what works (and what doesn't) with their current and potential clients.

d) Should Composer not do so, Library will register and clear all musical compositions embodied in the Works with the appropriate performing rights societies.

> The library will assume filing of PRO registrations if not already done by the composer.

e) Library shall not have the right to produce or authorize the production of sound recordings for retail sale to the general public through physical or electronic means, including digital phonorecord delivery, i.e., "digital downloads".

> The library may not sell copies of the composer's material directly to the public, either in physical or digital format.

5.   Duties of Composer: Composer agrees to act in good faith and to use its best efforts in the performance of the following duties during the Term:

Reciprocal good faith and best efforts clauses.

a)   Composer shall provide Library with all information and materials reasonably necessary in order for Library to comply with its duties as described herein and to promote Composer's Music & Sound Design Library, including, without limitation, sample CDs, content for brochures, writer/performer information, etc. Composer shall be solely responsible for all costs incurred in connection with the creation of Composer's Music & Sound Design Library and all Works contained therein.

The composer will supply all materials and pay for the creation of all music.

b)   Composer shall provide Library with (i) fully-mastered high-resolution copies of all musical compositions and sound recordings contained on Exhibit A; (ii) the Composer logo; (iii) other artwork elements necessary for Library to prepare promotional materials (with all materials to be provided to third parties subject to the mutual agreement of the parties); and (iv) names and contact information for all prospective licensees to which Composer wishes Library to contact in order to promote the Works.

This details the materials to be supplied by the composer to the library to assist the library in promoting and marketing the music. "Fully mastered" means that all elements of the sound recording, i.e. the instruments, equalization, any effects, etc., are fully included in the recordings being supplied. High resolution copies are necessary to use in television programs and motion pictures.

c)   Special events, travel and specialty marketing materials carried out for the specific request of Composer in connection with promoting and licensing Composer's Music & Sound Design Library outside the scope of Library's regular marketing plan shall be mutually approved by Library and Composer.

Extra events and materials by mutual consent of the parties.

d)   Promptly following receipt of its next statement from its previous administrator, Composer will (i) provide Library with the listing of license agreements provided by that previous administrator the terms of which continue beyond the commencement date of the Term and (ii) in connection with any prior licenses with terms that continue beyond the commencement of the Term and are not contained on the list provided to Composer by its previous administrator, use best efforts to provide Library with a complete listing of all such license agreements (along with the dates upon which the terms of such agreements will expire).

Since licenses to third parties can overlap administrators of the composer's library, the composer will supply a list to the library of deals in progress, expiration dates, and other details so that (i) the library doesn't attempt to market the composer to an existing client and (ii) the library can try to extend the deal when the current agreement expires.

Library's right to promote and license the Works in connection with such licensees will commence upon the expiration of such licenses.

After the previous agreements have expired, the library may exploit the composer's works.

6.   Compensation: In consideration of the services to be rendered by Library, payment shall be as follows:

a)   For fees and non-performance publishing royalties earned during the Term, Library shall (i) collect one hundred percent (100%) of gross receipts derived from and (ii) pay to Composer paid fifty percent (50%) of all net receipts of license fees and non-performance royalties from licenses entered into during the Term with third parties for the use of any part of Composer's Music & Sound Design Library.

For sync licenses, the library will collect all the fees and pay to the composer 50% of all income.

b)   As of the commencement date hereof, Library shall (i) collect one hundred percent (100%) of gross receipts derived from and (ii) pay to Composer fifty percent (50%) of the "publisher's share" of performance royalties received in connection with Composer's Music & Sound Design Library for all earnings for the period commencing as of the date of this agreement (such payments to be accompanied by a copy of the relevant provisions of performance royalty statements rendered to Library), including performance royalties received following the expiration of the Term on performances occurring during the Term.

For public performance royalties, the library will collect the entire publisher's share and pay to the composer 50% of net income.

Composer's compensation may intermittently include, but may not be limited to, the deduction of an expense to register Sound Recordings (masters) and Performing Arts (publishing) copyrights with the United States Copyright Office, as approved by Composer in writing.

The library shall have the right to deduct from the composer's share of income the costs of registering the works for copyright.

c)   Composer shall be entitled to collect one hundred percent (100%) of the "writer's share" of performance royalties received in connection with Composer's Music & Sound Design Library for all earnings.

The composer is paid 100% of the "writer's share" directly from their PRO.

d)   Synchronization license fees derived from the use of Composer's Music & Sound Design Library as described herein shall be paid to Library, and Library shall provide to Composer royalties due therefrom to Composer not later than thirty (30) days following its receipt thereof.

The composer is to be paid sync fees within 30 days after the library receives payment. Since the library has no rights of ownership in the music, having the composer pay for all the costs of copyrighting is appropriate.

In connection with " blanket license" royalties based upon fee payments received by Library, Library will calculate Composer's royalties therefrom on a quarterly basis (and account to and pay Composer therefrom within thirty [30] days following Library's receipt of quarterly reports pursuant to such "blanket licenses"),

A " blanket license" would be for the library's entire catalog, which would include the composer's works. In such cases, the fees are usually a one-time fee, not an individual fee every time a cue is used. The library will pay the composer within 30 days of getting reports from their client as to which cues were used.

by multiplying fifty percent (50%) of the gross sums received by Library for the prior quarter pursuant to any such " blanket license" agreement by a fraction, the numerator of which is the number of Composer licensee reported uses during such quarter of Works and the denominator of which is the total number of Library works uses (including Works uses) during such quarter.

The parties agree that, in connection with "weighting" sound design elements and fully orchestrated cues for the foregoing, one (1) fully orchestrated cue will have the same value as two (2) sound design elements.

Notwithstanding anything to the contrary contained herein, Library will not make any Works subject to any " blanket license" without first securing Composer's written approval, such approval not to be unreasonably withheld, delayed or conditioned; provided, however, Composer agrees that Library will have the right to enter into "blanket licenses" containing the Works with major networks that extend past the expiration of the Term up until December 31, 2015 when Library must do so to remain on any such network's "preferred list" without securing Composer's approval therefor. In the event that Library does so, it will notify Composer thereof.

The formula is to take 50% of the fees (the remaining 50% remains with the library) and multiply it by a fraction based upon the total number of cues used by the client and the number of composer's cues that are reported. For example, if the library had 1,000 uses and the composer's cues were 50 of those uses, the composer would get 5% of the 50% allocated to be paid to all composers.

For sound design cues, i.e., drum hits, cymbal whooshes, etc., the sound design cues are weighted as one-half of a fully orchestrated musical cue.

The composer must agree to have the works included in the blanket licenses. If so, the library must have the right to grant rights for the composer's works consistent with the licensing requirements of the major networks, which are usually multi-year deals.

e) A certified public accountant on either party's behalf shall have the right to examine the other party's books and records at the examining party's sole expense, upon thirty (30) days written notice, in connection with monies collected by each of the parties and/or paid out hereunder; the relevant party's records relating to any particular royalty statement may be examined as aforesaid during regular business hours where such records are regularly maintained within two (2) years after the date rendered. Each party shall have no obligation to permit the other to examine the books and records relating to any particular royalty statement more than once. Each party shall be deemed to have accepted and consented to all royalty statements and all other accountings rendered hereunder, and each such royalty statement or other accounting shall be conclusive, final, and binding, shall constitute an account stated, and shall not be subject to any objection for any reason whatsoever unless specific objection in writing, stating the basis thereof and is given by such party to the other party within two (2) years after the date rendered. Neither party shall commence or participate in any action, suit, or proceeding of any nature in respect of any royalty statement or other accounting rendered hereunder unless such action, suit, or proceeding is commenced in a court of competent jurisdiction within one (1) year of such party's receipt of said written objection.

> Standard audit provisions.

7. Warranties and Indemnification.

a) Composer warrants that it is the sole owner of Composer's Music & Sound Design Library; that it has not previously assigned, pledged or otherwise encumbered the same except for blanket licenses already in effect at the commencement of this Agreement; it has full power to enter into this Agreement;

that the Works are original and are not in the public domain;

that Composer is to be solely and exclusively responsible for paying all costs incurred in the creation of Composer's Music & Sound Design Library (including payments to third parties for services rendered); Composer shall be responsible for any and all payments due to the writers, performers and/or producers of the musical material contained in the Works;

> In situations like this, the composer may not be the sole writer of all the music in the library being licensed. As such, unlike the traditional songwriter agreement, the warranty is not that he wrote everything but that he owns everything in the library.
>
> It is not uncommon for music libraries to have versions of public domain works, so this language might need to be modified.
>
> The composer will pay all costs of creating the library as well as paying any third parties (including other composers) who contribute to its creation.

nothing in Composer's Music & Sound Design Library infringes upon any statutory or common law copyright or any other rights of any third party(ies); there are and will be no encumbrances, liens, conditions or restrictions upon or affecting Composer's Music & Sound Design Library; and Composer has not and will not violate any law, regulation or contractual obligation by entering into and performing this agreement and will not make any grant or assignment that can, will or might prevent or interfere with Library's full and complete enjoyment of rights and privileges granted hereunder, except for blanket licenses already in effect at the commencement of this Agreement.

More standard representations.

b)   Library warrants that it has the full power and right to enter into this agreement and that it shall be responsible for all aspects of the licensing and administration of Composer's Music & Sound Design Library as set forth herein.

The library represents that it will assume all duties involved with the licensing and administration of the composer's library.

The parties will at all times indemnify, defend and hold harmless each other and their owners, assignees and licensees from and against any and all claims, liabilities, suits, actions, costs and expenses (including reasonable legal costs and attorneys' fees) arising out of such party's performance hereunder and for any breach or alleged breach by such party of any warranty, representation or agreement hereunder which are reduced to final judgment or are settled with the approval of the indemnifying party (such approval not to be unreasonably withheld, delayed or conditioned).

Mutual indemnification clause.

Composer's Music & Sound Design Library shall not be deemed delivered to Library unless Composer has provided to Library documentation signed by all third party composers who render services in connection with Composer's Music & Sound Design Library.

If there are third party writers, the composer must prove to the library that it has the rights to the works created by those third parties. This could be an assignment of copyright or a work-made-for-hire agreement from the writer to the composer.

In the event of any claim, action or proceeding brought by a third party based upon an alleged violation of any of the foregoing warranties, (i) the indemnifying party shall have the right to defend the same through counsel of its own choosing; (ii) no settlement shall be effected without the prior written consent of indemnified party, which consent shall not unreasonably be withheld, delayed or conditioned, and (iii) the indemnifying party shall hold harmless the indemnified party, and any licensee of a subsidiary right, against any damages finally sustained.

In the event of a claim, the party against whom the claim is made has the right to select their own attorney, must approve of any settlement, and hold the other party harmless against any and all damages sustained.

If any such claim, action or proceeding is instituted, the indemnified party shall promptly notify the indemnifying party, who shall fully cooperate in the defense thereof.

These warranties and indemnities shall survive the expiration or termination of this Agreement.

8.   Assignment:

a)   Library may assign this Agreement to any corporation or other business entity, provided that _____ shall continue to perform Library's duties as described in this Agreement.

b)   Composer may assign this Agreement to any corporation or other business entity owned or controlled by Composer, provided that Composer shall notify Library at least thirty (30) days in advance of the assignment, and deliver to Library an assumption by the assignee of all of Composer's obligations hereunder. No such assignment shall affect or impair Library's rights hereunder.

9.   Composer's Current Direct Clients:

a)   The parties agree that Composer may continue to work directly with those client licensees listed on the attached Exhibit B, with which Composer is working directly as of the date of execution of this Agreement.

b)   Composer is entitled to collect and retain all revenues derived from such licensees. Composer shall not be obligated to pay to Library any portion of performance royalties received Composer in connection with performances of Works which are so licensed by Composer.

10.   General:

a)   This agreement will not be amended unless in writing signed by both parties hereto.

b)   The parties understand and agree that Composer will not be treated as an employee of Library. Accordingly, Library will not withhold any amount for taxes on any income paid to Composer.

Notice to the other party.

As some of the obligations of the parties, and rights granted to each other, extend beyond the expiration of the term, these indemnifications also extend beyond the date of termination or expiration.

A "key man" clause stating the library may assign the rights obtained as long as a principal of the library remains involved in the operations of the business.

The composer may also assign this agreement bit only if the obligations are assumed by the assignee.

For composers who have existing clients, sometimes there are provisions that the composer may continue to work with those clients independently of this agreement and the composer shall be entitled to collect all revenues from these clients without obligation to the library.

The composer is an independent contractor, not an employee, so standard income tax deductions will not be taken. The composer shall be responsible for all tax liabilities and obligations on their earnings. Beginning composers should consult with their tax advisers on procedures for paying self-employers taxes.

c)   Composer acknowledges that Library is not a signatory to, and has no present intention of becoming a party to, any guild, collective bargaining or similar agreement that might have jurisdiction over any services rendered by Composer hereunder.

As in many library agreements, there must be no union obligations attached to the use of the music by third parties.

d)   Composer acknowledges that its services hereunder are unique and extraordinary and agrees that any breach by Composer of the exclusivity provisions of this Agreement shall cause Library to suffer immediate and irreparable harm for which Library shall not have an adequate remedy at law. Accordingly, without limitation of its rights, it is agreed that Library shall be entitled to seek immediate injunctive or other equitable relief to prevent any such breach.

As in songwriter agreements, this is deemed to be a personal services contract and the composer is held to a higher standard, allowing the library to restrict them from working for anyone else in the event of a breach by allowing for injunctive relief.

e)   For the avoidance of doubt, Composer retains the right to collect the entire "writer's share" of public performance royalties (as paid directly to writer(s) by the appropriate PRO) derived from the Works.

This reaffirms the language in paragraph 6c, above.

f)   Neither party will be deemed to be in breach of this Agreement until (i) the aggrieved party notifies the other party of such alleged breach in writing and (ii) the allegedly breaching party has not cured such breach within thirty (30) days of its receipt of the aggrieved party's written notice.

Standard notice and cure period provisions.

This instrument constitutes the entire agreement between the parties and cannot be modified except by a written instrument signed by the parties hereto. This Agreement shall be governed and interpreted in accordance with the laws of the State of California.

IN WITNESS WHEREOF, the parties hereto have executed this Agreement on the date first written above.

_____   _____
Composer, d/b/a Composer's   Library
Music & Sound Design Library

MUSIC LIBRARY BLANKET LICENSE AGREEMENT

This agreement is between a library and a television network. It allows the network to use anything in the library in any program produced or initially broadcast on the network during the term of the agreement for a one-time flat fee, i.e., a "blanket" license agreement.

This MUSIC LIBRARY BLANKET LICENSE AGREEMENT (the "Agreement") is made and entered into effective as of _____ ("Effective Date") by and between XYZ THE NETWORK ("The Network"), located at _____ and MUSIC LIBRARY ("Library"), located at _____ (Fed Id #_____).

In consideration of the terms and conditions contained herein, the parties agree as follows:

1.   GRANT OF RIGHTS. In connection with programming and promotions on The Network's owned, operated and/or affiliated media properties and the Networks.

Library hereby grants The Network the non-exclusive worldwide license and right to:

A.   Use, reproduce and distribute the master recordings and musical compositions contained in Library's music library (" Library's music"), in connection with live and recorded programs, promotions and productions produced by, on behalf of or to benefit The Network (collectively referred to herein as the "Productions"), for purposes of exploitation pursuant to the terms of this Agreement.

To the degree that use of the Library's music by Library in a Production is construed a derivative work of the Library's music, The Network shall have the right to prepare derivative works.

Network shall have the right to edit and remix the Library's music, so long as The Network does not alter the fundamental character of the music and lyrics of any musical composition or use the title or subtitle of any musical composition as the title of the Production.

The grant to the network is for all programming and promotions on all network properties. Many television stations have different tiers of programming, such as ESPN and ESPN2, CNN and HLN (formerly Headline News), etc. This covers everything owned or affiliated with the network.

As with many synchronization licenses, this grant is non-exclusive and covers the entire world, even though the network may be based in the U.S.

As with most blanket agreements, the grant is pretty broad and includes live and pre-recorded programming, all promotions for the network, and any programs produced by the network or by third parties for broadcast on the network.

By its inclusion in another work, the music could now be considered part of a derivative work. Whether or not that is accurate, this paragraph covers the possibility and grants the network the right to secure copyright protection on the program with the music included.

Often, a broadcaster will need to edit a track for the specific use intended. Many libraries offer the same composition in varying lengths, i.e. 0:60, 0:30, 0:15, 0:10, and 0:05, so that they have the flexibility to use it in many different ways. This clause allows the network to achieve those variations if deemed necessary. That said, they cannot materially change the composition.

B.   Broadcast, telecast, syndicate, license, distribute, perform, sell and otherwise exploit the Productions with the master recordings and musical compositions contained in Library's music contained therein, by any and all means and methods now known or hereafter devised.

> This grants the network broad rights as to how it can distribute its programs that contain the music.

C.   Record on film, videotape, computer disk and/or any other medium and/or format, whether known or hereafter devised, Library's music in synchronization, timed relation or embodied within the Productions.

> Synchronization rights to the music within their programs.

2.   LICENSE FEE. The parties acknowledge that The Network shall not be required to make any additional payments or other remuneration whatsoever for the rights granted pursuant to this Agreement except as expressly provided below:

> Confirmation that this is a one-time payment for the rights being granted.

A.   Upon The Network's receipt of an appropriate invoice and appropriate tax identification form, _____ US Dollars ($ _____) payable as follows: (i) fifty percent (50%) of said License Fee within sixty (60) business days from the later of (a) execution of this Agreement or (b) commencement of the Term and (ii) the remaining fifty percent (50%) due upon completion of delivery of the Library Format ("Initial License Fee").

> Although this agreement contains the license fee and federal tax ID number, many companies still require an invoice and a W-9 tax form in order to facilitate payment of the fee. The library must wait up to 60 days for the initial payment of 50% of the fee, with the remaining 50% payable upon delivery of the music in the format required by the network (see paragraph 4a below).

B.   Pursuant to Section 3A and conditioned upon cue sheets reporting at least a ten percent (10%) increased use of the Library's music than in the Initial Term or immediately preceding Extension Term (if applicable), the amount specified in this Section 2B shall be increased, on an annual basis, by an amount equal to ten percent (10%) of the License Fee of the immediately preceding period ("Extension Term"), as established in paragraph 2 (A) above, and shall be payable within sixty (60) business days of commencement of the First Extension Term and any subsequent Extension Term (if any) and receipt of Library's invoice. The "Initial License Fee" and the Extension License Fee(s) (if any) shall be collectively referred to as the License Fee".

> If the amount of usage of the library's music goes up by 10% during the term (as defined below), the fee for any extension term also goes up by 10%.

C. Subject to the terms of Section 3B, One Thousand US Dollars ($1,000) shall be payable within sixty (60) business days of execution of the Agreement ("Extended License Fee"), and Library shall have the right to deduct Two US Dollars ($2) for each "Inadvertent Use" (as defined below) from the Extended License Fee. The Extended License Fee is understood to be a temporary means of allowing The Network "extended uses" of Library's music, and in no event shall allow extended uses for greater than one (1) calendar year following the termination of any Term.

This payment shall be a non-recoupable and final payment for any music in Library's catalog that is inadvertently used by The Network after the Term.

> This is a somewhat unusual clause. Once a library gets distributed to music editors and placed on hard drives in editing bays or on a centralized server, it is hard to delete efficiently and may be used "inadvertently." This clause provides an insurance policy to the network with a $1,000 premium paid to the library in the event that the library is used after the date of termination.

> Despite the language above about the right to deduct $2.00 for each inadvertent use, the fee of $1,000 is non-recoupable, so if the number of inadvertent uses does not add up to the full $1,000, the library gets to keep the remainder of the fee and does not have to pay it back to the network.

3. TERM.

> Initial term of one year.

A. The "Term" shall collectively refer to the Initial Term and Extension Term(s), if any, as provided below.

(i) The Initial Term ("Initial Term") of this Agreement shall be for a one (1) year period and shall commence on _____ and end on _____.

(ii) The Term shall extend automatically to include up to two (2) additional one (1) year periods (each an "Extension Term," sequentially numbered as "First Extension Term," "Second Extension Term," and so forth), unless The Network sends notice of termination of the Agreement to Library at least ninety (90) days prior to the commencement of the next applicable Extension Term. If applicable, each Extension Term shall commence immediately upon expiration of the preceding Extension Term or Initial Term, as applicable.

Upon one hundred eighty (180) days prior written notice, this Agreement may be terminated by The Network.

> An option for the term to extend for two additional terms of one year each that is automatically renewed unless notice is given by the network to the library no less than 90 days prior to the date of expiration of the then-current term.

> This agreement may be cancelled at any time upon 180 days notice from the network.

B.   Pursuant to Section 2(C), in the event of inadvertent use(s) of the Library's music after the Term ("Inadvertent Use(s)"), Library may deduct from the Extended License Fee such Inadvertent Uses. The Extended License Fee shall be deemed to extend the Term solely as to the specific musical compositions and master recordings that constitute the Inadvertent Use(s) and shall not be deemed to otherwise extend the Term as to the entirety of Library's music. For clarification, a single Inadvertent Use refers collectively to both the musical composition and the master recording.

This restates the concept of inadvertent uses and further states that the term is extended only for those tracks that are used inadvertently, not the entire catalog.

C.   For avoidance of doubt, the parties agree that The Network shall retain, in perpetuity and throughout the universe in all media now known or hereafter devised and without any remuneration, the rights to exploit Library's music in connection with any Productions created and embodying musical compositions and master recordings from Library's music during the Term.

Although the term of the agreement is only one year (plus extensions), the rights granted for use of the music in the programs are in perpetuity. This distinguishes the amount of time the network has rights to include the library in their program with how long the programs can be distributed containing the music.

4.   DELIVERY.

A.   Within seven (7) calendar days of execution of the Agreement, Library shall furnish and deliver The Network with such copies of Library's music in WAV format(s) and as requested by The Network ("Library Format")

along with accompanying metadata in the format required by Library. The Network may make copies of the Library Format subject to the terms of this Agreement, but the copies of the Library Format shall remain the exclusive property of Library.

The network has certain requirements about how the music is to be delivered. In this agreement, the music is in files in the WAV format. Other methods are on CD, DVD, or delivered via digital download.

Metadata is information embedded in the digital file that contains information the network needs to fill out music cue sheets, such as title, composer, publisher, PRO affiliations, and timing. In addition, it may also contain information such as the style of music, beats per minute, musical key, vocal or instrumental, and other identifiers to assist the music editors in selecting the right music for a particular use or scene without having to listen to every cue in the library.

B.   Upon expiration of this Agreement and upon Library's request, The Network shall make commercially reasonable efforts to return and/or destroy Library Format to Library within a reasonable time. However, The Network may retain a reasonable number of the copies of the Library Format for archival purposes.

Once the agreement expires, the network is not supposed to use the music, so returning or destroying it will help (but not completely) prevent inadvertent uses.

5.   USAGE REPORTS. The Network agrees to report to the appropriate performing rights societies The Network's usages of Library's music, pursuant to The Network's customary practices, for each calendar quarter within one hundred and twenty (120) days following the applicable quarter's end. Any inadvertent failure of comply with this Section 5 shall not be deemed a breach of this Agreement.

Although not technically music cue sheets, usage reports assist the library in tracking royalties to be received from the PROs as well as which music is used for purposes of allocating the income from the blanket license. There should also be a requirement that music cue sheets are supplied to the library as well as to the PROs. In addition, it would be advantageous for the cue sheets to be delivered within 90 days of the end of each quarter, as that is the requirement imposed by the PROs in order to make the next distribution.

A.   With respect to the promotional spots produced by The Network, Library waives and releases The Network from public performance reporting and payment obligation.

Since the PROs don't usually pay for music in promos, there is no need for this reporting.

6.   MUSIC PERFORMANCE RIGHTS. The Network agrees to obtain a public performance license issued by the PROs or directly from Library, where such performance license is required.

This obligates the network to negotiate licenses with the PROs or arrange for direct payment of performance royalties to the library. Either way, both the library and its composers receive public performance income.

7.   REPRESENTATIONS AND WARRANTIES.

A.   Library represents and warrants the following:

The library warrants that they own or control all music and has the right to grant this license.

(i)   Library owns and controls the Library and the full rights to license such assets to The Network. Library further represents and warrants that it has the full right, power and authority to enter into this Agreement and to grant the rights granted herein;

(ii)   The master recordings contained in Library's music are wholly owned or controlled by Library and Library has all rights necessary to enter into this Agreement; and,

This specifically addresses ownership or control of the master recordings.

(iii)   The Network's exercise of the rights granted to it herein does not and will not: (a) violate any applicable law, statute, ordinance, or regulation or (b) breach any rights of any person or entity including, without limitation, rights of intellectual property, publicity or privacy; or (c) subject The Network to any obligation or liability whatsoever, except as specifically set forth in this Agreement.

No laws will be violated by the network's use of the library.

(iv) The performance rights in all musical compositions contained in Library's music are (a) Available for license through the public performance rights society having the legal right to issue public performance licenses, namely American Society of Composers, Authors and Publishers (ASCAP), Broadcast Music, Inc. (BMI) or SESAC (or similar performing rights societies in foreign territories, as applicable) (collectively "PROs"); (b) In the public domain; or (c) controlled by Library to the extent necessary for the purposes of this Agreement.

All the music is covered under agreements with the PROs or the performing rights are available directly for the library.

(v) Library shall be solely responsible for any harm to The Network or resulting from any virus, worm, Trojan horse, defect or security breach caused or transmitted by the Library or Library Format; and

As many times files are delivered digitally, this makes the library responsible for any files that might corrupt the network's system, such as a virus.

(vi) Library's music was not recorded pursuant to any signatory to collective bargaining organization, labor unions or guilds (collectively "Guilds"), and The Network's use of the Library's music pursuant to the Agreement shall not subject The Network to any remuneration payable to the Guilds.

There are no union obligations to the network from the use of the library.

B. The Network represents and warrants that it has the full right, power and authority to enter into this Agreement.

8. INDEMNIFICATION.

Mutual indemnifications.

A. Library agrees to indemnify, defend and hold harmless The Network, its successors and assigns, and The Network's authorized productions, and each of its and their officers, directors, agents and employees from and against any and all liabilities, including, without limitation, reasonable attorneys' fees or disbursements, arising out of any claims, lawsuits or judgments, whether threatened or actual, fixed or contingent, arising out of the breach by Library of any representation, warranty or covenant of Library under this Agreement. Library shall not settle or otherwise participate in the final adjudication of a claim involving Library's music that adversely affects The Network's rights without the prior approval of The Network.

B.   The Network agrees to indemnify, defend and hold harmless Library, its The Networks, successors and assigns, and each of its and their officers, directors, agents and employees from and against any and all liabilities including, without limitation, reasonable attorneys' fees, arising out of any claims, lawsuits or judgments, whether threatened or actual, fixed or contingent, arising out of the breach by The Network of any representation or warranty by The Network under this Agreement. The Network shall not settle or otherwise participate in the final adjudication of a claim involving Library's music that adversely affects Library's rights without the prior approval of Library.

C.   In no event shall The Network be liable under this Agreement for any indirect, incidental, consequential, special, punitive, or exemplary damages arising out of or related to this Agreement.

9.   NOT GUILD SIGNATORY. Library acknowledges that The Network is not currently a signatory to any Guilds.

10.   ASSIGNMENT. This Agreement may be assigned by The Network, but in the event of any such assignment, The Network shall remain secondarily liable under this Agreement.

The agreement is assignable by the network. There is no language relating to the assignability by the library.

11.   REMEDIES. Library's rights and remedies in the event of breach or alleged breach of this Agreement by The Network shall be limited to Library's right, if any, to recover damages, and reasonable attorney's fees and disbursements, in an action at law and in no event shall Library be entitled by reason of any breach or alleged breach to enjoin, restrain or seek to enjoin or restrain the distribution or other exploitation of the Productions.

The library's remedy to any breach by the network shall be money damages only and no injunctive relief will be allowed.

12.   NOTICE AND CURE. The Network's failure to perform any of its obligations hereunder shall not be deemed a breach hereof, unless and until, Library has provided The Network with written notice of such failure and The Network does not cure (or take substantial steps to cure) such non-performance within thirty (30) business days following receipt of such notice. A courtesy copy of all notices shall be sent to:

Thirty-day period for the network to cure (or take substantial means to cure) any breaches.

Attn: Vice President
The Network

_____

_____

13.   GOVERNING LAW. This Agreement sets forth the complete under-standing between The Network and Library with respect to the subject matter hereof, and all prior agreements have been merged herein, whether written or oral, and may not be modified except by written instrument signed by the party to be charged. Library acknowl-edges that no representation or promise not expressly contained in this Agreement has been made by The Network or any of its agents, employees or representatives. This Agreement shall be construed and enforced in accordance with the laws of the State of California governing contracts to be wholly performed in California regardless of the actual place of execution or performance or the choice of law provisions. The parties consent to the sole and exclusive jurisdiction and venue of the state and federal courts located in the County of Los Angeles, California.

14.   MISCELLANEOUS. A waiver of any of the terms or conditions of this Agreement in any instance shall not be deemed or construed to be a waiver of such term or condition for the future. The headings at the beginning of each of the paragraphs hereof are for reference only and shall not affect the meaning or construction of this Agreement. Sections 1, 2C, 3B, 3C, 4B, 7 (Representations and Warranties), 8 (Indemnification), 9 (Not Guild Signatory), 10 (Assignment), 12 (Remedies), 13 (Notice and Cure), 14 (Governing Law) and 15 (Miscellaneous) shall be deemed to survive the expiration or termina-tion of this Agreement. For purposes of contractual interpretation, the Agreement shall be deemed the joint product of both parties hereto and no provision or term hereof shall be construed against any party hereto as the drafter, and the parties hereby unconditionally waive such defense or claim regarding the Agreement. This Agreement is binding upon and inures to the benefit of The Network and Library's respective assigns and successors.

> After expiration or termination of the agreement, certain terms will survive.

IN WITNESS WHEREOF, the parties have caused this Agreement to be executed as of the day and year first above written.

("Library")

BY: _____

TITLE: _____

DATE: _____

("The Network")

BY: _____

TITLE: _____

DATE: _____

CHAPTER 11
SAMPLING

"Sampling" is the practice of utilizing a portion of an existing musical composition, with or without a master recording of that composition, in a new work. The amount of the sample may be as small as a single drum beat or as large as the entire chorus or chord progression of a song. Historically a prevalent practice in rap and dance music, sampling is now being used in many different genres of music. The practice has been going on for so long that there are now second generation samples, i.e. songs that contain samples that contain other samples.

The term "sampling" began to be used only when a portion of an existing recording and musical composition was sampled for use with a new work. It has developed over time to include instances where only a portion of the underlying composition is being used, sung or played by new artists or musicians instead of using the complete original recording.

In the early days of sampling, it was an underground phenomenon, without proper licensing of the source material. The parties using the samples, when caught, would argue that no permissions or fees were necessary, as it was a Fair Use or they were paying tribute to the classic R&B artists being sampled, artists like James Brown, Parliament/Funkadelic, Ohio Players, and Earth, Wind & Fire. Once it came into the open, traditional music publishers and record companies were hesitant to engage in the lawful licensing of these samples until they realized that: (1) the practice was not going away; (2) the rappers doing the sampling were selling thousands, and sometimes hundreds of thousands, of albums through both conventional and non-conventional methods; and (3) the traditional parties were not making any money on these records. Sound familiar?

As publishers, record companies, and artists became more familiar and sophisticated about the use of samples, there was less argument from the new artists that a sample should be royalty-free. As with any other type of property, the use of a copyright requires payment and permission from the owner.

A request to issue a mechanical license is usually the first contact a publisher has with a party who wishes to sample a portion of that publisher's copyright as part of another work. Similarly, if a master recording is also being sampled, the party wishing to use a sample must contact the record company who owns the master. As publishing royalties and record royalties are based upon different types of calculations, there are usually not any Most Favored Nations clauses, as there might be for a synchronization license.

There are several issues to be considered when approached about granting a license for a sample. First, the party wishing to use the sample must make a determination whether the portion of the composition sampled from a recording is capable of copyright protection. A drum pattern, horn passage, or guitar lick may not be unique enough on its own to merit copyright protection **as a musical composition**. In this case, a mechanical license may not technically be necessary from the publisher of the composition that is the subject of the source recording. However, if the artist of the source recording is also the writer and/or publisher of the source composition, the prudent practice would be to also license the composition as well, rather than gamble on a court finding that the sample was or was not protectable.

Second, the length of the use and repetition of the use must be judged. If the new recording uses only 10 seconds of the source recording, but that 10-second section is looped throughout the entire recording, that could be considered a substantial use. In a similar manner, the use of the title lyric, chorus, or "hook" of a song is considered a substantial use. A good example of this is found in "U Can't Touch This" by MC Hammer. As the underlying basis of this entire work, Hammer utilized a portion of "Super Freak" by Rick James. Another example is "Shake" by Ying Yang Twins, which uses a substantial portion of both the composition and master recording of "Trommeltanz," aka "Din Daa Daa" by German techno artist George Kranz.

Based upon the use, the publisher of the source composition has the right to potentially be compensated using several different methods for the granting of a mechanical license. Unless the new artist is able, under the terms and requirements of the Copyright Act of 1976, to utilize the compulsory license provision and pay a full mechanical rate for the use of a sample, this compensation is negotiated with the original publisher. For a small use, the publisher may want a one-time, flat fee payment. For slightly larger uses, a mechanical royalty of X cents per copy might be required, payable quarterly or semiannually, for all copies sold and not returned.

For a substantial use, however, it is not uncommon for the publisher of the source composition to require partial ownership of the new work, which would entitle the publisher to mechanical royalties as well as a share of *all revenues* earned by the new work. This is founded upon the theory that an extensive use of a sample is really a derivative work based upon the original composition. For some samples, up to 50% to 75% of the new work is controlled by the source publisher. There are even cases in which the source publisher controls 100% of the new composition and the artist/writer of the new recording may or may not get partial writer's share of royalties.

An example of this last model is "Bittersweet Symphony," by The Verve, which incorporates a section of the composition "You Can't Always Get What You Want," by The Rolling Stones. As this song was not properly licensed at inception, the publishers for Stones writers Mick Jagger and Keith Richard insisted on total ownership of the new song, only giving Verve member Richard Ashcroft a portion of the writer's share of income. Because of this, many requests to use the recording of the song are denied by Ashcroft in retaliation for having to give up so much of the publishing rights.

Where the parties can agree to split the ownership of the new song, it is a prudent policy for the parties to enter into a co-publishing and co-administration agreement, clearly spelling out their shares of ownership and dictating how the new copyright is licensed and royalties are collected. As a co-publisher, the owner of the source composition has certain controls over the use of the new composition and is able to set fees for any potential licenses of the new composition. In addition, the added benefit of such an arrangement is being paid directly (and more quickly) for all sources of income and not having to rely on the other co-publisher to collect and pay shares when it does its next royalty distribution.

Under the co-publishing model, every sample adds additional writers and publishers to the new composition, diminishing the percentage of income retained by the writers and publishers using the sample. For samples used by certain artists with many members, like Parliament/Funkadelic and Earth, Wind & Fire, the songs by these artists frequently had many of the group members as co-writers, thereby potentially making everyone's shares very small.

One thing for the publisher of the source composition to keep in mind is that it is not necessarily subject to any controlled composition clause that might be in the artist's agreement with the record company. This allows the source publisher to charge its pro rata share of the full statutory rate for the mechanical license instead of having to reduce the mechanical rate to match the artist's controlled composition clause, which may result in a substantially lower royalty rate, especially if there are more than 10 tracks on the album.

Some of the same concepts apply to the sample of a master recording, for which a royalty and/or part ownership is given to the owner of the source recording. Under these circumstances, if there is a co-ownership of the new master, there are often restrictions placed on the owner of the newly created master regarding licensing the new master without the involvement of the owner of the source recording. For example, in these cases, the owner of the new recording cannot grant a synchronization license for a film or television program without the consent and negotiation by the sample owner. If there is co-ownership of the new master, the owner of the source recording must always be contacted for a license for the use of their recording.

Initially, the record companies undertook the responsibility to clear the samples that were included in their releases. This was a costly expense for the record companies, and it was no assurance that everything that needed to be cleared actually was being cleared. Given that the artist and producer of the new recording should be aware if samples have been included and the source of these samples, most record companies now make it the responsibility of the artist or producer to license these samples, as there is often no way for the record company to be able to identify the sampled material and clear it for use in the

CASE STUDY #1

I was contacted by a music clearance company about licensing a sample of my client's song "Trommeltanz," aka "Din Daa Daa" by German techno artist George Kranz, for use by Ying Yang Twins. At my request, I received a demo version of the song that incorporated all of my client's song's music and parts of the lyrics, with additional new lyrics being added. Using the common designation of 50/50 between music and lyrics, I felt that my clients were entitled to 75% of the new song (50% for music, 25% for half of the lyrics).

Before I could go to my clients for approval, I received a call from the art department of the record company, asking for credit information, as the artwork needed to be delivered in two days. At this point, I had a pretty good idea that the song was being used and went to my clients for approval on the terms described above.

The next day, I received a call from the attorney for Ying Yang Twins, who offered me 50% of the song. I explained that, since this was a derivative work and that I did not believe that the Copyright Act had changed that morning, we would instead grant permission and offered his clients 25% of the copyright in the new song. After a few moments of silence, he said he would get back to me. A day later, I received an email accepting the 75/25 split I had initially proposed.

Moral of the story: get your samples cleared well ahead of time, or any negotiating leverage you might have will be lost.

new recordings. As the attorney for those creative parties, it is incumbent on you to make these issues clear to your clients so that all necessary rights can be obtained in a timely manner.

The licensing of a sample for a successful recording artist can be extremely lucrative. In the case of "Shake," the album on which the song originally appeared sold over one million copies (i.e., platinum), was downloaded extensively, was used for ringtones, was included on several remix albums, was released as a single, received substantial radio play, and was licensed for use in several television programs. The amount of mechanical and master recording royalties from record sales, public performance income from radio and synchronization, master recording, and performance royalties in the years since the song was released have come to approximately $500,000.00, all this the result of a new artist using a 20-year-old German dance hit.

CASE STUDY #2

I was contacted by the attorney for a major rap artist about sampling a song by a 1980s group from Germany. I again asked to hear the track and was told that only the instrumentals had been recorded, but that the artist had not yet added his rap vocal. They could, however, supply a written copy of the rap for review.

I sent the lyrics to my clients, who approved the use. I again negotiated for 75% of the copyright, as the new song used the entire musical bed, the sung first verse and a repeatedly sung chorus from the original song.

The parties agreed on this split and the song was recorded and released under a different title so as not to cause confusion between the two songs, with the newer version listing the artist as an additional writer.

Upon release, my clients heard the song and found out that the lyrics they had approved were not the lyrics used, as the artist had "freestyled" new lyrics in the studio. In addition, they objected to the title change, even though I had previously authorized it for their own protection. I was never able to get a straight answer from the clients as to whether they objected to the content of the new lyrics or just on principle that they had not approved them previously. After a few weeks of negotiation with both the artist's attorney and my own clients, we were able to settle on an 82.5/17.5 split instead of 75/25.

Moral of the story: get approval on the actual music and lyrics you intend to use.

In this situation, the artist was about to release his first album in five years, with a major push, a televised live concert special, and a tour. The song was also released as a single and sold millions of copies in addition to being licensed for several additional television programs. This was a major source of income for my clients for several years.

CASE STUDY #3

Another client of mine (Writer 1) co-wrote a song with a second writer (Writer 2), with my client composing the music and the other writer creating rap lyrics. This gave each of the writers a 50% interest in the song. Then, another rapper (Writer 3) added some additional lyrics, and Writer 3 was given a 20% share in the song. Later, this song was passed to a major rap artist, who not only added more lyrics but added two more samples to his version of the recording. At the end of the day, Writer 1 ended up with only 6.67% of the song.

Moral of the story: have language in your agreement that does not allow your writer/publisher shares to be diminished with the addition of more samples, writers, and publishers. See paragraph 7b in the following agreement.

SAMPLING CO-ADMINISTRATION AGREEMENT

As mentioned above, often a sampling agreement evolves into a co-publishing agreement, with each party controlling their own shares of the new composition.

AGREEMENT made as of this __ day of _____, 20__, by and between _____ with offices at _____ _____ (hereinafter referred to as "Publisher I") and ___ _____ with offices at _____ _____ (hereinafter referred to as "Publisher II").

WITNESSETH:

Whereas, _____and_____ (hereinafter collectively referred to as "Composers") are co-writers of the musical composition entitled "_____" (hereinafter referred to as the "New Composition"), and

Whereas, the New Composition incorporates portions of the Original Composition (as defined in paragraph 1 below),

Now, therefore, in consideration of the mutual promises herein contained and other good and valuable consideration, the receipt and sufficiency of which the parties hereby acknowledge, it is agreed as follows:

1. The parties agree that the New Composition incorporates portions of a pre-existing composition entitled _____ _____written by_____, which is owned or co-owned by Publisher I (the "Original Composition").

The parties agree that the entire universe-wide right, title and interest in and to the New Composition, including the copyright therein, the right to copyright and all rights under copyright shall be owned in the percentages described below:

Percentages:

Publisher I:

Publisher II:

The term of the parties' right, title and interest in the New Composition shall be for the full term of copyright throughout the universe and any renewals, extensions or reversions thereof whether currently existing or coming into existence as the result of future legislation.

Nothing contained herein shall be deemed to grant Publisher II any right, title or interest in or to the Original Composition apart from the portion included in the New Composition hereunder.

Side notes:

As stated below, Publisher I is the owner of the composition being sampled and Publisher II is the company for the artists/writers using the sample in the new composition.

Writers and title of the new composition.

"Incorporates" here means "samples."

This identifies the writers and title of the original composition being sampled into the new composition.

Standard language used in a co-publishing situation, showing that all parties have shares in the new composition for all rights.

These percentages would be negotiated between Publisher I and Publisher II to determine the shares controlled by each party.

Again, standard language in a songwriter/publisher agreement, subject to the 35-year reversion rule under the Copyright Act for U.S. rights to the new composition.

The writers and Publisher II have no interest in the original composition, which remains 100% with Publisher I.

2.   Songwriter credits with respect to the New Composition shall be as follows:

Writer 1:

Writer 2:

Writer 3:

Writer 4:

These percentages are also negotiated between the parties. Usually, the publishing shares above would resemble the collective writer shares of their own writers. In addition, the writers of the original composition would retain the same ratio between themselves for this song as in the original.

3.   The Composition has been or shall be registered for copyright in the names of Publisher I and Publisher II in the Copyright Office of the United States of America.

As a co-published composition, the copyright is held in the names of both parties and should be registered as such.

4.   Each party hereto shall each have the right to administer its respective interest in and to the New Composition throughout the world during the full term of worldwide copyright, including renewals and extension, but only in accordance with all the terms and conditions of this agreement. Each party shall have the right throughout the world to enter into any and all exclusive and/or non-exclusive licenses and agreements only with respect to its respective interest in the New Composition (subject to Paragraph 5 hereof). The licensing party must notify its licensee that it must seek a license from the other party hereto with respect to such other party's interest in the New Composition.

Each publisher administers their own share (as stated above) of the new composition, throughout the world (see paragraph 6, below). They have the right to enter into licensing agreements only with respect to their share and have an affirmative duty to advise any potential licensees of the other publisher's interests in the new composition.

5.   Small performing rights in the New Composition, to the extent permitted by law, shall be assigned to and licensed by the performing rights society or societies to which each party belongs. Said society or societies shall be and is or are hereby authorized to collect and receive all monies earned from the public performance of the New Composition in the United States and Canada and shall be and is or are hereby directed (subject to its or their rules and regulations) to pay directly to Publisher I and Publisher II, in their respective shares, the amount allocated by said society or societies as the publisher's share of public performance fees for the New Composition for the United States and Canada.

Each publisher has the right to license their shares to their respective performing rights organizations, each of which is authorized to collect their member's share only.

6.   The parties hereto may each enter into sub-publishing or collection agreements with, and license or assign any of its rights hereunder and delegate any of its obligations hereunder to, any persons, firms or corporations for any one or more countries of the world, but solely with respect to its respective interest in the New Composition.

Each publisher has the right to enter into foreign sub-publishing agreements for their share.

7. (a) Each party hereto warrants and represents that:

      (i) It has all necessary right, title and authority to enter into this agreement, to grant the rights and interest herein granted, and to perform all of the obligations under this Agreement.

      (ii) It will pay or credit all royalties, and any other sums, if any, due to its respective writer of the New Composition, or to any other person or entity who may be contractually entitled to receive payment from the applicable party for the exploitation of the New Composition.

  (b) Publisher II warrants and represents that except for the "sample" of the Original Composition included in the New Composition, the New Composition is new, original and capable of copyright protection and will not violate or infringe upon any common law or statutory rights of any person, firm or corporation, including, without limitation, contractual rights, copyrights and rights of privacy.

8. (a) Publisher II hereby indemnifies and holds Publisher I harmless against any and all loss or damage, including without limitation, all court costs, penalties and reasonable attorneys' fees, incurred as a result of any claim or action by a third party pertaining to a breach or alleged breach of any warranty, representation, covenant or agreement made by Publisher II hereunder.

No claim affecting the ownership of the New Composition will be settled without the prior approval of the parties. In the event of any claim or action against Publisher I, Publisher II will have the right to participate in the defense of thereof with counsel of its own choice and at its expense, but Publisher I shall control the defense.

Margin notes:

Each party claims it has the right to enter into this agreement on behalf of its own interests.

Each publisher will be responsible for paying their respective writers their share of royalties.

A key clause. This makes Publisher II warrant that there are no other samples in the new composition that would diminish Publisher I's share of the song. As it is not uncommon for artists to use more than one sample in a composition, this puts the burden on the new writers and Publisher II to make sure that there are no other parties or, if there are, the third party's shares are deducted from Publisher II, not Publisher I. If there are multiple samples known by all parties, this agreement can be expanded to accommodate additional writers and publishers.

Since Publisher II has control over the new composition, they should indemnify Publisher I against all claims involving the new composition unless it can be shown that the source of the claim is actually about the original composition.

Since the new composition is co-owned, neither party has the right to settle any claims without the consent of the other party.

Without limiting the generality of the foregoing, Publisher II hereby indemnifies Publisher I against any claim by a third party regarding additional "sampling" embodied in the New Composition. Publisher II shall be solely responsible for any costs incurred in connection with such additional "sampling"; and in the event any share of the New Composition is required to be assigned to a third party in connection therewith, such share shall be deducted only from Publisher II's interest in the New Composition. There shall be no reduction in the interest therein owned by Publisher I.

See comment to 7b above.

ALTERNATIVE CLAUSE

[(b)   Publisher I hereby indemnifies and holds Publisher II harmless against any and all loss or damage, including without limitation, all court costs, penalties and reasonable attorneys' fees, incurred as a result of any claim or action by a third party pertaining to a breach or alleged breach of any warranty, representation, covenant or agreement made by Publisher I hereunder with respect to the Original Composition, which results in non-appealable judgment against Publisher II or which is settled with Publisher I's prior written consent. In the event of any claim or action against Publisher II, Publisher I will have the right to participate in the defense of thereof with counsel of its own choice and at its expense, but Publisher I shall control the defense.]

This is an indemnity from Publisher I to Publisher II regarding claims against the original composition. Note that the indemnity applies only to situations in which the claim results in a final judgment against Publisher II or is settled with Publisher I's written consent.

(c)   Any sums recouped by a party as a result of initiating an action affecting or respecting the New Composition shall be retained by that party unless any other party joins in bringing the action. The party receiving notice of any claim or initiating any claim respecting the New Composition shall give written notice thereof to the other party or parties.

In the event that either party initiates an action regarding the new composition, unless the other party joins in the action, the initiating party may keep all the proceeds from a successful outcome of the claim.

9.   (a)   Although the parties hereto have agreed to and provided herein for payment from any other person, licensee, assignee or grantee (hereinafter referred to as the "Payor") directly to each of the parties hereto, in the event either party hereto (for convenience herein referred to as the "Receiving Party") shall receive from a Payor monies which include the other party's appropriate share of monies, the Receiving Party shall hold the other Party's appropriate share of monies in trust for the benefit of the other party and shall immediately pay over to the other party said appropriate share of monies. In addition, the Receiving Party shall issue, at the same time, to the other party, a copy of all of the relevant portions of the accounting statements regarding the New Composition received by the Receiving Party from the Payor.

Although the agreement calls for each party to collect their own share of royalties, in the event that one party collects on behalf of both parties, the collecting party shall immediately pay over to the other party their share of income.

(b)   The parties hereto shall each have the right to audit the books and records of the other with respect to any monies received under Paragraph 8(a) hereof once during each year, provided that (i) the party desiring to conduct such audit shall give the other party thirty (30) days' prior notice of its desire to conduct such audit; (ii) said audit is conducted by a certified public accountant, and (iii) said audit is conducted at the expense of the party conducting same.

Reciprocal audit rights.

10.   The respective addresses of Publisher I and Publisher II for all purposes of this agreement shall be as set forth below until written notice of a new address shall be duly given:

PUBLISHER I

PUBLISHER II

All notices shall be in writing and shall either be delivered by hand (to an officer if the party to be served is a corporation) or by registered or certified mail (return receipt requested), postage prepaid, or by telegraph, all charges prepaid. The date of making personal service or of mailing or of deposit in a telegraph office, whichever shall be first, shall be deemed the date of service.

Standard notice provision.

11.   The parties hereto agree that Publisher I's share of the New Composition will not be subject to the "Controlled Compositions" provisions of any artist's recording agreement.

Since Publisher I does not represent the artist recording the new composition, they are not bound to the terms of the artist's controlled composition clause, thereby receiving their share of the full statutory rate in effect at the time.

12.   **[delete if not applicable]** The agreement of Publisher I to the terms and conditions hereof is conditioned upon Publisher II securing an agreement for the use of the Original Composition in the New Composition from any other co-owner of the Original Composition (other than Publisher I). In the event Publisher II has not secured an agreement from the co-owner as described above within thirty (30) days after the date of this agreement, this agreement shall be deemed null and void <u>ab initio</u>.

In situations where the original composition is itself co-published with another party besides Publisher I, Publisher II is responsible for negotiating with the co-publisher to ensure that all rights for the original composition are secured for use in the new composition. If these rights are not secured, this agreement becomes void and no rights are granted from Publisher I to Publisher II.

13.   This agreement shall not be deemed to give any right or remedy to any third party whatsoever unless said right or remedy is specifically granted to such third party by the terms hereof.

14.   The parties hereto shall execute any further documents including, without limitation, assignments of copyrights, and do all acts necessary to fully effectuate the terms and provisions of this agreement.

15.   This agreement sets forth the entire understanding between the parties, and cannot be changed, modified or canceled except by an instrument signed by the party sought to be bound.

No changes are allowed in the terms of this agreement unless agreed upon in writing by both parties.

This agreement shall be governed by and construed under the laws of the State of California applicable to agreements wholly per-formed therein.

Jurisdiction for any disputes shall be the laws of California.

16.   This agreement shall not be binding upon Publisher I or Publisher II until duly executed by both parties. Nothing herein contained shall constitute a partnership between or a joint venture by Publisher I and Publisher II. Neither party hereto shall hold itself out contrary to the terms of this paragraph, and neither party shall become liable for any obligation, act or omission of the other party contrary to the provisions hereof.

No agreement (and no rights granted) until signed by both parties.

If any provision of this agreement shall be declared invalid, same shall not affect the validity of the remaining provisions hereof. No waiver of any provision of this agreement or of any default hereunder shall affect the waiving party's rights thereafter to enforce such provision or to exercise any right or remedy in the event of any other default, whether or not similar.

In the event that any provision of this agreement is deemed invalid for some reason, the remaining terms of the agreement remain in full force and effect.

This agreement shall be binding on and inure to the benefit of the parties and their successors and assigns.

This implies that the agreement (and rights granted therein) is assignable by either party but is binding on any assignees.

      IN WITNESS WHEREOF, the parties have executed this agreement the day and year above set forth.

"PUBLISHER I"

By: _____

"PUBLISHER II"

By: _____

CHAPTER 12

DIGITAL MEDIA
Part 1

One of the trepidations in writing this section is that, as soon as it is finished, or by the time you read it, some of it may be out of date. Writing about the history, practices, and fee structures of digital deals will be helpful, but I also want to offer some editorial comments about the future of the music industry as I see it, again realizing that what is predicted today may be a reality tomorrow. Part two of this subject will focus on those areas.

Digital Delivery: Streaming and Downloading

Digital delivery of music to consumers comes in two basic ways: streaming and downloading. Streaming is the transmission of an audio file to the consumer without the reproduction of the file. The file does not reside on the user's computer and is "temporary" in that once streamed, in order for the consumer to hear the file again, it must be streamed again. There are two types of streaming: interactive and non-interactive. Non-interactive streaming is like radio, in that a streaming service (like Pandora) streams music to the user but the user does not select the individual songs that are played. Like radio, these services offer the consumer some choice as to the genre of music but not specific songs. Interactive streaming services (like Spotify) allow the consumer to select specific songs that they want to hear. Both types of services are considered public performances, not reproductions, and different fee structures for licensing are set for each type of service.

Downloading is the delivery of a digital phonorecord ("DPD") music file that resides on the user's computer system or device so that the user can replay the song at their discretion and access the file from a variety of devices. Downloading also comes in two varieties: permanent downloads and tethered downloads. A permanent download (like from iTunes) is a music file purchased by the consumer and is theirs to keep and use on a number of different devices. A tethered download is a file that also resides on the user's system but is tied (i.e., tethered) to a subscription service (like Rhapsody) and fee paid by the consumer to the service for as long as the consumer maintains the subscription. If the user's subscription lapses, the downloaded files are removed from the user's system.

There was much debate as to which kinds of licenses were needed by these two types of delivery. Downloads, like CDs, were clearly reproductions that required a mechanical license, while streaming, like radio, was clearly a public performance that required licenses from the PROs. However, in an effort to carve out a niche in the new digital space, the competing factions claimed that both types of delivery required both performance and mechanical licenses.

The (faulty) reasoning was that, while a file was streaming, a copy was made on the user's system that allowed the file to "buffer" for more consistent playback, and that this temporary file was a reproduction and required a mechanical license. Conversely, the PROs maintained that the transmission of a down-loaded file from a centralized server to the consumer was a public performance in the same way that a radio or television program was considered such and required a license from the PROs. Over time, and via court decisions in the U.S. (*U.S. v. ASCAP*, 485 F. Supp. 2d 438 S.D.N.Y. 2007), these issues have now been settled for domestic delivery so that streaming is now defined as a public performance while downloading is a reproduction, with no crossing the license between the two. In foreign countries, since in many countries the performing rights society and mechanical society are the same organization, the issue is less complex and more settled.

Aside from the licensing implications, there was also debate amongst publishers and writers on the same issue due to the differences in how these types of royalties were paid out. Public performance royalties are paid directly and separately to the writer and publisher so payments to the writer would not be subject to recoupment of advances from the publisher. If deemed a mechanical royalty, the publisher would collect 100% of the income, which would make the writer's share subject to recoupment.

A Brief History of Digital Delivery

The past 15 years have shown remarkable changes in the music industry, in the way that music is delivered, in the way that consumers listen to music, and in the methods by which record companies, artists, publishers, and songwriters get paid for the music they create. The music establishment, i.e., the record companies, publishers, and licensing organizations, made (in my opinion) a huge tactical error in not embracing digital technologies sooner, leading to a proliferation of illegal services by which consumers could obtain music for free via "file sharing" services such as Napster and its offspring. In fact, there is now a whole generation of listeners who believe that music should always be free.

The availability of DPDs to the consumer is a relatively recent development, hindered in the past by the relatively slow speed of data transfer technology and the unwillingness of the record companies and publishers to enter into licensing agreements with companies willing to offer individual songs or complete albums via digital download. In the early stages of the Internet, less bandwidth and slower download speeds contributed to there being less of a demand for downloads, as it could take 45–60 minutes to download a single track over the dial-up technologies available at the time. With high-speed Internet access, file transfer time has diminished to a couple of minutes per track (and it's getting faster), depending on the size of the file and the speed of the connection. In addition, the availability of high speed broadband has made streaming both easier and quicker.

The Illegal Downloading of Music

The more important hindrance to downloads was the reluctance of the record companies to make available CD quality tracks that could be copied and distributed with impunity without payment to the record companies or publishers. There is an old saying by Aristotle that "nature abhors a vacuum," and the absence of legal digital music led to the development of illegal services. It was this reluctance to legally offer downloads that led to the development of Napster, a peer-to-peer service that operated between June 1999 and July 2001 and allowed consumers to "share" tracks between themselves by making illegal copies. Napster made it easy for consumers to download copies of songs that were otherwise difficult to obtain, such as older songs, unreleased recordings, and songs from concert bootleg recordings. Some users felt that, since they had already purchased legal versions of songs in other formats, such as LPs, cassette tapes, and compact disc, they were justified in downloading digital copies of these same recordings.

These reasons aside, many other users simply enjoyed getting music for free. They were able to download any number of songs without cost and without there being any royalties paid to the record company/artist or publisher/composer. As many colleges gave free Internet access to students in their dormitories, high-speed networks at colleges became overloaded, with as much as 80% of external network traffic consisting of MP3 file transfers. Many colleges blocked its use for this reason, as the record industry began threatening that the colleges be held liable for facilitating copyright violations on campus. After several individual artists sued Napster for copyright violations, the record companies, through their trade group, the Recording Industry Association of America (RIAA), filed suit against Napster in 2000 for copyright infringement under Section 512 of the Copyright Act, titled the Digital Millennium Copyright Act (DMCA). The RIAA made the following claims against Napster:

1. That its users were directly infringing the plaintiffs' copyrights.

2. That Napster was liable for contributory infringement of the plaintiffs' copyrights.

3. That Napster was liable for vicarious infringement of the plaintiffs' copyrights.

At that time, Hank Barry, Napster's CEO, while speaking to a legal seminar conducted by the State Bar of Texas, stated that Napster had over 100 million unique users. According to Barry, their research indicated that 50% of those users would be willing to pay a subscription fee of $5.00 per month for an unlimited, all-you-can-eat music model, and that Napster was willing to enter into negotiations with the music industry that would give 85% of that income to the rights holders, i.e. labels and publishers. If those figures proved to be true, that would equal approximately $2.5 billion in royalties to the rights holders annually. Despite revenues significantly dropping due to online piracy and the loss of billions of dollars already, the music industry turned Napster down flat.

Napster lost the case and appealed to the U.S. Court of Appeals for the Ninth Circuit. Although the appeals court found that Napster was capable of some commercially significant non-infringing uses, it affirmed the lower court's decision. On remand, the lower court ordered that Napster block access to infringing material when notified of that material's location. However, Napster was unable to follow this directive and shut down in July 2001.

More illegal services followed in the wake of Napster, like Grokster, Aimster, and many others. Lawsuits have been brought against many of them and, to a large degree, the services were found to be illegal and eventually shut down. The battle still rages today, as there are always new services that think they have a different business model and somehow fall within the law or that their services do not require licensing and payments.

Members of the public have also been sued by the music industry for illegally uploading or downloading music. While possibly not the best approach in terms of public relations, the RIAA has brought litigation against individuals who they believe to have illegally distributed music.

Legal Online Music Download Services

The issue of "file sharing" is one that has caused great division between the owners of musical content and the users of musical content. If an artist wishes to allow their fans to make copies of their music for free, as the copyright owner that is their choice. But that's a choice for the artist to make, not someone who bought a copy or illegally downloaded the artist's work.

These "file sharing" services allowed consumers to upload digital files so that thousands of people could download them at no cost. This is where I must disagree with the term "file sharing." If I buy a CD and loan it to you to listen to, I'm sharing. If I make thousands of copies of that CD, or allow others to do the same, we're not sharing. The copyrights of the record company and publisher are being infringed upon. In other words, to be blunt, file sharing is stealing.

Some of the issues raised by consumers to justify their activities were (i) that CDs cost too much and that there were usually only a few songs on the CD that the listener actually would play over and over, thereby diminishing even further the value of the CD, (ii) artists made enough money and their music should be given away, and (iii) implying Fair Use, that it "wasn't fair" that they couldn't make copies of the music.

In 2002, Universal Music Group and Sony Music Enterprises created Pressplay, an online music store that provided music by subscription. A rival service, MusicNet, was created by Warner Music Group, BMG, EMI, and other independent labels and operated on the same basic structure. One of the problems with these two services was that they did not feature music from the labels of their opposition, making it necessary for the consumer to join both services in order to get the music desired. This complicated model earned Pressplay and MusicNet spots on *PCWorld's* 2006 list of the "25 Worst Tech Products of All Time," stating that "the services' stunningly brain-dead features showed that the record companies still didn't get it." (Dan Tynan, "The 25 Worst Tech Products of All Time," *PC World Magazine*, Mar. 3, 2006).

iTunes was introduced by Apple Inc. on January 9, 2001. First only available for Apple's MacIntosh computers, it was developed for Windows-based PCs as well. Now somewhat ubiquitous, it was the first online music system that was both easy to use and legal. Apple entered into licensing agreements with the record companies and offered a wide variety of music from many sources, eliminating some of the issues with Pressplay and MusicNet. By virtue of these deals, Apple paid the record companies who, in turn, paid the publishers.

Once legal services for downloading became available and easy to use, some consumers began to take advantage of features that these services offered. With a relatively low price of $0.99 per individual download or $9.99 for an entire album (or less), consumers now had a choice that made more sense to them and iTunes was an immediate success. Other similar services followed, but today iTunes still dominates the download market. At the time of this writing, iTunes has now sold upwards of 10 billion tracks.

At some point a few years ago, the record labels, buoyed by the success of iTunes and finally seeing some income from the digital market, began to feel that the iTunes price of $0.99 per track was too low and began to demand that iTunes increase its price for certain categories of music (such as more current releases) to $1.49 per track. Apple resisted this attempt and refused to raise their prices, causing at least one major record company to withdraw their material from iTunes. Shortly thereafter, however, once the label saw their drop in digital income, they withdrew their demand.

Concurrently, once the public began to buy music again, there was still substantial debate in the industry about digital rights management ("DRM") and whether the consumer should be able to transfer the legally purchased files to other devices that they own. Consumers felt that, since they had paid for the tracks, they should be able to maintain copies on their desktop computer and their laptop as well as their iPod. At first, the record companies and publishers were adamant that DRM had to be encoded into these purchased music files, to prevent multiple copies being made without additional fees paid. EMI Music, one of the major labels, decided, however, that DRM could be removed if the consumer was willing to pay a slightly higher fee for a downloaded track. The other labels soon followed this model and now tracks purchased from iTunes can be reproduced on up to five devices owned by the same person.

Currently, the different download services offer a variety of pricing options, depending on the artist, label, and nature of the catalogs they represent. Fees now range from $0.69 to $1.49 per track, depending on a variety of factors. It should be noted, however, that this increase in the price for downloads has not translated into higher mechanical rates to publishers, leaving more money in the pockets of the labels without any financial benefit to the publishers. While there are still a few artists who refuse to allow downloading of their material, an overwhelming majority of artists and labels now embrace the digital market as a way of maintaining the income source of consumers purchasing music.

While credit should be given to Apple and its late founder, Steve Jobs, for their ability to finally be able to strike deals with the labels for digital distribution, what should also be noted is that Apple is not in the music business in the same way that a record company is. Apple's main source of revenue is not iTunes, but the sale of hardware, like the iPod or iPad, that will play the music for the consumer. Their interest in selling downloads is not necessarily directly tied to the benefits to the artist, label, publisher, and songwriters, but to sell devices. From Apple's perspective, any benefits to the music copyright holders are purely secondary.

Conflicts Within the Music Industry

Whatever the problems the industry has with outside sources, there are internal conflicts that have inhibited the development of a digital market as well. Artists have disputed the royalties that the record companies have paid them for DPDs, publishers have battled with record companies over mechanical royalties, copyright owners have sued consumers over illegally downloading music, and both the record companies and publishers have fought with the digital industry about rates payable for reproduction and public performance.

Artists vs. Record Companies

Although this book focuses on music publishing and not record companies and artists, there were several lawsuits brought against the record companies by artists that might also have a bearing on the music publishing industry.

The typical language in an artist agreement is that the artist gets a royalty for sales of their recording based upon a percentage of either the retail or wholesale price of the sale. If the record company licenses the artist's music to a third party, like a motion picture, television program, or to another record company for a soundtrack or compilation album, the usual language is that the artist gets 50% of the net license fee paid to their record company.

The issue in question is whether a digital download is a sale (paying a royalty to the artist) or comes about as a result of a license between the record company and the digital distributor (calling for a 50/50 division of income). The record companies argued that a consumer purchase of a DPD via iTunes is no different than a consumer buying a CD at a retail location, which would clearly be dealt with as a "sale." One of the issues is that the early agreements between Apple and the labels actually calls the grant of rights to iTunes a "license." The difference between these two models can be substantial, as follows:

Record Company vs. Artist—The Economics Of iTunes	
Retail Price for Individual Download	$0.9900
Amount Paid to Record Company	$0.6500
Less Mechanical Royalty to Publisher	($0.0910)
Net to record company	$0.5590
Example #1—Artist Gets Royalty as if a Retail Sale	
Royalty = 12% of Retail Sales Price	$0.1188
Example #2—Artist Gets 50% of Net Licensing Receipts	
50% Share of Net Licensed Income ($0.5590)	$0.2795
Difference Between License vs. Royalty	**($0.1607)**

A difference of over $0.16 per track (or more than $1.60 per album) is a huge difference to the artists, most of whom have advances and costs that need to be recouped before actually being paid any additional record royalties.

There have been several settlements between artists and record companies before going into court for a judge or jury to determine this issue. In March of 2012, music giant Sony BMG ended its five-year battle with musicians including The Allman Brothers, Cheap Trick, and The Youngbloods, but there has been at least one case as of this writing—involving the production company for artist Eminem, *F.B.T. Productions, LLC, et al. v. Aftermath Records, et al.* 621 F.3d 958—in which a court decided that this transaction is based on language classifying digital downloads under the license provision of the agreement instead of considering it a sale. There are currently other lawsuits pending on this issue.

Record Companies vs. Publishers

In 2008, the previously negotiated mechanical royalty provisions and rates were set to expire. The record labels, to no surprise, wanted a reduction in the rate of $0.091 per copy while the publishers desired an increase in the rates, as historically had been previously negotiated.

The argument from the record company perspective was as follows: instead of selling a CD for $18.99, albums were now available via download for $9.99. In addition, single songs could now be purchased for $0.99 instead of a CD single for $2.99. Due to these lower prices, the record companies argued that their income was being reduced and the amount of the mechanical royalty should also be reduced. The record companies suggested either a reduction to about $0.06 per copy (the rate in 1992) or a percentage of the wholesale price, similar to the published price to dealer ("PPD") concept in Europe.

Conversely, the publishers argued that the costs to the record companies had been reduced considerably for digital distribution, as they no long had to pay for materials, manufacturing, distribution, and returns. As a result, the publishers requested that the rate be increased to $0.12 per copy.

After months of negotiations, a settlement was finally reached that the mechanical rate would remain at $0.91 until the end of 2012. Oddly enough, both sides claimed victory. In the summer of 2012, the parties agreed to extend these rates for another five years, to the end of 2017.

In a more recent action, a music publisher has sued, among others, Apple, Amazon, Google, and Microsoft over whether the digital distribution services need to have licenses directly with the music publishers, as the mechanical licenses from publishers to record companies do not usually allow for an assignment of the rights under that license. Currently, the digital services pay the record companies their share of the sales price and the record companies then pay mechanical royalties to the publishers, causing a delay in payment to the publishers of 6–12 months. In addition, for catalog product, a new license may mean an updated and increased mechanical royalty. The arguments being made are similar to the ones between record companies and artists (see above) as to whether a DPD purchase is a sale or under a license.

Copyright Owners vs. Consumers

In order to amplify the need of the consumer to obtain music legally, one of the strategies of the copyright owners has been to identify users who have illegally downloaded music and attempt to settle with them for the infringements involved. The settlements offered have been relatively low, this being used as an educational tool rather than a money-making operation by the record companies. While admittedly a heavy-handed approach to this issue, and perhaps not the best public relations tactic, these cases illustrate that downloading and offering downloads to others via file sharing is, indeed, illegal.

In a few cases, however, the parties who have downloaded the music have refused to settle, forcing the record companies to bring lawsuits against them. In 2005, the RIAA sent a cease-and-desist letter and settlement offer of $5,000 to Jammie Thomas (now Jammie Thomas-Rasset) for illegally downloading and sharing songs via Kazaa, an illegal downloading site. Thomas declined to settle, so suit was brought on behalf of the record companies by the RIAA in Minnesota, where Thomas resided. *Capitol Records Inc. v. Thomas*, 579 F.Supp.2d 1210, 1228 (D.Minn.2008). Thomas initially claimed that the Kazaa account was not hers, then that her computer system was hacked or that others (i.e., her boyfriend or children) had access to her computer and downloaded the files. (*Author's note*: Pick a defense and stick with it.) Thomas was found guilty of infringement by a jury and assessed damages in the amount of $222,000.00. This verdict was set aside by the judge due to what was an error in the language in the instructions given to the jury.

A second trial was held and Thomas was again found liable by a jury, this time in the amount of $1.92 million. This award was later slashed by the judge to $54,000 because his opinion was that the award was out of proportion to the actual damages suffered by the record companies. A few days later, the RIAA again attempted to settle for $25,000 but Thomas declined. The RIAA appealed the reduction of the award, leading to a third trial.

The third trial focused not on whether Thomas was guilty of infringement but solely on the amount of the damages. In this case, a jury awarded damages in the amount of $1.5 million, which the court again reduced to $54,000. In September of 2012, the court of appeals ruled that recording companies were entitled to the remedies they sought: damages of $222,000 and a broadened injunction that forbids Thomas to make available sound recordings for distribution. "The protection of copyrights is a vindication of the public interest," wrote the U.S. Court of Appeals for the Eighth Circuit.

A second case involved Harvard University student Joel Tenenbaum, *Sony BMG v. Tenenbaum*, No. 07cv11446-NG (D. Mass. Dec. 7, 2009). Tenenbaum, like Jammie Thomas, was accused of using Kazaa to download and upload music files illegally. He was offered the chance to settle for $3,500 for the 31 music files at issue in this case. Tenenbaum counteroffered $500, which was rejected by the RIAA.

At trial, Tenenbaum admitted downloading and distributing the files, so the court held that liability was no longer an issue and the only issue left for consideration by the jury was the amount of damages. Tenebaum's attorney argues that his client did not intend any harm, nor did he understand the copyright law. Tenenbaum was found liable in the amount of $675,000, with the jury taking the middle ground between the statutory minimum ($22,500 total) and maximum ($4.5 million) for willful infringement. The trial court reduced the award to $67,500 but the court of appeals (*Sony BMG Music Entertainment, et al v. Joel Tenenbaum*, no. 10-1947, Court of Appeals for the First Circuit), reinstated the award after denying various arguments made by Tenenbaum relating to a violation of due process and the constitutionality of the Copyright Act. A further appeal was made to the U.S. Supreme Court, which declined to hear the case.

Copyright Owners vs. Digital Services

On August 6, 2007, the NMPA and certain music publisher plaintiffs joined a putative class action lawsuit against YouTube/Google in the U.S. District Court for the Southern District of New York, captioned *The Football Association Premier League Limited, et al. v. YouTube, Inc., et al.*, which included a number of music publishers as plaintiffs. In the suit, NMPA and music publisher plaintiffs alleged that YouTube infringed publishers' copyrights through the unauthorized use of copyrighted music works. Prior to certification of a plaintiff class, the district court issued a decision granting YouTube's motion for summary judgment and entered judgment in YouTube's favor.

In August 2011, in exchange for consideration received from YouTube, NMPA and the other plaintiffs settled with YouTube, despite the fact that the decision was on appeal. NMPA and the other plaintiffs have dismissed their appeal and released YouTube from all past copyright infringement claims and entered into a licensing agreement with YouTube. Other publishers who choose to enter into the license agreement with YouTube will likewise release YouTube for all copyright claims (with some exceptions) that accrued through the date of the license agreement, and forgo any right to participate in any ongoing copyright lawsuits against YouTube or benefit from any judgments or future settlements that may result from those suits, including the litigation.

The overall idea of the licensing agreement is to allow music publishers and the organizations that collect payments for songwriters and composers to identify videos on YouTube that use their compositions, and then get a split of YouTube's advertising revenue from the video. The record labels, which represent the artists that perform the songs, already have similar deals going.

One of the main complaints from digital services is that there is no centralized way of clearing the rights they might need. In the area of performing rights for streaming, that issue has been dealt with through recent negotiations between the NMPA and the digital industry. For synchronization rights for audiovisual productions, however, the process is still a song-by-song negotiation with the record companies and publishers for the rights and fees to be paid. Many have said that this has greatly inhibited the development of the digital use of music in audio visual productions. The counterargument, however, is that the copyright owners still retain the right to approve any such uses and negotiate a fee agreed upon between the parties. There is merit to both arguments, but no movement on changing the system as of this date.

In another twist involving digital rights, ReDigi, Inc. sought to build a market for consumers to resell their "used" digital songs. Under the first-sale doctrine, a party who legally purchased copyrighted material has the right to re-sell that material without permission or compensation to the owner of the copyright. ReDigi claimed that they had technology to delete files from the original purchasers' drives so that there would be no duplicate copies made by the original purchaser.

However, in *Capitol Records, LLC v. ReDigi Inc.* (S.D.N.Y., Mar. 30, 2013, 12 CIV. 95 RJS), the court recently held that the first-sale doctrine did not apply to digital media and that, in addition, ReDigi would have to make an additional copy for storage on the ReDigi servers, thereby violating the rights of the copyright owners.

Other Sources of Digital Revenue

Ringtones, Mastertones, and Ringbacks

These types of music uses grew out of the increased popularity of mobile phones and their ability to use music files as signals to those using them. A "ringtone" is a MIDI-generated music file that plays an instrumental version of a song. A "mastertone" is a file that uses an original master recording as the source of the music instead of computer generated music. Both of these are heard by the owner of the phone to signal an incoming call. A "ringback" is music chosen by the user to play to the party making the call, i.e., until the person being called answers, the caller hears music chosen by the person being called. Quite popular for a while, these allowed the users to customize their phones by being able to select their own music.

A ringtone was determined to be a mechanical reproduction available under a compulsory license but, unlike DPDs, the rate was set at $0.24 per copy, possibly due to the fact that ringtones cost anywhere from $0.99 to $1.99 each, depending on the perceived value of the song by the carriers. For some reason, mastertones and ringbacks were not categorized in the same way and are subject to negotiations between the carriers and the music publishers, which usually end up being the greater of $0.12 per copy or 10% of the retail sales price, with these files selling from between $1.99 to $2.99 each.

Apps

Mobile applications, or "apps" are the latest areas in which music is being used. One of the issues in licensing apps is whether a copy of the music is being reproduced as embedded in the app obtained by the user (either by purchase or for free), or whether the app merely accesses a single copy on the app developers' servers for streaming by the user. In this case, the costs of the app developer also come into play in determining what the royalty to the music publisher might be. As usual, the answers are unclear and vary from app to app.

Online Video Services

With increased access to broadband delivery of content to the user and the low cost of digitizing video, online video services like YouTube, Hulu, or VEVO are becoming outlets for videos, many of which contain music. With full-blown versions of motion pictures and episodes of television programs being made available for streaming and downloading via these services, as well as via Amazon and iTunes, more and more musical content contained in these productions is also available, which should increase the amount of royalties earned by the music publishers.

Recently, The National Academy of Recording Arts and Sciences (NARAS) made available online through VEVO archival footage from past Grammy Awards programs that had not been seen since the original broadcast dates. Older television programs that are no longer in syndication due to low licensing fees to the studios or on DVD due to the costs of manufacturing and distributing physical copies are now available online, generating income for all parties involved, including the music industry. As with the streaming services, the dollars are not huge, but an asset that has been underexploited can now generate some income where none was being earned.

Audio Greeting Cards

Due to the increased capacity of small sound chips, it has been possible for greeting card companies to include an audio chip as part of a card that plays a portion of a popular song and the master recording when the consumer opens the card. Stevie Wonder's "Happy Birthday," Billy Joel's "Just The Way You Are," and Kool & the Gang's "Celebration" are among the most popular songs include in these cards. The greeting card companies pay royalties to both the publisher and record company for each card sold, usually at a rate much higher than a statutory mechanical license royalty, thereby making these cards a possible source of revenue. And as the costs of the sound chips continue to decrease, the card companies will be licensing more and more songs for this type of use.

Micro Licensing

There has been an increase in licensing of music for uses in wedding videos, school concert videos and CDs, and other uses where the proposed uses don't allow for a high license fee. As such, many publishers and record companies now offer "micro-licenses," i.e., licenses at vastly reduced fees for these smaller uses. Many times, the license restricts the number of copies that can be reproduced (example: no more than 10 copies of a wedding DVD, or 100 copies of a school concert for choir members and their families), but still allows the uses to be properly licensed. It is unlikely that any single use will generate a significant amount of income, but the accumulated totals could amount to decent money.

How these new sources will generate income, and the formulas for calculating this income, will be discussed in the next chapter. In total, however, there are some new opportunities for music publishers to earn income for themselves and their writers, if the publishers can abandon some old ideas and embrace the new delivery methods.

DIGITAL RIGHTS AGREEMENTS

This is an agreement between a record company and a publisher involving the rights to a composition previously licensed to the record company under a mechanical license. The record company seeks to digitally exploit their master in a variety of ways and wants to "pre-clear" with the publisher the ability to include the composition in the record company's grant of rights for digital uses as specified in the agreement.

DATE: _____

In order to take mutual and maximum advantage of the present growth of ringtone, ringback and digital music video sales,

This agreement deals with mobile uses as well as digital video streams and sales.

we are requesting, on behalf of XYZ Recordings, Inc. and its affiliates, successors, assigns and licensees ("XYZ"), the right to use your musical compositions(s) (the "Composition(s)") in XYZ's recordings in connection with the advertising, distribution and sale of:

The record company is requesting permission of the publisher for the use of their composition for:

(1)   **Audio and audiovisual "master" ringtones** (e.g., excerpt of a Composition is used to reveal an incoming call or other communication and which is downloaded or transmitted to a phone or other communications device);

Ringtones are the sounds played on a mobile device when the phone rings. Since the record company owns the master recording of this particular version of the composition, they are interested in licensing mastertones, not just ringtones of the composition.

(2)   **Audio and audiovisual "master" ringbacks** (e.g., excerpt of a Composition is transmitted and heard by a caller when they are calling a phone or other communications device); and

A ringback is what the caller hears when waiting for the party being called to answer. Again, here the record company wants to utilize their master recording as the audio source of the ringback.

(3)   **Digital music videos** (e.g., permanent music video downloads, limited music video downloads and commercial music video streaming).

Despite being originally created for promotional use, such as on MTV, music videos are now being sold and streamed on sites that feature advertising, thereby generating income and no longer being considered strictly promotional.

All audiovisual material used in conjunction with ringtones, ringbacks and digital music videos shall be footage owned by, controlled by or licensed to XYZ (e.g., MTV-type video or live concert footage).

All the video content is either already owned by the record company or licensed to them from other sources, such as concert footage the record company did not create.

Such ringtones, ringbacks and digital music videos shall be referred to herein collectively as "Digital Products."

Combines the three types of rights granted into one defined term.

Please sign where indicated below, and return a copy to XYZ via fax to accept all of the terms found herein in exchange for the royalties and other consideration offered by XYZ, and to enter into a license with XYZ.

Composition(s): _____

Writer(s): _____

Publisher(s): _____

_____

_____

Administrative Share(s): _____%

(If you license less than 100% of a Composition to XYZ, the royalty rates payable to you shall be appropriately reduced to correspond to the percentage of your administrative share.)

Usage Timing: Not to exceed 45 seconds per usage for ringtones and ringbacks, and up to full use for digital music videos

Requested Rights: XYZ will have the non-exclusive right

to edit, reproduce, distribute, synchronize (if applicable) and perform the Compositions(s) in connection with the distribution, sale, and promotion of any number of versions of the Digital Products embodying the Composition(s) via any medium, means or method now known or hereafter discovered.

Territory: United States and Canada (and their respective territories and possessions)

Term: Perpetuity

Signing below indicates acceptance of the terms of this agreement and gives the record company the right to include the rights to the composition in their grant of rights for the master.

Specifies the information for the composition covered under this agreement.

Defines the share of the composition owned by this publisher. Note the language that the royalties listed below will be paid on a *pro rata* basis only for the share owned by this publisher.

As most ringtones do no last more than 30–45 seconds, the grant here is limited to that amount of time. Music videos last for the full length of the master.

The grant of rights is non-exclusive, which means that the publisher may license this same composition to others for similar rights.

A broad grant of rights, consistent with the record company position that they should control all uses of the composition based on the use of their master.

As ringtones are deemed mechanical licenses, only U.S. (and maybe Canadian) rights can be granted.

As the business structures of many digital licenses are still being developed, a grant of rights in perpetuity would seem to be ill advised. A term of 2–3 years would be suggested instead.

Royalty Rates: **Audio "master" ringtones:**

The royalty for audio "master" ringtones shall be the minimum statutory mechanical royalty rate in the United States, or the minimum mechanical license rate agreed to by the major recording companies and the major music publishers in Canada (as applicable) in effect at the time of sale or license of the particular audio master ringtone.

Notwithstanding the foregoing, if a different U.S. statutory rate and/or Canadian license rate is established specifically for audio master ringtone products during the Term, then such rate(s) shall apply prospectively as of the effective date of such rate(s).

All other audio and audiovisual "master" ringtones and ringbacks:

The greater of: (i) 10% of the retail price per successfully completed sale or license; or

(ii) 20% of XYZ's receipts from sales and exploitations (10% if XYZ sells direct-to-consumer), subject to the following minimums:

Minimum Royalty in the United States and its territories and possessions, per successfully completed sale or license: (a) 10¢ (USD) [where retail price is less than or equal to $1.00 (USD)]; or (b) 12.5¢ (USD) [where retail price is greater than $1.00 (USD)].

Notwithstanding the foregoing, if a different U.S. statutory rate and/or Canadian license rate is established specifically for any ringtone products described hereunder during the Term, then such rate(s) shall apply prospectively as of the effective date of such rate(s).

All Digital Music Videos –

Ten percent (10%) of XYZ's receipts from successfully completed sales or commercial exploitations allocated to the Composition(s)

The U.S. statutory rate for ringtones is $0.24 per copy. In this agreement, the licensee is also agreeing to pay the same rate for mastertones, although they are not necessarily covered under the statutory rate. For Canada, an industry consensus will govern the rate.

If the rate changes, the new rate (either higher or lower) will apply prospectively to all sales during the remainder of the term.

Here is where the royalty calculation begins to get interesting. The agreement sets out a couple of parameters by which a royalty is calculated by a percentage, but also establishes a floor, i.e., minimum, based on a penny rate.

The royalty for these uses will be based upon the larger of several factors, the first being a percentage of the retail sales price of a completed sale to a consumer.

The second factor will be 20% of the income the record company receives from a distributor or 10% of the record company receipts from direct sales to a consumer.

The above formulas notwithstanding, there is also a minimum royalty paid in the United States if the calculations above fall below these minimums for sales under or over $1.00 USD.

If the rate changes, the new rate (either higher or lower) will apply prospectively to all sales during the remainder of the term.

A straight percentage calculation based upon receipts of the record company.

Accountings: XYZ shall account to you on a quarterly basis, within 45 days after the end of each quarter. Upon no less than 30 days notice, you shall have the right to audit no more frequently than once per calendar year and no more than once per accounting statement. Unless objected to, each statement shall become binding 2 years after your receipt of such statement.

Quarterly accountings with standard audit rights.

Miscellaneous: This agreement represents the final expression of the parties' intent with respect to the subject matter hereof, and all prior and contemporaneous agreements are merged herein.

This agreement and the royalty rates herein are not meant to set precedent and will be without prejudice to any rights and arguments.

Because these are relatively new business models, neither side wants to establish a precedent that might affect changes in the way future deals might be structured. However, as mentioned above, since the term of this agreement is in perpetuity, it has the effect of setting the deal terms for similar exploitations in the future, at least for the songs covered under this agreement.

You represent and warrant that you exclusively own or control the above Administrative Share(s) of the work(s) and that the exercise by XYZ or its successors, licensees, or assigns of the rights granted to it hereunder will not infringe upon the rights of any third party. You will indemnify and hold XYZ and its successors, licensees, or assigns harmless from any third party claim, cost, or expense arising out of any breach of the foregoing representation and warranty.

Standard warranties, representations, and indemnification by the publisher to the record company.

This agreement has been entered into in the State of California. The validity, interpretation and legal effect of this agreement is governed by the laws of the State of California applicable to contracts entered into and performed entirely within such State. The California courts (state and federal), only, will have jurisdiction over any controversies regarding this agreement, and the parties hereto consent to the jurisdiction of said courts.

XYZ reserves the right to revoke this proposal if it is not executed and returned by you within forty five (45) days from the date hereof.

Any license fee with the respect to the royalties as described herein that are currently payable by XYZ to your co-publisher, for substantially the same territory, shall in no event be greater than the license fees payable hereunder to you.

A Most Favored Nations clause, limited only to any co-publishers of this composition, but not necessarily to all similar deals made by the label. Given the structure of the deal, a broader MFN clause would be preferable.

ACCEPTED AND AGREED:

By: _____
      (An Authorized Signatory)

Print Name: _____

Title: _____

Date: _____

ACCEPTED AND AGREED
XYZ Recordings, Inc.

By: _____

CHAPTER 13

DIGITAL MEDIA
Part 2

The music industry is still trying to figure out the best ways to deliver music to people and monetize these methods. The consumers are equally trying to decide the best ways to receive music while keeping their costs reasonable. Developments such as (i) ringtones, ringbacks, and mastertones (as was discussed in the previous chapter), (ii) videogames played by single users, multiple users in one location, or multiple users online, (iii) music in applications ("apps") for mobile devices, and (iv) streaming video sites are all relatively new methods of exploiting music and generating income for the copyright owners.

Performing Rights License Rates

The three Performing Rights Organizations in the U.S. all have slightly different methods of calculating the costs of an Internet website's public performance license. Factors include whether the site is interactive or passive, if the site is primarily a music site or music is ancillary to the main purpose of the site, and if the site generates revenues from sponsors or users of the site. There are alternative methods of calculating the rates based on either a percentage of income (as defined in the licenses), a per-use payment based on the number of "sessions" or page views (also as defined), or an annual minimum fee. Also factored into these equations is the amount of music controlled by the PRO in relationship to the total amount of music performed on the site.

There are advantages and disadvantages to the various methodologies involved. If the music use is small, the minimum annual fee might be sufficient to cover all the uses. And there are multiple ways of calculating the fees, based on an annual election by the site operator. But no matter which method is chosen, it appears that the licenses require that the income calculations and session calculations are all necessary for each option in order to determine the actual fee, so while these seem like alternative methods of reporting, they are, in fact, all required in order to calculate the appropriate fees. Given digital technologies, keeping track of the number of sessions might not be that difficult, and certainly the sites would be keeping track of their income, but the task is still burdensome to smaller sites that might not have the ability to keep track of all the details necessary for proper reporting, and leaves uncertain the actual amount of the license fees to be paid until the calculations are completed and methods compared to each other.

It should be noted that the costs of the PRO licenses are deducted from the license fees due under the Section 115 settlement agreements discussed below.

Each PRO has information on their sites about their own methodologies and rules for calculations but, at least conceptually, all follow the general guidelines listed above. Below are some samples of how the license fees are calculated by the different PROs.

SESAC

As the smallest of the PROs, SESAC's formulas are actually the easiest to calculate. For audio-only sites, the gross revenue of the site is multiplied by 0.0057, with an annual minimum fee of $225. SESAC requires the following additional information to assist in their reporting of performances and payment to the applicable parties.

For Audio Performances

Program records, server logs or similar records listing the particular musical compositions performed and the number of times each composition was performed.

For Audiovisual Performances

1. The unique number assigned to each program by the licensee that identifies the source of each program.

2. The name of the source of each program.

3. The unique number assigned to each program by the licensee that identifies the particular program.

4. The title of the particular program (i.e., the title of the series, movie, sporting event, etc.).

5. The number assigned to each episode of the program by the program producer.

6. The name assigned to the each episode of the program by the program producer.

7. The date each such performance occurs.

8. The number of performances that occurred during the reporting period summarized by source, program, episode, and date.

In effect, the above information is the same type of information required on a music cue sheet for a program broadcast on television for the same purposes.

BMI

For corporate image websites, where the music use would be minimal, the fees are calculated as follows (at the user's option).

1. Page Impression Calculation: License fee = page impressions x $0.40/1,000

2. Music Page Impressions Calculation: License fee = Music page impressions x $0.60/1000

3. Annual Minimum License Fee for 2012 is $335.

For sites where music is a key component, the fees are as follows (again, at user's option).

1. Gross Revenue Calculation: License fee = gross revenue x 1.75%

2. Music Revenue Calculation: License fee = the greater of (a) music revenue x 2.5% and (b) (music page impressions/1,000) x $0.12

3. Annual Minimum License Fee for 2012 is $335.

For non-profit organizations, the rates are as follows.

1. Page Impression Calculation: License fee = page impressions x $0.08/1,000

2. Music Page Impressions Calculation: License fee = music page impressions x $0.12/1000

3. Annual Minimum License Fee for 2012 is $335.

BMI also requires music use reports that provide similar information as the SESAC report listed above.

ASCAP

The ASCAP licenses are far and away the most complicated of the three PROs, offering three different calculation methods, each based on three different sets of calculations. One example is as follows.

REVENUE BASED LICENSE FEE CALCULATION FOR RATE SCHEDULE "A"

1. Sponsor Revenue $_____

2. Adjustment to Sponsor Revenue $_____

3. Net Sponsor Revenue (line 1 minus line 2) $_____

4. User Revenue $_____

5. Service Revenue (add lines 3 and 4) $_____

6. Rate Based on Service Revenue x 0.030 $_____

7. Revenue Based License Fee (multiply lines 5 by line 6) $_____

SESSION BASED LICENSE FEE CALCULATION FOR RATE SCHEDULE "A"

SESSION VALUE

8. Number of Service Sessions   _____

9. Rate Based on Service Sessions x 0.0009 $_____

10. Session Based License Fee (multiply line 8 by line 9) $_____

LICENSE FEE CALCULATION FOR RATE SCHEDULE "A"

11. Licensee Fee (enter line 7 or line 10, whichever is greater) $ _____

12. Minimum License Fee (not subject to pro-ration) $340.00

13. LICENSE FEE DUE (enter amount from line 11
    or line 12, whichever is greater) $ _____

The above rates are based on one variation (Schedule A) for interactive sites. There are also calculations based upon a Schedule B and Schedule C. Rather than reprint them all here, the rates can be found at: ascap.com/~/media/Files/Pdf/licensing/digital/InteractiveLicenseAgreement_R2_1.pdf. In addition, there are calculations for non-interactive sites that are similar in concept but with different rates.

Like the other PROs, ASCAP requires reporting of various types of uses that mimic the reports that radio and television stations supply to determine which music was performed on the sites and, therefore, which songs to credit for the income received.

Recent Negotiated Settlements and Digital Rates Under Section 115

The PROs, National Music Publishers Association/Harry Fox Agency, and SoundExchange have entered into agreements with the digital carriers for licensing of performance and/or mechanical rights and continue to find more creative ways to generate licensing income. In October 2008, the NMPA and the Digital Media Association (DiMA) entered into an agreement that fell under the compulsory licensing provisions Section 115 of the Copyright Act and would set new mechanical and streaming rates until December 31, 2012. Mechanical royalties for DPDs have been discussed previously as being paid at the statutory rate of $0.091 per copy, with ringtones paid at $0.24 per copy. Rates for interactive streams and limited (or "tethered") downloads were also set at that time.

More recently, in early 2012, the same parties extended the rates agreed upon in 2008 until December 31, 2017, and also instituted new rates for media and business models that had been developing since the 2008 settlement, such as "cloud-based" streaming services, "locker" services in which users could store their own music (either previously purchased online or uploaded from their existing CD libraries) for access from any Internet-connected device, different mixed services that are bundled together, and new subscription service models. These rates are calculated by determining a wide variety of factors, such as the retail prices of items sold, per-subscriber rates, net revenue to the service from all sources, including any equity, advances or other monetary and nonmonetary consideration, costs of payments to the record companies and PROs, and many other factors. The documents and charts attached provide a detailed (and complicated) analysis of the formulas used. In addition, the allowable length of a free promo stream was increased from 30 seconds to 90 seconds.

The key to all of this is that the music publishers and digital services have *finally* been able to agree on formulas for payment that, while each side feels that they are either too high or too low, allows the music industry to move forward and develop these new business models.

When the mechanical rate was set at $0.02 per copy until 1977, there was a saying that "the music publishing business is a penny business." Well, now it's a micro-penny business, as the payments generated by these other uses of music are, at least for the moment, miniscule.

Licensing these various services now falls under a compulsory license, with the fees paid by the services calculated at a statutory rate, based on a number of factors and different methods of calculation and on the type of delivery methods the services offer, as summarized below and outlined in more detail in the documents relating to the 2008 and 2012 settlements attached to this chapter. (Many of the terms contained in these documents are defined in the Electronic Code of Federal Regulations, which is attached at the end of this book, with additional definitions contained in the 2012 settlement analysis attached at the end of this chapter.) Under the 2008 settlement, five types of services were identified and rates were set as described below. These services are:

1. Standalone Non-Portable Subscriptions, Streaming Only

2. Standalone Non-Portable Subscriptions, Mixed Use

3. Standalone Portable Subscriptions, Mixed Use

4. Bundled Subscription Services

5. Free Non-Subscription / Ad-Supported Services

Calculating Rates under the 2008 Settlement

The calculation of the rates payable by these services is a complicated formula. Factors include the greater of the applicable Service Type Minimum or a fixed percentage of revenue collected (currently 10.5% less the costs of performing rights royalties) paid to publishers divided by the number of "plays" on the service. Another method is comparing the calculation above with a flat rate per subscriber, with the higher payment considered the royalty. (For the Free Non-Subscription / Ad-Supported Services, there is obviously no subscriber fee to be used as a basis for the royalty). This can be as low as $0.00130 per play, which will require hundreds of thousands of plays for there to be any measurable income.

1. Calculate All-In Royalty For Service as greater of:

    (a) applicable % of Services Revenue = 10.5%

    and (**Author's note**: although this language is written as "and," it really means "or," as in "the greater of (a) <u>or</u> (b)")

    (b) applicable Service Type Minimum if pass thru license, 18% of service roy. exp. for label, if not pass thru, 22% of service roy. exp. for label

2. Subtract from All-In Royalty for Offering PRO royalties re: licensed activities

3. Payable Royalty Pool ($ payable for all musical works used in the period) =

    (a) Greater of:

        i.   Step 2 Result, or

        ii. $.XX per Subscriber Month*

4. Per Work Royalty Allocation for Each Relevant Work, applicable to all offering types:

    (a) Payable Royalty Pool for an offering divided by the total number of plays of all musical works through the offering (other than promo rate plays) to yield a per-play allocation

    (b) Multiply per-play allocation times the number of plays each musical work (other than promo rate plays). After 10/01/10 the number of plays for musical works with a playing time of over 5 minutes shall be counted to that each actual play is counted as 1 plus 0.2 for each minute or portion thereof in excess of 5 minutes.

* - Subscriber Month for all offerings except bundled subscription services shall be calculated for the accounting period, taking into account all end users who were subscribers for complete calendar months, prorating in the case of end users who were subscribers for only part of a calendar month, and deducting on a prorated basis for end users covered by a free trial period subject to the promo royalty rate. For bundled subscription services, determined with respect to active subscribers (i.e., each end user who made at least one play of a licensed work during such month).

Based on a recent statement received for one of our clients for the Apple cloud service:
114,000 plays = $86.00 in royalties.

The 2012 Settlement

Under the 2012 settlement, the following services were identified and added to the list:

1. Mixed Service Bundle

2. Paid Locker Service

3. Purchased Content Locker

4. Limited Offering

5. Music Bundle

Calculation of the rates under the 2012 settlement follow the same type of protocols as the 2008 rates, i.e., some formulas based on the greater of one method vs. another, with the rates being different for the different types of services.

For record labels, the numbers are small as well, about $0.0017 per play with the artist getting 15% of that income, or $0.000255 per play. This is why some artists have refused to license their music to some of the new streaming services, feeling that the service is diluting the value of their music.

For major companies, who are used to dealing with royalties in the thousands of dollars, these micropayments are a huge source of frustration, as it takes as much work to process a statement for $1.00 as it does for $10,000. For major copyright owners, there are now millions, if not billions, of line items on the statement from the digital services, requiring much more work for much less income.

Are You In or Out?

Is getting some money from digital services, no matter how small, better than not getting any money at all? The conundrum for *all* companies is whether to withdraw from licensing to these systems entirely or get whatever money they can while they can. For example, The Beatles did not license their songs to iTunes for 10 years. While no one is feeling sorry for them financially, imagine how many downloads they could have sold in that 10-year period. For an artist or publisher *not* to license their material to the new digital services is to eliminate a potential source of income that did not exist a few years ago.

And it needs to be noted that publishers need to take a long range view of the income streams that might be developing. The question is not how much a publisher earns in one quarterly statement, but how much they might make over the lifetime of a song's popularity, despite the possible decline in the number of people streaming the song. For fans of the song, the age of the song isn't important; what is important is that they can listen to it over and over, whenever they want to. This is the type of continuing income that publishers and writers hope for.

One of the current issues the streaming services face, however, is that a majority of their income goes towards paying royalties to publishers and record companies for the rights being granted, either through negotiation or compulsory licensing. According to an August 28, 2012, article by Ben Sisario in *The New York Times*, in 2011 Pandora paid approximately 54% of its revenue for licensing royalties. In the same article, it was reported that Spotify paid approximately 70% of its income in licensing fees.

"Cloud-based" services are also becoming more prevalent. These services allow the user to store copies of their music, photos, or documents that they own by uploading the files to a remote server (or "locker") and access them via web-connected devices. In some cases, the service scans the user's hard drive for files and matches them with files already stored on the server, making the need for uploading unnecessary and the service easier to use. These services require licenses from the publishers and record companies, as copies are being made on the server for access by the user. What is not allowed, however, are files that are illegally obtained by the user, or for the user to be able to access copies of files on the server for songs that the user does not already own, also known as "sideloading."

What should also be remembered, however, is that these services are in their infancy and, assuming that the licensing fees don't become too high and put them out of business (a real danger, by the way—see above), the increased mobility of music users will probably allow the services to grow and generate more plays for the artists. In order for that to happen, the music industry must be patient and allow this growth to monetize the use of music.

A correlation can be drawn to the early days of cable television in the early 1980s. The license fees charged by the PROs to HBO, Showtime, and similar services in those days was a fraction of what was being charged to the major networks, as the cable broadcasters had significantly fewer viewers. As the cable industry grew, more people had access to cable, and viewership rose, the PROs were able to negotiate higher fees with the cable companies. It was this early business model, however, that allowed the cable companies to continue in business and grow their viewership and revenues.

For promotional "MTV-style" music videos, publishers have traditionally granted a gratis synchronization license to the record companies, as the exploitation of these music videos was mutually beneficial. With the advent of the services listed above, however, the use of these videos has transformed from promotion to commercial, with the labels earning sometime substantial license fees as a result of their deals with the video services. In some cases, these fees are advances against a share of advertising revenue generated by the services which, due to technology, can now be attributed to the individual videos in question. As a result, the publishers are now claiming that their gratis license no longer covers this type of use and are requesting a share of record companies' revenue stream.

At this time, this is a fairly recent development, but it has led to a new business practice by the labels. Publishers, instead of licensing to the video services directly, are now being asked to grant the labels the right to license their video content containing the publishers' music in exchange for a share of revenue generated. The share is different from company to company but, like the controlled composition clause, an industry standard is being developed. The licenses state that the publishers will receive a percentage of the labels' revenue, pro rata to the number of performances of the publishers' songs in comparison to all the songs performed. Again, while the amounts of money being generated by advertising online are still relatively small, it is hoped that these amounts will grow as the model develops.

The Future of Digital Delivery

As stated by artist Usher in the online magazine *Singersroom*, **"Evolve or evaporate."** (singersroom.com/content/2012-06-11/Ushers-Career-Reflection-Evolve-or-Evaporate/). The ability (or inability) of the major music companies to adapt to the changes in the way consumers listen to music holds the key. The dinosaurs couldn't evolve, so they evaporated. Will the record companies be able to escape the same fate?

The ability of independent artists to have web presence or to have their music on the digital services is a great advance in their ability to get their music heard by more people, possibly generating more income. However, as my law partner, Ron Sobel, frequently says, **"You have to get people to pay attention before they pay royalties."** With access to tens of thousands of artists on thousands of music sites available to the listening public for streaming or downloading, how does an independent artist get eyeballs and ears to where their music is located?

The term "screen-agers" has evolved out the habits of young people whose attention spans are being diverted. They watch television, while doing their homework on their laptop, while texting on their smartphones, while listening to music on their digital players.

An artist must now understand how to use the Internet for their own gain by communicating directly with their fans and figuring out how to get viewers to their sites. A physical sale at Walmart, a digital sale on iTunes or Amazon, or a stream on Spotify is indirect and the artist (or their label) gains no information about the people listening to their music. With everyone wired in, it is easier for an artist to make contact if they have the right tools.

In the early days of downloading, when it took hours just to get one song via a dial-up service, Tom Petty offered a free download of his new single in exchange for a fan's email address and ZIP code. There were reportedly 350,000 downloads in a few days until Petty's label, as owners of the master recordings, shut down the site. But what Petty was able to do was to connect directly with his fans, people who already knew and loved his music. With this information, he was able to communicate directly with a targeted audience. Emails could be sent, based on ZIP codes, saying, "Hey, (name of town), I'm coming to your city next month. Here's where to buy tickets and here's a link to my site in case you want to buy my new album or a t-shirt to wear to the concert." The data became as valuable as any currency, as Petty was able to drive his fans to sites that could make him money.

With the increased use of search engines like Google, Yahoo, and Bing, the artist must try to have their sites listed on the first page when a user is searching for a particular type of music or sound. The artist must use Search Engine Optimization, or SEO, to embed their sites with key words or phrases that can be identified by the search engines and boost the artist's site to the top of the list of potential pages that qualify under the search terms.

Storage vs. Access

In addition, the idea of "storage" of music (as opposed to "access" to music) is becoming more of an issue, as the consumers want to hear what they want, when they want it, wherever they are.

Storage would be the purchasing and downloading of digital files on a device such as a computer, laptop, iPod, mobile device, or tablet (or, to go old school, to buy CDs), so that the user could listen to the music whenever they had the ability to use their device. Some of these devices are portable, while some require being connected in the location of the device. A user's device is limited to only that music which the user has loaded on to the device. If someone wants to hear Barry White, but has not already downloaded Barry White, they will miss the experience they were hoping for in that instant.

Access, on the other hand, means that the user is connected via Internet or other wireless transmission to a service that streams music to them, either on demand or in a non-interactive method, like radio or Pandora. As long as the user can connect, they have access to the music, whether they own it or not. Whether a service stores the user's music in a cloud-based server or merely streams the music, the user has the ability to listen to much more music than they own and have via storage.

Survival Strategies

In order for the music industry to survive, music must be available to all consumers via digital technology. These issues bring us to the following opinions:

1. While there will still be some parties who will feel the need to be able to touch a CD and hold the jewel case in their hands, many consumers will switch to the digital delivery model if simple and affordable. Therefore, delivery must be easy to accomplish and a straight line from the services to the consumer without interference from any intermediary parties.

2. The average consumer doesn't have much interest in the technology involved in receiving their music, so the process should seem invisible to the consumer.

3. The costs of receiving digital music should "feel free." Most consumers these days have cable television or mobile phones that require a fee to be paid to their carrier, but these devices have become so common that the payment of a cable TV or cellular phone bill is no longer deemed a luxury, but almost a necessity, as if it were a utility like electricity or water. Adding a small charge to a cable TV or Internet service provider bill would have the same effect in that those bills are being paid already and a small additional charge would be virtually un-noticed by the consumer.

There is also another model already in existence that can be utilized here: television. Virtually everyone in the U.S. has a television set and receives programming in one of three ways: either (1) they get their television signals without cost via antenna, subject to having to watch commercials; (2) they subscribe to a cable or satellite service for a relatively small fee in order to receive their over-the-air stations in addition to other basic cable programming like CNN, MTV, or Animal Planet, still having to endure watching commercials; or (3) they pay a higher fee to get premium programming like HBO or Showtime that is shown without commercials. In all of these services, money is paid, either by the consumers or the advertisers, that supports the costs of producing the programming, paying all associated costs of production and broadcasting (such as public performance and synchronization fees).

A similar model could be used for streaming services, in which the consumer could listen to music with commercials for no fee or pay a subscription fee to eliminate the commercials. Again, money comes into the pipeline to pay for the music rights from record companies and publishers needed for these services to operate. These systems are already in place and are used by some consumers already, with the usage rate increasing rapidly.

In the future, these services will become more widely used and the purchase of music may become less relevant. If the consumer can hear anything they want, anywhere they want, any time they want, do they need to buy music? And, more importantly, do they need to steal music?

Yet, with all the talk of the digital jukebox and cloud-based storage, problems still remain. In order to utilize these streaming or cloud-based systems, the user must be connected to an Internet or wireless service at all times, which eliminates certain geographic areas where service may not be available and (currently) most airplane travel, when listening to music is a great way to pass the time while flying from one place to another. The transmission of music involves the transfer of huge amounts of data so, with the mobile companies moving away rapidly from unlimited data plans, connectivity will become more expensive in addition to the fees paid for the digital services.

So maybe storage isn't such a bad idea after all. Hard disc space is relatively cheap, flash drives have more capacity while taking up little physical space, and mobile devices have increasing storage capabilities as the costs of technology keep coming down. These alternative theories only highlight the difficulty the music business and consumer are having in trying to figure out the best way to deliver and listen to music.

In summary, the future of the music industry is in the digital space and, in some ways, levels the playing field between independent artists and major label artists in terms of having the ability to have their music listened to and possibly purchased. And for music publishers, with the use of music increasing every time there is some new development in technology, the future is brighter than it has been since the early days of music piracy.

HFA Ready to Implement New Digital Era Mechanical Royalty Rates

October 2, 2008 – The Harry Fox Agency, Inc. (HFA), a leading U.S. music rights licensing organization, applauds today's decision of the Copyright Royalty Judges (CRJ), and is ready to implement the new digital era mechanical royalty rates, including the first-ever statutory royalties for on-demand streams, limited downloads, and ringtones, as well as for physical recordings and permanent downloads. 180 days after the rates take effect, record labels, online music services, and other licensees will include these royalties in their quarterly reports. This will include the payment of all of the retroactive royalties for subscription services, which HFA has been licensing since 2001.

"HFA has more than 80 years' experience licensing, collecting, and distributing royalties – we have evolved with every rate and music delivery format in the history of the U.S. recording industry, and we have already issued millions of licenses for online music services. With this decision from the Copyright Royalty Judges, we're very pleased to finally be able to distribute these long-awaited royalties," said Gary Churgin, HFA's President and CEO. "Our systems are ready to handle these more complex royalty reports, and we also have the added strength of our highly skilled Collections and Royalty Compliance teams to ensure the application of the correct rate structure. Publishers and licensees can trust HFA to deliver for them as we have for nearly a century."

The new schedule of mechanical rates, which will be in effect after final publication in the Federal Register until December 31, 2012, is:

> Physical recordings: 9.1 ¢ for recordings five minutes or less; for recordings over 5 minutes, 1.75 ¢ for each minute, rounded up.

> Permanent Digital Downloads: 9.1 ¢ for recordings five minutes or less; for recordings over 5 minutes, 1.75 ¢ for each minute, rounded up.

> Mastertone Ringtunes: 24¢ (for non-derivative uses)

Rates for limited downloads and on-demand streams vary by service offering; see attached chart.

Mechanical licenses are required under U.S. Copyright Law if one wants to duplicate and distribute a recording of a song that is owned by someone else whether in a physical or digital configuration. Through proper licensing, the publisher, and ultimately, the songwriter, are compensated for the use of their work. HFA is the largest mechanical rights agent in the U.S. Cumulatively, HFA administers over 15.2 million licenses for the almost 36,000 publisher catalogs it represents. In addition to mechanicals, HFA licenses a variety of formats, including lyrics, tablature, and more.

About HFA
Established in 1927 by the National Music Publishers' Association, HFA represents almost 36,000 music publishers for their licensing needs in the United States, issuing licenses and collecting and distributing the associated royalties. In addition to being the premier mechanical licensing agent in the U.S., which includes CDs, ringtones, digital downloads, interactive streams, limited downloads and more, HFA is dedicated to finding new ways for its affiliated publishers to recognize value for their catalogs, including lyrics and tablature. Further, HFA provides collection and monitoring services to its publisher clients for music distributed and sold in over 95 territories around the world. For more information about HFA, or to become an affiliate publisher or a licensee, see www.harryfox.com.

(used by permission)

Royalty Rates for the Use of Musical Works in Services Providing Interactive Streaming and Limited Downloads

Calculation Steps:	Offering Type				
	Standalone Non-Portable Subscriptions, Streaming Only	Standalone Non-Portable Subscriptions, Mixed Use	Standalone Portable Subscriptions, Mixed Use	Bundled Subscription Services	Free Non-Subscription / Ad-Supported Services
1. Calculate **All-In Royalty For Service** as <u>greater of</u>: (a) applicable % of Service's Revenue,† and	(a) pre-12/31/07: 8.5%, 10.5% thereafter	(a) pre-12/31/07: 8.5%, 10.5% thereafter	(a) pre-12/31/07: 8.5%, 10.5% thereafter	(a) pre-12/31/07: 8.5%, 10.5% thereafter	(a) pre-12/31/07: 8.5%, 10.5% thereafter
(b) applicable Service Type Minimum	(b) <u>Lesser of</u> $ .50 per subscriber per month, and if pass thru license, 18% (14.53% if pre-01/08) of service roy. exp. for label, if not pass thru, 22% (17% if pre-01/08) of service roy. exp. for label	(b) <u>Lesser of</u> $ .50 per subscriber per month, and if pass thru license, 17.36% (14.53% if pre-01/08) of service roy. exp. for label, if not pass thru, 21% (17% if pre-01/08) of service roy. exp. for label	(b) <u>Lesser of</u> $ .80 per subscriber per month, and if pass thru license, 17.36% (14.53% if pre-01/08) of service roy. exp. for label, if not pass thru, 21% (17% if pre-01/08) of service roy. exp. for label	if pass thru license, 17.36% (14.53% if pre-01/08) of service roy. exp. for label, if not pass thru, 21% (17% if pre-01/08) of service roy. exp. for label	if pass thru license, 18% (14.53% if pre-01/08) of service roy. exp. for label, if not pass thru, 22% (17% if pre-01/08) of service roy. exp. for label
2. Subtract from All-In Royalty for Offering	PRO royalties re. licensed activities	PRO royalties re. licensed activities	PRO royalties re. licensed activities	PRO royalties re. licensed activities	PRO royalties re. licensed activities
3. **Payable Royalty Pool** ($ payable for all musical works used in the period) =	<u>Greater of:</u> 1. Step 2 Result, or 2. $.15 per Subscriber Month *	<u>Greater of:</u> 1. Step 2 Result, or 2. $.30 per Subscriber Month *	<u>Greater of:</u> 1. Step 2 Result, or 2. $.50 per Subscriber Month *	<u>Greater of:</u> 1. Step 2 Result, or 2. $.25 per Subscriber Month *	Step 2 Result
4. Per Work Royalty Allocation for Each Relevant Work, applicable to all offering types: (a) Payable Royalty Pool for an offering divided by the total number of plays of all musical works through the offering (other than promo rate plays) to yield a per-play allocation. (b) Multiply per-play allocation times the number of plays each musical work (other than promo rate plays). After 10/01/10 the number of plays for musical works with a playing time of <u>over 5 minutes</u> shall be counted as 1 plus 0.2 for each minute or portion thereof in excess of 5 minutes.					

(used by permission)

* - Subscriber Month for all offerings except bundled subscription services shall be calculated for the accounting period, taking into account all end users who were subscribers for complete calendar months, prorating in the case of end users who were subscribers for only part of a calendar month, and deducting on a prorated basis for end users covered by a free trial period subject to the promo royalty rate. For bundled subscription services, determined with respect to active subscribers (i.e., each end user who made at least one play of a licensed work during such month).

† Author's note—the use of the word "and" above actually means "or," i.e., "the greater of (a) or (b)"

Summary Sheet of 2012 Section 115 CRB Settlement
prepared by Bobby Rosenbloum and Charmaine Smith,
Greenberg, Traurig, LLC Atlanta
Used by Permission

This summary sheet is intended to convey the general parameters of the settlement of the CRB Section 115 rate-setting proceeding.

Existing Subparts A and B of 37 CFR 385:

- Rollover of all existing rates and terms, except that the permitted length of promotional clips is extended to 90 seconds.

  o "Sound Recording Payment Integrity" — Language confirming that for purposes of computing royalties based on a service's payments to record companies (the "TCC" royalty calculation), the royalty base is to be viewed as encompassing the full range of GAAP expenses.

- The royalty base will include anything of value given for the identified rights to undertake the licensed activity, including, without limitation, ownership equity, monetary advances, barter or any other monetary and/or nonmonetary consideration, whether such consideration is conveyed via a single agreement, multiple agreements and/or agreements that do not themselves authorize the licensed activity but nevertheless provide consideration for the identified rights to undertake the licensed activity, and including any such value given to an affiliate of a record company for such rights to undertake the licensed activity.

- Late Fees — The existing late fee term will be extended.

New Subpart C:
A new Subpart C, generally patterned on Subpart B, addresses several new types of offerings (and also includes Sound Recording Payment Integrity language as described above).

- Mixed Service Bundle

  o Definition: An offering of one or more of permanent digital downloads, ringtones, locker services, or limited offerings, together with one or more of non-music services (e.g., Internet access service, mobile phone service) or non-music products (e.g., a device such as a phone) of more than token value, that is provided to users as part of one transaction without pricing for the music services or music products separate from the whole offering.

  o All-in rate (inclusive of PRO fees) is greater of:

    › 11.35% of service revenue; and

    › 21% of a service's payments to record companies for sound recording rights only.

  o Service revenue allocation — Similar to the bundle revenue allocation methodology in the current definition of "service revenue," but subject to a floor of 50% of the standalone published price of the licensed music component of the bundle, or 40% in the case of a bundle that has (or is reasonably expected to have) 750,000 subscribers.

- Paid Locker Service
  - Definition: A locker service that is user subscription based. A "locker service" is a service providing access to sound recordings of musical works in the form of interactive streams, ringtones, permanent digital downloads or downloads that may not be retained and played on a permanent basis, where the service has reasonably determined that phonorecords of the applicable sound recordings have been purchased by the end user or are otherwise in the possession of the end user prior to the end user's first request to access such sound recordings by means of the service. The term locker service does not extend to any part of a service otherwise meeting this definition as to which a license is not obtained for the applicable reproductions and distributions of musical works.
  - All-in rate (inclusive of PRO fees) is greater of:
    - 12% of service revenue;
    - 20.65% of a service's payments to record companies for sound recording rights only; and
    - $0.17 per sub per month.
- Purchased Content Locker
  - Definition: A locker service made available to end-user purchasers of permanent digital downloads, ringtones or physical phonorecords, at no incremental charge, whereby the locker service enables the purchaser to (1) receive one or more additional phonorecords of such purchased sound recordings of musical works in the form of permanent digital downloads or ringtones at the time of purchase, or (2) subsequently access such purchased sound recordings of musical works in the form of interactive streams, ringtones, additional permanent digital downloads, or downloads that may not be retained and played on a permanent basis. The permanent digital downloads, ringtones or physical phonorecords must be purchased from a qualifying seller having a sufficient connection to the provider of the locker service through a written agreement (or in the case of physical phonorecords the provision of the locker and sale of the physical phonorecord must be part of an integrated offering). Further, in the case of a locker service made available to the purchaser of a physical phonorecord, the seller must permanently part with possession of the phonorecord.
  - All-in rate (inclusive of PRO fees) is greater of:
    - 12% of incremental service revenue (e.g., advertising on relevant pages); and
    - 22% of a service's incremental payments to record companies (above the otherwise applicable payments for the permanent digital downloads) for sound recording rights only.

- Limited Offering
  - Definition: A subscription service providing interactive streams or limited downloads where (1) an end user is not provided the opportunity to listen to a particular sound recording chosen by the user at a time chosen by the user (i.e., the service does not provide interactive streams of individual recordings that are on-demand, and any limited downloads are rendered only as part of programs rather than as individual recordings that are on-demand); or (2) the particular sound recordings available to the end user over a period of time are substantially limited relative to services in the marketplace providing access to a comprehensive catalog of recordings (e.g., a service limited to a particular genre, or permitting interactive streaming only from a monthly playlist consisting of a limited set of recordings).
  - All-in rate (inclusive of PRO fees) is greater of:
    - 10.5% of service revenue;
    - 21% of a service's payments to record companies for sound recording rights only; and
    - $0.18 per sub per month.
- Music Bundles
  - Definition: An offering of two or more of physical phonorecords, permanent digital downloads or ringtones provided to users as part of one transaction (e.g., download plus ringtone, CD plus downloads). A music bundle must contain at least two different product configurations and cannot be combined with any other offering containing licensed activity under subpart B or subpart C.
  - In the case of music bundles containing one or more physical phonorecords, the physical phonorecord component of the music bundle must be sold under a single catalog number, and the musical works embodied in the digital phonorecord delivery configurations in the music bundle must be the same as, or a subset of, the musical works embodied in the physical phonorecords; provided that when the music bundle contains a set of digital phonorecord deliveries sold by the same record company under substantially the same title as the physical phonorecord (e.g. a corresponding digital album), up to 5 sound recordings of musical works that are included in the stand-alone version of such set of digital phonorecord deliveries but are not included on the physical phonorecord may be included among the digital phonorecord deliveries in the music bundle. In addition, the seller must permanently part with possession of the physical phonorecord or phonorecords sold as part of the music bundle.
  - In the case of music bundles composed solely of digital phonorecord deliveries, the number of digital phonorecord deliveries in either configuration cannot exceed 20, and the musical works embodied in each configuration in the music bundle must be the same as, or a subset of, the musical works embodied in the configuration containing the most musical works.
  - All-in rate (inclusive of PRO fees) is greater of:
    - 11.35% of service revenue; and
    - 21% of a service's payments to record companies for sound recording rights only.
  - Royalty pool allocated based on ratio of standalone prices and number of tracks in each configuration.

Electronic Code of Federal Regulations

Title 37: Patents, Trademarks, and Copyrights

PART 385—RATES AND TERMS FOR USE OF MUSICAL WORKS UNDER COMPULSORY LICENSE FOR MAKING AND DISTRIBUTING OF PHYSICAL AND DIGITAL PHONORECORDS

Contents

AUTHORITY: 17 U.S.C. 115, 801(b)(1), 804(b)(4).

SOURCE: 74 FR 4529, Jan. 26, 2009, unless otherwise noted.

Subpart A—Physical Phonorecord Deliveries, Permanent Digital Downloads and Ringtones

§ 385.1 General.

(a) *Scope.* This subpart establishes rates and terms of royalty payments for making and distributing phonorecords, including by means of digital phonorecord deliveries, in accordance with the provisions of 17 U.S.C. 115.

(b) *Legal compliance.* Licensees relying upon the compulsory license set forth in 17 U.S.C. 115 shall comply with the requirements of that section, the rates and terms of this subpart, and any other applicable regulations.

(c) *Relationship to voluntary agreements.* Notwithstanding the royalty rates and terms established in this subpart, the rates and terms of any license agreements entered into by Copyright Owners and Licensees shall apply in lieu of the rates and terms of this subpart to use of musical works within the scope of such agreements.

§ 385.2 Definitions.

For purposes of this subpart, the following definitions apply:

Copyright owners are nondramatic musical work copyright owners who are entitled to royalty payments made under this subpart pursuant to the compulsory license under 17 U.S.C. 115.

Digital phonorecord delivery means a digital phonorecord delivery as defined in 17 U.S.C. 115(d).

Licensee is a person or entity that has obtained a compulsory license under 17 U.S.C. 115, and the implementing regulations, to make and distribute phonorecords of a nondramatic musical work, including by means of a digital phonorecord delivery.

Permanent digital download means a digital phonorecord delivery that is distributed in the form of a download that may be retained and played on a permanent basis.

Ringtone means a phonorecord of a partial musical work distributed as a digital phonorecord delivery in a format to be made resident on a telecommunications device for use to announce the reception of an incoming telephone call or other communication or message or to alert the receiver to the fact that there is a communication or message.

§ 385.3 Royalty rates for making and distributing phonorecords.

a) *Physical phonorecord deliveries and permanent digital downloads.* For every physical phonorecord and permanent digital download made and distributed, the royalty rate payable for each work embodied in such phonorecord shall be either 9.1 cents or 1.75 cents per minute of playing time or fraction thereof, whichever amount is larger.

(b) *Ringtones.* For every ringtone made and distributed, the royalty rate payable for each work embodied therein shall be 24 cents.

§ 385.4 Late payments.

A Licensee shall pay a late fee of 1.5% per month, or the highest lawful rate, whichever is lower, for any payment received by the Copyright Owner after the due date set forth in (201.19(e)(7)(i) of this title. Late fees shall accrue from the due date until payment is received by the Copyright Owner.

Subpart B—Interactive Streaming, Other Incidental Digital Phonorecord Deliveries and Limited Downloads

§ 385.10 General.

(a) *Scope.* This subpart establishes rates and terms of royalty payments for interactive streams and limited downloads of musical works by subscription and nonsubscription digital music services in accordance with the provisions of 17 U.S.C. 115.

(b) *Legal compliance.* A licensee that makes or authorizes interactive streams or limited downloads of musical works through subscription or nonsubscription digital music services pursuant to 17 U.S.C. 115 shall comply with the requirements of that section, the rates and terms of this subpart, and any other applicable regulations.

§ 385.11 Definitions.

For purposes of this subpart, the following definitions shall apply:

Interactive stream means a stream of a sound recording of a musical work, where the performance of the sound recording by means of the stream is not exempt under 17 U.S.C. 114(d)(1) and does not in itself or as a result of a program in which it is included qualify for statutory licensing under 17 U.S.C. 114(d)(2).

Licensee means a person that has obtained a compulsory license under 17 U.S.C. 115 and its implementing regulations.

Licensed activity means interactive streams or limited downloads of musical works, as applicable.

Limited download means a digital transmission of a sound recording of a musical work to an end user, other than a stream, that results in a specifically identifiable reproduction of that sound recording that is only accessible for listening for—

(1) An amount of time not to exceed 1 month from the time of the transmission (unless the service, in lieu of retransmitting the same sound recording as another limited download, separately and upon specific request of the end user made through a live network connection, reauthorizes use for another time period not to exceed 1 month), or in the case of a subscription transmission, a period of time following the end of the applicable subscription no longer than a subscription renewal period or 3 months, whichever is shorter; or

(2) A specified number of times not to exceed 12 (unless the service, in lieu of retransmitting the same sound recording as another limited download, separately and upon specific request of the end user made through a live network connection, reauthorizes use of another series of 12 or fewer plays), or in the case of a subscription transmission, 12 times after the end of the applicable subscription.

(3) A limited download is a general digital phonorecord delivery under 17 U.S.C. 115(c)(3)(C) and (D).

Offering means a service's offering of licensed activity that is subject to a particular rate set forth in § 385.13(a) (e.g., a particular subscription plan available through the service).

Promotional royalty rate means the statutory royalty rate of zero in the case of certain promotional interactive streams and certain promotional limited downloads, as provided in § 385.14.

Publication date means January 26, 2009.

Record company means a person or entity that

(1) Is a copyright owner of a sound recording of a musical work;

(2) In the case of a sound recording of a musical work fixed before February 15, 1972, has rights to the sound recording, under the common law or statutes of any State, that are equivalent to the rights of a copyright owner of a sound recording of a musical work under Title 17, United States Code;

(3) Is an exclusive licensee of the rights to reproduce and distribute a sound recording of a musical work; or

(4) Performs the functions of marketing and authorizing the distribution of a sound recording of a musical work under its own label, under the authority of the copyright owner of the sound recording.

Relevant page means a page (including a Web page, screen or display) from which licensed activity offered by a service is directly available to end users, but only where the offering of licensed activity and content that directly relates to the offering of licensed activity (e.g., an image of the artist or artwork closely associated with such offering, artist or album information, reviews of such offering, credits and music player controls) comprises 75% or more of the space on that page, excluding any space occupied by advertising. A licensed activity is directly available to end users from a page if sound recordings of musical works can be accessed by end users for limited downloads or interactive streams from such page (in most cases this will be the page where the limited download or interactive stream takes place).

Service means that entity (which may or may not be the licensee) that, with respect to the licensed activity,

(1) Contracts with or has a direct relationship with end users in a case where a contract or relationship exists, or otherwise controls the content made available to end users;

(2) Is able to report fully on service revenue from the provision of the licensed activity to the public, and to the extent applicable, verify service revenue through an audit; and

(3) Is able to report fully on usage of musical works by the service, or procure such reporting, and to the extent applicable, verify usage through an audit.

Service revenue. (1) Subject to paragraphs (2) through (5) of the definition of "Service revenue," and subject to U.S. Generally Accepted Accounting Principles, *service revenue* shall mean the following:

(i) All revenue recognized by the service from end users from the provision of licensed activity;

(ii) All revenue recognized by the service by way of sponsorship and commissions as a result of the inclusion of third-party "in-stream" or "in-download" advertising as part of licensed activity (i..e., advertising placed immediately at the start, end or during the actual delivery, by way of interactive streaming or limited downloads, as applicable, of a musical work); and

(iii) All revenue recognized by the service, including by way of sponsorship and commissions, as a result of the placement of third-party advertising on a relevant page of the service or on any page that directly follows such relevant page leading up to and including the limited download or interactive streaming, as applicable, of a musical work; provided that, in the case where more than one service is actually available to end users from a relevant page, any advertising revenue shall be allocated between such services on the basis of the relative amounts of the page they occupy.

2) In each of the cases identified in paragraph (1) of the definition of "Service revenue," such revenue shall, for the avoidance of doubt,

(i) Include any such revenue recognized by the service, or if not recognized by the service, by any associate, affiliate, agent or representative of such service in lieu of its being recognized by the service;

(ii) Include the value of any barter or other nonmonetary consideration;

(iii) Not be reduced by credit card commissions or similar payment process charges; and

(iv) Except as expressly set forth in this subpart, not be subject to any other deduction or set-off other than refunds to end users for licensed activity that they were unable to use due to technical faults in the licensed activity or other bona fide refunds or credits issued to end users in the ordinary course of business.

(3) In each of the cases identified in paragraph (1) of the definition of "Service revenue," such revenue shall, for the avoidance of doubt, exclude revenue derived solely in connection with services and activities other than licensed activity, provided that advertising or sponsorship revenue shall be treated as provided in paragraphs (2) and (4) of the definition of "Service revenue." By way of example, the following kinds of revenue shall be excluded:

(i) Revenue derived from non-music voice, content and text services;

(ii) Revenue derived from other non-music products and services (including search services, sponsored searches and click-through commissions); and

(iii) Revenue derived from music or music-related products and services that are not or do not include licensed activity.

(4) For purposes of paragraph (1) of the definition of "Service revenue," advertising or sponsorship revenue shall be reduced by the actual cost of obtaining such revenue, not to exceed 15%.

(5) Where the licensed activity is provided to end users as part of the same transaction with one or more other products or services that are not a music service engaged in licensed activity, then the revenue deemed to be recognized from end users for the service for the purpose of the definition in paragraph (1) of the definition of "Service revenue" shall be the revenue recognized from end users for the bundle less the standalone published price for end users for each of the other component(s) of the bundle; provided that, if there is no such standalone published price for a component of the bundle, then the average standalone published price for end users for the most closely comparable product or service in the U.S. shall be used or, if more than one such comparable exists, the average of such standalone

prices for such comparables shall be used. In connection with such a bundle, if a record company providing sound recording rights to the service

(i) Recognizes revenue (in accordance with U.S. Generally Accepted Accounting Principles, and including for the avoidance of doubt barter or nonmonetary consideration) from a person or entity other than the service providing the licensed activity and;

(ii) Such revenue is received, in the context of the transactions involved, as consideration for the ability to make interactive streams or limited downloads of sound recordings, then such revenue shall be added to the amounts expensed by the service for purposes of § 385.13(b). Where the service is the licensee, if the service provides the record company all information necessary for the record company to determine whether additional royalties are payable by the service hereunder as a result of revenue recognized from a person or entity other than the service as described in the immediately preceding sentence, then the record company shall provide such further information as necessary for the service to calculate the additional royalties and indemnify the service for such additional royalties. The sole obligation of the record company shall be to pay the licensee such additional royalties if actually payable as royalties hereunder; provided, however, that this shall not affect any otherwise existing right or remedy of the copyright owner nor diminish the licensee's obligations to the copyright owner.

Stream means the digital transmission of a sound recording of a musical work to an end user—

(1) To allow the end user to listen to the sound recording, while maintaining a live network connection to the transmitting service, substantially at the time of transmission, except to the extent that the sound recording remains accessible for future listening from a streaming cache reproduction;

(2) Using technology that is designed such that the sound recording does not remain accessible for future listening, except to the extent that the sound recording remains accessible for future listening from a streaming cache reproduction; and

(3) That is also subject to licensing as a public performance of the musical work.

Streaming cache reproduction means a reproduction of a sound recording of a musical work made on a computer or other receiving device by a service solely for the purpose of permitting an end user who has previously received a stream of such sound recording to play such sound recording again from local storage on such computer or other device rather than by means of a transmission; provided that the user is only able to do so while maintaining a live network connection to the service, and such reproduction is encrypted or otherwise protected consistent with prevailing industry standards to prevent it from being played in any other manner or on any device other than the computer or other device on which it was originally made.

Subscription service means a digital music service for which end users are required to pay a fee to access the service for defined subscription periods of 3 years or less (in contrast to, for example, a service where the basic charge to users is a payment per download or per play), whether such payment is made for access to the service on a standalone basis or as part of a bundle with one or more other products or services, and including any use of such a service on a trial basis without charge as described in § 385.14(b).

§ 385.12 Calculation of royalty payments in general.

(a) *Applicable royalty.* Licensees that make or authorize licensed activity pursuant to 17 U.S.C. 115 shall pay royalties therefor that are calculated as provided in this section, subject to the minimum royalties and subscriber-based royalty floors for specific types of services provided in § 385.13, except as provided for certain promotional uses in § 385.14.

(b) *Rate calculation methodology.* Royalty payments for licensed activity shall be calculated as provided in paragraph (b) of this section. If a service includes different offerings, royalties must be separately calculated with respect to each such offering. Uses subject to the promotional royalty rate shall be excluded from the calculation of royalties due, as further described in this section and the following § 385.13.

(1) *Step 1*: Calculate the All-In Royalty for the Service. For each accounting period, the all-in royalty for each offering of the service is the greater of

(i) The applicable percentage of service revenue as set forth in paragraph (c) of this section (excluding any service revenue derived solely from licensed activity uses subject to the promotional royalty rate), and

(ii) The minimum specified in § 385.13 of the offering involved.

(2) *Step 2*: Subtract Applicable Performance Royalties. From the amount determined in step 1 in paragraph (b)(1) of this section, for each offering of the service, subtract the total amount of royalties for public performance of musical works that has been or will be expensed by the service pursuant to public performance licenses in connection with uses of musical works through such offering during the accounting period that constitute licensed activity (other than licensed activity subject to the promotional royalty rate). While this amount may be the total of the service's payments for that offering for the accounting period under its agreements with performing rights societies as defined in 17 U.S.C. 101, it will be less than the total of such public performance payments if the service is also engaging in public performance of musical works that does not constitute licensed activity. In the latter case, the amount to be subtracted for public performance payments shall be the amount of such payments allocable to licensed activity uses (other than promotional royalty rate uses) through the relevant offering, as determined in relation to all uses of musical works for which the public performance payments are made for the accounting period. Such allocation shall be made on the basis of plays of musical works or, where per-play information is unavailable due to bona fide technical limitations as described in step 4 in paragraph (b)(4) of this section, using the same alternative methodology as provided in step 4.

(3) *Step 3*: Determine the Payable Royalty Pool. This is the amount payable for the reproduction and distribution of all musical works used by the service by virtue of its licensed activity for a particular offering during the accounting period. This amount is the greater of

(i) The result determined in step 2 in paragraph (b)(2) of this section, and

(ii) The subscriber-based royalty floor resulting from the calculations described in § 385.13.

(4) *Step 4*: Calculate the Per-Work Royalty Allocation for Each Relevant Work. This is the amount payable for the reproduction and distribution of each musical work used by the service by virtue of its licensed activity through a particular offering during the accounting period. To determine this amount, the result determined in step 3 in paragraph (b)(3) of this section must be allocated to each musical work used through the offering. The allocation shall be accomplished by dividing the payable royalty pool determined in step 3 for such offering by the total number of plays of all musical works through such offering during the accounting period (other than promotional royalty rate plays) to yield a per-play allocation, and multiplying that result by the number of plays of each musical work (other than promotional royalty rate plays) through the offering during the accounting period. For purposes of determining the per-work royalty allocation in all calculations under this step 4 only (i.e. , after the payable royalty pool has been determined), for sound recordings of musical works with a playing time of over 5 minutes, each play on or after October 1, 2010 shall be counted as provided in paragraph (d) of this section. Notwithstanding the foregoing, if the service is not capable of tracking play information due to bona fide limitations of the available technology for services of that nature or of devices useable with the service, the per-work royalty allocation may instead be accomplished in a manner consistent with the methodology used by the service for making royalty payment allocations for the use of individual sound recordings.

(c) *Percentage of service revenue.* The percentage of service revenue applicable under paragraph (b) of this section is 10.5%, except that such percentage shall be discounted by 2% (i.e. , to 8.5%) in the case of licensed activity occurring on or before December 31, 2007.

(d) *Overtime adjustment.* For licensed activity on or after October 1, 2010, for purposes of the calculations in step 4 in paragraph (b)(4) of this section only, for sound recordings of musical works with a playing time of over 5 minutes, adjust the number of plays as follows:

(1) 5:01 to 6:00 minutes—Each play = 1.2 plays

(2) 6:01 to 7:00 minutes—Each play = 1.4 plays

(3) 7:01 to 8:00 minutes—Each play = 1.6 plays

(4) 8:01 to 9:00 minutes—Each play = 1.8 plays

(5) 9:01 to 10:00 minutes—Each play = 2.0 plays

(6) For playing times of greater than 10 minutes, continue to add .2 for each additional minute or fraction thereof.

(e) *Accounting.* The calculations required by paragraph (b) of this section shall be made in good faith and on the basis of the best knowledge, information and belief of the licensee at the time payment is due, and subject to the additional accounting and certification requirements of 17 U.S.C. 115(c)(5) and § 201.19 of this title. Without limitation, a licensee's statements of account shall set forth each step of its calculations with sufficient information to allow the copyright owner to assess the accuracy and manner in which the licensee determined the payable royalty pool and per-play allocations (including information sufficient to demonstrate whether and how a minimum royalty or subscriber-based royalty floor pursuant to § 385.13 does or does not apply) and, for each offering reported, also indicate the type of licensed activity involved and the number of plays of each musical work (including an indication of any overtime adjustment applied) that is the basis of the per-work royalty allocation being paid.

§ 385.13 Minimum royalty rates and subscriber-based royalty floors for specific types of services.

(a) *In general.* The following minimum royalty rates and subscriber-based royalty floors shall apply to the following types of licensed activity:

(1) *Standalone non-portable subscription—streaming only.* Except as provided in paragraph (a)(4) of this section, in the case of a subscription service through which an end user can listen to sound recordings only in the form of interactive streams and only from a non-portable device to which such streams are originally transmitted while the device has a live network connection, the minimum for use in step 1 of § 385.12(b)(1) is the lesser of subminimum II as described in paragraph (c) of this section for the accounting period and the aggregate amount of 50 cents per subscriber per month. The subscriber-based royalty floor for use in step 3 of § 385.12(b)(3) is the aggregate amount of 15 cents per subscriber per month.

(2) *Standalone non-portable subscription—mixed.* Except as provided in paragraph (a)(4) of this section, in the case of a subscription service through which an end user can listen to sound recordings either in the form of interactive streams or limited downloads but only from a non-portable device to which such streams or downloads are originally transmitted, the minimum for use in step 1 of § 385.12(b)(1) is the lesser of the subminimum I as described in paragraph (b) of this section for the accounting period and the aggregate amount of 50 cents per subscriber per month. The subscriber-based royalty floor for use in step 3 of § 385.12(b)(3) is the aggregate amount of 30 cents per subscriber per month.

(3) *Standalone portable subscription service.* Except as provided in paragraph (a)(4) of this section, in the case of a subscription service through which an end user can listen to sound recordings in the form of interactive streams or limited downloads from a portable device, the minimum for use in step 1 of § 385.12(b)(1) is the lesser of subminimum I as described in paragraph (b) of this section for the accounting period and the aggregate amount of 80 cents per subscriber per month. The subscriber-based royalty floor for use in step 3 of § 385.12(b)(3) is the aggregate amount of 50 cents per subscriber per month.

(4) *Bundled subscription services.* In the case of a subscription service made available to end users with one or more other products or services as part of a single transaction without pricing for the subscription service separate from the product(s) or service(s) with which it is made available (e.g., a case in which a user can buy a portable device and one-year access to a subscription service for a single price), the minimum for use in step 1 of § 385.12(b)(1) is subminimum I as described in paragraph (b) of this section for the accounting period. The subscriber-based royalty floor for use in step 3 of § 385.12(b)(3) is the aggregate amount of 25 cents per month for each end user who has made at least one play of a licensed work during such month (each such end user to be considered an "active subscriber").

(5) *Free nonsubscription/ad-supported services.* In the case of a service offering licensed activity free of any charge to the end user, the minimum for use in step 1 of § 385.12(b)(1) is subminimum II described in paragraph (c) of this section for the accounting period. There is no subscriber-based royalty floor for use in step 3 of § 385.12(b)(3).

(b) *Computation of subminimum I.* For purposes of paragraphs (a)(2), (3) and (4) of this section, and with reference to paragraph (5) of the definition of "service revenue" in § 385.11 if applicable, subminimum I for an accounting period means the aggregate of the following with respect to all sound recordings of musical works used in the relevant offering of the service during the accounting period—

(1) In cases in which a record company is the licensee under 17 U.S.C. 115 and a third-party service has obtained from the record company the rights to make interactive streams or limited downloads of a sound recording together with the right to reproduce and distribute the musical work embodied therein, 17.36% of the total amount expensed by the service in accordance with U.S. Generally Accepted Accounting Principles, which for the avoidance of doubt shall include the value of any barter or other nonmonetary consideration provided by the service, for such rights for the accounting period, except that for licensed activity occurring on or before December 31, 2007, subminimum I for an accounting period shall be 14.53% of the amount expensed by the service for such rights for the accounting period.

(2) In cases in which the relevant service is the licensee under 17 U.S.C. 115 and the relevant service has obtained from a third-party record company the rights to make interactive streams or limited downloads of a sound recording without the right to reproduce and distribute the musical work embodied therein, 21% of the total amount expensed by the service in accordance with U.S. Generally Accepted Accounting Principles, which for the avoidance of doubt shall include the value of any barter or other nonmonetary consideration provided by the service, for such sound recording rights for the accounting period, except that for licensed activity occurring on or before December 31, 2007, subminimum I for an accounting period shall be 17% of the amount expensed by the service for such sound recording rights for the accounting period.

(c) *Computation of subminimum II.* For purposes of paragraphs (a)(1) and (5) of this section, subminimum II for an accounting period means the aggregate of the following with respect to all sound recordings of musical works used by the relevant service during the accounting period—

(1) In cases in which a record company is the licensee under 17 U.S.C. 115 and a third-party service has obtained from the record company the rights to make interactive streams and limited downloads of a sound recording together with the right to reproduce and distribute the musical work embodied therein, 18% of the total amount expensed by the service in accordance with U.S. Generally Accepted Accounting Principles, which for the avoidance of doubt shall include the value of any barter or other nonmonetary consideration provided by the service, for such rights for the accounting period, except that for licensed activity occurring on or before December 31, 2007, subminimum II for an accounting period shall be 14.53% of the amount expensed by the service for such rights for the accounting period.

(2) In cases in which the relevant service is the licensee under 17 U.S.C. 115 and the relevant service has obtained from a third-party record company the rights to make interactive streams or limited downloads of a sound recording without the right to reproduce and distribute the musical work embodied therein, 22% of the total amount expensed by the service in accordance with U.S. Generally Accepted Accounting Principles, which for the avoidance of doubt shall include the value of any barter or other nonmonetary consideration provided by the service, for such sound recording rights for the accounting period, except that for licensed activity occurring

on or before December 31, 2007, subminimum II for an accounting period shall be 17% of the amount expensed by the service for such sound recording rights for the accounting period.

(d) *Computation of subscriber-based royalty rates.* For purposes of paragraph (a) of this section, to determine the minimum or subscriber-based royalty floor, as applicable to any particular offering, the service shall for the relevant offering calculate its total number of subscriber-months for the accounting period, taking into account all end users who were subscribers for complete calendar months, prorating in the case of end users who were subscribers for only part of a calendar month, and deducting on a prorated basis for end users covered by a free trial period subject to the promotional royalty rate as described in § 385.14(b)(2), except that in the case of a bundled subscription service, subscriber-months shall instead be determined with respect to active subscribers as defined in paragraph (a)(4) of this section. The product of the total number of subscriber-months for the accounting period and the specified number of cents per subscriber (or active subscriber, as the case may be) shall be used as the subscriber-based component of the minimum or subscriber-based royalty floor, as applicable, for the accounting period.

§ 385.14 Promotional royalty rate.

(a) *General provisions.* (1) This section establishes a royalty rate of zero in the case of certain promotional interactive streaming activities, and of certain promotional limited downloads offered in the context of a free trial period for a digital music subscription service under a license pursuant to 17 U.S.C. 115. Subject to the requirements of 17 U.S.C. 115 and the additional provisions of paragraphs (b) through (e) of this section, the promotional royalty rate shall apply to a musical work when a record company transmits or authorizes the transmission of interactive streams or limited downloads of a sound recording that embodies such musical work, only if—

(i) The primary purpose of the record company in making or authorizing the interactive streams or limited downloads is to promote the sale or other paid use of sound recordings by the relevant artists, including such sound recording, through established retail channels or the paid use of one or more established retail music services through which the sound recording is available, and not to promote any other good or service;

(ii) Either—

(A) The sound recording (or a different version of the sound recording embodying the same musical work) is being lawfully distributed and offered to consumers through the established retail channels or services described in paragraph (a)(1)(i) of this section; or

(B) In the case of a sound recording of a musical work being prepared for commercial release but not yet released, the record company has a good faith intention of lawfully distributing and offering to consumers the sound recording (or a different version of the sound recording embodying the same musical work) through the established retail channels or services described in paragraph (a)(1)(i) of this section within 90 days after the commencement of the first promotional use authorized under this section (and in fact does so, unless it can demonstrate that notwithstanding its bona fide intention, it unexpectedly did not meet the scheduled release date);

(iii) In connection with authorizing the promotional interactive streams or limited downloads, the record company has obtained from the service it authorizes a written representation that—

(A) In the case of a promotional use commencing on or after October 1, 2010, except interactive streaming subject to paragraph (d) of this section, the service agrees to maintain for a period of no less than 5 years from the conclusion of the promotional activity complete and accurate records of the relevant authorization and dates on which the promotion was conducted, and identifying each sound recording of a musical work made available through the promotion, the licensed activity involved, and the number of plays of such recording;

(B) The service is in all material respects operating with appropriate license authority with respect to the musical works it is using for promotional and other purposes; and

(C) The representation is signed by a person authorized to make the representation on behalf of the service;

(iv) Upon receipt by the record company of written notice from the copyright owner of a musical work or agent of the copyright owner stating in good faith that a particular service is in a material manner operating without appropriate license authority from such copyright owner, the record company shall within 5 business days withdraw by written notice its authorization of such uses of such copyright owner's musical works under the promotional royalty rate by that service;

(v) The interactive streams or limited downloads are offered free of any charge to the end user and, except in the case of interactive streaming subject to paragraph (d) of this section in the case of a free trial period for a digital music subscription service, no more than 5 sound recordings at a time are streamed in response to any individual request of an end user;

(vi) The interactive streams and limited downloads are offered in a manner such that the user is at the same time (e.g., on the same Web page) presented with a purchase opportunity for the relevant sound recording or an opportunity to subscribe to a paid service offering the sound recording, or a link to such a purchase or subscription opportunity, except—

(A) In the case of interactive streaming of a sound recording being prepared for commercial release but not yet released, certain mobile applications or other circumstances in which the foregoing is impracticable in view of the current state of the relevant technology; and

(B) In the case of a free trial period for a digital music subscription service, if end users are periodically offered an opportunity to subscribe to the service during such free trial period; and

(vii) The interactive streams and limited downloads are not provided in a manner that is likely to cause mistake, to confuse or to deceive, reasonable end users as to the endorsement or association of the author of the musical work with any product, service or activity other than the sale or paid use of sound recordings or paid use of a music service through which sound recordings are available. Without limiting the foregoing, upon receipt of written notice from the copyright owner of a musical work or agent of the copyright owner stating in good faith that a particular use of such work under this section violates the limitation set forth in this paragraph (a)(1)(vii), the record company shall promptly cease such use of that work, and within 5 business days withdraw by written notice its authorization of such use by all relevant third parties it has authorized under this section.

(2) To rely upon the promotional royalty rate, a record company making or authorizing interactive streams or limited downloads shall keep complete and accurate contemporaneous written records of such uses, including the sound recordings and musical works involved, the artists, the release dates of the sound recordings, a brief statement of the promotional activities authorized, the identity of the service or services where each promotion is authorized (including the Internet address if applicable), the beginning and end date of each period of promotional activity authorized, and the representation required by paragraph (a)(1)(iii) of this section; provided that, in the case of trial subscription uses, such records shall instead consist of the contractual terms that bear upon promotional uses by the particular digital music subscription services it authorizes; and further provided that, if the record company itself is conducting the promotion, it shall also maintain any additional records described in paragraph (a)(1)(iii)(A) of this section. The records required by this paragraph (a)(2) shall be maintained for no less time than the record company maintains records of usage of royalty-bearing uses involving the same type of licensed activity in the ordinary course of business, but in no event for less than 5 years from the conclusion of the promotional activity to which they pertain. If the copyright owner of a musical work or its agent requests a copy of the information to be maintained under this paragraph (a)(2) with respect to a specific promotion or relating to a particular sound recording of a musical work, the record company shall provide complete and accurate documentation within 10 business days, except for any information required under paragraph (a)(1)(iii)(A) of this section, which shall be provided within 20 business days, and provided that if the copyright owner or agent requests information concerning a large volume of promotions or sound recordings, the record company shall have a reasonable time, in view of the amount of information requested, to respond to any request of such copyright owner or agent. If the record company does not provide required information within the required time, and upon receipt of written notice citing such failure does not provide such information within a further 10 business days, the uses will be considered not to be subject to the promotional royalty rate and the record company (but not any third-party service it has authorized) shall be liable for any payment due for such uses; provided, however, that all rights and remedies of the copyright owner with respect to unauthorized uses shall be preserved.

(3) If the copyright owner of a musical work or its agent requests a copy of the information to be maintained under paragraph (a)(1)(iii)(A) of this section by a service authorized by a record company with respect to a specific promotion, the service shall provide complete and accurate documentation within 20 business days, provided that if the copyright owner or agent requests information concerning a large volume of promotions or sound recordings, the service shall have a reasonable time, in view of the amount of information requested, to respond to any request of such copyright owner or agent. If the service does not provide required information within the required time, and upon receipt of written notice citing such failure does not provide such information within a further 10 business days, the uses will be considered not to be subject to the promotional royalty rate and the service (but not the record company) will be liable for any

payment due for such uses; provided, however, that all rights and remedies of the copyright owner with respect to unauthorized uses shall be preserved.

(4) The promotional royalty rate is exclusively for audio-only interactive streaming and limited downloads of musical works subject to licensing under 17 U.S.C. 115. The promotional royalty rate does not apply to any other use under 17 U.S.C. 115; nor does it apply to public performances, audiovisual works, lyrics or other uses outside the scope of 17 U.S.C. 115. Without limitation, uses subject to licensing under 17 U.S.C. 115 that do not qualify for the promotional royalty rate (including without limitation interactive streaming or limited downloads of a musical work beyond the time limitations applicable to the promotional royalty rate) require payment of applicable royalties. This section is based on an understanding of industry practices and market conditions at the time of its development, among other things. The terms of this section shall be subject to de novo review and consideration (or elimination altogether) in future proceedings before the Copyright Royalty Judges. Nothing in this section shall be interpreted or construed in such a manner as to nullify or diminish any limitation, requirement or obligation of 17 U.S.C. 115 or other protection for musical works afforded by the Copyright Act, 17 U.S.C. 101 *et seq.*

(b) *Interactive streaming and limited downloads of full-length musical works through third-party services.* In addition to those of paragraph (a) of this section, the provisions of this paragraph (b) apply to interactive streaming, and limited downloads (in the context of a free trial period for a digital music subscription service), authorized by record companies under the promotional royalty rate through third-party services (including Web sites) that is not subject to paragraphs (c) or (d) of this section. Such interactive streams and limited downloads may be made or authorized by a record company under the promotional royalty rate only if—

(1) No cash, other monetary payment, barter or other consideration for making or authorizing the relevant interactive streams or limited downloads is received by the record company, its parent company, any entity owned in whole or in part by or under common ownership with the record company, or any other person or entity acting on behalf of or in lieu of the record company, except for in-kind promotional consideration used to promote the sale or paid use of sound recordings or the paid use of music services through which sound recordings are available;

(2) In the case of interactive streaming and limited downloads offered in the context of a free trial period for a digital music subscription service, the free trial period does not exceed 30 consecutive days per subscriber per two-year period; and

(3) In contexts other than a free trial period for a digital music subscription service, interactive streaming subject to paragraph (b) of this section of a particular sound recording is authorized by the record company on no more than 60 days total for all services (*i.e.*, interactive streaming under paragraph (b) of this section of a particular sound recording may be authorized on no more than a total of 60 days, which need not be consecutive, and on any one such day, interactive streams may be offered on one or more services); provided, however, that an additional 60 days shall be available each time the sound recording is re-released by the record company in a remastered form or as a part of a compilation with a different set of sound recordings than the original release or any prior compilation including such sound recording.

(4) In the event that a record company authorizes promotional uses in excess of the time limitations of paragraph (b) of this section, the record company, and not the third-party service it has authorized, shall be liable for any payment due for such uses; provided, however, that all rights and remedies of the copyright owner with respect to unauthorized uses shall be preserved. In the event that a third-party service exceeds the scope of any authorization by a record company, the service, and not the record company, shall be liable for any payment due for such uses; provided, however, that all rights and remedies of the copyright owner with respect to unauthorized uses shall be preserved.

(c) *Interactive streaming of full-length musical works through record company and artist services.* In addition to those of paragraph (a) of this section, the provisions of this paragraph (c) apply to interactive streaming conducted or authorized by record companies under the promotional royalty rate through a service (e.g., a Web site) directly owned or operated by the record company, or directly owned or operated by a recording artist under the authorization of the record company, and that is not subject to paragraph (d) of this section. For the avoidance of doubt and without limitation, an artist page or site on a third-party service (e.g., a social networking service) shall not be considered a service operated by the record company or artist. Such interactive streams may be made or authorized by a record company under the promotional royalty rate only if—

(1) The interactive streaming subject to this paragraph (c) of a particular sound recording is offered or authorized by the record company on no more than 90 days total for all services (*i.e.* , interactive streaming under this paragraph (c) of a particular sound recording may be authorized on no more than a total of 90 days, which need not be consecutive, and on any such day, interactive streams may be offered on one or more services operated by the record company or artist, subject to the provisions of paragraph (b)(2) of this section); provided, however, that an additional 90 days shall be available each time the sound recording is re-released by the record company in a remastered form or as part of a compilation with a different set of sound recordings than prior compilations that include that sound recording;

(2) In the case of interactive streaming through a service devoted to one featured artist, the interactive streams subject to this paragraph (c) of this section of a particular sound recording are made or authorized by the record company on no more than one official artist site per artist and are recordings of that artist; and

(3) In the case of interactive streaming through a service that is not limited to a single featured artist, all interactive streaming on such service (whether eligible for the promotional royalty rate or not) is limited to sound recordings of a single record company and its affiliates and the service would not reasonably be considered to be a meaningful substitute for a paid music service.

(d) *Interactive streaming of clips.* In addition to those in paragraph (a) of this section, the provisions of this paragraph (d) apply to interactive streaming conducted or authorized by record companies under the promotional royalty rate of segments of sound recordings of musical works with a playing time that does not exceed the greater of:

(1) 30 seconds, or

(2) 10% of the playing time of the complete sound recording, but in no event in excess of 60 seconds. Such interactive streams may be made or authorized by a record company under the promotional royalty rate without any of the temporal limitations set forth in paragraphs (b) and (c) of this section (but subject to the other conditions of paragraphs (b) and (c) of this section, as applicable). For clarity, this paragraph (d) is strictly limited to the uses described herein and shall not be construed as permitting the creation or use of an excerpt of a musical work in violation of 17 U.S.C. 106(2) or 115(a)(2) or any other right of a musical work owner.

§ 385.15 [Reserved]

§ 385.16 Reproduction and distribution rights covered.

A compulsory license under 17 U.S.C. 115 extends to all reproduction and distribution rights that may be necessary for the provision of the licensed activity, solely for the purpose of providing such licensed activity (and no other purpose).

§ 385.17 Effect of rates.

In any future proceedings under 17 U.S.C. 115(c)(3)(C) and (D), the royalty rates payable for a compulsory license shall be established *de novo*.

EXCERPTS OF THE COPYRIGHT ACT OF 1976

(TITLE 17, UNITED STATES CODE)

§ 101. Definitions

As used in this title, the following terms and their variant forms mean the following:

An "anonymous work" is a work on the copies phonorecords of which no natural person is identified as author.

"Audiovisual works" are works that consist of a series of related images which are intrinsically intended to be shown by the use of machines or devices such as projectors, viewers, or electronic equipment, together with accompanying sounds, if any, regardless of the nature of the material objects, such as films or tapes, in which the works are embodied.

The "Berne Convention" is the Convention for the Protection of Literary and Artistic Works, signed at Berne, Switzerland, on September 9, 1886, and all acts, protocols, and revisions thereto.

The "best edition" of a work is the edition, published in the United States at any time before the date of deposit, that the Library of Congress determines to be most suitable for its purposes.

A person's "children" are that person's immediate offspring, whether legitimate or not, and any children legally adopted by that person.

A "collective work" is a work, such as a periodical issue, anthology, or encyclopedia, in which a number of contributions, constitutes an original work of authorship. The term "compilation" includes collective works.

A "compilation" is a work formed by the collection and assembling of preexisting materials or of data that are selected, coordinated, or arranged in such a way that the resulting work as a whole constitutes an original work of authorship. The term "compilation" includes collective works.

A "computer program" is a set of statements or instructions to be used directly or indirectly in a computer in order to bring about a certain result.

"Copies" are material objects, other than phonorecords, in which a work is fixed by any method now known or later developed , and from which the work can be perceived, reproduced, or otherwise communicated, either directly or with the aid of a machine or device. The term "copies" includes the material object, other than a phonorecord, in which the work is first fixed.

"Copyright owner", with respect to any one of the exclusive rights comprised in a copyright, refers to the owner of that particular right.

A work is "created" when it is fixed in a copy or phonorecord for the first time; where a work is prepared over a period of time, the portion of it that has been fixed at any particular time constitutes the work as of that time, and where the work has been prepared in different versions, each version constitutes a separate work.

A "derivative work" is a work based upon one or more preexisting works, such as a translation, musical arrangement, dramatization, fictionalization, motion picture version, sound recording, art reproduction, abridgment, condensation, or any other form in which a work may be recast, transformed, or adapted. A work consisting of editorial revisions, annotations, elaborations, or other modifications, which as a whole, represent an original work of authorship, is a "derivative work".

A "device", "machine", or "process" is one now known or later developed.

A "digital transmission" is a transmission in whole or in part in a digital or other non-analog format.

To "display" a work means to show a copy of it, either directly or by means of a film, slide, television image, or any other device or process or, in the case of a motion picture or other audiovisual work, to show individual images nonsequentially.

An "establishment" is a store, shop, or any similar place of business open to the general public for the primary purpose of selling goods or services in which the majority of the gross square feet of space that is nonresidential is used for that purpose, and in which nondramatic musical works are performed publicly.

A "food service or drinking establishment" is a restaurant, inn, bar, tavern, or any other similar place of business in which the public or patrons assemble for the primary purpose of being served food or drink, in which the majority of the gross square feet of space that is nonresidential is used for that purpose, and in which nondramatic musical works are performed publicly.

A work is "fixed" in a tangible medium of expression when its embodiment in a copy or phonorecord, by or under the authority of the author, is sufficiently permanent or stable to permit it to be perceived, reproduced, or otherwise communicated for a period of more than transitory duration. A work consisting of sounds, images, or both, that are being transmitted, is "fixed" for purposes of this title if a fixation of the work is being made simultaneously with its transmission.

The "Geneva Phonograms Convention" is the Convention for the Protection of Producers of Phonograms Against Unauthorized Duplication of Their Phonograms, concluded at Geneva, Switzerland, on October 29, 1971.

The "gross square feet of space" of an establishment means the entire interior space of that establishment, and any adjoining outdoor space used to serve patrons, whether on a seasonal basis or otherwise.

The terms "including" and "such as" are illustrative and not limitative.

An "international agreement" is—

    (1) the Universal Copyright Convention;

    (2) the Geneva Phonograms Convention;

    (3) the Berne Convention;

    (4) the WTO Agreement;

    (5) the WIPO Copyright Treaty;

    (6) the WIPO Performances and Phonograms Treaty; and

    (7) any other copyright treaty to which the United States is a party.

A "joint work" is a work prepared by two or more authors with the intention that their contributions be merged into inseparable or interdependent parts of a unitary whole.

"Literary works" are works, other than audiovisual works, expressed in words, numbers, or other verbal or numerical symbols or indicia, regardless of the nature of the material objects, such as books, periodicals, manuscripts, phonorecords, film, tapes, disks, or cards, in which they are embodied.

"Motion pictures" are audiovisual works consisting of a series of related images which, when shown in succession, impart an impression of motion, together with accompanying sounds, if any.

To "perform" a work means to recite, render, play dance, or act it, either directly or by means of any device or process or, in the case of a motion picture or other audiovisual work, to show its images in any sequence or to make the sounds accompanying its audible.

A "performing rights society" is an association, corporation, or other entity that licenses the public performance of nondramatic musical works on behalf of copyright owners of such works, such as the American Society of Composers, Authors and Publishers (ASCAP), Broadcast Music, Inc. (BMI), and SESAC, Inc.

"Phonorecords" are material objects in which sounds, other than those accompanying a motion picture or other audiovisual work, are fixed by any method now known or later developed, and from which the sounds can be perceived, reproduced, or otherwise communicated, either directly or with the aid of a machine or device. The term "phonorecords" includes the material object in which the sounds are first fixed.

"Pictorial, graphic, and sculptural works" include two-dimensional and three-dimensional works of fine, graphic, and applied art, photographs, prints and art reproductions, maps, globes, charts, diagrams, models, and technical drawings, including architectural plans. Such works shall include works of artistic craftsmanship insofar as their form but not their mechanical or utilitarian aspects are concerned; the design of a useful article, as defined in this section, shall be considered a pictorial, graphic, or sculptural features that can be identified separately from, and are capable of existing independently of, the utilitarian aspects of the article.

For purposes of Section 513, a "proprietor" is an individual, corporation, partnership, or other entity, as the case may be, that owns an establishment or a food service or drinking establishment, except that no owner or operator of a radio or television station licensed by the Federal Communications Commission, cable system or satellite carrier, cable or satellite carrier service or programmer, provider of online services or network access or the operator of facilities therefore, telecommunications company, or any other such audio or audiovisual service or programmer now known or as may be developed in the future, commercial subscription music service, or owner or operator of any other transmission service, shall under any circumstances be deemed to be a proprietor.

A "pseudonymous work" is a work on the copies or phonorecords of a work to the public by sale or other transfer of ownership, or by rental, lease, or lending. The offering to distribute copies or phonorecords to a group of persons for purposes of further distribution, public performance, or public display, constitutes publication. A public performance or display of a work does not of itself constitute publication.

"Publication" is the distribution of copies or phonorecords to the public by sale or other transfer of ownership, or by rental, lease, or lending. The offering to distribute copies or phonorecords to a group of persons for purposes of further distribution, public performance, or public display constitutes publication. A public performance or display of a work does not of itself constitute publication.

To perform or display a work "publicly" means—

(1) to perform or display it at a place open to the public or at any place where a substantial number of persons outside of a normal circle of a family and its social acquaintances is gathered; or

(2) to transmit or otherwise communicate a performance or display of the work to a place specified by clause (1) or to the public, by means of any device or process, whether the members of the public capable of receiving the performance or display receive it in the same place or in separate places and at the same time or at different times.

"Registration," for purposes of sections 205(c)(2), 405, 406, 410(d), 411, 412, and 506(e), means a registration of a claim in the original or the renewed and extended term of copyright.

"Sound recordings" are works that result from the fixation of a series of musical, spoken, or other sounds, but not including the sounds accompanying a motion picture or other audiovisual work, regardless of the nature of the material objects, such as disks, tapes, or other phonorecords, in which they are embodied.

"State" includes the District of Columbia and the Commonwealth of Puerto Rico, and any territories to which this title is made applicable by an Act of Congress.

A "transfer of copyright ownership" is an assignment, mortgage, exclusive license, or any other conveyance, alienation, or hypothecation of a copyright or of any of the exclusive rights comprised in a copyright, whether or not it is limited in time or place of effect, but not including a nonexclusive license.

A "treaty party" is a country or intergovernmental organization other than the United States that is a party to an international agreement.

A "transmission program" is a body of material that, as an aggregate, has been produced for the sole purpose of transmission to the public in sequence and as a unit.

To "transmit" a performance or display is to communicate it by any device or process whereby images or sounds are received beyond the place from which they are sent.

The "United States", when used in a geographical sense, comprises the several States, the District of Columbia and the Commonwealth of Puerto Rico, and the organized territories under the jurisdiction of the United States Government.

A "useful article" is an article having an intrinsic utilitarian function that is not merely to portray the appearance of the article or to convey information. An article that is normally part of a useful article is considered a "useful article".

For purposes of section 411, a work is a "United States work" only if —

(1) in the case of a published work, the work is first published —

(A) in the United States;

(B) simultaneously in the United States and another treaty party or parties, whose law grants a term of copyright protection that is the same as or longer than the term provided in the United States;

(C) simultaneously in the United States and a foreign nation that is not a treaty party; or

(D) in a foreign nation that is not a treaty party, and all of the authors of the work are nationals, domiciliaries, or habitual residents of, or in the case of an audiovisual work legal entities with headquarters in, the United States;

(2) in the case of an unpublished work, all the authors of the work are nationals, domiciliaries, or habitual residents of the United States, or, in the case of an unpublished audiovisual work, all the authors are legal entities with headquarters in the United States; or

(3) in the case of a pictorial, graphic, or sculptural work incorporated in a building or structure, the building or structure is located in the United States.19

The author's "widow" or "widower" is the author's surviving spouse under the law of the author's domicile at the time of his or her death whether or not the spouse has later remarried.

The "WIPO Copyright Treaty" is the WIPO Copyright Treaty concluded at Geneva, Switzerland, on December 20, 1996.

The "WIPO Performances and Phonograms Treaty" is the WIPO Performances and Phonograms Treaty concluded at Geneva, Switzerland, on December 20, 1996.

A "work of the United States government" is a work prepared by an officer or employee of the United States Government as part of that person's official duties.

A "work made for hire" is—

(1) a work prepared by an employee within the scope of his or her employment; or

(2) a work specially ordered or commissioned for use as a contribution to a collective work, as a part of a motion picture or other audiovisual work, as a translation, as a supplementary work, as a compilation, as an instructional text, as a test, as answer material for a test, or as an atlas, if the parties expressly agree in a written instrument signed by them that the work shall be considered a work made for hire. For the purpose of the foregoing sentence, a "supplementary work" is a work prepared for publication as a secondary adjunct to a work by another for the purpose of introducing, concluding, illustrating, explaining, revising, commenting upon, or assisting in the use of the other work, such as forewards, afterwards, pictorial illustrations, maps, charts, tables, editorial notes, musical arrangements, answer material for tests, bibliographies, appendixes, and indexes, and "instructional text" is a literary, pictorial, or graphic work prepared for publication and with the purpose of use in systematic instructional activities.

In determining whether any work is eligible to be considered a work made for hire under paragraph (2), neither the amendment contained in section 1011(d) of the Intellectual Property and Communications Omnibus Reform Act of 1999, as enacted by section 1000(a)(9) of Public Law 106-113, nor the deletion of the words added by that amendment —

(A) shall be considered or otherwise given any legal significance, or

(B) shall be interpreted to indicate congressional approval or disapproval of, or acquiescence in, any judicial determination, by the courts or the Copyright Office. Paragraph (2) shall be interpreted as if both section 2(a)(1) of the Work Made For Hire and Copyright Corrections Act of 2000 and section 1011(d) of the Intellectual Property and Communications Omnibus Reform Act of 1999, as enacted by section 1000(a)(9) of Public Law 106-113, were never enacted, and without regard to any inaction or awareness by the Congress at any time of any judicial determinations.

The terms "WTO Agreement" and "WTO member country" have the meanings given those terms in paragraphs (9) and (10), respectively, of section 2 of the Uruguay Round Agreements Act.

§ 103. Subject matter of copyright: Compilations and derivative works

(a) the subject matter of copyright as specified by section 102 includes compilations and derivative works, but protection for a work employing preexisting material has been used unlawfully.

(b) The copyright in a compilation or derivative work extends only to the material contributed by the author of such work, as distinguished from the preexisting material. The copyright in such work is independent of, and does not affect or enlarge the scope, duration, ownership, or subsistence of, any copyright protection in the preexisting material.

§ 106. Exclusive rights in copyrighted works

Subject to sections 107 through 120, the owner of copyright under this title has the exclusive rights to do and to authorize any of the following:

(1) to reproduce the copyrighted work in copies or phonorecords;

(2) to prepare derivative works based upon the copyrighted work;

(3) to distribute copies or phonorecords of the copyrighted work to the public by sale or other transfer of ownership, or by rental, lease, or lending;

(4) in the case of literary, musical, dramatic, and choreographic works, pantomimes, and motion pictures and other audiovisual works, to perform the copyrighted work publicly;

(5) in the case of literary, musical, dramatic, and choreographic works, pantomimes, and pictorial, graphic, or sculptural works, including the individual images of a motion picture or other audiovisual work, to display the copyrighted work publicly; and

(6) in the case of sound recordings, to perform the copyrighted work publicly by means of a digital audiotransmission

§ 107. Limitations on exclusive rights: Fair use

Notwithstanding the provisions of sections 106 and 106A, the fair use of a copyrighted work, including such use by reproduction in copies or phonorecords or by any other means specified by that section, for purposes such as criticism, comment, news reporting, teaching (including multiple copies for classroom use), scholarship, or research, is not an infringement of copyright. In determining whether the use made of a work in any particular case is a fair use the factors to be considered shall include—

(1) the purpose and character of the use, including whether such use is of a commercial nature or is for nonprofit educational purposes;

(2) the nature of the copyrighted work;

(3) the amount and substantiality of the portion used in relation to the copyrighted work as a whole; and

(4) the effect of the use upon the potential market for or value of the copyrighted work.

The fact that a work is unpublished shall not itself bar a finding of fair use if such finding is made upon consideration of all the above factors.

§ 109. Limitations on exclusive rights: Effect of transfer of particular copy or phonorecord

(a) Notwithstanding the provisions of section 106(3), the owner of a particular copy or phonorecord lawfully made under this title, or any person authorized by such owner, is entitled, without the authority of the copyright owner, to sell or otherwise dispose of the possession of that copyright or phonorecord.

(b)(1)(A) Notwithstanding the provisions of subsection (a), unless authorized by the owners of copyright in the sound recording or the owner of copyright in a computer program (including any tape, disk, or other medium embodying such program), and in the case of a sound recording in the musical works embodied therein, neither the owner of a particular phonorecord nor any person in possession of a particular copy of a computer program (including any tape, disk, or other medium embodying such program), may, for the purposes of direct or indirect commercial advantage, dispose of, or authorize the disposal of, the possession of that phonorecord or computer program (including any tape, disk, or other medium embodying such program), by rental, lease, or lending, or by any other act or practice in the nature of rental, lease, or lending. Nothing in the preceding sentence shall apply to the rental, lease, or lending of a phonorecord for nonprofit purposes by a nonprofit library or nonprofit educational institution. The transfer of possession of a lawfully made copy of a computer program by a nonprofit educational institution to another nonprofit educational institution or to faculty, staff, and students does not constitute rental, lease, or lending for direct or indirect commercial purposes under this subsection.

. . . .

(4) Any person who distributes a phonorecord or a copy of a computer program (including any tape, disk, or other medium embodying such program), in violation of paragraph (1) is an infringer of copyright under section 501 of this title and is subject to the remedies set forth in sections 502, 503, 504, 505, and 509. Such violation shall not be a criminal offense under section 506 or cause such person to be subject to the criminal penalties set forth in section 2319 of title 18.

(c) Notwithstanding the provisions of section 106(5), the owner of a particular copy lawfully made under this title, or any person authorized by such owner, is entitled, without the authority of the copyright owner, to display that copy publicly, either directly or by the projection of no more than one image at a time, to viewers present at the place where the copy is located.

(d) The privileges prescribed by subsections (a) and (c) do not, unless authorized by the copyright owner, extend to any person who has acquired possession of the copy or phonorecord from the copyright owner, by rental, lease, loan, or otherwise, without acquiring ownership of it.

§ 110. Limitations on exclusive rights: Exemption of certain performances and displays

Notwithstanding the provisions of section 106, the following are not infringements of copyright:

(1) performance or display of a work by instructors or pupils in the course of face-to-face teaching activities of a nonprofit educational institution, in a classroom or similar place devoted to instruction, unless, in the case of a motion picture or other audiovisual work, the performance, or the display of individual images, is given by means of a copy that was not lawfully made under this title, and that the person responsible for the performance knew or had reason to believe was not lawfully made;

(2) performance of a nondramatic literary or musical work or display of a work, by or in the course of a transmission, if—

(A) the performance or display is a regular part of the systematic instructional activities of a governmental body or a nonprofit educational institution; and

(B) the performance or display is directly related and of material assistance to the teaching content of the transmission; and

(C) the transmission is made primarily for—

(i) reception in classrooms or similar places normally devoted to instruction, or

(ii) reception by persons to whom the transmission is directed because their disabilities or other special circumstances prevent their attendance in classrooms or similar places normally devoted to instruction, or

(iii) reception by officers or employees of governmental bodies as a part of their official duties or employment;

(3) performance of a nondramatic literary or musical work or of a dramatico-musical work of a religious nature, or display of a work, in the course of services at a place of worship or other religious assembly;

(4) performance of a nondramatic literary or musical work otherwise than in a transmission to the public, without any purpose of direct or indirect commercial advantage and without payment of any fee or other compensation for the performance to any of its performers, promoters, or organizers, if—

(A) there is no direct or indirect admission charge; or

(B) the proceeds, after deducting the reasonable costs of producing the performance, are used exclusively for educational, religious, or charitable purposes and not for private financial gain, except where the copyright owner has served notice of objection to the performance under the following conditions;

(i) the notice shall be in writing and signed by the copyright owner or such owner's duly authorized agent; and

(ii) the notice shall be served on the person responsible for the performance at least seven days before the date of the performance, and shall state the reasons for the objection; and

(iii) the notice shall comply, in form, content, and manner of service, with requirements that the Register of Copyrights shall prescribe by regulation;

(5)(A) except as provided in subparagraph (B), communication of a transmission embodying a performance or display of a work by the public reception of the transmission on a single receiving apparatus of a kind commonly used in private homes, unless—

(i) a direct charge is made to see or hear the transmission; or

(ii) the transmission thus received is further transmitted to the public;

(B) communication by an establishment of a transmission or retransmission embodying a performance or display of a nondramatic musical work intended to be received by the general public, originated by a radio or television broadcast station licensed as such by the Federal Communications Commission, or, if an audiovisual transmission, by a cable system or satellite carrier, if—

(i) in the case of an establishment other than a food service or drinking establishment, either the establishment in which the communication occurs has less than 2,000 gross square feet of space (excluding space used for customer parking and for no other purpose), or the establishment in which the communication occurs has 2,000 or more gross square feet of space (excluding space used for customer parking and for no other purpose) and—

(I) if the performance is by audio means only, the performance is communicated by means of a total of not more than 6 loudspeakers, of which not more than 4 loudspeakers are located in any 1 room or adjoining outdoor space; or

(II) if the performance or display is by audiovisual means, any visual portion of the performance or display is communicated by means of a total of not more than 4 audiovisual devices, of which not more than 1 audiovisual device is located in any 1 room, and no such audiovisual device has a diagonal screen size greater than 55 inches, and any audio portion of the performance or display is communicated by means of a total of not more than 6 loudspeakers, of which not more than 4 loudspeakers are located in any 1 room or adjoining outdoor space;

(ii) in the case of a food service or drinking establishment, either the establishment in which the communication occurs has less than 3,750 gross square feet of space (excluding space used for customer parking and for no other purpose), or the establishment in which the communication occurs has 3,750 gross square feet of space or more (excluding space used for customer parking and for no other purpose) and

(I) if the performance is by audio means only, the performance is communicated by means of a total of not more than 6 loudspeakers, of which not more than 4 loudspeakers are located in any 1 room or adjoining outdoor space; or

(II) if the performance or display is by audiovisual means, any visual portion of the performance or display is communicated by means of a total of not more than 4 audiovisual devices, of which not more than one audiovisual device is located in any 1 room, and no such audiovisual device has a diagonal screen size greater than 55 inches, and any audio portion of the performance or display is communicated by means of a total of not more than 6 loudspeakers, of which not more than 4 loudspeakers are located in any 1 room or adjoining outdoor space;

(iii) no direct charge is made to see or hear the transmission or retransmission;

(iv) the transmission or retransmission is not further transmitted beyond the establishment where it is received; and

(v) the transmission or retransmission is licensed by the copyright owner of the work so publicly performed or displayed;

(6) performance of a nondramatic musical work by a governmental body or a nonprofit agricultural or horticultural organization, in the course of an annual agricultural or horticultural fair or exhibition conducted by such body or organization; the exemption provided by this clause shall extend to any liability for copyright infringement that would otherwise be imposed on such body or organization, under doctrines of vicarious liability or related infringement, for a performance by a concessionaire, business establishment, or other person at such fair or exhibition, but shall not excuse any such person from liability for the performance;

(7) performance of a nondramatic musical work by a vending establishment open to the public at large without any direct or indirect admission charge, where the sole purpose of the performance is to promote the retail sale of copies or phonorecords of the work, or of the audiovisual or other devices utilized in such performance, and the performance is not transmitted beyond the place where the establishment is located and is within the immediate area where the sale is occurring;

. . . .

(10) notwithstanding paragraph 4 above, the following is not an infringement of copyright: performance of a nondramatic literary or musical work in the course of a social function which is organized and promoted by a nonprofit veterans' organization or a nonprofit fraternal organization to which the general public is not invited, but not including the invitees of the organizations, if the proceeds from the performance, after deducting the reasonable costs of producing the performance, are used exclusively for charitable purposes and not for financial gain. For purposes of this section the social functions of any college or university fraternity or sorority shall not be included unless the social function is held solely to raise funds for a specific charitable purpose.

The exemptions provided under paragraph (5) shall not be taken into account in any administrative, judicial, or other governmental proceeding to set or adjust the royalties payable to copyright owners for the public performance or display of their works. Royalties payable to copyright owners for any public performance or display of their works other than such performances or displays as are exempted under paragraph (5) shall not be diminished in any respect as a result of such exemption.

§ 112. Limitations on exclusive rights: Ephemeral recordings

(a)(1) Notwithstanding the provisions of section 106, and except in the case of a motion picture or other audiovisual work, it is not an infringement of copyright for a transmitting organization entitled to transmit to the public a performance or display of a work, under a license, . . . that makes a broadcast transmission of a performance of a sound recording in a digital format on a nonsubscription basis, to make no more than one copy or phonorecord of a particular transmission program embodying the performance or display, if —

(A) the copy or phonorecord is retained and used solely by the transmitting organization that made it, and no further copies or phonorecords are reproduced from it; and

(B) the copy or phonorecord is used solely for the transmitting organization's own transmissions within its local service area, or for purposes of archival preservation or security; and

(C)   unless preserved exclusively for archival purposes, the copy or phonorecord is destroyed within six months from the date the transmission program was first transmitted to the public.

. . . .

§ 115. Scope of exclusive rights in nondramatic musical works: Compulsory license for making and distributing phonorecords

In the case of nondramatic musical works, the exclusive rights provided by clauses (1) and (3) of section 106, to make and to distribute phonorecords of such works, are subject to compulsory licensing under the conditions specified by this section.

(a) AVAILABILITY AND SCOPE OF COMPULSORY LICENSE.—

(1) When phonorecords of a nondramatic musical work have been distributed to the public in the United States under the authority of the copyright owner, any other person, including those who make phonorecords or digital phonorecord deliveries, may, by complying with the provisions of this section, obtain a compulsory license to make and distribute phonorecords of the work. A person may obtain a compulsory license only if his or her primary purpose in making phonorecords is to distribute them to the public for private use, including by means of a digital phonorecord delivery. A person may not obtain a compulsory license for use of the work in the making of phonorecords duplicating a sound recording fixed by another, unless:

(i) such sound recording was fixed lawfully; and

(ii) the making of the phonorecords was authorized by the owner of copyright in the sound recording or, if the sound recording was fixed before February 15, 1972, by any person who fixed the sound recording pursuant to an express license from the owner of the copyright in the musical work or pursuant to a valid compulsory license for use of such work in a sound recording.

(2) A compulsory license includes the privilege of making a musical arrangement of the work to the extent necessary to conform it to the style or manner of interpretation of the performance involved, but the arrangement shall not change the basic melody or fundamental character of the work, and shall not be subject to protection as a derivative work under this title, except with the express consent of the copyright owner.

(b) NOTICE OF INTENTION TO OBTAIN COMPULSORY LICENSE.—

(1) Any person who wishes to obtain a compulsory license under this section shall, before or within thirty days after making, and before distributing any phonorecords of the work, serve notice of intention to do so on the copyright owner. If the registration or other public records of the Copyright Office do not identify the copyright owner and include an address at which notice can be served, it shall be sufficient to file the notice of intention in the Copyright Office. The notice shall comply, in form, content, and manner of service, with requirements that the Register of Copyrights shall prescribe by regulation.

(2) Failure to serve or file the notice required by clause (1) forecloses the possibility of a compulsory license and, in the absence of a negotiated license, renders the making and distribution of phonorecords actionable as acts of infringement under section 501 and fully subject to the remedies provided by sections 502 through 506 and 509.

(c) ROYALTY PAYABLE UNDER COMPULSORY LICENSE.—

(1) To be entitled to receive royalties under a compulsory license, the copyright owner must be identified in the registration or other public records of the Copyright Office. The owner is entitled to royalties for phonorecords made and distributed after being so identified, but is not entitled to recover for any phonorecords previously made and distributed.

(2) Except as provided by clause (1), the royalty under a compulsory license shall be payable for every phonorecord made and distributed in accordance with the license. For this purpose and other than as provided in paragraph (3), a phonorecord is considered "distributed" if the person exercising the compulsory license has voluntarily and permanently parted with its possession. With respect to each work embodied in the phonorecord, the royalty shall be either two and three-fourths cents, or one-half of one cent per minute of playing time or fraction thereof, whichever amount is larger.[1]

(3)(A) A compulsory license under this section includes the right of the compulsory licensee to distribute or authorize the distribution of a phonorecord of a nondramatic musical work by means of a digital transmission which constitutes a digital phonorecord delivery, regardless of whether the digital transmission is also a public performance of the sound recording under section 106(6) of this title or of any nondramatic musical work embodied therein under section 106(4) of this title. For every digital phonorecord delivery by or under the authority of the compulsory licensee—

(i) on or before December 31, 1997, the royalty payable by the compulsory licensee shall be the royalty prescribed under paragraph (2) and chapter 8 of this title; and

(ii) on or after January 1, 1998, the royalty payable by the compulsory licensee shall be the royalty prescribed under subparagraphs (B) through (F) and chapter 8 of this title.

(B) Notwithstanding any provision of the antitrust laws, any copyright owners of nondramatic musical works and any persons entitled to obtain a compulsory license under subsection (a)(1) may negotiate and agree upon the terms and rates of royalty payments under this paragraph and the proportionate division of fees paid among copyright owners, and may designate common agents to negotiate, agree to, pay or receive such royalty payments. Such authority to negotiate the terms and rates of royalty payments includes, but is not limited to, the authority to negotiate the year during which the royalty rates prescribed under subparagraphs (B) through (F) and chapter 8 of this title shall next be determined.

(C) During the period of June 30, 1996, through December 31, 1996, the Librarian of Congress shall cause notice to be published in the Federal Register of the initiation of voluntary negotiation proceedings for the purpose of determining reasonable terms and rates of royalty payments for the activities specified by subparagraph (A) during the period beginning January 1, 1998, and ending on the effective date of any new terms and rates established pursuant to subparagraph (C), (D) or (F), or such other date (regarding digital phonorecord deliveries) as the parties may agree. Such terms and rates shall distinguish between (I) digital phonorecord deliveries where the reproduction or distribution of a phonorecord is incidental to the transmission which constitutes the digital phonorecord

---

1   The rates have been adjusted pursuant to regulations enacted by the Copyright Royalty Tribunal as prescribed by Chapter 8 of the Copyright Act and by the 1997 Mechanical Rate Adjustment Proceeding. A table of statutory rates for mechanical licenses appears on page 38.

delivery, and (ii) digital phonorecord deliveries in general. Any copyright owners of nondramatic musical works and any persons entitled to obtain a compulsory license under subsection (a)(1) may submit to the Librarian of Congress licenses covering such activities. The parties to each negotiation proceeding shall bear their own costs.

(D) In the absence of license agreements negotiated under subparagraphs (B) and (C), upon the filing of a petition in accordance with section 803(a)(1), the Librarian of Congress shall, pursuant to chapter 8, convene a copyright arbitration royalty panel to determine and publish in the Federal Register a schedule of rates and terms which, subject to subparagraph (E), shall be binding on all copyright owners of nondramatic musical works and persons entitled to obtain a compulsory license under subsection (a)(1) during the period beginning January 1, 1998, and ending on the effective date of any new terms and rates established pursuant to subparagraph (C), (D) or (F), or such other date (regarding digital phonorecord deliveries) as may be determined pursuant to subparagraphs (B) and (C). Such terms and rates shall distinguish between (I) digital phonorecord deliveries where the reproduction or distribution of a phonorecord is incidental to the transmission which constitutes the digital phonorecord delivery, and (ii) digital phonorecord deliveries in general. In addition to the objectives set forth in section 801(b)(1), in establishing such rates and terms, the copyright arbitration royalty panel may consider rates and terms under voluntary license agreements negotiated as provided in subparagraphs (B) and (C). The royalty rates payable for a compulsory license for a digital phonorecord delivery under this section shall be established de novo and no precedential effect shall be given to the amount of the royalty payable by a compulsory licensee for digital phonorecord deliveries on or before December 31, 1997. The Librarian of Congress shall also establish requirements by which copyright owners may receive reasonable notice of the use of their works under this section, and under which records of such use shall be kept and made available by persons making digital phonorecord deliveries.

(E)(i) License agreements voluntarily negotiated at any time between one or more copyright owners of nondramatic musical works and one or more persons entitled to obtain a compulsory license under subsection (a)(1) shall be given effect in lieu of any determination by the Librarian of Congress. Subject to clause (ii), the royalty rates determined pursuant to subparagraph (C), (D) or (F) shall be given effect in lieu of any contrary royalty rates specified in a contract pursuant to which a recording artist who is the author of a nondramatic musical work grants a license under that person's exclusive rights in the musical work under sections 106 (1) and (3) or commits another person to grant a license in that musical work under sections 106 (1) and (3), to a person desiring to fix in a tangible medium of expression a sound recording embodying the musical work.

(ii) The second sentence of clause (i) shall not apply to—

(I) a contract entered into on or before June 22, 1995, and not modified thereafter for the purpose of reducing the royalty rates determined pursuant to subparagraph (C), (D) or (F) or of increasing the number of musical works within the scope of the contract covered by the reduced rates, except if a contract entered into on or before June 22, 1995, is modified thereafter for the purpose of increasing the number of musical works within the scope of the contract, any contrary royalty rates specified in the contract shall be given effect in lieu of royalty rates determined pursuant to subparagraph (C), (D) or (F) for the number of musical works within the scope of the contract as of June 22, 1995; and

(II) a contract entered into after the date that the sound recording is fixed in a tangible medium of expression substantially in a form intended for commercial release, if at the time the contract is entered into, the recording artist retains the right to grant licenses as to the musical work under sections 106(1) and 106(3).

(F) The procedures specified in subparagraphs (C) and (D) shall be repeated and concluded, in accordance with regulations that the Librarian of Congress shall prescribe, in each fifth calendar year after 1997, except to the extent that different years for the repeating and concluding of such proceedings may be determined in accordance with subparagraphs (B) and (C).

(G) Except as provided in section 1002(e) of this title, a digital phonorecord delivery licensed under this paragraph shall be accompanied by the information encoded in the sound recording, if any, by or under the authority of the copyright owner of that sound recording, that identifies the title of the sound recording, the featured recording artist who performs on the sound recording, and related information, including information concerning the underlying musical work and its writer.

(H)(i) A digital phonorecord delivery of a sound recording is actionable as an act of infringement under section 501, and is fully subject to the remedies provided by sections 502 through 506 and section 509, unless—

(I) the digital phonorecord delivery has been authorized by the copyright owner of the sound recording; and

(II) the owner of the copyright in the sound recording or the entity making the digital phonorecord delivery has obtained a compulsory license under this section or has otherwise been authorized by the copyright owner of the musical work to distribute or authorize the distribution, by means of a digital phonorecord delivery, of each musical work embodied in the sound recording.

(ii) Any cause of action under this subparagraph shall be in addition to those available to the owner of the copyright in the nondramatic musical work under subsection (c)(6) and section 106(4) and the owner of the copyright in the sound recording under section 106(6).

(I) The liability of the copyright owner of a sound recording for infringement of the copyright in a nondramatic musical work embodied in the sound recording shall be determined in accordance with applicable law, except that the owner of a copyright in a sound recording shall not be liable for a digital phonorecord delivery by a third party if the owner of the copyright in the sound recording does not license the distribution of a phonorecord of the nondramatic musical work.

(J) Nothing in section 1008 shall be construed to prevent the exercise of the rights and remedies allowed by this paragraph, paragraph (6), and chapter 5 in the event of a digital phonorecord delivery, except that no action alleging infringement of copyright may be brought under this title against a manufacturer, importer or distributor of a digital audio recording device, a digital audio recording medium, an analog recording device, or an analog recording medium, or against a consumer, based on the actions described in such section.

(K) Nothing in this section annuls or limits

(i) the exclusive right to publicly perform a sound recording or the musical work embodied therein, including by means of a digital transmission, under sections 106(4) and 106(6),

(ii) except for compulsory licensing under the conditions specified by this section, the exclusive rights to reproduce and distribute the sound recording and the musical work embodied therein under sections 106(1) and 106(3), including by means of a digital phonorecord delivery, or (iii) any other rights under any other provision of section 106, or remedies available under this title, as such rights or remedies exist either before or after the date of enactment of the Digital Performance Right in Sound Recordings Act of 1995.

(L) The provisions of this section concerning digital phonorecord deliveries shall not apply to any exempt transmissions or retransmissions under section 114(d)(1). The exemptions created in section 114(d)(1) do not expand or reduce the rights of copyright owners under section 106 (1) through (5) with respect to such transmissions and retransmissions.

(4) A compulsory license under this section includes the right of the maker of a phonorecord of a nondramatic musical work under subsection (a)(1) to distribute or authorize distribution of such phonorecord by rental, lease, or lending (or by acts or practices in the nature of rental, lease, or lending). In addition to any royalty payable under clause (2) and chapter 8 of this title, a royalty shall be payable by the compulsory licensee for every act of distribution of a phonorecord by or in the nature of rental, lease, or lending, by or under the authority of the compulsory licensee. With respect to each nondramatic musical work embodied in the phonorecord, the royalty shall be a proportion of the revenue received by the compulsory licensee from every such act of distribution of the phonorecord under this clause equal to the proportion of the revenue received by the compulsory licensee from distribution of the phonorecord under clause (2) that is payable by a compulsory licensee under that clause and under chapter 8. The Register of Copyrights shall issue regulations to carry out the purpose of this clause.

(5) Royalty payments shall be made on or before the twentieth day of each month and shall include all royalties for the month next preceding. Each monthly payment shall be made under oath and shall comply with requirements that the Register of Copyrights shall prescribe by regulation. The Register shall also prescribe regulations under which detailed cumulative annual statements of account, certified by a certified public accountant, shall be filed for every compulsory license under this section. The regulations covering both the monthly and the annual statements of account shall prescribe the form, content, and manner of certification with respect to the number of records made and the number of records distributed.

(6) If the copyright owner does not receive the monthly payment and the monthly and annual statements of account when due, the owner may give written notice to the licensee that, unless the default is remedied within thirty days from the date of the notice, the compulsory license will be automatically terminated. Such termination renders either the making or the distribution, or both, of all phonorecords for which the royalty has not been paid, actionable as acts of infringement under section 501 and fully subject to the remedies provided by sections 502 through 506 and 509.

(d) DEFINITION—As used in this section, the following term has the following meaning: A "digital phonorecord delivery" is each individual delivery of a phonorecord by digital transmission of a sound recording which results in a specifically identifiable reproduction by or for any transmission recipient of a phonorecord of that sound recording, regardless of whether the digital transmission is also a public performance of the sound recording or any nondramatic musical work embodied therein. A digital phonorecord delivery does not result from a real-time, non-interactive subscription transmission of a sound recording where no reproduction of the sound recording or the musical work embodied therein is made from the inception of the transmission through to its receipt by the transmission recipient in order to make the sound recording audible.

§ 201. Ownership of copyright

(a) INITIAL OWNERSHIP.—Copyright in a work protected under this title vests initially in the author or authors of the work. The authors of a joint work are co owners of copyright in the work.

(b) WORKS MADE FOR HIRE.—In the case of a work made for hire, the employer or other person for whom the work was prepared is considered the author for purposes of this title, and, unless the parties have expressly agreed otherwise in a written instrument signed by them, owns all of the rights comprised in the copyright.

(c) CONTRIBUTIONS TO COLLECTIVE WORKS.—Copyright in each separate contribution to a collective work is distinct from copyright in the collective work as a whole, and vests initially in the author of the contribution. In the absence of an express transfer of the copyright or of any rights under it, the owner of copyright in the collective work is presumed to have acquired only the privilege of reproducing and distributing the contribution as part of that particular collective work, any revision of that collective work, and any later collective work in the same series.

(d) TRANSFER OF OWNERSHIP.—

(1) The ownership of a copyright may be transferred in whole or in part by any means of conveyance or by operation of law, and may be bequeathed by will or pass as personal property by the applicable laws of intestate succession.

(2) Any of the exclusive rights comprised in a copyright, including any subdivision of any of the rights specified by section 106, may be transferred as provided by clause (1) and owned separately. The owner of any particular exclusive right is entitled, to the extent of that right, to all of the protection and remedies accorded to the copyright owner by this title.

(e) INVOLUNTARY TRANSFER.—When an individual author's ownership of a copyright, or of any of the exclusive rights under a copyright, has not previously been transferred voluntarily by that individual author, no action by any governmental body or other official or organization purporting to seize, expropriate, transfer, or exercise rights of ownership with respect to the copyright, or any of the exclusive rights under a copyright, shall be given effect under this title except as provided under Title 11.

§ 202. Ownership of copyright as distinct from ownership of material object

Ownership of a copyright, or of any of the exclusive rights under a copyright, is distinct from ownership of any material object in which the work is embodied. Transfer of ownership of any material object, including the copy or phonorecord in which the work is first fixed, does not of itself convey any rights in the copyrighted work embodied in the object; nor, in the absence of an agreement, does transfer of ownership of a copyright or of any exclusive rights under a copyright convey property rights in any material object.

§ 204. Execution of transfers of copyright ownership

(a) A transfer of copyright ownership, other than by operation of law, is not valid unless an instrument of conveyance, or a note or memorandum of the transfer, is in writing and signed by the owner of the rights conveyed or such owner's duly authorized agent.

(b) A certificate of acknowledgment is not required for the validity of a transfer, but is prima facie evidence of the execution of the transfer if—

(1) in the case of a transfer executed in the United States, the certificate is issued by a person authorized to administer oaths within the United States; or

(2) in the case of a transfer executed in a foreign country, the certificate is issued by a diplomatic or consular officer of the United States, or by a person authorized to administer oaths whose authority is proved by a certificate of such an officer.

§ 205. Recordation of transfers and other documents

(a) CONDITIONS FOR RECORDATION.—Any transfer of copyright ownership or other document pertaining to a copyright may be recorded in the Copyright Office if the document filed for recordation bears the actual signature of the person who executed it, or if it is accompanied by a sworn or official certification that it is a true copy of the original, signed document.

(b) CERTIFICATE OF RECORDATION.—The Register of Copyrights shall, upon receipt of a document as provided by subsection (a) and of the fee provided by section 708, record the document and return it with a certificate of recordation.

(c) RECORDATION AS CONSTRUCTIVE NOTICE.—Recordation of a document in the Copyright Office gives all persons constructive notice of the facts stated in the recorded document, but only if—

(1) the document, or material attached to it, specifically identifies the work to which it pertains so that, after the document is indexed by the Register of Copyrights, it would be revealed by a reasonable search under the title or registration number of the work; and

(2) registration has been made for the work.

(d) PRIORITY BETWEEN CONFLICTING TRANSFERS.—As between two conflicting transfers, the one executed first prevails if it is recorded, in the manner required to give constructive notice under subsection (c), within one month after its execution in the United States or within two months after its execution outside the United States, or at any time before recordation in such manner of the later transfer. Otherwise the later transfer prevails if recorded first in such manner, and if taken in good faith, for valuable consideration or on the basis of a binding promise to pay royalties, and without notice of the earlier transfer.

(e) PRIORITY BETWEEN CONFLICTING TRANSFER OF OWNERSHIP AND NONEXCLUSIVE LICENSE.—A nonexclusive license, whether recorded or not, prevails over a conflicting transfer of copyright ownership if the license is evidenced by a written instrument signed by the owner of the rights licensed or such owner's duly authorized agent, and if—

(1) the license was taken before execution of the transfer; or

(2) the license was taken in good faith before the recordation of the transfer and without notice of it.

§ 302. Duration of copyright: Works created on or after January 1, 1978

(a) IN GENERAL.—Copyright in a work created on or after January 1, 1978, subsists from its creation and, except as provided by the following subsections, endures for a term consisting of the life of the author and 70 years after the author's death.

(b) JOINT WORKS.—In the case of a joint work prepared by two or more authors who did not work for hire, the copyright endures for a term consisting of the life of the last surviving author and 70 years after such last surviving author's death.

(c) ANONYMOUS WORKS, PSEUDONYMOUS WORKS, AND WORKS MADE FOR HIRE.—In the case of an anonymous work, a pseudonymous work, or a work made for hire, the copyright endures for a term of 95 years from the year of its first publication, or a term of 120 years from the year of its creation, whichever expires first. If, before the end of such term, the identity of one or more of the authors of an anonymous or pseudonymous work is revealed in the records of a registration made for that work under subsections (a) or (d) of section 408, or in the records provided by this subsection, the copyright in the work endures for the term specified by subsection (a) or (b), based on the life of the author or authors whose identity has been revealed. Any person having an interest in the copyright in an anonymous or pseudonymous work may at any time record, in records to be maintained by the Copyright Office for that purpose, a statement identifying one or more authors of the work; the statement shall also identify the person filing it, the nature of that person's interest, the source of the information recorded, and the particular work affected, and shall comply in form and content with requirements that the Register of Copyrights shall prescribe by regulation.

(d) RECORDS RELATING TO DEATH OF AUTHORS.—Any person having an interest in a copyright may at any time record in the Copyright Office a statement of the date of death of the author of the copyrighted work, or a statement that the author is still living on a particular date. The statement shall identify the person filing it, the nature of that person's interest, and the source of the information recorded, and shall comply in form and content with requirements that the Register of Copyrights shall prescribe by regulation. The Register shall maintain current records of information relating to the death of authors of copyrighted works, based on such recorded statements and, to the extent the Register considers practicable, on data contained in any of the records of the Copyright Office or in other reference sources.

(e) PRESUMPTION AS TO AUTHOR'S DEATH.—After a period of seventy-five years from the year of first publication of a work, or a period of 120 years from the year of its creation, whichever expires first, any person who obtains from the Copyright Office a certified report that the records provided by subsection (d) disclose nothing to indicate that the author of the work is living, or died less than 70 years before, is entitled to the benefit of a presumption that the author has been dead for at least 70 years. Reliance in good faith upon this presumption shall be a complete defense to any action for infringement under this title.

§ 303. Duration of copyright: Works created but not published or copyrighted before January 1, 1978

Copyright in a work created before January 1, 1978, but not theretofore in the public domain or copyrighted, subsists from January 1, 1978, and endures for the term provided by section 302. In no case, however, shall the term of copyright in such a work expire before December 31, 2002; and, if the work is published on or before December 31, 2002, the term of copyright shall not expire before December 31, 2047.

§ 304. Duration of copyright: Subsisting copyrights

(a) COPYRIGHTS IN THEIR FIRST TERM ON JANUARY 1, 1978.—

(1)(A) Any copyright, the first term of which is subsisting on January 1, 1978, shall endure for 28 years from the date it was originally secured.

(B) In the case of—

(i) any posthumous work or of any periodical, cyclopedia, or other composite work upon which the copyright was originally secured by the proprietor thereof, or

(ii) any work copyrighted by a corporate body (otherwise than as assignee or licensee of the individual author) or by an employer for whom such work is made for hire, the proprietor of such copyright shall be entitled to a renewal and extension of the copyright in such work for the further term of 67 years.

(C) In the case of any other copyrighted work, including a contribution by an individual author to a periodical or to a cyclopedia or other composite work—

(i) the author of such work, if the author is still living,

(ii) the widow, widower, or children of the author, if the author is not living,

(iii) the author's executors, if such author, widow, widower, or children are not living, or

(iv) the author's next of kin, in the absence of a will of the author,

shall be entitled to a renewal and extension of the copyright in such work for a further term of 67 years.

(2)(A) At the expiration of the original term of copyright in a work specified in paragraph (1)(B) of this subsection, the copyright shall endure for a renewed and extended further term of 67 years, which—

(i) if an application to register a claim to such further term has been made to the Copyright Office within 1 year before the expiration of the original term of copyright, and the claim is registered, shall vest, upon the beginning of such further term, in the proprietor of the copyright who is entitled to claim the renewal of copyright at the time the application is made; or

(ii) if no such application is made or the claim pursuant to such application is not registered, shall vest, upon the beginning of such further term, in the person or entity that was the proprietor of the copyright as of the last day of the original term of copyright.

(B) At the expiration of the original term of copyright in a work specified in paragraph (1)(C) of this subsection, the copyright shall endure for a renewed and extended further term of 67 years, which—

    (i) if an application to register a claim to such further term has been made to the Copyright Office within 1 year before the expiration of the original term of copyright, and the claim is registered, shall vest, upon the beginning of such further term, in any person who is entitled under paragraph (1)(C) to the renewal and extension of the copyright at the time the application is made; or

    (ii) if no such application is made or the claim pursuant to such application is not registered, shall vest, upon the beginning of such further term, in any person entitled under paragraph (1)(C), as of the last day of the original term of copyright, to the renewal and extension of the copyright.

(3)(A) An application to register a claim to the renewed and extended term of copyright in a work may be made to the Copyright Office—

    (i) within 1 year before the expiration of the original term of copyright by any person entitled under paragraph (1)(B) or (C) to such further term of 67 years; and

    (ii) at any time during the renewed and extended term by any person in whom such further term vested, under paragraph (2)(A) or (B), or by any successor or assign of such person, if the application is made in the name of such person.

(B) Such an application is not a condition of the renewal and extension of the copyright in a work for a further term of 67 years.

(4)(A) If an application to register a claim to the renewed and extended term of copyright in a work is not made within 1 year before the expiration of the original term of copyright in a work, or if the claim pursuant to such application is not registered, then a derivative work prepared under authority of a grant of a transfer or license of the copyright that is made before the expiration of the original term of copyright may continue to be used under the terms of the grant during the renewed and extended term of copyright without infringing the copyright, except that such use does not extend to the preparation during such renewed and extended term of other derivative works based upon the copyrighted work covered by such grant.

    (B) If an application to register a claim to the renewed and extended term of copyright in a work is made within 1 year before its expiration, and the claim is registered, the certificate of such registration shall constitute prima facie evidence as to the validity of the copyright during its renewed and extended term and of the facts stated in the certificate. The evidentiary weight to be accorded the certificate of a registration of a renewed and extended term of copyright made after the end of that 1-year period shall be within the discretion of the court.

(b) Copyrights in Their Renewal Term at the Time of the Effective Date of the Sonny Bono Copyright Term Extension Act.—Any copyright still in its renewal term at the time that the Sonny Bono Copyright Term Extension Act becomes effective shall have a copyright term of 95 years from the date copyright was originally secured.

(c) Termination of Transfers and Licenses Covering Extended Renewal Term.—In the case of any copyright subsisting in either its first or renewal term on January 1, 1978, other than a copyright in a work made for hire, the exclusive or nonexclusive grant of a transfer or license of the renewal or any right under it, executed before January 1,1978, by any of the persons designated by the subsection (a)(1)(C) of this section, otherwise than by will, subject to termination under the following conditions:

(1) In the case of a grant executed by a person or persons other than the author, termination of the grant may be effected by the surviving person or persons who executed it. In the case of a grant executed by one or more of the authors of the work, termination of the grant may be effected, to the extent of a particular author's share in the ownership of the renewal copyright, by the author who executed it or, if such author is dead, by the person or persons who, under clause (2) of this subsection, own and are entitled to exercise a total of more than one-half of that author's termination interest.

(2) Where an author is dead, his or her termination interest is owned, and may be exercised, as follows:

(A) the widow or widower owns the author's entire termination interest unless there are any surviving children or grandchildren of the author, in which case the widow or widower owns one-half of the author's interest;

(B) the author's surviving children, and the surviving children of any dead child of the author, own the author's entire termination interest unless there is a widow or widower, in which case the ownership of one-half of the author's interest is divided among them;

(C) the rights of the author's children and grandchildren are in all cases divided among them and exercised on a per stirpes basis according to the number of such author's children represented; the share of the children of a dead child in a termination interest can be exercised only by the action of a majority of them.

(D) In the event that the author's widow or widower, children, and grandchildren are not living, the author's executor, administrator, personal representative, or trustee shall own the author's entire termination interest.

(3) Termination of the grant may be effected at any time during a period of five years beginning at the end of fifty-six years from the date copyright was originally secured, or beginning on January 1, 1978, whichever is later.

(4) The termination shall be effected by serving an advance notice in writing upon the grantee or the grantee's successor in title. In the case of a grant executed by a person or persons other than the author, the notice shall be signed by all of those entitled to terminate the grant under clause (1) of this subsection, or by their duly authorized agents. In the case of a grant executed by one or more of the authors of the work, the notice as to any one author's share shall be signed by that author or his or her duly authorized agent or, if that author is dead, by the number and proportion of the owners of his or her termination interest required under clauses (1) and (2) of this subsection, or by their duly authorized agents.

(A) The notice shall state the effective date of the termination, which shall fall within the five-year period specified by clause (3) of this subsection, or, in the case of a termination under subsection (d), within the five-year period specified by subsection (d)(2), and the notice shall be served not less than two or more than ten years before that date. A copy of the notice shall be recorded in the Copyright Office before the effective date of termination, as a condition to its taking effect.

(B) The notice shall comply, in form, content, and manner of service, with requirements that the Register of Copyrights shall prescribe by regulation.

(5) Termination of the grant may be effected notwithstanding any agreement to the contrary, including an agreement to make a will or to make any future grant.

(6) In the case of a grant executed by a person or persons other than the author, all rights under this title that were covered by the terminated grant revert, upon the effective date of termination, to all of those entitled to terminate the grant under clause (1) of this subsection. In the case of a grant executed by one or more of the authors of the work, all of a particular author's rights under this title that were covered by the terminated grant revert, upon the effective date of termination, to that author or, if that author is dead, to the persons owning his or her termination interest under clause (2) of this subsection, including those owners who did not join in signing the notice of termination under clause (4) of this subsection. In all cases the reversion of rights is subject to the following limitations:

(A) A derivative work prepared under authority of the grant before its termination may continue to be utilized under the terms of the grant after its termination, but this privilege does not extend to the preparation after the termination of other derivative works based upon the copyrighted work covered by the terminated grant.

(B) The future rights that will revert upon termination of the grant become vested on the date the notice of termination has been served as provided by clause (4) of this subsection.

(C) Where the author's rights revert to two or more persons under clause (2) of this subsection, they shall vest in those persons in the proportionate shares provided by that clause. In such a case, and subject to the provisions of subclause (D) of this clause, a further grant, or agreement to make a further grant, of a particular author's share with respect to any right covered by a terminated grant is valid only if it is signed by the same number and proportion of the owners, in whom the right has vested under this clause, as are required to terminate the grant under clause (2) of this subsection. Such further grant or agreement is effective with respect to all of the persons in whom the right it covers has vested under this subclause, including those who did not join in signing it. If any person dies after rights under a terminated grant have vested in him or her, that person's legal representatives, legatees, or heirs at law represent him or her for purposes of this subclause.

(D) A further grant, or agreement to make a further grant, of any right covered by a terminated grant is valid only if it is made after the effective date of the termination. As an exception, however, an agreement for such a further grant may be made between the author or any of the persons provided by the first sentence of clause (6) of this subsection, or between the persons provided by subclause (C) of this clause, and the original grantee or such grantee's successor in title, after the notice of termination has been served as provided by clause (4) of this subsection.

(E) Termination of a grant under this subsection affects only those rights covered by the grant that arise under this title, and in no way affects rights arising under any other Federal, State, or foreign laws.

(F) Unless and until termination is effected under this subsection, the grant, if it does not provide otherwise, continues in effect for the remainder of the extended renewal term.

(d) Termination Rights Provided in Subsection (C) Which Have Expired on or Before the Effective Date of the Sonny Bono Copyright Term Extension Act—In the case of any copyright other than a work made for hire, subsisting in its renewal term on the effective date of the Sonny Bono Copyright Term Extension Act for which the termination right provided in subsection (c) has expired by such date, where the author or owner of the termination right has not previously exercised such termination right, the exclusive or nonexclusive grant of a transfer or license of the renewal copyright or any right under it, executed before January 1, 1978, by any of the persons designated in subsection (a)(1)(C) of this section, other than by will, is subject to termination under the following conditions:

(1) The conditions specified in subsections (c) (1), (2), (4), (5), and (6) of this section apply to terminations of the last 20 years of copyright term as provided by the amendments made by the Sonny Bono Copyright Term Extension Act.

(2) Termination of the grant may be effected at any time during a period of 5 years beginning at the end of 75 years from the date copyright was originally secured.

§ 305. Duration of copyright: Terminal date

All terms of copyright provided by sections 302 through 304 run to the end of the calendar year in which they would otherwise expire.

§ 708. Copyright Office fees

(a) The following fees shall be paid under the Register of Copyrights:

(1) on filing each application under section 408 for registration of a copyright claim or for a supplementary registration, including the issuance of a certificate of registration if registration is made;

(2) on filing each application for registration of a claim for renewal of a subsisting copyright in under section 304(a), including the issuance of a certificate of registration if registration is made;

(3) for the issuance of a receipt for a deposit under section 407;

(4) for the recordation, as provided by section 205, of a transfer of copyright ownership or other document;

(5) for the filing, under section 115(b), of a notice of intention to obtain a compulsory license;

(6) for the recordation, under section 302(c), of a statement revealing the identity of an author of an anonymous or pseudonymous work, or for the recordation, under section 302(d), of a statement relating to the death of an author;

(7) for the issuance, under section 706, of an additional certificate of registration;

(8) for the issuance of any other certification; and

(9) for the making and reporting of a search as provided by section 705, and for any related services.

The Register of Copyrights is authorized to fix the fees for preparing copies of Copyright Office records, whether or not such copies are certified, on the basis of the cost of such preparation.

(b) In calendar year 1995 and in each subsequent fifth calendar year, the Register of Copyrights, by regulation, may increase the fees specified in subsection (a) by the percent change in the annual average, for the preceding calendar year, of the Consumer Price Index published by the Bureau of Labor Statistics, over the annual average of the Consumer Price Index for the fifth calendar year preceding the calendar year in which such increase is authorized.

(c) The fees prescribed by or under this section are applicable to the United States Government and any of its agencies, employees, or officers but the Register of Copyrights has discretion to waive the requirement of this subsection in occasional or isolated cases involving relatively small amounts.

(d)(1) Except as provided in paragraph (2), all fees received under this section shall be deposited by the Register of Copyrights in the Treasury of the United States and shall be credited to the appropriations for necessary expenses of the Copyright Office. Such fees that are collected shall remain available until expended. The Register may, in accordance with regulations that he or she shall prescribe, refund any sum paid by mistake or in excess of the fee required by this section.

(2) In the case of fees deposited against future services, the Register of Copyrights shall request the Secretary of the Treasury to invest in interest-bearing securities in the United States Treasury any portion of the fees that, as determined by the Register, is not required to meet current deposit account demands. Funds from such portion of fees shall be invested in securities that permit funds to be available to the Copyright Office at all times if they are determined to be necessary to meet current deposit account demands. Such investments shall be in public debt securities with maturities suitable to the needs of the Copyright Office, as determined by the Register of Copyrights, and bearing interest at rates determined by the Secretary of the Treasury, taking into consideration current market yields on outstanding marketable obligations of the United States of comparable maturities.

(3) The income on such investments shall be deposited in the Treasury of the United States and shall be credited to the appropriations for necessary expenses of the Copyright Office.

INTERNET COPYRIGHT AND PUBLISHING RESOURCES

General Information About Copyright

10 Big Copyright Myths Explained (by Brad Templeton)
www.templetons.com/brad/copyright.html

Kohn on Music Licensing (by Al Kohn and Bob Kohn)
www.kohnmusic.com

Government

United States Copyright Office—Library of Congress
lcweb.loc.gov/copyright/

Her Majesty's Stationery Office—The Copyright Unit
www.hmso.gov.uk/copy.htm

Canadian Intellectual Property Office
cipo.gc.ca

Music Publishers' Organizations

National Music Publishers' Association, Inc. (NMPA)
www.nmpa.org

Music Publishers' Organization of the United States (MPO)
www.mpa.org

U.S. Music Rights Organizations

American Society of Composers, Authors and Publishers (ASCAP) (performing)
www.ascap.com

Broadcast Music Incorporated (BMI) (performing)
www.bmi.com

SESAC, Inc. (performing)
www.sesac.com

The Harry Fox Agency, Inc. (HFA) (mechanical)
www.harryfox.com

International Music Rights Organizations

Australasia

Australasian Mechanical Copyright Owners' Society (AMCOS)
www.amcos.com.au

Australasian Performing Right Association (APRA)
www.apra.com.au

Belgium

Société d'Auteurs Belge/Belgische Auteurs Matschappij (SABAM) (both)
www.sabam.be/HtmlEn/index_e.html

British Isles

Irish Music Rights Organisation (IMRO) (performing)
www.imro.ie

PRS for Music
www.prsformusic.com

Canada

Canadian Musical Reproduction Rights Agency Ltd. (CMRRA)
www.cmrra.ca

Society of Composers, Authors and Music Publishers of Canada (SOCAN)
www.socan.ca

France

Société des Auteurs, Compositeurs et Éditeurs de Musique (SACEM) (both)
www.sacem.org/english/index.html

Germany

Gesellschaft für musikalische Aufführungs-und mechanische Vervielfältigungsrechte (GEMA) (both)
www.gema.de/eng/index.html

Italy

Societá Italiana degli Autori ed Editori (SIAE) (both, not limited to music)
www.siae.it

Japan

Japanese Society for Rights of Authors, Composers and Publishers (JASRAC) (both)
www.jasrac.or.jp/ejhp

Netherlands

> BUMA (performing)/STEMRA (mechanical)
> **www.buma.nl**

Scandinavia & Baltic States

> Komponister i Danmark (KODA) (Denmark) (performing)
> **www.koda.dk**
>
> Samband tónskálda og eigenda flutningsréttar (STEF) (Iceland) (performing)
> **www.stef.is**
>
> Säveltäjäin Tekijänoikeustoimisto Teosto r.y. (TEOSTO) (Finland) (performing)
> **www.teosto.fi**
>
> (TONO) (Norway) (performing)
> **www.tono.no**
>
> Svenska Tonsättares Internationella MusikbyrD (STIM) (Sweden) (performing)
> **www.stim.se**
>
> Nordisk Copyright Bureau (mechanical)
> **www.ncb.dk/english/index.htm**

Spain

> Sociedad General Autores y Editores (SGAE) (performing, not limited to music)
> **www.sgae.es**

Switzerland & Liechtenstein

> SUISA (both, not limited to music)
> **www.suisa.ch/index.html**

Worldwide Associations

> Confédération Internationale des Socétés d'Auteurs et Compositeurs (CISAC) (performing)
> **www.cisac.org**
>
> Bureau International des Sociétés Gerant les Droits d'Enregistrement et de Réproduction Mécanique (BIEM) (mechanical)
> **www.biem.org**

Related Music Organizations

Recording Industry Association of America (RIAA)
www.riaa.com

The National Academy of Recording Arts & Sciences, Inc.
grammy.com

Songwriters' Guild of America
www.songwritersguild.com

Country Music Association
www.countrymusic.org

California Copyright Conference (CCC)
www.theccc.org

Association of Independent Music Publishers (AIMP)
www.aimp.org

Music Industry Publications

Billboard
www.billboard.com

The Hollywood Reporter
www.hollywoodreporter.com

Music Connection
www.musicconnection.com

Music Newswire
www.musicnewswire.com

Other Author & Clearance Organizations

Authors' Licensing and Collecting Society, United Kingdom (ALCE)
www.alcs.co.uk

The Authors Registry
www.authorsregistry.org

Copyright Clearance Center (CCC)
www.copyright.com

Motion Picture Licensing Corporation (MPLC)
www.mplc.com

National Writers Union Publications Right Clearinghouse
www.nwu.org/publications-rights-clearinghouse

Writers, Artists, and Their Copyright Holders (WATCH)
www.lib.utexas.edu/Libs/HRC/WATCH/

International Federation of Reproduction Rights Organisations' (IFRRO)
www.ifrro.org

Christian Copyright Licensing International (CCLI)
www.ccli.com

LIST OF FOREIGN PERFORMING AND MECHANICAL RIGHTS SOCIETIES

Country	Type	Society	Full Name	Territories	Website
Albania	Mechanical	ALBAUTOR	Société Albanaise des Droits de l'Auteur des Droits Voisins	Republic of Albania	N/A
	Performing				
Argentina	Mechanical	SADAIC	Sociedad Argentina de Autores y Compositores de Música	Republic of Argentina	www.sadaic.org.ar
	Performing				
Australia	Mechanical	AMCOS	Autralasian Mechanical Copyright Owners Society Ltd.	Ashmore Island, Australia, Australian Antarctic Territory, Cartier Island, Christmas Island, Cocos (Keeling) Islands, Fiji, Heard Island, Kiribati, Macquarie Island, McDonald Island, Nauru, New Guinea, New Zealand, Niue (Savage) Island, Norfolk Island, Papua, Ross Dependency, Solomon Islands, Tokelau (Union) Islands, Tonga, Tuvalu, Vanuatu and Samoa	www.apra-amcos.com.au
	Performing	APRA	Australasian Performing Right Association Limited	Ashmore Island, Australia, Australian Antarctic Territory, Cartier Island, Christmas Islands, Cocos (Keeling) Islands, Cook, Fiji Islands, Heard Islands, Kiribati, Macquarie Island, McDonald Island, Nauru, New Zealand, Niue (Savage) Island, Norfolk Island, Papua-New Guinea, Ross Dependence, Solomon Islands, Tokelau (Union) Islands, Tuvalu, Western Samoa	www.apra-amcos.com.au

Country	Type	Society	Full Name	Territories	Website
Austria	Mechanical	AUSTRO-MECHANA	Gesellschaft zur Wahrnehmung mechanisch-musikalischer Urheberrechte GmbH	Austria	www.herold.at/gelbe-seiten/wien/SHqsw/austro-mechana-gesellschaft-zur-wahrnehmung-mechanisch-musikalischer-urheberrechte-gesmbh/
	Performing	AKM	Autoren, Komponisten und Musikverleger		www.akm.at
Belgium	Mechanical	SABAM	Société Belge des Auteurs Compositeurs et Éditeurs	Belgium	www.sabam.be
	Performing				
Brazil	Mechanical	UBC	União Brasileira de Compositores	Brazil	www.ubc.org.br
	Performing				
Bulgaria	Mechanical	MUSICAUTOR	Bulgarian Society of Authors and Composers for Performing and Mechanical Rights	Bulgaria	www.musicautor.org
	Performing				
Burkina Faso	Mechanical	BBDA	Bureau Burkinabe du Droit d'Auteur	Burkina Faso	www.bbda.bf
	Performing				
Canada	Mechanical	CMRRA	Canadian Musical Reproduction Rights Agency Limited	Canada	www.cmrra.ca
		SODRAC	Société du droit reproduction des auteurs, compositeurs et éditeurs au Canada	Canada	www.sodrac.ca
	Performing	SOCAN	Society of Composers, Authors and Music Publishers of Canada	Canada	www.socan.ca

Country	Type	Society	Full Name	Territories	Website
Chile	Mechanical	SCD	Sociedad Chilena del Derecho de Autor	Chile	www.scd.cl
	Performing				
China	Mechanical	MCSC	Music Copyright Society of China	People's Republic of China	www.mcsc.com.cn
	Performing				
Colombia	Mechanical	SAYCO	Sociedad de Autores y Compositores de Colombia	Colombia	www.sayco.org
	Performing				
Costa Rica	Mechanical	ACAM	Asociación de Compositores y Autores Musicales de Costa Rica	Costa Rica	www.acam.cr
	Performing				
Croatia	Mechanical	HDS ZAMP	Hrvatsko Drustvo Skladatelja Croatian Composers' Society	Croatia	www.zamp.hr
	Performing	HDS	Hrvatsko Drustvo Skladatelja Croatian Composers' Society	Croatia	www.hds.hr
Czech Republic	Mechanical	OSA	Ochranny Svaz Autorsky	Czech Republic	www.osa.cz
	Performing				
Denmark	Mechanical	NCB	Nordisk Copyright Bureau	Denmark, Estonia, Finland, Iceland, Latvia, Lithuania, Norway, Sweden, Faroe Islands	www.ncb.dk
	Performing	KODA	Selskabet Til Forvaltning af International Komponistrettigheder I Denmark	Denmark, Faroe Islands, Greenland	www.koda.dk

Country	Type	Society	Full Name	Territories	Website
England	Mechanical	MCPS	Mechanical Copyright Protection Society	Anguilla, Antigua, Ascension Island, Bahamas, Bangladesh, Barbados, Barbuda, Belize, Bermuda, British Antarctic Territory, British Indian Ocean Territory, British Virgin Islands, Brunel, Cayman Islands, Channel Islands, Cyprus, Diego Garcia, Dominica, Falkland Islands, Ghana, Gibraltar, Grenada, Guyana, India, Jamaica, Kenya, Malawai, Malta, Man (Isle of), Monserrat, Nigeria, Pakistan, Pitcairn Islands, Seychelles, Sierra Leone, South Georgia, South Sandwich Islands, Sri Lanka, St. Helena, St. Kitts-Nevis, St. Lucia, St. Vincent, Tanzania, Tonga, Trinidad & Tobago, Tristan da Cunha, Turks and Caicos Islands, Uganda, United Kingdom, Zambia, Zimbabwe	www.prsformusic.com
	Performing	PRS	The Performing Rights Society Ltd.		www.prsformusic.com
Estonia	Mechanical	NCB	Nordisk Copyright Bureau	Denmark, Estonia, Finland, Iceland, Latvia, Lithuania, Norway, Sweden, Faroe Islands	www.ncb.dk
	Performing	EAU	Eesti Atoritie Uhing	Estonia	www.eau.org
Finland	Mechanical	NCB	Nordisk Copyright Bureau	Denmark, Estonia, Finland, Iceland, Latvia, Lithuania, Norway, Sweden, Faroe Islands	www.ncb.dk
	Performing	Teosto	Saveltajain Tekijanoikeustoimisto	Finland	www.teosto.fi

Country	Type	Society	Full Name	Territories	Website
France	Mechanical	SDRM	Société pour l'administration du Droit de Reproduction Mécanique	France and its overseas departments (Guadeloupe, Guyane, Martinique, Reunion), Polynesia, Wallis and Futuna, New Caledonia, Mayotte, Saint-Pierre and Miquelon, French Austral and Antartic territories (TAAF). B. Luxembourg, Monaco, Andorra, Lebanon. C. Benin (BUBEDRA), Burkina Faso (BBDA), Cameroon, Central African Rep. (BUCADA), Congo (BCDA), Ivory Coast (BURIDA), Egypt (SACERAU), Guinea (BGDA), Madagascar (OMDA), Mali (BUMDA), Morocco (BMDA), Niger (BNDA), Senegal (BSDA), Togo (BUTODRA)	www.sdrm.fr
	Mechanical	SACEM	Société des Auteurs, Compositeurs et Éditeurs de Musique		www.sacem.fr
	Performing	SACEM	Société des Auteurs, Compositeurs et Éditeurs de Musique	French Republic: France, French Austral and Antarctic Possessions, French Guyana, French Polynesia (via the intermediary of SPACEM), Guadeloupe, Martinique, Mayotte, New Caledonia and dependencies, Reunion, Saint-Pierre and Miquelon, Wallis and Futuna, Andorra, Guinea (via BGDA), Lebanon (via SACEML), Luxembourg, Monaco, Morocco (via BMDA)	www.sacem.fr
Germany	Mechanical	GEMA	Gesellschaft für Musikalische Aufführungs-und Mechanische Vervielfältigungsrechte	Germany	www.gema.de
	Performing				
Greece	Mechanical	AEPI	Société Hellénique pour la Protection de la Propriété Intellectuelle S.A.	Greece	www.aepi.gr
	Performing				

Country	Type	Society	Full Name	Territories	Website
Holland	Mechanical	BUMA/STEMRA	Vereniging Buma en Stichting STEMRA zijn de auteursrecht-organisaties van componisten, tekstdicht	Netherlands	www.bumastemra.nl
	Performing	BUMA	Vereniging Buma	French Republic: France, French Austral and Antarctic Possessions, French Guyana, French Polynesia (via the intermediary of SPACEM), Guadeloupe, Martinique, Mayotte, New Caledonia and dependencies, Reunion, Saint-Pierre and Miquelon, Wallis and Futuna, Andorra, Guinea (via BGDA), Lebanon (via SACEML), Luxembourg, Monaco, Morocco (via BMDA)	
Hong Kong	Mechanical	CASH	Composers and Authors Society of Hong Kong	Hong Kong	www.cash.org.hk
	Performing				
Hungary	Mechanical	ARTISJUS	Bureau Hongrois pour la protection des Droits d'Auteur	Hungary	www.artisjus.hu
	Performing				
Iceland	Mechanical	NCB	Nordisk Copyright Bureau	Denmark, Estonia, Finland, Iceland, Latvia, Lithuania, Norway, Sweden, Faroe Islands	www.ncb.dk
	Performing	STEF	Samband Tonskalda Og Eigenda Flutningsrettar	Iceland	www.stef.is
Ireland	Mechanical	MCPS-Ireland	Mechanical Copyright Protection Society-Ireland	Ireland	www.mcps.ie
	Performing	IMRO	Irish Music Rights Organisation Limited	Ireland	www.imro.ie

Country	Type	Society	Full Name	Territories	Website
Israel	Mechanical	ACUM	Société des Auteurs, Compositeurs et Éditeurs de Musique en Israël	Israel	www.acum.org.il
	Performing				
Italy	Mechanical	SIAE	Società Italiana degli Autori ed Editori	Italy, Republic of San Marino, Vatican City	www.siae.it
	Performing				
Japan	Mechanical	JASRAC	Japanese Society for Rights of Authors, Composers and Publishers	Japan	www.jasrac.or.jp
	Performing				
Korea	Mechanical	KOMCA	Korea Music Copyright Association	Republic of Korea (South Korea)	www.komca.or.kr
	Performing				
Latvia	Mechanical	NCB	Nordisk Copyright Bureau	Denmark, Estonia, Finland, Iceland, Latvia, Lithuania, Norway, Sweden, Faroe Islands	www.ncb.dk
	Performing	AKKA/LAA	Copyright and Communication Consulting Agency/Latvian Copyright Agency	Latvia	www.akka-laa.lv
Lithuania	Mechanical	NCB	Nordisk Copyright Bureau	Denmark, Estonia, Finland, Iceland, Latvia, Lithuania, Norway, Sweden, Faroe Islands	www.ncb.dk
	Performing	LATGA-A	Agency of Lithuanian Copyright Protection Association	Republic of Lithuania	www.latga.lt
Malaysia	Mechanical	MACP	Music Authors' Copyright Protection Berhad	Malaysia	www.macp.com.my
	Performing				
Mexico	Mechanical	SACM	Sociedad de Autores y Compositores de Música	Mexico	www.sacm.org.mx
	Performing				

Country	Type	Society	Full Name	Territories	Website
Norway	Mechanical	NCB	Nordisk Copyright Bureau	Denmark, Estonia, Finland, Iceland, Latvia, Lithuania, Norway, Sweden, Faroe Islands	www.ncb.dk
	Performing	TONO	Norsk Komponistforenings Internasjonale Musikkbyra	Bear Islands, Hope Island, Jan Mayen Island, Norway, Spitsbergen	www.tono.no
Peru	Mechanical	APDAYC	Asociación Peruana de Autores y Compositores	Peru	www.apdayc.org.pe
	Performing				
Philippines	Mechanical	FILSCAP	Filipino Society of Composers, Authors and Publishers, Inc.	Philippine Republic	www.filscap.com.ph
	Performing				
Poland	Mechanical	ZAISKS	Stowarzyszenie Autorow	Poland	www.zaiks.org.pl
	Performing				
Portugal	Mechanical	SPA	Sociedade Portuguesa de Autores	Azores, Madeira, Portugal	www.spautores.pt
	Performing				
Romania	Mechanical	UCMR-ADA	Romanian Musical Performing and Mechanical Rights Society	Romania	www.ucmr-ada.ro
	Performing				
Russia	Mechanical	RAO	Russian Author' Society	Russia	rp-union.ru
	Performing				
Singapore	Mechanical	COMPASS	Composers and Authors Society of Singapore	Singapore	www.compass.org.sg
	Performing				

Country	Type	Society	Full Name	Territories	Website
Slovak Republic	Mechanical	SOZA	Slovensky Ochranny Zvaz Autorsky	Slovak Republic	www.soza.sk
	Performing				
Slovenia	Mechanical	SAZAS	Société des Compositeurs, Auteurs et Éditeurs de Slovenie	Slovenia	www.sazas.org
	Performing				
South Africa	Mechanical	SAMRO	Southern African Music Rights Organisation	South Africa	www.samro.org.za
	Performing				
Spain	Mechanical	SGAE	Sociedad General de Autores y Editores	Spain	www.sgae.es
	Performing				
Sweden	Mechanical	NCB	Nordisk Copyright Bureau	Denmark, Estonia, Finland, Iceland, Latvia, Lithuania, Norway, Sweden, Faroe Islands	www.ncb.dk
	Performing	STIM	Svenska Tonsattares Intenrationalla Musikbyra	Sweden	www.stim.se
Switzerland	Mechanical	SUISA	Société Suisse pour les Droits d'Auteurs d'Oeuvres Musicales	Liechtenstein, Switzerland	www.suisa.ch
	Performing				
Taiwan	Mechanical	MUST	Music Copyright Society of Chinese Taipei	Taiwan	www.must.org.tw
	Performing	CHA	Copyright Holder's Association of the Republic of China	Taiwan, Republic of China	
Thailand	Mechanical	MCT	Music Copyright Thailand Limited	Thailand	www.mct.in.th
	Performing				

Country	Type	Society	Full Name	Territories	Website
Uruguay	Mechanical	AGADU	Asociación General Autores del Uruguay	Uruguay	www.agadu.com.uy
	Performing				
Venezuela	Mechanical	SACVEN	Sociedad de Autores y Compositores de Venezuela	Venezuela	www.sacven.org
	Performing				
Yugoslavia	Mechanical	SOJOK	Savez Organizacija Kompozitora Jugoslavije	Yugoslavia	www.sokoj.rs
	Performing				
Zaire	Mechanical	SACEM	Société des Auteurs, Compositeurs et Éditeurs de Musique	France and its overseas departments (Guadeloupe, Guyane, Martinique, Reunion), Polynesia, Wallis and Futuna, New Caledonia, Mayotte, Saint-Pierre and Miquelon, French Austral and Antartic territories (TAAF). B. Luxemburg, Monaco, Andorra, Lebanon. C. Benin (BUBEDRA), Burkina Faso (BBDA), Cameroon, Central African Rep. (BUCADA), Congo (BCDA), Ivory Coast (BURIDA), Egypt (SACERAU), Guinea (BGDA), Madagascar (OMDA), Mali (BUMDA), Morocco (BMDA), Niger (BNDA), Senegal, (BSDA), Togo (BUTODRA), France, Martinique, Guadeloupe, Guyana, Réunion, Mayotte, Polynesia, New Caledonia, Saint-Pierre and Miquelon, Wallis and Futuna, Andorra, Luxembourg, Monaco, Algeria, Tunisia, Morocco, Egypt, Ivory Coast, Guinea, Madagasgar, Lebanon, Benin, Nigeria, Congo, Senegal, Chad, Mali, Cameroun, Zaire	
	Performing	SONECA	Société Nationale des Éditeurs, Compositeurs et Auteurs	Zaire	

GLOSSARY

administration fee: Charge for the professional service of administration.

Advance payment: Payment of royalties in anticipation of earning royalties in the future.

affidavit: A sworn statement in writing made under oath before an official authorized to take oaths and affirmations; often a *declaration* made under penalty of perjury serves the same purpose.

agent: One who acts for or in the place of another with authority; a representative.

album: A collection of sound recordings of songs or other musical works.

arranger: Person engaged to transpose keys, elaborate on chord structures, or even make creative contributions to enhance the popularity of a song.

ASCAP: *American Society of Composers, Authors and Publishers*; a U.S. performing rights society; *see* BMI, SESAC.

Assignment: A transfer to another.

author: One who writes the words of a musical work; LYRICIST; *cf.* COMPOSER; by statute, any creator of a copyrightable work.

BMI: *Broadcast Music, Inc.*; a U.S. performing rights society; *see* ASCAP, SESAC.

budget package: Product sold at a greater value (more quantity for the same money or same the quantity for less money).

collaborator: One who works jointly with another, as in creating a musical work.

compilation: A collection of existing works, each of which is a separate and independent work in itself, which may or may not be created by the same person(s).

compositions: Musical works, *i.e.*, songs, with or without lyrics.

composer: One who writes the music of a song; *cf.* AUTHOR.

composite work: A work consisting of distinctly separable components.

compulsory license: A license obtained upon payment of a statutorily fixed royalty rate and in compliance with all other requirements imposed by law; compulsory licenses are available only for certain uses, primarily for use in PHONORECORDS (but not COPIES).

copy: Any tangible embodiment of a work subject to copyright laws, *except* PHONORECORDS; includes any printed matter or tangible embodiment of an audiovisual work, such as a film or video cassette tape.

copyright: Exclusive legal right to reproduce, distribute, sell in any manner or form, or publicly perform (or display), a literary or artistic work.

cover recording: A sound recording other than the original version of a musical work.

cut: *See* SIDE; synonym: track.

demo: An illustrative sound recording of the merits of a musical work to prospective users.

digital download: A file sent via the Internet and stored on the user's hard drive or other storage media; *cf.* STREAMING.

digital phonorecord delivery (DPD): A music file delivered via digital download.

encumbrance: A claim or lien upon property rights.

exclusive: Limited to control or use by a single individual or group.

grand rights: The rights associated with dramatic musical works; generally, a performance is nondramatic when it is removed from a dramatic context and unrelated to a larger plot structure, although the entire drama need not be developed to render a performance dramatic; *cf.* SMALL RIGHTS.

gross receipts: Generally, all sums a publisher receives for the exploitation of a work, although the precise definition may vary according to the terms of the contract.

Harry Fox Agency: The licensing and auditing arm of the National Association of Music Publishers.

infringement: The act of violation, encroachment, or trespass on a right or privilege, especially copyright.

interactive streaming: The process whereby the user has direct input as to which files are *streamed* to their devices; *cf.* NON-INTERACTIVE STREAMING

lead sheet: A copy that shows the melody and lyrics of a song, used by the "lead" in a performance or recording session.

license: A permission to act, granted by competent authority; a document evidencing such a permission granted.

lyricist: One who writes the words of a song; *cf.* AUTHOR.

master: Any recording of sound that is or is intended to be embodied in or on a record; sometimes may include a recording coupled with a visual image; also known as a "master recording" or "recording."

mechanical income: Royalties for the reproduction of a musical work in PHONORECORDS.

nonexclusive: Not limited to control by a single individual or group.

non-interactive streaming: The process where the user had no (or limited) input as to which files are *streamed* to their devices. In the analog world, "radio" would be considered non-interactive.

original recording: *cf.* COVER RECORDING.

performance income: Royalties for the public performance of a nondramatic musical work, collected and distributed by performing rights societies.

permanent download: A download that is owned by the user and remains on the user's storage device (hard drive, iPod, etc.) until removed by the user.

phonorecord: A tangible object in which performances of musical works (or other sound recordings) are embodied as sounds (except in motion pictures or other audiovisual works), such as a tape, vinyl phonograph record, or compact disc; *cf.* COPY.

premium package: Something given free or at a reduced price with the purchase of a product.

publication: To place on sale, sell, or publicly distribute.

public domain: Property rights that belong to the community at large, are unprotected by copyright or patent, and are subject to appropriation by anyone.

publisher royalties: The publisher's share of royalties paid for by the exploitation of a copyrighted *musical work*; *publishing* royalties are divided between publisher royalties and writer royalties; *record* or *artist* royalties are entirely different, and are paid for the exploitation of copyrighted *sound recordings*.

rate: Charge, payment, or price fixed according to a ratio, scale, or standard.

record: *See* PHONORECORD; sometimes includes configurations of sound that technically fall under the definition of COPY.

registration: To make or secure official entry in a register.

reversion: The act or process of returning as to former condition.

rights period: The time during which an agreement is in effect.

royalty: A share of the product or profit reserved by the grantor; a payment made to an author or composer for each exploitation of his or her work, whether by sale of copies or phonorecords or by public performance.

SESAC: SESAC, Inc. (formerly *Society of European Stage Authors and Composers*); a U.S. performing rights society; *see* ASCAP, BMI.

side: A term sometimes used to refer to a single song or a single track on an album or single, often with a contractually-specified minimum length; *see* CUT; TRACK.

small rights: The public performance rights of musical works that are not performed dramatically; also known as *small performing rights*; *cf.* GRAND RIGHTS.

sound recording: A work that results from the fixation of a series of musical, spoken, or other sounds, but not including the sounds accompanying a motion picture or other audiovisual work, regardless of the nature of the material objects—such as disks, tapes, or other phonorecords—in which they are embodied.

split publishing: Joint ownership of a copyright.

statement: A report showing a financial summary of royalties earned or costs incurred by an artist or songwriter.

streaming: The transmission of a file from a server to the user that is not stored on the user's devices but that can simultaneously accessed by the user for viewing or listening purposes; *cf.* DOWNLOAD.

sub-publishing: The leasing of rights in copyrights, usually in a foreign territory.

synchronization: Fixing musical works with motion pictures or other audiovisual works.

term: The time during which an agreement is in effect.

territory: Geographic area delimiting a scope of rights

tethered download: A file that temporarily resides on the user's storage media for as long as the user complies with certain requirements, such as maintaining a subscription service. Once these requirements are no longer met, the file is automatically deleted form the user's devices.

writer royalties: *cf.* PUBLISHER ROYALTIES.

INDEX

ABOUT THE AUTHOR

With over 30 years experience as an attorney in the music industry, Steven Winogradsky is a partner in Winogradsky/Sobel in Studio City, Calif., providing global media and music business affairs & legal support for composers; songwriters; music publishers; recording artists; and television, film, video, and multi-media producers. In addition to an entertainment law practice, the company handles music clearance and licensing in all media for many production companies, worldwide administration of the publishing catalogs for a number of clients, and new media strategies and revenue modeling.

Prior to being in solo practice with The Winogradsky Company from 1992 to 2009, Mr. Winogradsky had served as Director of Music Business Affairs for Hanna-Barbera Productions, Inc.; Managing Director of Music, Legal & Business Affairs for MCA Home Entertainment; Director of Music Licensing and Administration for Universal Pictures and Universal Television; and Vice President of Business Affairs for The Clearing House, Ltd.

He was twice elected President of the California Copyright Conference, after spending nine years on the Board of Directors, and also served for four years as President of The Association of Independent Music Publishers.

Mr. Winogradsky was awarded the 2012 Texas Star Award by the Entertainment and Sports Law Section of the State Bar of Texas for his contributions to legal education in Texas. Mr. Winogradsky was also named as one of the Outstanding Instructors in Entertainment Studies and Performing Arts at UCLA Extension, where he has taught since 1997.

He has written numerous magazine articles on the subject of music for motion pictures and television and has lectured on a variety of music-related topics at MIDEM; University of Houston Law Foundation (1993, 1994, and 1997); Texas State Bar Entertainment Law Seminar (1994–2012); American Bar Association Entertainment & Sports Law Conference; University of Southern California Entertainment Law Institute; *The Hollywood Reporter* Film and Television Music Conference (1997–2000); *Billboard* Film and Television Music Conference; NARAS; The Society of Composers and Lyricists; Loyola Law School; Southwestern Law School; California Lawyers for the Arts; American Film Institute; LMNOP (New Orleans); Toronto International Film Festival; Canadian Music Week; Musicians Institute; McNally Smith College of Music; California State University, Northridge (CSUN); NARIP; Copyright Society of the USA; and various other symposia.

In addition, he is a guitarist, singer, and songwriter who is both a composer and publisher member of ASCAP.